THE KEYS OF POWER

STUDIES IN RHETORIC/COMMUNICATION
Thomas W. Benson, Series Editor

THE KEYS OF POWER

The Rhetoric and Politics of Transcendentalism

Nathan Crick

THE UNIVERSITY OF SOUTH CAROLINA PRESS

Published by the University of South Carolina Press
Columbia, South Carolina 29208

www.sc.edu/uscpress

Manufactured in the United States of America

26 25 24 23 22 21 20 19 18 17
10 9 8 7 6 5 4 3 2 1

Library of Congress Cataloging-in-Publication Data
can be found at http://catalog.loc.gov/.

ISBN 978-1-61117-778-7 (cloth)
ISBN 978-1-61117-779-4 (ebook)

This book was printed on recycled paper with
30 percent postconsumer waste content.

For my mother,
for whom melody is beauty
and art lives in the hand

And with these forms, the spells of persuasion, the keys of power are put into his hands.

Ralph Waldo Emerson, *Nature*

CONTENTS

SERIES EDITOR'S PREFACE

In *The Keys of Power*, Nathan Crick examines the work of six nineteenth-century American Transcendentalists who responded to the social upheavals and historical challenges of their time by developing theories of politics and who in turn theorized and enacted genres of rhetoric through which their political visions could be realized. Professor Crick develops his argument with studies of six leading figures—Sampson Reed, Amos Bronson Alcott, Orestes Brownson, Ralph Waldo Emerson, Margaret Fuller, and Henry David Thoreau—and concludes with a chapter on Frederick Douglass and the legacy of Transcendentalism. In these figures Crick finds an abundance of reflection, speculation, and inspiration about an American rhetoric suitable to its own understandings of universal imperatives and historical urgencies.

The story begins with Sampson Reed, who in August 1821 delivered an M.A. address at Harvard, calling on his audience, which included a young Ralph Waldo Emerson, to embrace genius and eloquence and prefiguring Transcendentalism. Reed himself later pursued a career not in the university or the pulpit, but as an entrepreneur of the New England pharmaceutical market—the Transcendental hero as a middle-class businessman. Amos Bronson Alcott was a teacher who led his Temple School in defining and enacting a vision of education as the dialogic cultivation of genius and education in a classroom experience that continues to influence progressive educators. For Alcott the true genius was a radical reformer who awakened the faculties of children through dialogue. Orestes Brownson was a restlessly energetic ideological critic and reformer who grew into and out of Transcendentalism in a search for unity. Ralph Waldo Emerson has long been fascinating to philosophers and rhetorical theorists. In his 1943 essay on Emerson in the second volume of *A History and Criticism of Public Address*, Cornell professor Herbert A. Wichelns wrote with admiration and eloquence that "No speaker, it would seem, ever found and held an audience, even a small and select one, as Emerson's essentially was, on terms so independent of it."

Nathan Crick enriches our understanding of the seeming contradiction between rhetorical power and independence of thought and spirit, reading Ralph Waldo Emerson as an advocate of gradualist social change and as committed to an eloquence that sought not for immediate effects but for the articulation of a higher truth that speaks to a universal audience. Margaret Fuller is identified as a committed Transcendentalist who brought to her rhetoric of reform her prescient understandings of the contradictions of unjust power and whose increasingly radical and influential writing on the rights of women, slaves, Native Americans, and laborers was cut short during its developement while she was still a young woman. Henry David Thoreau, younger than the first Transcendentalists, developed early and underwent profound changes in the range and tenor of his thought and action, with a commitment to principles and a keen understanding of how developing technologies challenged those principles while yielding opportunities to the radical thinker for leverage and influence.

Nathan Crick's *The Keys of Power* is a compelling exercise in sympathetic and critical understanding that will lead readers back to the American Transcendentalists and stimulate them in their own search for principled and effective thought and action, perhaps to redeem the "faith of the Transcendentalists that" for them too "the many tendencies their age could be controlled and directed by eloquence."

THOMAS W. BENSON

PREFACE

The stone foundation of the old farmhouse had been abandoned for so long that a thirty-foot oak tree had stood where the floor should have been. All that had remained were three sides of the foundation constructed out of the large stones that the receding glaciers had long ago dumped over Western Massachusetts. Sometime in the 1800s, someone had cleared the area at the base of what is now Vining Hill Road to build that house and raise a family. The hard labor of many months had built a rock wall that extended from the road about two hundred yards back into the forest. And the original well had remained perfectly preserved in the woods, a cement slab placed over the top to prevent children from falling inside.

I grew up on the other side of that rock wall in a small house my parents had bought just before I was born. The wall represented simply one side of our property. Our house was alone on our side of the street and bordered by three sides by woods. To the west was a pond that was populated by small frogs. Behind our house the woods stretched back a quarter mile until it encountered the next road. And to the east was the rock wall and just beyond that the foundation and the well. During the fall, after my brother, my sister, and I helped rake the yard, we would drag a plastic sheet piled with leaves through the gap in the wall and up a small path and dump them into the remains of the old farmstead. It had become for us simply a place to put nature. We rarely thought much else about it.

The well was a different story. The cement slab had long ago cracked into pieces so that one could actually climb down inside—which one of my brother's friends did as a teenager, considering himself something of a rock climber. The well was about fifteen yards away from the foundation deeper into the woods. As a child this seemed a great distance. Sometimes I would go off by myself to try to find it, never quite remembering its location. The stone slab made the well seem mysterious and dangerous. I would peer down inside to see the reflection of the sunlight off the water below and drop stone pebbles to hear them tick tack on the stone and plink into the puddle. The well was a gateway to something below and yet something above.

However it was the land behind the old farmstead—that stretched back into the woods—that represented our childhood world. When our home had first been built, much of the land was still a field, so much of it having been cleared for so long. Although it was not our property, we made use of it. My mother grew vegetables in a small patch of soil that we would grudgingly help weed in order to crunch on fresh cucumbers. My father, meanwhile, had cleared a place to play football and Wiffle ball during the summer and fall. To get there we had to walk through a short path until we emerged on a slightly inclined field that was completely surrounded by trees. During the height of summer, when the leaves were thick, you could only just barely see the back of our house and no other. We were alone. During the winter, after a thick snowfall, I would often walk through the path into the field and listen to the silence. I remember the silence most of all.

When I returned from college one day in 1992, all of this was gone. The entire property beyond the wall had been bulldozed flat—the field, the foundation, the well. A few months later a square, unremarkable house went up, filled with equally unremarkable people. Eventually my mother sold the house to live at the highest rather than the lowest part of town.

But somewhere under the carpet of grass, the stones of that farmhouse and of that well still exist. Their part in history is not yet over. Just as deep in our memories, the experiences that have made us who we are still provide us a living foundation on which to build our selves, and our world, anew. I still can see my father in his white T-shirt, triumphantly using a crowbar to pull out yet another stone. I can taste the salty burst of a fresh tomato that my mother had sliced and laid out for lunch. I can feel the gritty sting of the gravel after skinning my knee playing basketball in the backyard with my brother. And I can smell the pine needles in the tree that my sister and I had just climbed as part of our "Tree Climbing Club." All of this is Nature. All of this is History. All of this speaks the language of Love. For all of it I am grateful.

Introduction

"Eloquence is forever a power"—
Transcendentalism and the Search for New Gods

When we have lost our God of tradition & ceased from our God of rhetoric
then may God fire the heart with his presence.

Ralph Waldo Emerson, *Journals,* 1834

The early nineteenth century in the United States was a battlefield between gods
old and new. As Ralph Waldo Emerson told the Harvard graduating class of 1837,
theirs was "the age of Revolution; when the old and the new stand side by side
and admit of being compared; when the energies of all men are searched by fear
and by hope; when the historic glories of the old can be compensated by the rich
possibilities of the new era."[1] But Emerson had already summed up the nature
of this revolutionary moment in his journal three years prior to his commencement address. Reflecting on his experience of a cool November evening at his
home in Concord, Massachusetts, he recorded "how shone the moon & her little
sparklers last eve. There was a light in the selfsame vessels which contained it a
million years ago." The moon having transported Emerson from his comfortable
home to the dark vastness of space and ancient history, he now looked back at
his own life and "perceived in myself this day with a certain degree of terror the
prompting to retire." But by "retiring" Emerson did not mean putting himself out
to pasture; he used the word in the utopian sense of nineteenth-century reformers, such as those in Brook Farm, who had sought to retire from society. Even his
friends did not understand the pull of isolation on Emerson that would make even
the company of a *few* the company of too many: "They who urge you to retire
hence would be too many for you in the center of the desert or on top of a pillar.
How dear how soothing to man arises the Idea of God peopling the lovely place,
effacing the scars of our mistakes & disappointments."[2] It is thus in response to
the image of himself alone in the desert with a direct and unmediated connection
with the divine that he imagines a battle between this new "Idea of God" and the

old gods of tradition and rhetoric. Only when the old gods have been overcome might an individual become so fully emancipated from mere egotism and social pressures that God would fire the heart with his presence.

One name that Emerson gave to this new god was "Eloquence." Eloquence spoke with abandon of the truth and beauty of things, piercing the veil of appearances and revealing the hidden immunity that binds together all phenomena, of which humans are but a part. For the old gods, eloquence had nothing but contempt and exerted nothing but power. As Emerson wrote in his journal of 1856, "Eloquence is forever a power that shoves usurpers from their thrones, & sits down on them by allowance & acclaim of all."[3] The old usurper god, rhetoric, knew nothing but dry logic and formulaic style. Like the genteel Edward Everett, whom Emerson held up as an example, the god of rhetoric only had "charms for the dull" while possessing "neither intellectual nor moral principles to teach."[4] How different it was when eloquence spoke through the voice of the true orator. For a "true orator will instantly show you that all the states & kingdoms in the world, all the senators, lawyers, & rich men are caterpillars' webs & caterpillars, when seen in the light of the same despised & imbecile truth, Grand grand truth! The orator himself becomes a shadow & a fool before this light which lightens through him. It shines backward & forward; diminishes, annihilates everybody, and the prophet so gladly, so sublimely feels his personality lost in this gaining triumphing godhead."[5] For Emerson, and for the Transcendentalists as a whole, the nineteenth century was a time of revolution in which the god of tradition, and its handmaiden, the god of rhetoric, would be revealed as caterpillars in the light of grand truth that would illuminate the world through prophetic eloquence.

What Emerson disparagingly referred to as the god of rhetoric was not the self-conscious art of crafting persuasive discourse but rather the calcified and formulaic traditions that had remained in place even up through the eighteenth century. This style of rhetoric had dominated speech and writing prior to the American Revolution. Still constrained by what were essentially medieval humanistic traditions, rhetoric prior to the writing of the Declaration of Independence was seen not as a democratic art of addressing and rallying the people but rather an elite form of literacy "addressed to specialized legal, political, or religious audiences with their own formalist codes." Consequently early eighteenth-century writers adhered to what Jay Fliegelman describes as "a circumscribed, ceremonial view of rhetoric as but figures and tropes serving as handmaidens charged with the artful presentation of ideas determined by a master logic and expressed through the conventions of grammar."[6] Rhetoric served a function within power, but it facilitated action in concert not by exciting, animating, and motivating a mass audience of citizens—to say nothing of individual genius—but rather by refining the technical means by which a literary elite managed the affairs of state and kept the people from choosing to assert their own power through various forms of mob violence.[7]

When the future Supreme Court justice Oliver Wendell Holmes Jr. remarked of Emerson's "The American Scholar" that "this grand oration was our intellectual Declaration of Independence," he may have been more accurate than he knew.[8] Jefferson had not only declared independence for the nation but also for language, specifically the political language of persuasion. By redefining political authority in a republican setting as something that emerges from the voluntary consent of the governed, the Declaration had also inaugurated a new kind of rhetoric that was more than simply a proper and decorous use of figures and tropes intended to be consumed and evaluated by a literary elite. Jefferson's Declaration introduced to the United States what Fliegelman calls a "new rhetoric of persuasion" that "sought to recover classical rhetoric, broadly understood as the active art of moving and influencing men, of galvanizing their passions, interests, biases, and temperament."[9] But in the late eighteenth century, this rhetoric of persuasion, even while emancipated from aristocratic diction, was still limited by the practical-minded demos that consisted mainly of yeoman farmers whose horizon of experience did not go far beyond the boundaries of their farmstead and village. For them this new rhetoric of persuasion was characterized by a kind of Yankee sensibility marked by a "nakedness of truth, a true beauty, a self-evidence that required no judgment, the ultimate Protestant plain style."[10] Emerson's call for a new kind of eloquence was thus a demand for a second revolution in language that would violate every norm of this plain style so as to give to genius access to the full range of expression and grant it the freedom to speak truth with power, come what may.

Transcendentalism was the movement that heard that call. Constituted by a new generation of American artists, intellectuals, ministers, and reformers, the Transcendentalists included Orestes Brownson, Theodore Parker, Margaret Fuller, Amos Bronson Alcott, Elizabeth Peabody, George Ripley, and Henry David Thoreau. During their short heyday in the 1830s and 1840s, they represented, in Perry Miller's opinion, "the most energetic and extensive upsurge of the mind and spirit enacted in America until the intellectual crisis of the 1920s."[11] Although difficult to define neatly due to the wide range of interests and attitudes the movement encompassed, Transcendentalism can nonetheless be said to be held together by a common commitment to self-culture that sought to actualize the innate potentialities of the human spirit through free thought and experimental action. In the words of Transcendentalist poet and artist Christopher Pearse Cranch, "true Transcendentalism is that living and always new *spirit* of truth, which is ever going forth on its conquests into the world" and "which is thus in the only sense *transcendental,* when it labors to *transcend* itself, and soar ever higher and nearer the great source of Truth."[12] The Transcendentalists were thus what Lawrence Buell characterized as "the first American youth movement, the nation's first counterculture" dedicated to what was then a radical notion that "youthful vision and vigor should count for more than the stodgy so-called wisdom of the elders."[13] They were members of the first American youth move-ment to ask, in Emerson's words, the question that would be asked by every subsequent generation: "Why should not we also enjoy an original relation to the universe?"[14]

Many would argue that this question has taken on even more significance in the twenty-first century. This is certainly so for a critic such as Harold Bloom, for whom Emerson in particular remains a source of salvation for the American spirit. Emerson advanced, in Bloom's reading, not a specific kind of revolution, person, knowledge, or even structure of power, all of which would reproduce another form of the old gods, but rather a universal notion that the expression of individual power is self-justifying. For Bloom "Emerson remains the American theoretician of power—be it political, literary, spiritual, economic—because he took the risk of exalting transition for its own sake."[15] To do battle with the old gods that would have writers merely parrot the behaviors and speech patterns of others, quite irrespective of the virtues of such imitation, is for Bloom the sign of a decadence to be continually resisted. Bloom thus equates imitation with decadence and individualism with virtue—even as he acknowledges the latter's vices: "Individualism, whatever damages its American ruggedness continues to inflict on our politics and social economy, is more than ever the only hope for our imaginative lives."[16] Citing the same passage in Emerson's journal that opens this chapter, he thus calls on readers to resist the god of tradition, which belongs "to the political clerics and the clerical politicians," as well as the god of rhetoric, which belongs today "to the academies, where he is called by the name of the Gallic Demiurge, Language," so that we might finally leave "the American imagi-nation free as always to open itself to the third God of Emerson's prayer."[17] That god is eloquence.

What exactly the nature of this third god? For Bloom eloquence is not a personal god but a gnosis, a kind of knowledge that "is not rational knowledge, but like poetic knowledge."[18] Reminiscent of Plato's conception of God as the god of forms, as a sublime encounter with truth and beauty that in its fullness can only be contemplated as one would the sun, gnosis reveals a knowledge that transcends the empirical sciences or even traditional religion. Gnosis emancipates people from the bounds of their particular lives and reveals a whole that tran-scends the limits of conventional language. It is for this reason that eloquence, as an expression of gnosis, expresses itself in a way that "transcends the epistemol-ogy of tropes, the cognitive aspects of rhetoric."[19] The latter are the purview of the old gods that eloquence seeks to depose. The old gods defined power as its maintenance and so valorized a kind of language that maintained tradition by the repetition of the same. Rhetoric itself became an old god. Indeed any rhetorical theory, for Bloom, is a way of maintaining the status quo, including those postmodern theories that oppose the status quo through ironic textuality. For Emerson, however, "power is an affair of crossings, of thresholds or transitional moments, evasions, substitutions, mental dilemmas resolved only by arbitrary acts of will." Consequently, Bloom suggests, "what a Gnosis of rhetoric, like Emerson's, prophetically wars against is every philosophy of rhetoric, and so now against the irony of irony and the randomness of all textuality."[20] In the place of rhetorical theory, Bloom's, Emerson asserts only one principle for those who would follow the new god: "Every fall is a *fall forward,* neither fortunate nor unfortunate, but forward, without effort, impelled to the American truth, which is that the stream of power and wisdom flowing as life is eloquence."[21]

There is something enduring about this image of that Bloom paints of Emerson, as a heroic individual speaking truth with beauty, revealing kingdoms to be caterpillars, and losing oneself in the light of the divine spirit only to be reconstituted again as a triumphant and eloquent genius who seeks only the power to become something new. Attractive, too, is the notion that one replaces the false idols of a god of rhetoric with the gnostic revelations of a god of eloquence, in which "power is in the traversing of the black holes of rhetoric, where the interpreter reads his own freedom to read."[22] For this type of rhetoric, one needs no Aristotle. It requires no understanding of a situated exigence, commits people to no psychological theory of audience, is not limited by historical or economic conditions, demands no faithfulness to motive, and restricts language to nothing more than people's capacity for freedom and the power to express what they feel with the resources that language puts before them. In his journal Emerson wrote, "Men quarrel with your rhetoric. Society chokes with a trope, like a child with the croup. They much prefer Mr Prose, & Mr Hoarse-as-Crows, to the dangerous conversation of Gabriel and archangel Michael perverting all rules, & bounding continually from earth to heaven."[23] Here is a norm of transcendental eloquence that speaks to the prophetic impulse in all people—let society choke on everyone's tropes as they bound ever more freely from earth to heaven in continual self-making.

Picking up on this sentiment, Richard T. Poirier argues that the unique power of Emerson's writing represents what he calls the act of "troping," or the "turning of a word in directions or detours it seemed destined otherwise to avoid."[24] Troping embodies an act of impiety toward the old god of rhetoric, whose laws established clear boundaries on language and suggested detours that at best simply delight the ear or please the eye. Yet the new god of eloquence turned language to different ends so that "by the turning, the troping of it, language can be made into a sign not of human subservience but human power."[25] Troping is thus an expression of a kind of abandonment, not of language itself but of the demand that it be consistent, transparent, and unified. Emerson, Poirer suggests, "recommends that we abandon one discourse for another, give up one tone of voice for another, change or trope the vocabulary that has also been found to be at least procedurally useful."[26] People should abandon these things not to embrace their opposite, pure irony or chaos, but rather to acknowledge "that such contradictions are inherent to the mystery of human existence."[27] The act of twisting language, of wrenching words from their traditional usages and thrusting them in new directions, represents the acknowledgment that society is thrown into a world of becoming in which words are not mirrors of reality but catalysts for change.

What does this new god of eloquence, so contemptuous of the old gods of tradition and rhetoric, herald for the understanding of democracy, of people's capacity to live together? One view suggests that these consequences are fully democratic. For instance John Dewey, in an egalitarian reading of Emerson, declared him the "Philosopher of Democracy," namely because of his willingness to find truth on the highway where all can experience and access it freely: "Against creed and system, convention and institution, Emerson stands for restoring to the common man that which in the name of religion, of philosophy, of art and of morality, has been embezzled from the common store and appropriated to sectarian and class use."[28] A second reading, however, finds Dewey's interpretation too close to the more egalitarian spirit of American pragmatism. For someone such as Richard Rorty, Emerson in his praise of the new god actually stands for a completely different set of virtues: those of individual heroic reinvention. At bottom, he argues, "Emerson, like his disciple Nietzsche, was not a philosopher of democracy but a private self-creation, of what he called 'the infinitude of the private man.' Godlike power was never far from Emerson's mind. His America was not so much a community of fellow citizens as a clearing in which Godlike heroes could act out self-written dramas."[29] Or as Stanley Cavell summarizes the difference, whereas Deweyan pragmatism tends to "address a situation of unintelligence" and seeks to use a scientifically informed politics to reorder the world, Emersonian individualism "discerns a scene of what he variously called conformity, timidity, and shame" and calls for provocative experimentation in order to overcome despair and aspire for genius.[30] For a rhetoric that might restore democracy and achieve social justice, Rorty and Cavell suggest, one should go to Dewey and the pragmatists; but for an eloquence that might inspire individual acts of private self-creation, Emerson—and by association the Transcendentalists —should be the exemplars.

As important are these distinctions are between the spirit of Pragmatism and Transcendentalism, between rhetoric and eloquence, I prefer a more comic interpretation of their relationship inspired by Kenneth Burke. For Burke comedy always complicates stark dualisms and simplistic oppositions by placing characters in complex situations with overlapping motives, such that what seems praiseworthy at one moment is blameworthy in the next, and vice versa. By thus acknowledging the forensic complexity of any dramatic action performed in the company of others, comedy is thus "neither wholly euphemistic, nor wholly debunking—hence it provides the charitable attitude toward people that is required for purposes of persuasion and co-operation."[31] Burke's view of comedy grows out of his understanding of the original Greek context of comedy, which is particularly notable here because of the idea of the transition between gods (or kings). As Francis Macdonald Cornford has shown, Greek comedy had its origins in archaic fertility festivals that dramatized "the succession of a new divine King to one who stands for the old year whose powers have failed in the decay of winter," the conclusion being the marriage of the new king to the daughter of the old and a welcoming of the new year.[32] The clash between the old king and the new king thus did not produce any revolution but merely a cyclical restoration of a familiar order under new management, with all the strife and conflict in the initial clash of the two orders coming to some reconciliation in the end. Similarly, although Emerson called for his readers to cease from their god of rhetoric, the god of eloquence that he inaugurates is still married to tradition and has assumed all of the powers of the old god. Eloquence, for all intents and purposes, is but the next generation of the older god.

Similarly the pragmatic faith in intelligence as a method of reforming moral, social, and political life is not discontinuous with the poetic spirit of transcendentalism but actually an extension of it. This goes as much for Emerson as any of the other Transcendentalists. Indeed what makes the movement of such rhetorical interest is how this youthful spirit of rebellion found expression in what were then radically new forms of advocacy and eloquence by individuals passionately committed to social and political change. The Transcendentalists were not simply nineteenth-century rebels without a cause; they were what Philip Gura calls "one of the nation's first coherent intellectual groups: movers and shakers in the forefront of educational reform; proselytizers for the rights of women, laborers, prisoners, and the indigent and infirm; and agitators for the abolition of slavery."[33] Much different than the familiar commodification of youthful rebellion in today's popular culture, the Transcendentalist notion of counterculture committed its members to reform. As Joel Myerson explains, the spirit of reform was a logical deduction from Transcendentalist principles, for "if we live in a religious environment in which we can perceive God directly by cultivating our innate divinity, if we act on the basis of intuition rather than sensory experience, if we believe in self-culture and self-reliance (which is, after all, god reliance), and if we wish to eliminate those who try to deny us all these things by insisting that only a credentialed intermediate body can interpret them for us, then, naturally, the result is religious, philosophical, literary, and social change."[34] To be a Transcendentalist meant to commit oneself to the politics of transcendence whereby one harnessed the critical and constitutive capacities of eloquent rhetoric to shatter and remake existing structures of power and thereby enable the pursuit of self-culture both for oneself and for others. As Roger Thompson argues, even in Emerson one can find a "rhetoric whose function is the formation of a just society" and that is "at the center of the center of action because it provides the means through which participation and social change can be prompted."[35] This kind of rhetoric is eloquence.

This book narrates how individual Transcendentalists each articulated a unique rhetoric and politics that applied their philosophical reflections and poetic practices to affairs of persuasive eloquence and social justice. By the politics of Transcendentalism, I mean the degree to which the ideas of many of the leading Transcendentalists—including Emerson—were not simply applied to the controversies of their day after the fact but were actually developed as a reaction and response to them. According to Harald Wydra, the politics of transcendence arises within "liminal" moments of history in which "people experience existential uncertainty when confronted with territorial disintegration, moral collapse, or the threat of civil war."[36] The politics of transcendence inevitably arises during these periods of rapid transition and uncertainty, such as those decades leading up to the Luther's Reformation, the French Revolution, or the American Civil War. These are times when people became frustrated with existing forms of power and engaged in a "quest for recognition and meaning in extraordinary politics."[37] To accomplish its aims, the politics of transcendence makes strategic use of the twofold meaning of "going beyond" in order to mobilize an audience to action. On the one hand, the politics of transcendence "is transgressive and performative. It consists of breaking of boundaries that had 'controlled' and 'protected' the habits, procedures, and values but also differentiated the sectors of action—private and public, religious and secular—in a given community."[38] On the other hand, it is always "reflective and creative of new meanings," thus providing a new foundation or promise on which to act and to hope.[39] In this way the politics of transcendence is simultaneously destructive and creative, gratifying the pent-up bodily energy that yearns to sweep away the vestiges of the old while fulfilling the appetites of the mind to envision and struggle toward a new world designed by the architecture of principle. Transcendentalism, I argue, was therefore not only a literary genre of poetic writing to be consumed in private, although it certainly lends itself to that mode of reception; it was also a rhetorical genre of public advocacy whose full power and vibrancy can only be understood in the light of its politics.

By the rhetoric of Transcendentalism, I mean the self-conscious and public use of symbols to move people to collective action. The rhetoric of transcendence also accomplishes political aims, but it does so through use of a specific rhetorical strategy. For Kenneth Burke, for instance, transcendence neither means argument by principle, which deduces the consequences of committing oneself to adherence to some higher law, nor tragic catharsis, whereby a divided audience is purged and unified through the ritual imitation of the image. Transcendence for Burke is a way of crossing a divide or reconciling a contradiction through a radical act of imagination whereby people are able to see and judge themselves from the perspective of some distant and different "beyond." As an example Burke cites a passage from Virgil's *Aeneid* in which the dead in the underworld, who could not be ferried across the river because they remain unburied, "stretched forth their hands, through love of the farther shore." This is the pattern of transcendence. Burke explains: "whether there is or is not an ultimate shore towards which we, the unburied, would cross, transcendence involves dialectical processes whereby something HERE is interpreted in terms of something THERE, something beyond itself." And this is exactly the kind of transcendence he sees in the language of Emerson, the kind of transcendence implicit in the nature of language itself. According to Burke "the machinery of language is so made that, either rightly or wrongly, either grandly or in fragments, we stretch forth our hands through love of the farther shore."[40] The accomplishment of Emerson and the Transcendentalists is to make this stretching forth a self-conscious rhetorical strategy whereby an audience would "find itself" by interpreting its present from a future time and distant place, by looking at the part from the perspective of the whole, by seeing the particular in light of the universal, or by seeing existence from the distance of a star.

This book will explore the life and work of six of the most important figures in the Transcendentalist movement—Sampson Reed, Bronson Alcott, Orestes Brownson, Ralph Waldo Emerson, Margaret Fuller, and Henry David Thoreau—and conclude with a reflection on the movement through the writings of Frederick Douglass. However, unlike other books that explore the Transcendentalist movement as a whole, as for instance the excellent treatments by Barbara Packer and Philip Gura, my aim is not to provide an overarching summary of the movement in history. It is more narrowly to dramatize and elucidate how each of these figures developed a unique theoretical perspective on rhetoric and politics that was both a reaction to the circumstances of their time and prophetic of contemporary understandings of rhetoric and politics that arose in the context of modernity. Although I will dedicate a chapter to each of these individuals, I do not intend to provide a comprehensive review of their lives and works. Rather the biographies of each individual are situated within the context of a specific social, political, or economic controversy of the early nineteenth-century United States and will be narrated only up until the point to provide the rhetorical context for interpreting a specific text that I believe is representative of one of their major contributions to rhetorical theory and practice. Moreover each chapter will conclude at a progressively later period in history, thus giving the book a sense of qualitative form that begins after the war of 1812 and leads up to and then beyond the American Civil War. One of the overarching themes of the book is thus how each Transcendentalist developed theories of rhetoric and politics that became increasingly revolutionary precisely because they were formed in response to the increasing crises in American political culture (and, for Fuller, European culture) that by the time of Thoreau had made violence seemed inevitable.

There are several audiences for this book. For rhetoricians I believe the Transcendentalists represent an untapped resource for understanding the historical roots of rhetorical theory and practice in the United States. I will thus be using the term *rhetoric* not to refer to the practices of the old gods but more generally to what Burke calls "the use of words by human agents to form attitudes or induce actions in other human agents."[41] A rhetorical perspective is thus one that recognizes the full extent to which people are immersed in a rhetorical landscape and how even, in the Transcendentalist sense, nature itself can act rhetorically upon them when it is experienced as a symbol that unleashes their power. For those in literature, philosophy, or American studies who may be familiar with the life and work of the Transcendentalists but have not interpreted them in terms of the rhetorical exigencies of their day, my contribution will be less to challenge current literary theories and more to complement those with current rhetorical theory. Lastly, I have a desire to make this book appealing to a general readership. I believe that it is in the spirit of Transcendentalism itself to argue that an important contribution of scholarship is simply to dramatize ideas and people in history in such a way that it expands the horizons of experience and introduces readers to a world that is not their own so that they might see their lives differently—and perhaps more connectedly.

A simple restatement of the Transcendentalist principle is that people live in a cosmos and must ever seek beyond the limitations of their particular horizons to try to link themselves with a greater whole. This principle must continually be revived in a culture that celebrates the interconnectedness of a global economy at the same time that it provides evermore sophisticated ways of "retiring" to private technological and ideological utopias. Transcendentalism is no cure for the problems of the United States. Indeed, looking at the Transcendentalist legacy today, one can even say that the myth of the heroic individual genius they often promoted has become fully absorbed within the system of economic exploitation that individuals like Brownson and Thoreau utterly rejected. But encountered as agents acting in their own rhetorical history, and not simply as myths to be consumed, the Transcendentalists can be encountered again as complex and contradictory individuals struggling for what they believed to be a vision of truth, beauty, and goodness that could lift Americans out of the mire of tradition, break the chains of bigotry, and pierce the veil of ignorance that kept them sleepwalking through life. Transcendentalism did not represent any system of thought, but rather an attitude—specifically an attitude that made one dissatisfied with oneself, eager to expand the horizons of experience to encompass the experience of the other and willing to judge one's life as if viewed from the perspective of an immanent ideal of perfection. To adopt the Transcendentalist attitude today is thus to look out at the world with similar eyes, to speak a language that challenges the old gods, and to commit oneself to crafting a form of eloquence whereby collective transcendence might be possible, even if only to the degree that we might stretch forth our hands a bit closer to the farther shore.

CHAPTER I

"Eloquence is the language of love"

Sampson Reed and the Calling of Genius

> The world was always busy; the human heart has always had love of some kind; there has always been fire on the earth. There is something in the inmost principles of an individual, when he begins to exist, which urges him onward; there is something in the center of the character of a nation, to which the people aspire; there is something which gives activity to the mind in all ages, countries, and worlds. This principle of activity is love; it may be the love of good or evil; it may manifest itself in saving life or in killing; but it is love.
>
> Sampson Reed, "Genius," 1821

In the month of August 1821, love was in the air. On August 4 the first issue of the *Saturday Evening Post* appeared in the United States. Sold for just a nickel, the *Post* was the makeover of Benjamin Franklin's original 1754 *Pennsylvania Gazette,* to be published as a four-page newspaper that contained essays, poems, stories, and advertisements. Soon to become the most widely read publication in the United States, the *Post* was the model for a new kind of American periodical that spoke with the voice not of a region or class but of the nation. And its debut could not have been more timely. On August 10 Missouri peaceably became the twenty-fourth state of the Union. Finally admitted as a slave state over strenuous objections from the North, its integration had only been made possible by the Missouri Compromise of 1820 that forbid slavery in any subsequent territories above 36°30' north latitude. The Missouri Compromise was delivered with a promise that the nation would continue expanding West without further discord and strife. And farther south Stephen Austin was making his way to the Texas capital of New Spain, San Antonio de Béxar, following in the steps of his father, Moses Austin, who had earlier been authorized by Spanish authorities to bring American colonists into Texas to help populate its sparse landscape. Then he heard the news. On August 20 Juan O'Donojú, captain general of New Spain and representative of the Spanish Crown, signed the Treaty of Córdoba, which granted independence to Mexico and ended the decade-long Mexican War of Independence. In a few years, Austin, with the permission of the new Mexican government, would bring about fifteen hundred families from the United States into the territory, where they eventually outnumbered Hispanic *tejanos* more than two to one.[1] In August 1821 Americans were falling in love with their growing nation, which seemed to be increasing in scope and power by the day.

Few people were feeling more amorous that month than Sampson Reed (1800–1880). The son of a Massachusetts clergyman, Reed had been on his way to graduating from Harvard College in 1818 and then entering the fledgling Divinity School at Cambridge to become a Unitarian minister. But something happened to him in the privacy of his study that would change the course of his life: he fell in love with the idea of love. Specifically he discovered the writings of Swedish visionary and mystic Emmanuel Swedenborg, who, after a long career studying metallurgy and mining, had suddenly prophesized the coming of a New Jerusalem and the final unity of the two worlds of matter and spirit, which had too long been kept separate. But the day was dawning, imagined Swedenborg, when humanity would discover the key that would interpret the true correspondences between language, nature, and God. On that day human beings would no longer simply be detached observers of nature and passive imitators of religious texts; they would instead be active interpreters of "the vast allegory we behold as the universe" and the medium by which the power of the divine spirit would be made manifest.[2] For Reed reading Swedenborg was a revelation; it had disclosed to him that the true power of the universe that guided all things was not strife or matter or law or chance, but love.

And so it was that love guided Reed to the podium that August to deliver his address, "Oration on Genius," on reception of his MA from Harvard. Perry Miller described his address as his "farewell to academic security and respectability," effectively announcing to his own graduating class that he cared nothing for pursuing a life of a gentleman minister.[3] But in another way it was a manifesto for those who would gain a different kind of security and respectability in the new nation that was just being born. His oration was delivered to give confidence and direction to all those like him who wished to strike out on their own to seek power through an original, creative, and direct encounter with nature not for the sake of contemplation but for the sake of transformation and power. The language of divine love gave him this confidence and direction, for it represented that "fire on the earth" that had always given "activity to the mind in all ages, countries, and worlds."[4] One's power potential was thus not measured by physical size but by the degree to which one lives by and channels this force. Nor did it matter *what* one loved, whether it be good or evil, life or killing. People's continual doubts about whether or not they love the right object are self-imposed limitations, artificial constraints that prevent them from tapping into the power of their innate activity. But genius knows no constraint, for it is the uninhibited disclosure of the power and truth of love in history.

To the graduates of Harvard, including in attendance one BA student named Ralph Waldo Emerson, Reed defined for them a new calling much in the way that Emerson would do sixteen years later. That calling was genius, which was both the perception of the light of divine truth through the "intellectual eye of man" and the public disclosure of that truth through the language of eloquence.[5] In contradistinction to both the scholastic philosopher who buries insights into indecipherable tomes of learning and the celebrity dilettante who exists mainly to flatter the people, true genius seeks a higher form of communication: "Here is no sickly aspiring after fame,—no filthy lust after philosophy, whose very origin is an eternal barrier to the truth. But sentiments will flow from the heart warm as its blood, and speak eloquently; for eloquence is the language of love."[6] Unenlightened society, of course, continued to reiterate the stale dualistic pieties that "greatness is one thing, and goodness another; that philosophy is divorced from religion; that truth is separated from its source; that that which is called goodness is sad, and that which is called genius is proud." But Reed tells those geniuses of a new generation not to give up hope: "The time is not far distant. The cock has crowed. I hear the distant lowing of the cattle which are grazing on the mountains. 'Watchman, what of the night? Watchman, what of the night? The watchmen saith, the morning cometh.'"[7] And when morning comes, the eloquence of genius will shine forth.

The relatively elusive figure of Reed serves as an appropriate introduction to the rhetoric and politics of Transcendentalism for two reasons. First, although never formally a member of the inner circle of the Transcendentalists, Reed was the first to give public expression to many themes that would be central to their attitudes and assumptions. Arthur Wrobel identifies these shared romantic characteristics as "a philosophical optimism that viewed nature as existing for the soul's use, a faith in the inherent godlikeness of man, the belief in the unique genius of each individual, and a confidence that all the elements of the creation are linked together according to a benevolent divine order."[8] And these characteristics would have practical effects in terms of how individuals were to understand their political relationships to each other and the form and function of eloquence within that system. Reed's vision of a divine order of love, for instance, "aroused expectations of mankind's spiritual rejuvenation, elevated intuition over Lockean empiricism, asserted that the genius of the individual's mind links him to the infinite, exalted the uniqueness of each individual and his potential for greatness, and proposed that lasting art has its foundation in nature."[9] For Reed, then, genuine politics was not a struggle between partisan interests but an arena whereby individual geniuses would display through eloquence their intuited visions of perfection rooted in nature's laws and God's love.

Perhaps more important, however, Reed is significant because his actual life and times reveal a great deal about the social and economic conditions that make his prophetic vision a suitable myth for ambitious individuals like himself in the decades following the War of 1812. This is because even though Reed produced only two important rhetorical texts, his oration "Genius" and his 1826 essay, "The Growth of the Mind," in his life he embodied in many ways the spirit of his place and time, illuminating important changes in the nation that prefigure the emergence of Transcendentalism as a social movement. Reed was not, like other Transcendentalists, a minister, writer, or public intellectual. After his epic pronouncements about love, he followed his own genius by eventually becoming the leading wholesale druggist of New England under the firm Reed, Cutter, and Company. He thus participated not only in the intellectual and religious movements surrounding Swedenborg, but also in the new market economy of the Northeast that promised to remake the entire economic and social landscape of the United States. His pronouncements about love are thus misunderstood if their meaning is restricted to emotional or spiritual growth. Love for Reed was a force not only of the spiritual but also of the natural world, and therefore of the world of technology, economy, finance, and politics. To investigate him in his time is to establish at the beginning the intimate relationship between Transcendentalism and a rapidly changing nation and to discover in his conception of eloquence a language that endeavors to remake the nation by transforming the latent capacities of love into practical and political power.

Rather than beginning with the context of New England Unitarianism, then, it is more valuable to begin with a figure such as Reed, who more directly places the movement within the larger changes in American politics and economy. Transcendentalism did not arise simply out of religious controversies involving the nature of miracles or philosophical debates about the meaning of Lockean empiricism; it became a popular movement because it channeled the actual ambitions and desires of individuals who saw before them new opportunities in a developing nation that were being obstructed by the recalcitrance of old gods. The United States in the 1820s was saying farewell to the old myth of Jeffersonian agrarianism. The South was entrenching itself into a conservative plantation aristocracy, while the North was rapidly embracing the transportation, communication, and market revolutions that were pushing the nation spreading westward at a rapid rate. Reed's conception of love was thus a symbol of a latent power that was now transforming the continent through a union of technology and ideas and seemed to make it possible for a few individuals to remake themselves and their environment in their own image of God. That each of the Transcendentalists would develop his or her own image to pursue makes each worthy of particular attention; but that they all thought to tap into this newfound power for the sake of their own self-culture makes them consistent with Reed's conception of politics and rhetoric in an age in which eloquence had finally come into its own.

In May 1834 Emerson wrote a letter to his friend Thomas Carlyle in England, in which he promised to send forthwith a copy of the speeches of Daniel Webster, "a good man and as strong as if he were a sinner," who "begins to find himself at the centre of a great and enlarging party."[10] The volume of Webster included his famous "Second Reply to Hayne," delivered in response to the 1829 Foot Resolution, a resolution supported by Jacksonian Democrats that would have handed federal land over to the states to be parceled out and sold as quickly as possible to white settlers eager to "civilize" the land. But the resolution was defeated, in large part because of the eloquence of Webster, a leader in the emerging Whig Party, whose speech Emerson rightly notes "the Americans have never done praising."[11] In fact newspaper reprints and pamphlets of Webster's "Second Reply" made the artifact the most widely circulated speech in history up until that point, with at least one hundred thousand copies sold in addition to those reprints that were recorded in schoolbooks and memorized by grammar students for almost a century afterward.[12]

What made the speech so remarkable was that Webster had taken what might have seen initially as a minor policy dispute and turned it into a referendum on whether the United States was simply a confederation of individual states, each pursuing its own self-interest, or an entire nation guided by shared ideals. Webster championed the latter. In his closing he made his famous declaration of nationalistic sentiment: "Liberty *and* Union, now and forever, one and inseparable!"[13] In Webster, Emerson placed his hope; after years of having endured the regime of Andrew Jackson, "the most unfit person in the Presidency" who has been "doing the worst things," he perceived that finally "now things seem to mend."[14]

But the Webster volume was not the only book that he sent to Carlyle. He included "with it the little book of my Swedenborgian druggist of whom I told you."[15] This was Reed's *The Growth of the Mind.* Of the two books he received, Carlyle was more struck by Reed's. Webster seemed to him a man he "can recognize: a sufficient, effectual man, whom one must wish well to, and prophecy well of." But Reed was altogether different: "he is a faithful thinker, that Swedenborgian Druggist of yours, with really deep ideas, who makes me too pause and think, were it only to consider what type of man *he* must be, in what manner of thing, after all, Swedenborgianism must be." To express his wonder at Reed's thought, he then quotes a line from Reed's pamphlet: "Through the smallest window look well, and you can look out into the Infinite."[16] A few months later, Emerson followed up with a letter praising to Carlyle the novelty of Reed and his "New Church," which challenged all separations and dualisms in the world and instead viewed "the Natural World as strictly the symbol or exponent of the Spiritual, and part for part; the animals to be incarnations of certain affections; and scarce a popular expression seemed figurative, but they affirm to be the simple statement of fact."[17] Although not perfect by any means, Emerson acknowledges, Reed and his sect "must contribute more than all of the other sects to the new faith which must arise out of all."[18] It was Emerson's hope that through this faith everything that had been kept apart for so long would be suddenly brought together—and if not with liberty and union, then with a love by some other name.

The pairing of Webster and Reed may have been coincidental by Emerson, but it was also fitting. Reed's significance to the Transcendentalist movement cannot be understood apart from the economic and political changes catalyzed by what Charles Sellers wryly refers to as "that hired gun of wealth and power, Webster."[19] Born to a New Hampshire family a few years before the signing of the Constitution and graduating from Dartmouth College just after the turn of the nineteenth century, Webster quickly rose to power as a lawyer specializing in a defense of corporate interests and rights, famously winning the case of *Dartmouth College vs. Woodward* (1819) by persuading the Supreme Court to declare that a corporation was an "artificial being" endowed with characteristics of "immortality and, if the expression be allowed, individuality," which made it an independent agent that had contractual rights that could not be modified at whim by the states.[20] Chief Justice John Marshall even went so far as to express wonder that a "perpetual succession of individuals are capable of acting for the promotion of the particular object, like one immortal being."[21] By the time Webster was elected to Congress in 1823, he had replaced the old conservatism of aristocratic Federalism, which had been based on a firm distinction between the propertied and nonpropertied classes, with a new conservatism of capitalistic Whiggery that dissolved this distinction by reinterpreting every citizen as a potential corporate shareholder: "by the 1830s, he came to understand that by appealing for an even broader diffusion of property—to be achieved by sound conservative business policies and not by destructive Jacksonian foolishness—the experiment of democracy might be rendered safe."[22]

Of all the Transcendentalists, it was Reed who took this faith to heart and dedicated his life to its realization. The most detailed early account of his life is not found in any history or biography; it is found in the pages of volume 43 of the *American Druggist and Pharmaceutical Record,* published on November 23, 1903. Under the title "Sampson Reed, Emerson's Swedenborgian Druggist" and written by James O. Jordan, PhG, the one-page eulogy celebrates the life and accomplishment of Reed in order to bring to "light an interesting personality" and celebrate one of the founding entrepreneurs of the New England pharmaceutical industry. The basic facts of his life are uncomplicated. After graduating from Harvard, Reed was "entirely destitute of means and was under the necessity of seeking some other occupation for subsistence." He thus spent several years searching for occupation, first teaching school, then trying out medicine, until finally, through an acquaintance, he gained a position with apothecary William B. White in Boston, for whom he worked for three years. Finally, after gaining a temporary loan of nine hundred dollars, he was able to open his own business under the partnership of Lowe and Reed, where "they sold on the first day one stick of licorice for 1 cent." But business picked up, and after relocating and changing the names of partners several times, he "amassed what was in those days a competency" and handed interest of the business to his son, Thomas (a business that in 1901 merged with the Eastern Drug Company). During that time Reed was also active in public affairs, serving on the school committee as an alderman and taking part in the Massachusetts Constitutional Convention in 1853; he kept a steady interest in the affairs of the other members of his Harvard class; and he "was untiring in his devotion to the cause of Swedenborg," publishing several works and investing most of his fortune to promoting the church.[23]

It was this final point, clearly, that made Reed an "interesting personality" to Jordan. The writer spends considerable space describing Reed's influence on Emerson, quoting many of the same passages from the letters to and from Carlyle. And to further bolster Reed's significance, Jordan cites the conclusion of an essay by Alex Japp, "The Gift of Emerson," which had appeared in the voluminous 1882 edition (more than seven hundred pages) of the *Gentleman's Magazine*. Japp had compared side-by-side excerpts from Reed and Emerson, concluding that "Emerson efficiently developed and applied what Reed had only suggested."[24] With this line of influence from Reed to Emerson authoritatively verified, Jordan then worked up to his eloquent conclusion: "Mr. Reed died in Boston, July 8, 1880. He was a man of much energy and force of character, one who when he had made up his mind of the right, acts according to his views. Of intense industry and application, he found time from business cares to devote to literary and public work. One wonders what stature he might have attained had the conditions been such that he could have developed his own suggestion instead of having, as Japp avows, Emerson do it for him.[25] Such was the legacy of Reed, Emerson's Swedenborgian druggist, a man both of action and of thought, who not only became one of the most successful capitalist entrepreneurs of New England during his lifetime, but also, to quote Japp, "was one of those who sowed seeds, some of which rose to stately flowers in his own garden, and thus attested their inherent value and vitality."[26] Reed ended up being praised in a pharmaceutical journal less for being a druggist than for being a Swedenborgian, showing how the ethos of the contemplative life had rhetorical authority even for an audience arguably committed to a practical one.

Yet if druggists might find Reed interesting because of his role in influencing the history of ideas, rhetoricians have good reason to find him more interesting because of how his ideas were in fact intimately connected with sanctioning and celebrating his ethos as a capitalist entrepreneur. It is easy, that is to say, to separate Reed's abstract writings from the immediate economic and political context of his time and interpret them as poetic contemplations about the meaning of the universe; it is quite another to see them as specific rhetorical interventions in the controversies of his time. Reed had not spent years cultivating a specific spiritual vision of genius simply because he was interested in abstract metaphysical questions; he did so, at least in part, in order to construct a new mythology in which he, and others like him, could play the role of hero. And this hero was the middle-class businessman. Reed was thus part of an effort of a numerous and rising class of small-scale bourgeois enterprisers who "claimed hegemony over all classes" by dissolving the old feudal boundaries between the nobility, the priesthood, and the common people and establishing in their place a market society that rewarded each according to his effort. As Sellers explains, "scorning both the handful of idle rich in the multitude of dissolute poor, they apotheosized a virtuous middle class of the effortful."[27] Thus what made Reed unique among the Transcendentalists is that he took this mythology literally. Whereas Emerson interpreted it figuratively by his own brand of poetic iconoclasm and critics such as Thoreau or Brownson explicitly condemned it as inaugurating a society of self-interested busybodies, Reed actually dedicated his life to achieving its aims and embodying its values, eventually becoming enshrined in the pages of *American Druggist and Pharmaceutical Record* as an early bourgeois hero.

Far from existing in a separate sphere of contemplation, then, his proto-Transcendentalist ideas functioned rhetorically in the sphere of action by defining a new calling consistent with what Max Weber calls the "spirit of capitalism," or the spiritual ethos of an economic system. According to Weber the development of modern capitalism was not simply based on individual desires for wealth, power, and accumulation, desires that have always played a role in human history. Rather capitalism grows out of a uniquely Protestant conception of a calling, which represented "the fulfillment of the obligations imposed upon the individual by his position in the world."[28] The stress here is upon the phrase *his position in the world.* In traditional Catholicism worldly morality, a calling while important to uphold, was not the way to God; that route was through ritual participation in church sacraments and in extreme cases a kind of "monastic asceticism" in which one renounced worldly affairs in order to dedicate oneself fully to the love of

God.[29] The Protestant ethic reversed this entire system by identifying "the valuation of the fulfillment of duty in worldly affairs as the highest form which the moral activity of the individual could assume."[30] In this way one's calling was no longer universal and otherworldly (that is to say "to love God") but particular to the role one was assigned to play in this world. In the Protestant ethic, one was put on this earth not to imitate rituals handed down from the centuries, but to labor publicly for the glory of God, in whatever capacity one found oneself.

However it is important to keep in mind that in the original conception of the Protestant ethic, which was still operative in the eighteenth-century New England economy populated by individual members of an artisan class such as Paul Revere or Thomas Paine, this labor was done for its own sake and not for any excessive material gain or worldly power. In fact this self-restraint is the key contribution of the Protestant ethic to the spirit of capitalism—its religious sanction of a "rational organization of free labor under regular discipline," an organization that was able to prosper precisely because it reined in the uncontrolled and unbridled pursuit of gain.[31] One's calling was not to get rich at all costs but to uphold the strict and sober norms of a capitalist system governed by the rules of free exchange, exact calculation, and reliable bookkeeping. Indeed in opposition to the attitude of the more traditional "capitalist adventurer" who sought above all "the acquisition of booty, whether directly in war or in the form of continuous physical booty by exploitation of subjects," the figure of sober bourgeois capitalism actually found increased possessions to be a burden rather than a source of immediate pleasure.[32] Weber explains that "the idea of man's duty to his possessions, to which he subordinates himself as an obedient steward, or even as an acquisitive machine, bears with chilling weight on his life. The greater the possession the heavier, if the ascetic attitude toward life stands the test, the feeling of responsibility for them, for holding them undiminished for the glory of God and increasing them by restless effort."[33] In this way the Puritan ethic could balance the seemingly paradoxical demands of ascetic self-denial and capitalistic acquisition. In the spirit of capitalism, the struggle was not "against the rational acquisition, but against the irrational use of wealth."[34] In other words in the Puritan ethic, it was more sinful for the poor to squander what little they had on idle pleasures than for the rich to accumulate inordinate wealth that was invested wisely, even if never actually used for any end productive of the social good.

One can only appreciate the radicalism of Reed's transformation of this ethic by first understanding what purpose it served for so long for Americans in the colonial setting. Although this conception of life seems drab and depressing to modern sensibilities—particularly when paired with Calvinist fatalism, which taught that only a few elect were predetermined by God to be saved, an elect in part identified by their successful accumulation of wealth and adherence to the Protestant ethic—it was fitting for a democratically minded people who had to endure a hard and frugal existence. This remained the lifestyle for most free citizens in the United States up until the early years of the nineteenth century. Howe writes that "life in America in 1815 was dirty, smelly, laborious, and uncomfortable. People spent most of their waking hours working, with scant opportunity for the development of individual talents and interests unrelated to farming."[35] It thus made sense that "the prevailing versions of Protestantism preached a stern morality and self-control." Negatively this ethic served to ward off the distractions of frivolous leisure that could only serve to waste precious time and energy. Positively, however, it upheld certain democratic sensibilities insofar as it "did foster literacy for Bible-reading, broad participation in decision-making, and a sense of equality among the lay members."[36] The puritanical sensibility helped level hierarchies (namely because everyone felt themselves, at some level, to be a member of the elect), increase the overall level of education (in order to read the Bible), and interpret a difficult and Spartan lifestyle into a method of praising God and proving oneself to be chosen for election to heaven (which had the added benefit of revealing wealthy nobles and aristocratic sensualists to be headed the other way). In short the Protestant ethic as applied to early capitalism gave religious sanction for the individual pursuit of wealth at the same time that it suppressed excessive individuality, leveled hierarchies, shunned the development of fine arts, and provided the foundation for an austere kind of local democracy with its equally austere form of political rhetoric.

Reed challenged this austere Protestant ethic on every point. Against the Calvinist notion of a judgmental, mysterious, and personal God, he posited that God is loving and rational and exists not as a person but as a principal activity. Against the conceptions of Original Sin that profess that the world is "immersed in darkness" because of the fallenness of human beings, Reed suggested that light can be brought into the world and that in fact "the light is the effect of the innate strength of the human intellect." Against the Puritan view of nature that sees it as a source of evil and temptation, he argued that "nature is full of God." Against the ascetic ideal of self-discipline that denies the pleasures of the body, he celebrated the genius of the kind one finds "in the language of licentious passion, in the songs of chivalry, in the descriptions of heroic valor, in the mysterious wildness of Ossian." Against the democratic ethic of Protestantism that sees every individual as equally sinful before God and needful of grace, he suggested that geniuses actually exist and that their excellence is due precisely because they have seen the light of God and internalized the principles of love. And finally, countering the Christian warning against pride and self-love, Reed suggested that there exists what he called a "humility which exalts," which is a characteristic of a genius that occurs "not when the man thinks that he is God, but when he acknowledges that his powers are from God."[37] Clearly his own address was meant to stand as an example of this new form of genius to inspire the next generation.

But what acted as the most direct challenge to the god of tradition more than any single act of eloquence was Reed's subsequent life. The fact that he went from being "entirely destitute of means" to becoming the largest wholesale druggist in New England in a matter of two short decades showed how much things had changed since the drab and sober sixteenth-century world of John Calvin—or for that matter even the eighteenth-century world of that other thrifty capitalist, Benjamin Franklin. Reed lived in an age in which, relative to the past, it seemed that the gap between the ideal and the actual, the fantastic and the possible, had begun to close if not completely collapse. This process of change is what he called the "growth of the mind" in the pamphlet that Emerson had sent to Carlyle. Here are his opening passages:

> Nothing is a more common subject of remark than the changed condition of the world. There is a more extensive intercourse of thought, and a more powerful action of mind upon mind, than formerly. The good and wise of all nations are brought nearer together, and begin to exert a power, which, though yet feeble as infancy, is felt throughout the globe. Public opinion, that helm which directs the progress of events by which the world is guided to its ultimate destination, has received a new direction. The mind has attained an upward and onward look, and is shaking off the errors and prejudices of the past. . . . The moral and intellectual character of man has undergone, and is undergoing, a change; and as this is effected, it must change the aspect of all things, as when the position-point is altered from which a landscape viewed. We appear to be approaching an age which will be the silent pause of merely physical force before the powers of the mind; the timid, subdued, awed condition of the brute, gazing on the erect and godlike form of man.[38]

Nothing could be more antithetical to the Calvinist mind-set than the idea that progress is a real character of the world, that public opinion is a voice to be respected and obeyed, that the wisdom of the past should be cast away, that the individual human mind is a source not of sin but of power, and that ultimately one should gaze with awe upon the "erect and godlike form of man." Here was a vision of history and virtue grounded not in dutiful labor to glorify God but rather creative acts of genius that revealed humans to be not obedient to God but like God. This was an age in which the powers of the mind were to harness the mechanisms of physical force, including the forces of nature, to remake the world in its own image. Reed's oration on "genius" was a reflection of and reaction to these conditions, acting as a vision of perfection that inspired him to become a prime example of the new breed of hero who could not only speak the truth but could disseminate that truth (with the profits earned from a successful joint-stock company).

Reed is important, in other words, because he shows the logic whereby one can transcend the apparent contradiction of being both the inspiration for a generation of young idealists such as Emerson and a tough-minded businessman who sought to corner the market on New England pharmaceuticals. Reed is a symbol for that frequently uncomfortable relationship at the heart of Transcendentalism between the selfless desire to attain aesthetic and intellectual union with the divine and the individualistic ambition to seek power through the rigorous pursuit of self-culture in a rapidly growing nation. Unfortunately too often it is only the poetic idealism of the Transcendentalists that is emphasized—namely by situating them solely within the context of liberal Unitarianism and the theological debates between ministers in Boston. This approach undoubtedly illuminates many key features of the theological and philosophical origins of Transcendentalism, but I do not believe one can understand the political and rhetorical significance of the movement without a broader understanding of the political economy of the United States at the beginning of the nineteenth century that brought that powerful and well-educated class into being. That Reed became a member of this class and was also the first to embody a form of transcendental eloquence is indicative of the fact that Transcendentalism had its roots in the revolutionary changes occurring in the United States. For someone such as Reed, in fact, a true Transcendentalist was neither a poet nor an entrepreneur but a fusion of the two of them together; one needed a poetic consciousness in order truly to visualize how to impose a new order of nature through the power of the mind.

The clearest indication that Transcendentalism as an intellectual movement was closely aligned with these changes is the fact that a hero to both Reed and Emerson was the spokesperson for the new political party of their age, Daniel Webster of the National Republicans. Webster in many ways was the embodiment of the dramatic shift in the political landscape that occurred in the wake of the War of 1812. Prior to the war, there still existed a division between two colonial parties: the Hamilton-styled Federalists, who favored a European-style executive federal government with its power in urban centers, and the Jeffersonian Republicans, who favored a decentralized model that championed the virtues of rural agrarianism. When the Federalist Party collapsed after the war (a collapse accelerated by its perceived collusion with the British) and the Republicans became ascendant, there emerged within their ranks a new nationalistic wing of the party called National Republicans (soon to morph into the Whigs). Embodying that spirit of love that was expanding the nation westward, the National

Republicans absorbed the former Federalists by turning their gaze from the East to the West: "Where Federalist nationalism, facing toward Europe, had feared the westward extension of the Democratic farming populace, National Republicanism staked out a continental base for the most extensive free market the world had yet seen."[39] And the basis of this turn toward the West was the main thing that traditional Jeffersonian Republicans were against: an active federal government that would invest in a series of internal improvements to bind the entire nation together into an interconnected economic and political power that would extend eventually across the continent. As South Carolinian John C. Calhoun put it (in his early nationalistic phase, before he became the leading proponent of Southern secession), "let us then bind the Republic together with a perfect system of roads and canals. Let us conquer space."[40] In fact, during the years that Reed studied at Harvard, the Fourteenth Congress, in cooperation with President James Monroe, "not only charter[ed] a bank but push[ed] national developmentalism far beyond anything envisioned by the parochial federalism of Port elites," directing the nation "irrevocably toward its capitalist destiny."[41] Webster was the spokesperson for this new destiny.

But Webster and his political party were themselves the product of three interconnected revolutions that made this capitalist destiny possible—those in transportation, communication, and markets. The first of these, the transportation revolution, made it possible to spread what Reed called the "centre of the character of the nation" across great expanses of physical space. By the turn of the nineteenth century, networks of trade and commerce remained largely crude and undeveloped due to the difficulty of moving goods through dirt roads and undeveloped natural waterways using largely horse and wind power. For instance "because of roads and bridges few in number and poor in condition—and rivers running north-south rather than east-west—long-distance trade between coast and hinterland was slow and expensive. In 1817, it took nearly 3 weeks to move a ton of goods from Buffalo to New York City."[42] But soon the invention of steamships and railroads, bridges and canals, and turnpikes and gravel roads cut travel time in most cases by a third and in some cases to a fifth of what it was previously. When the Erie Canal, the symbol of majestic internal improvements, was completed in 1825, New York governor DeWitt Clinton "boarded the canal boat *Seneca Chief* in Lake Erie and arrived at Albany a week later, having been cheered in every town along the way."[43] The canal soon exceeded everyone's expectations. Within nine years the total cost had already been collected in tolls, the skeptical urban artisans of New York City had embraced the canal because it increased a market for their products, and cities along the route had exploded in size: "between 1820 and 1850, Rochester grew in population from 1,502 to 36,403; Syracuse, from 1,814 to 22,271; Buffalo, from 2,095 to 42,261."[44]

The change in lifestyle was drastic: "where earlier settlers had been to some extent 'self-sufficient'—eking out a subsistence and making do with products they made themselves or acquired locally—people now could produce for a market, specialize in their occupations, and enjoy the occasional luxury brought in from outside."[45] This was just one of many examples of the transportation revolution, which cut distances between North and South, Europe and the United States, and the coast and the Midwest—and eventually the Atlantic and Pacific Oceans.

The revolution in communication facilitated the spread of what Reed called "the language of love" across this new space in order to bind its people together with a common language. The founding of the United States had been contingent on its own earlier communication revolution, which occurred with the dramatic rise of print culture and popular literacy around 1750. Michael Warner writes that whereas in the early part of the eighteenth century there were no press, newspapers, or magazines in Virginia or any of the southern plantations and only nine master printers in the northern cities, by 1760 the number had risen to forty-two throughout the colonies. At the same time, literacy for white men had rapidly increased, with almost the entire white male population of New England achieving literacy by midcentury. By 1765 "print had come to be seen as indispensable to political life, and could appear to men such as Adams to be the primary agent of world emancipation."[46] Bernard Bailyn offers a glimpse into how this enlarged print culture lay the groundwork for revolutionary public opinion that made the Declaration of Independence such a national spectacle:

> Every medium of written expression was put to use. The newspapers, of which by 1775 there were thirty-eight in the mainland colonies, were crowded with columns of arguments and counter-arguments appearing as letters, official documents, extracts of speeches, and sermons. Broadsides—single sheets on which there were often printed not only large letter notices but, in three or four columns of minuscule type, essays of several thousand words—appeared everywhere; they could be found posted or passing from hand-to-hand in the towns of every colony. Almanacs, workaday publications universally available in the colonies, carried, in odd corners and occasional columns, a considerable freight of political comment.[47]

The overall effect of this flood of newspapers, broadsides, and almanacs on the national consciousness was of far more significance than any particular argument that appeared in them. It created what Benedict Anderson describes as that "imagined political community" called a nation.[48] An illiterate farmer working the fields typically thought only of his own immediate interests in the small area bounded by his physical horizons, but a citizen reading a newspaper had a totally different experience. Knowing that the exact replica of this newspaper was being read by thousands of others across a vast geographic space, the citizen was able to think of him- or herself as an American, a person with common identification and interests despite living hundreds of miles apart. Such a common public consciousness was essential to the success of the American Revolution.

The communication revolution of the early nineteenth century thus built on the foundations of eighteenth-century print culture but (to borrow the language of Marshall McLuhan) rapidly expanded the scale, increased the pace, and changed the pattern of public communication. These changes occurred through a combination of technology and organization. Technologically the first cylinder press driven by a steam engine, invented in 1811, could print two thousand papers an hour, thus signaling the end of the old hand-driven Gutenberg press of Benjamin Franklin. The mechanization of making paper from rags, as well as the discovery of how to produce paper on a continuous roll instead of separate sheets, also served to reduce printing costs and increase the rate of publishing, such that by 1833 the *New York Sun* could reach out "for a truly mass audience by charging only a penny a copy and selling individual copies on the street instead of by subscription."[49] Organizationally the expansion of the United States Post Office then allowed for easy transportation and dissemination of newspapers across the country. By the 1820s delivering the mail was the largest activity of the federal government and "employed more people than the peacetime armed forces and more than all the rest of the civilian bureaucracy put together."[50] The number of post offices between 1815 and 1830 had more than doubled from three thousand to eight thousand, most of them located in tiny villages that reached deep into rural America.[51] The postal system pushed for improvements in transportation even when major development bills were vetoed in the Congress and, in combination with the subsidizing of low-cost delivery of newspapers and the increase in publishing technology, helped to create in the United States more newspaper readers than in any other country by 1822.[52] There was thus truth to the remark by Alexis de Tocqueville that the typical American was "a very civilized man prepared to take up a temporary home in the woods, plunging into the wilderness of the New World with his Bible, axe, and newspapers."[53] The transportation and communication revolutions made this venture possible.

The combined effect of these two revolutions was to bring about the radical changes in American economic, political, religious, and cultural life that have been characterized by the term *market revolution*. Narrated with the most dramatic flair by Charles Sellers, the market revolution represented a shift from a largely rural, agrarian, patriarchal culture in which yeoman farmers created goods largely for their own subsistence or for a highly circumscribed trading economy—the idyll of Jefferson's Republicanism—to a capitalistic market economy in which farmers,

merchants, and artisans became individualistic entrepreneurs dedicated to producing and trading single specialized goods that would generate profits through
exploiting the expanding national and international trade markets. Whereas "subsistence culture fostered family obligation, communal cooperation, and reproduction over generations of a modest comfort," the newer market ethics "fostered
individualism and competitive pursuit of wealth by open-ended production of
commodity values that could be accumulated as money."[54] In short, according to
Sellers, by "establishing capitalist hegemony over economy, politics, and culture,
the market revolution created ourselves and most of the world we know."[55]

Once again this social transformation can be made sense of in reference
to the original Protestant ethic that dominated early New England culture. In
its early form, the notion of a calling was not at all consonant with a search to
advance oneself up the social ladder, as one might think today of the American
dream. As Eric Foner points out, although the early Protestant ethic placed a
"stress on economic success as a sign of divine approval," the notion of one's
calling was still "associated with the idea of an hierarchical social order, with
more or less fixed classes."[56] Consequently one was bound to work for wealth and
advancement in one's chosen profession, not to change professions, invent new
ones, or change the rules of the game. All of this was upset, however, with the
market revolution. Now an individual with a calling would be prepared to cast off
this limitation and "was driven by an inordinate desire to improve his condition
in life, and by boundless confidence that he could do so."[57] Thus while many of
the moral qualities of the Protestant ethic remained, such as honesty, frugality,
temperance, piety, and punctuality, Americans increasingly viewed these virtues
as means to social mobility, economic advancement, and individual growth rather
than ends in themselves. In short "as God seemed kindlier, the environment more
manageable, and their fate more dependent on their own abilities, they could no
longer see themselves as sinners helplessly dependent on the arbitrary salvation
of an all-powerful God."[58] Indeed liberal Unitarians such as Dr. William Ellery
Channing came to see salvation as contingent on remaking themselves in God's
image, a message that clearly spoke to ambitious young men such as Sampson
Reed.

One can thus find in Reed's prophetic oration the definition of a new calling for this revolutionary time. In fact he made this explicit when he argued that
"there is something which everyone can do better than anyone else; and it is the
tendency and must be the end of human events, to assign to each his true calling."[59] But to recognize one's true calling required an awareness that times had
changed. His most explicit commentary on the revolutionary transformations
then occurring in the American society appears in his "Growth of the Mind":
"the world is beginning to be changed from what it was. Physical power instead

of boasting of its deeds of prowess, and pointing with the tomahawk or the lance to the bloody testimonies of its strength, is beginning to leave its image on the rugged face of nature, and to feel the living evidence of its achievements, in the happy circle of domestic life." Here Reed indicates the degree to which technology had changed its focus from the traditionally masculine sphere of war to the traditionally feminine sphere of domestic life and the maintenance of a healthy society. Physical power was now being used not only to build roads and dig canals but also create instruments that aided in the care of the home. But Reed astutely recognized that making use of these new powers required a new type of calling that relied more on the intellect than on physical strength. As he explains, "it remains for intellectual strength to lose the consciousness of its existence in the passions subdued, and to reap the reward of his labors, not in the spoils of any, but in the fruits of honest industry. It remains for us to become more thoroughly acquainted with the laws of moral mechanism."[60]

What Reed announced in his conception of genius, then, was a calling for those prepared to cast off the shackles of Calvinism and embrace a new kind of god that demanded a new vocation. The old Calvinist God had remained an impenetrable mystery and was represented as a judge who created a world of nature largely for the purposes of temptation. But for Reed, God was only one thing: love. That is to say, God ceased to be a person and became a principle of activity, a form of power, and an expression of light. God was not a detached judge but an active creator, and through God all things were not only made but continually remade, thus allowing people to witness God's light through every act of creation, both human and natural. As he writes, "Because God is love, nature exists; because God is love, the Bible is poetry. If, then, the love of God creates the scenery of nature, must not he whose mind is most open to this love be most sensible to natural beauties?"[61] Completely refuting the worldly asceticism of Calvinism, Reed thus encouraged not only observation of nature but a study of all of the arts of human invention, however imperfect their expression, because they all referred to "the source from which they came," which is the love of God.[62]

One need not question the sincerity of Reed's oration to see his triumphant embrace of genius as a reflection of his revolutionary era. While still embedded in the tradition of Protestant ethics and piety, he also channeled the confidence, ambition, and individualism of his time, downplaying traditional obligations to family, community, profession, and church in order to strike out on his own, to seek enlightenment and power as he could find it, and to redefine the true servant of God as the genius with the intellect and talent to perceive and to disclose the laws of God's principle of activity, which is love. The new calling of genius was thus not to be content with a sober exhibition of Protestant virtues in order to reveal oneself to be the chosen elect of God; it was to be an active discoverer of the divine light of spirit that pervades the works of nature and man and to channel that power into every activity of life in order to unify parts of the world, bring order out of chaos, and remake oneself and one's nation in the image of God and through the power of love.

Central to understanding how this perspective influenced the rhetoric and politics of the Transcendentalists, however, is grasping what Reed meant by love. The best way to understand his conception of love as eros is to contrast it with the traditional Christian notions of agape love. Jesus had instructed his followers to love each other as both God and Jesus had loved them, meaning in effect that love was a social virtue that dealt with one's relationship to other individuals. Reinhold Niebuhr, for instance, outlined four qualities of love in the Christian tradition. First, Christian love is universal because it "cannot be limited to partial communities of nature and history, to family, tribe, or nation." Second, love is sacrificial insofar as "perfect love has no logical limit short of the readiness to sacrifice the self for the other." Third, love is forgiveness of the kind that "justifies the love of the enemy in terms of the imitation of a God whose mercy cuts across every conception of justice." Fourth, love is willingness to stand in the place of the other, a virtue of embodying a "relation between persons in which one individual penetrates imaginatively and sympathetically into the life of another."[63] Christian love is "the capacity to recognize the social substance of human existence, and to realize that the unique self is intimately related to all human creatures."[64] Inspired by Jesus's own sacrifice, traditional Christian love represents that pure possibility of giving one's life for another human being for no other reason than that he or she is a thinking and feeling being created in the image of God.

Much of Reed's classically educated audience must have been struck by the degree to which his conception of eros largely departed from this Christian notion of love in favor of one that derived from the Greek pre-Socratic tradition, specifically that of Empedocles. For Empedocles love was not primarily representative of a human or even godly emotion; it represented a divine force of nature. In his epic cosmological book, *On Nature,* he tells a story of how all things began in the chaotic separateness of hate until love (eros) drew the elements together into a vortex. And thus the world exists in a constant tension between these two divine forces, which, in his words, "never cease their continual interchange, now through *Eros* all coming together into one, now again each carried apart by the hatred of Strife."[65] In the cosmology of Empedocles, there is no place for a personal god or savior. There is hardly even a place for human emotion at all, as eros represents not some individual desire but rather an impersonal cosmic force that brings the many together into the harmony of the one. To bear witness to this eros is thus not to gaze upon God's divine love of humankind or the willingness to sacrifice oneself for another; it is to be overwhelmed by the eternal recurrence of the coming together and taking apart of the universe, of the cycles of birth and death, of creation and destruction, all without desire or pity. That is why Reed says that this love of which he speaks "may be the love of good or evil; it may manifest itself in saving life or in killing."[66] The categories of good and evil are merely human terms of moral judgment; but eros represents a cosmic principle of activity that transcends mere human morality.

Here can be found both the roots of what Bloom calls the Emersonian gnosis as well as the basis for the type of eloquence that Friedrich Nietzsche attributed to "aesthetic man." For Bloom this replacement of the personal Judeo-Christian God with the impersonal creative force of the pre-Socratics not only generates that experience in which "space, time and mortality flee away, to be replaced by 'the knowing,'" but also lays the foundations for the new god of transcendental eloquence or that tropological rhetoric that "achieves persuasion by the trick of affirming identity with a wholly discontinuous self, one which *knows* only the highest moments in which it *is* a vision."[67] This is precisely what Nietzsche perceives in the attitude of another pre-Socratic philosopher, Heraclitus. According to Nietzsche, Heraclitus believed that the creative fire of the logos, or the divine world order, performs the same function of love and strife in Empedocles insofar as it "exhibits coming-to-be and passing away, structuring and destroying, without any moral additive, in forever equal innocence."[68] Thus Nietzsche would agree with Reed that it takes a rare individual to be able to perceive the world this way and speak about it with words that are unconstrained by the old gods of tradition and rhetoric. He writes that "only aesthetic man can look thus at the world, a man who has experienced in artists and in the birth of art objects how the struggle of the many can yet carry rules and laws inherent in itself, how the artist stands contemplatively above and at the same time actively within his work, how necessity and random play, oppositional tension and harmony, must pair to create a work of art."[69] Reed's conception of eloquence thus anticipates the type of art produced by Nietzsche's aesthetic man.

The rhetorical significance of Reed's reinterpretation of Christian love as eros can be identified through four consequences it has for his conception of transcendental eloquence. Only the first consequence can be said to have direct resonance with its Christian counterpart. That is to say, transcendental eloquence does not adapt itself to the biases of this or that social group but speaks to a universal audience of all humankind, thereby channeling the universality of Christian love that shatters the limits of the tribe or race. Reed argued that "all minds, whatever may be their condition, are not unconnected with God; and consequently not unconnected with each other. All nations, under whatever system of government, and in whatever state of civilization, are under the Divine

Providence, surely but almost imperceptibly advancing to a moral and political order, such as the world has not yet seen."[70] Consequently the one who speaks of this coming order should not stoop to adapt one's language to the immediate audience, as the decorous teachers of traditional rhetoric might counsel. Instead the "poet should be free and unshackled as the eagle; whose wings, as he soars in the air, seem merely to serve the office of a helm, while he moves on simply by the agency of the will."[71] The universality of the influence of love on all people demands nothing less than a universal form of speech.

The next three consequences, however, depart significantly from those of traditional Christian love. The second is that transcendental eloquence guided by eros replaces the Christian ethic of sacrifice for the sake of the other with a gnostic ethic that the present self should sacrifice its petty, worldly desires for the sake of the growth of a future, more universal, self. It is this kind of sacrifice that Reed referred to when argued that it was the duty of "intellectual strength to lose the consciousness of its existence in the passions subdued, and to reap the reward of its labors, not in the spoils of an enemy, but in the fruits of honest industry."[72] But Reed did not restrict such rewards to merely honest industry. Sacrificing one's precious sense of individuality and all its passions has wider rewards—namely the capacity to perceive a higher knowledge and to produce a more beautiful art. He writes that "when the heart is purified from all selfish and worldly affections" and "the human mind is cleansed of its lusts, truth will permit and invoke its approach, as the coyness of the virgin subsides into the tender love of the wife. The arts will spring full-grown beauty from Him who is the source of beauty."[73] The sacrifice of genius is thus, ironically, to get rid of that prideful ambition and lust for personal fame often associated with it. In its place will thus be a "humility which exalts" and springs forth eloquence precisely because it acknowledges that the source of beauty comes not from the self but from God.

Third, the erotic love that inspires eloquence does not bestow forgiveness upon sinners for their trespasses but rather calls on them to redeem themselves by overcoming their limitations through the acquisition of power. In Christian love all must forgive because all are irredeemably sinful. But in Reed's conception the reason for sin is the failure to perceive and to channel the light of God's love through the innate power of the human intellect. This is not something to forgive but something to blame and then to correct. At no point does Reed ever acknowledge a reason that human beings need to be forgiven. He only chastises society for disseminating false beliefs that conceal from people the true power of the light (and individuals for believing them). In particular he has harsh words for the church, which he calls a "graveyard" on which "the finger of death has rested." Rather than cheerfully pronouncing the capacity for the human intellect to perceive the light of love and translate it into practical power, "the bell which calls men to worship is to toll at their funerals, and the garments of the priests are of the color of the hearse and the coffin. Whether we view her in the strange melancholy that sits on her face, in her mad reasonings about truth, or in the occasional convulsions that agitate her limbs, there are symptoms, not of life, but of disease and death."[74] Transcendental eloquence calls on people to leave such institutions behind—forgiving them, perhaps, for their ignorance—so that they might seek the light for themselves and by so doing earn the praise of others.

Lastly Reed's conception of transcendental eloquence replaces the demand to see the world from the perspective of the other with the imperative to view any part of the world from the perspective of the whole of nature. The reason for this imperative grows out of his replacement of a personal, anthropomorphic god that stands above and apart from nature with an impersonal creative force of eros that is immanent in nature itself. To express God's love from this perspective thus requires more than a simple expression of affection as from a parent to a child; it rather requires a capacity for language to reveal humanity's place within the totality of the natural (and thereby divine) universe. Somewhat paradoxically, then, it is only through natural science—or the study of nature's laws and relations—that the human mind can understand the nature of love. Reed writes that when this new science comes into being, "science will be full of life, as nature is full of God. She will wring from her locks the dew which was gathered in the wilderness."[75] Eloquence is thus the wringing of the locks of nature into a new language of love, for "eloquence is the language of love. There is a unison of spirit and nature. The genius of the mind will descend, and unite with the genius of the rivers, lakes, and the woods. Thoughts fall to the earth with power, and make a language of nature."[76] In other words eloquence is the product of a genius mind not only capable of perceiving, through experience of natural phenomena such as rivers, lakes and woods the totality of God's love, but also able to create a language of nature—a rhetoric of tropes—that conveys the spirit of this totality with a beauty and power.

It is this last characteristic of transcendental eloquence that came to distinguish the rhetoric of the Transcendentalists from other reformist discourse of the time. Although the degree to which natural imagery pervaded their discourse varied from person to person, with Thoreau on one end of the spectrum and Brownson on the other, all of the Transcendentalists assumed that genuine eloquence never proceeded from part to part but always attempted to see the part from the perspective of the whole—namely a whole that lay beyond. Negatively this meant that they never ceased to condemn followers of the old god of rhetoric that demanded plenty of quotations from authoritative texts to establish principles followed by a clear and rigorous exposition of facts. Reed, for instance, waves dismissively at the dictums of the old rhetorical handbooks: "Syllogistic reasoning is passing away. It has left no permanent demonstration but that of his own worthlessness. . . . Few minds can now endure the tediousness of being led blindfold to a conclusion and of being satisfied with the result merely from the recollection of having been satisfied on the way to it."[77] This dissatisfaction is rooted in the nature of the human mind itself: "The mind requires to view the parts of the subject, not only separately but together; and the secret in the exercise of those powers of arrangement by which a subject is presented in its just relations to other things, takes the name of reason."[78] Reason, then, is the innate ability to see subjects together as a whole in their totality of relations, and eloquence is the type of rhetoric that appeals directly to that faculty.

Positively, then, transcendental eloquence represented what Reed called the language "not of words but of things." The ground of this language of things is the principle that nature itself speaks a type of pure language that transcends the limits of words and by so doing addresses itself directly to reason. As he writes, "the natural world was precisely and perfectly adapted to invigorate and strengthen the intellectual and moral man."[79] Consequently eloquence "draws her fire from natural imagery" and uses "poetry to enliven the imagination. There is the secret of all her power."[80] Reed thus denies the false division between dry and dusty reason and showy but empty style. This was but a product of the old gods. With the new gods, there will be "union of reason and eloquence." In this new age of eloquence "we neither wish to see an anatomical plate of bare muscles, nor the gaudy daubings of finery; but a happy mixture of strength and beauty." By recapturing the language of things, which is inspired by the revelation of love, a revolution will occur whereby "the imagination (which is called the creative power of man) shall coincide with the active creative will of God, [and] reason will be clothed with eloquence, as nature is with verdure."[81] For Reed the language of love finds inspiration from every facet of the world, from science, nature, poetry, and every other objective emanation and reflection of the world spirit.

Finally when the mind perceives the love of God through the correspondences of nature, the language eloquence expresses will be one of power, which of course is an expression of eros, that cosmic force that urges one onward and inspires the character of individuals, countries, ages, and worlds. Eloquence thus deals with no trivial affairs and does not concern itself merely with dressing up arguments with tropes and figures to make them attractive to an audience. Eloquence by definition is the language of power, which is to say the language that uses reason to discern the unity between the parts, uses imagination to clothe that unity with beauty and uses the force of love to direct and channel of the collective will in order to make real the promises of God. And of course the means by which those promises would be made real was "public opinion, that helm which directs the progress of events by which the world is guided to its ultimate destination."[82] Eloquence is the form of speech that seeks to alter this position point of public opinion, shifting the entire perspective of a public so that it can adequately see the full panorama of things illuminated by the light of love. When that happens, the full power of the public can be put to use as a means by which events are directed and the world molded in the revelation of genius.

Reed's "Genius" received a mixed response on that Harvard graduation day of 1821. Almost five decades later, in 1870, Emerson reminisced in his journal that he "became much acquainted with Reed, who talked very seriously with me, both at his counting room & my own house."[83] Reed's oracular style and bold pronouncements seemed for the most part lost on his audience, accustomed as it was to traditional commencement addresses that waxed nostalgic about youth before bidding the graduates a fond and optimistic farewell. Emerson reflects on the listeners' sour response: "I heard on the day when I graduated at Cambridge, in 1821, Sampson Reed, who on that day took his Master's degree, deliver his oration on Genius. It was poorly spoken, as A. Adams said, 'in a meeching way,' & the audience found it very dull & tiresome. John Quincy Adams who sat on the platform (his son George Washington A. graduating on that day) clapped Reed's oration with emphasis, & I doubt if anyone joined him."[84] For the receptive few to whom the call of genius resonated, however, Reed's oration was a rallying cry. Emerson says of his own response that "I was much interested in it, &, at my request, my brother William, of Reed's class, borrowed afterwards the manuscript, & I copied the whole of it, & kept it as a treasure."[85] Over the years this manuscript circulated among the initiated until it finally appeared in print in 1849 in the only issue of Elizabeth Peabody's *Aesthetic Papers*. Despite its poor delivery and overly grand style, Reed's oration came to be known as the first recognizable example of transcendental eloquence that served as a model and ideal for Emerson and all of his circle to follow.

But as inspiring as the oration was for the small circle of New England intellectuals in 1820s, something in Emerson's 1870 journal entry brings attention back to the larger national context in which the speech was delivered. Reed had delivered his oration just a year after the Missouri Compromise, which was supposed to have saved the Union and put to rest forever the question of slavery. Yet Emerson notes that he ran into Reed again three decades later, right after the Compromise of 1850, which purported to do the same. Championed by senators Henry Clay, Stephen Douglas, and Daniel Webster through the rhetoric of nationalism, the 1850 Compromise formalized the boundaries of Texas as a slave state, admitted California as a free state, and created territorial governments in New Mexico and Utah that would determine their position on slavery through popular sovereignty. But it also enacted a new Fugitive Slave Law, which coerced all free states to be complicit in returning fugitive slaves to their owners. This compromise infuriated Emerson, and so Reed's response disappointed him: "In 1851, after Webster's March speech in the U.S. Senate pronouncing for the fugitive slave law, I met Sampson Reed in the Boston Athenaeum, & deplored to him this downfall of our great man, &c. he replied, that 'he thought it his best speech, & the greatest action of his life.' So there were my two greatest men both down in the pit together."[86] The man who had inspired ecstatic transcendence in Emerson now inspired only disgust and disappointment by wallowing in the pit of compromise with slave power along with Emerson's former Whig political hero, Webster.

What Emerson referred to as the "pit," however, might more generally refer to the ordinary political reality of the United States by the middle of the nineteenth century. The Compromise of 1850 was a desperate act to preserve the Union in the face of an increasingly bold and recalcitrant slave power in the South and an expanding and ambitious monetary power in the North. While Southern leaders such as John C. Calhoun talked of secession in the face of Northern aggression, Northern senators such as William Henry Seward began appealing to a "higher law" than the Constitution, which to many sounded like a "new and unnerving radical claim, that the godly forces of antislavery were above the law" and thus had the right to pursue any means necessary to ensure that "slavery was doomed."[87] When Webster stood up to speak, in his words, "not as a Massachusetts man, not as a northern man, but as an American," he thus rejected both radicalisms in order to bolster "the view that some sort of compromise was required to keep the nation from falling apart."[88] That Reed applauded Webster's speech from the pit of political realism suggests that his practical sense as a businessman had overridden his youthful idealism. For him the Union had to be preserved at all costs because that was good for business, no matter what any higher law of love might demand.

Although it is easy to condemn Reed as a hypocrite, it is also important to recognize that the same conditions that inspired the lofty spirit of his transcendental eloquence were also responsible for his success as a businessman and his compromising stance of the politician. In his youthful oration on genius, he had struck a delicate balance between praising the godlike capacities of individuals and cautioning against the dangers of overweening ambition and pride. "Let ambition and the love of the world be plucked up by their roots," he wrote. "How can he love his neighbor, who desires to be above him? He may love him for a slave; but that is all. Let not the shrouds of death be removed, till the living principle has entered. It was not till Lazarus was raised from the dead, and had received the breath of life, that the Lord said 'Loose him, and let him go.'"[89] That is to say, only when Americans had fully purged themselves of merely worldly ambition, which cloaks them in the shrouds of death, could they fully emerge in the light of love to be resurrected as geniuses. Until that time they would merely reproduce the worldly hierarchies that create opposition between neighbors. Reed pronounced this optimistic vision precisely because the revolutionary transformations of the early nineteenth-century United States had presented before ambitious men such as himself a new path of success and prosperity. In his idealism Reed constructed a beautiful vision of the genius who could simultaneously attain power in a new age while seeking power over no one. Yet the same power that was driving the nation westward into Texas, Missouri, Kansas, Oregon, and California, binding the nation together through railways, newspapers, steamships, and eloquence also produced in its wake slavery, Indian removal, the Mexican war, subsistence-wage labor, the exploitation of women, and the rise of a new, rapacious bourgeois capitalism. Reed has closed his oration by announcing that "the morning cometh." But what the dawn revealed in the coming decades was something less than the triumph of love. Indeed it could just as well be seen as the triumph of strife. What is clear, at least, is that this period of love and strife would witness the rise of Transcendentalism.

CHAPTER 2

"Jesus was a teacher"

The Dialogic Rhetoric of Amos Bronson Alcott

Jesus was a teacher; he sought to renovate Humanity. His method commends itself to us. It is a beautiful exhibition of his Genius, bearing the stamp of naturalness, force, and directness. It is popular. Instead of seeking formal and austere means, he rested his influence chiefly on the living word, writing spontaneously in the soul, and clothing itself at once, in the simplest, yet most commanding forms. He was a finished extemporaneous speaker. His manner and style are models.

Amos Bronson Alcott, *The Doctrine and Discipline of Human Culture*, 1836

In 1836, as Sampson Reed busied himself with channeling his own spark of genius into his growing regional pharmaceutical empire, a different kind of genius was shining its light in the rooms on the top floor of Boston's Masonic Temple. There the largely self-taught Amos Bronson Alcott (1799–1888), inspired by the model of Jesus, was attempting to use the power of the living word to awaken in a handful of children a sense of their own latent divinity. He sought to imitate a particular method of Jesus's: "the Art—so long lost in our Consciousness—of unfolding its powers into the fullness of God."[1] But Alcott's practice of the art was not performed as part of a church service or Bible reading; it was part of the regular workings of his "Temple School," designed to compete with other Boston private schools for six- to twelve-year-olds of the city's upper middle class. Alcott's promise to offer a radically new sort of pedagogical experience was advertised by the structure of the classroom. Out were the mechanical rows of uncomfortable chairs designed to facilitate rote memorization of authoritative lectures by a taciturn schoolmaster; in were custom-made individual desks with swing-out blackboards arranged in a circle in a great and stately room to encourage engagement, reflection, and dialogue. And at the center was Alcott, seated at his master's desk with a cast of Christ in bas-relief hanging behind him and the busts of Socrates, John Milton, William Shakespeare, and Sir Walter Scott ornamenting the corners of the room. Here, the classroom design announced, one was to experience an education modeled on the great pedagogues of the past and designed to cultivate genius in the youth of the present.

Thus in Alcott the light of genius expressed a very different kind of love—through a very different kind of speech—than that of Reed. In a fashion that helps distinguish American Transcendentalism from Reed's Swedenborg-inspired visions, Alcott did not lose sight of the individual human beings in front of him, even as he, like Reed, sang hymns to the spirit. For Reed, that is to say, the love that was God often felt very unlovely, either because of the piercing cold of its objectivity or the fierce heat of its creative and destructive force. His was a love fit for giants of industry like the railroad barons to come, who in the fashion of the eros of Empedocles would bind the nation together with threads of steel. By contrast Alcott believed that the true expression of divine love is not found in the building of a nation but in the teaching of a child. It is on this principle that he found inspiration in the Bible story in which "the Star led the Wise Men to the Infant Jesus." Against Calvinist pessimism that saw in children the seed of Original Sin and the mark of Cain, Alcott saw them as pure and as virtuous as was Jesus at his birth. And for this he is joyous: "so is the hour approaching, and it lingers not on its errand, when the Wise and the Gifted, shall again surround the cradle of the New Born Babe, and there proffer, as did the Magi, their gifts of reverence and of love to the Holiness that hath visited the earth, and shines forth with a celestial glory around their heads."[2] As a teacher Alcott saw himself as the reincarnation of a magus (albeit a magus who also possessed the art of Jesus) who would unfold the powers of the city's sons and daughters so that they might strive toward the fullness of God.

Alcott exhibited what might be called the unalloyed spirit of Transcendentalism. Donald Nelson Koster calls him the "quintessential Transcendentalist, great in heart, lofty in spirit, and unflinching in optimism until the day he died."[3] Perhaps more important than his lofty spirit, however, was the fact that he dedicated himself more than any other Transcendentalist to the mission that most set it apart from Reed's prophetic brand of eloquence. This mission was one of education, which he and Transcendentalists saw not simply as the transmission of textual knowledge from a teacher to a student but the lifelong unfolding of one's powers through experience, reflection, action, and communication. In fact, modifying Perry Miller's claim that Transcendentalism could be most accurately defined as a religious demonstration, Wesley Mott argues that "so fundamental to the Transcendentalists were teaching and learning—as profession, calling, and trope—that the movement might be just as fairly defined as an *educational* demonstration."[4] In other words Transcendentalism can be seen as a movement that sought not only to inspire educational growth through the writings and practices of its members, but also to leave a demonstration of the type of growth that was possible when the rigid and hierarchical methods of the old gods were replaced with the progressive and egalitarian methods of the new. In a journal entry of 1835, Alcott wrote: "He who kindles the fire of genius on the altar of the young heart unites his own prayers for humanity with every ascending flame that is emitted from it through succeeding time. He prays with the Universal Heart, and his prayers bring down blessings on all the race below."[5] This is the paradigmatically Transcendentalist view of the role of the teacher as one who kindles the fire of genius on the altar of the young, a view that has inspired many educational reformers from John Dewey to Jonathan Kozol, both of whom "acknowledge the influence of the Transcendentalists in defining their commitment to human dignity and the inherent value of education."[6]

It was not simply any form of education that Alcott and the Transcendentalists praised, however, but what Paulo Freire calls a "dialogic" education. Although Freire has never acknowledged his connection with Alcott, one can find in his concept of dialogue the modern manifestation of the Transcendentalist model of education. Like Alcott, Freire challenges traditional "banking" concepts of education in which "the teacher issues communiqués and makes deposits which the students patiently receive, memorize, and repeat."[7] This method was consistent with the attitude of the old god of tradition that prefers monologue to dialogue, insists that any speech and thought stay within the accepted parameters of argumentation and style, and looks at students as fixed units whose fundamental character does not change. In contradistinction dialogic education "affirms men and women as beings in the process of *becoming*—as unfinished, uncompleted beings in and with a likewise unfinished reality."[8] Moreover dialogue is not simply as a back and forth exchange of words; rather it is "the encounter in which the united reflection and action of the dialoguers are addressed to the world which is to be transformed and humanized."[9] Dialogue thus involves a cooperative and loving act by which the participants create a new vocabulary to describe themselves and the world, both of which are in a process of becoming something other than what they were. One can thus identify the spirit of Alcott's Transcendentalism in Freire particularly when the latter argues that true dialogue "requires an intense faith in humankind, faith in their power to make and remake, to create and re-create, faith in their vocation to be more fully human (which is not the privilege of an elite, but the birthright of all)."[10] It is the existence of this faith, combined with the willingness to express it in eloquence and put it into practice in education, that both characterizes Transcendentalism as a historical movement and shows its continued relevance to contemporary pedagogical reforms.

Even with this relationship between Alcott and contemporary progressive pedagogy, it may nonetheless seem unusual to begin an inquiry into the rhetoric and politics of the leading Transcendentalists by focusing on his work—particularly since he wrote neither about politics nor rhetoric. More typical is to begin with Emerson's idealistic critique of Unitarianism and to mention Alcott as an interesting but secondary educational application of these same principles. But there are three reasons for beginning with Alcott. First, he far more than Emerson adapted his ideas in direct relationship to the political, social, and economic changes in the early nineteenth century. Indeed placing Alcott after Emerson is highly misleading, precisely because, as his biographer Odell Shepard put it, by the 1820s Alcott "was an idealist without having read a word of Plato. He was a transcendentalist without having heard the name of Emerson."[11] Far from being derivative of Emerson, the older Alcott actually anticipated many of his ideas, because they were developed in direct response to the revolutionary currents of his age. Specifically the method of Alcott's school combined the two aspects of his experience with religion and economy. From the "inner light" of the Second Great Awakening, he acquired a belief in the innate divinity of individual souls and their capacity to channel the power of God; from the market economy, he learned a method of tapping into those capacities that mirrored not only the Jesus of the Gospels but also the sales techniques of New England peddlers. Second, his vigorous defense of the Transcendentalist pedagogy of his Temple School was rhetorical in practice and challenged many of the prevailing attitudes of the day. As Mott observes, many of the recorded conversations of his class "dealt frankly with questions about the origin of spirit and human life—topics that precariously approached the taboo matters of religion and sexuality."[12] Although such controversy eventually put an end to Alcott's career as a teacher, his effort to justify his methods to the public was one of the first examples of transcendental eloquence being used to defend and advance a particular form of controversial social practice.

Alcott's educational methods embodied and advanced a form of "dialogic rhetoric." According to James Philip Zappen, dialogic rhetoric replaces a narrow view of persuasion as a speaker's attempt to dominate others with a more cooperative view in which a speaker must be willing to engage in the "testing, contesting, and creating of ideas" and "to hear and to engage in the ongoing exchange of voices."[13] Inspired by the Socratic ideal of dialogue, this perspective admits "the possibility of reconnecting dialogue to the rhetorical tradition, not my rhetoricizing dialogue and thus reducing it to monologue but by dialogizing rhetoric: by introducing the voices of others into rhetorical discourse, by showing how these voices test and contest and create or re-create ideas tacitly and unreflectively held to be true, by asking those of us who speak and write to render ourselves accountable to others in an ongoing exchange of voices."[14] For Alcott this kind of dialogic rhetoric was embodied in the figure of what he called "Jesus for

Conversation," whose art represented "the fittest organ of utterance."[15] Rejecting the one-way models of pulpit oratory, epistolary composition, and street-corner harangue, he celebrated a dialogic form of rhetoric in which "man faces his fellow man. He holds a living intercourse. He feels the quickening life and light."[16] Here is an art of the word that bears the properties of naturalness, force, and directness; that is unabashedly popular rather than arcane; that uses the living words of present speech rather than the dead ones of old books; that rises spontaneously in the soul and clothes itself in simple yet commanding forms. Here was a dialogic rhetoric that would find its sources of invention in the places in which a person stands, lives, labors, and loves, humbling itself before the divinity of the other in order to bring them to the realization that all is in fact one.

To look at Alcott's early life is to catch a glimpse of the old god of tradition that Alcott himself would have a hand in usurping. He was born in the dying days of the eighteenth century, on November 29, 1799, in a town that had remained unchanged since pioneer times. Wolcott, Connecticut, was twenty-five miles north of New Haven and thirty miles from the state's western line, perched on a hill nine hundred feet above sea level and therefore well away from the new ideas and people that flowed along the waterways of New England. Populated by what Shepard characterized as "a rugged, sufficiently honest, hard-working, moderately temperate, and not very intelligent lot," Wolcott was a tightly knit small community that struggled to prosper by farming the hard and rocky New England soil.[17] Unlike Daniel Webster's constituency of urban traders and manufacturers, these were people largely disconnected from the accumulation of wealth through market innovations. Although limited trade at nearby markets was certainly not unusual, for the most part the economy was local: "They grew their own food among the rocks of the hilltop. They ground their own corn at the gristmill on Mad River. They spun, wove, dyed, and fashioned their own clothing. They made what simple tools they needed for the workshop, hearth, and field."[18] In 1799 nothing could have been more foreign to the people of Wolcott than Reed's grandiose visions of progress. "In speech and thought, in knowledge and culture, the community was not noticeably different from any that might have been found in one of the older Connecticut towns toward the end of the seventeenth century."[19] Little during the year of Alcott's birth signaled that any change was coming.

His own family was representative of a typical larger community in turn-of-the-century America. His great-grandfather, John Alcocke, had moved to the area in 1731 to escape from the malarial fevers caused by the lowland dampness of Waterbury. There he founded the farm that would be inherited by his son Joseph Chatfield Alcox, who married Anna Bronson. The farm was located in a part of Wolcott called Spindle Hill (named because of the household crafts associated with it), and it did its part to uphold the tradition, making "plows, rakes, boxes, baskets, and brooms for local sale."[20] Although by no means wealthy, Joseph and Anna were fortunate to raise ten healthy children, of whom Bronson was the oldest. As with almost all families in rural agricultural communities, the children were expected to labor with and for the family, whose patriarch had the right to the entirety of his child's earnings until the age of twenty-one. Bronson was no exception: "While still a child himself he began to work for his father— folding the sheep under the great rock on the hillside, guiding the oxen along the furrow, mending the stone walls that surrounded the woodland pastures, husking corn, flailing grain, milking cows, molding candles, bringing water from the well, and doing whatever else might be asked of him between dawn and dark."[21] Although given a rudimentary state-funded public school education in a one-room schoolhouse from age six to age ten, followed by a few more winter sessions at a district school, by the age of thirteen, Bronson had become valuable enough as a laborer that his regular schooling came to an end. Looked at from a distance, then, little on the outside might have marked him as being led toward a fate significantly different than the many generations of Wolcott inhabitants who had come before him.

The fact that Alcott's life took a radically different path—and that this path was determined by no one specific influence—is indicative of the atmosphere of restlessness that pervaded early nineteenth-century New England. Somehow, without ever having spent significant time outside of Wolcott, Alcott as a youth had already begun to develop that sense of dissatisfaction and alienation, on one hand, and of yearning for a new kind of communion, on the other, that lies at the core of Transcendentalism. It is not enough to blame his restlessness on the strict, uncomfortable, and unimaginative pedagogy that went on at the Spindle Hill school. This kind of pedagogy was certainly not new, and Alcott was by no means alone among his peers in being less than enthusiastic about enduring its trials, which included sitting still on uncomfortable backless benches most of the day, clustered together in a room that was alternately freezing and hot as a furnace, memorizing facts from Nathaniel Dwight's *Geography* or sounding out words from Noah Webster's *Speller* and occasionally enduring physical punishment such as "holding down a nail in the floor" in a painful stooping position. In time, of course, Alcott came to despise and challenge these practices, blaming a "low estimate of human nature, and consequent want of reverence and regard for it," for adults' having developing institutions of learning based on training the young to "repeat the vices and reproduce the opinions of parents."[22] But at the time of his own youth, he was just one more student—although a remarkably precocious one—who had to endure the drudgery and discipline of a poorly funded public school education.

A better way to understand Alcott's personal development (and in turn the development of Transcendentalism in general) is to look at three outstanding aspects of his life that also illuminate essential aspects of how the communication revolution helped give rise to the Transcendentalists. The first thing about Alcott that set him apart from his peers was that he had outlets from schooling not only in the traditional boyhood play or farm labor but in the realm of ideas and letters. He had the rare good fortune to find a kindred spirit in his second cousin, William Andrus Alcott (who later grew up to be an educator, educational reformer, author, and physician) and the two boys built a world of their own. In a town in which few people "read anything more than passages from the Bible and rarely wrote anything but their names," Amos and William "kept journals, borrowed books, and relished intellectual discussions."[23] Always the smartest boys in the class and the winners of the town spelling bee, they would also walk two miles every weekend to obtain New Haven newspapers—not only to gain an insight on the goings-on of the wider world but also to learn new styles of writing that would set them apart from the local farmers and their uncultivated colloquial speech. Indicative of their intellectual ambition and their heightened sense of themselves, on their own initiative they built a small "Juvenile Library" in town, with Amos as president, William as secretary and treasurer, and the two of them as the sole subscribers and beneficiaries of the institution, which consisted of around a hundred volumes they had accumulated by scouring the "kitchens of their kinsfolk."[24] These volumes included John Bunyan's *Pilgrim's Progress,* Milton's *Paradise Lost,* James Hervey's *Meditations among the Tombs,* Daniel Defoe's *Robinson Crusoe,* and James Burgh's *Dignity of Human Nature.* With William's help, then, Alcott was able to create for himself his own intellectual world within the bounds of his conservative community. He "later claimed that his happiest experiences as a youth took place in the south room of the homestead, where he could retire to read and write."[25]

The second formative influence on Alcott was an atmosphere of religious freedom and experimentation that was a result of the currents of the Second Great Awakening. Like the First Great Awakening of the 1730s and 1754s, led by Jonathan Edwards, the Second Great Awakening was a rejection of overly rational and institutionalized forms of religious worship, placing emphasis instead on the direct authority of the Bible and a personal and emotional conversion experience brought about in large part through revivals, sermons, and the distribution of evangelical literature. But as indicated by Edwards's famous sermon "Sinners in the Hands of an Angry God," the First Great Awakening tended to put parishioners in a "passive mood, as if to underscore God's action upon them. They saw themselves so hopelessly mired in sin that they could not even reach out to accept God's offers of grace."[26] Although there was a sense in which the choice to accept God was one's own, it was ultimately up to God to judge whose souls would be saved. But times had changed for Americans since then: "As God seemed kindlier, the environment more manageable, and their fate more dependent on their own abilities, they could no longer see themselves as sinners helplessly dependent on the arbitrary salvation of an all-powerful God."[27] Thus there arose a new kind of "Armenianism," named after "Dutch theologian Arminius and relating salvation to human capability and effort."[28] As a result, "in dramatic contrast, the preachers of the Second Great Awakening routinely suggested that God had already given sinners the ability to accept grace when he offered it."[29] Although rejecting eighteenth-century rationalism and deism that tended to speak to the head rather than the heart, these preachers nonetheless integrated Enlightenment notions that human beings through their own moral and intellectual agency could work for their own salvation—and equally important, the salvation of others as well.

Alcott's most direct encounter with the Second Great Awakening came in his meeting with one of its leaders, Lyman Beecher, who preached the ordination sermon for the pastor, John Keyes, who succeeded Israel Beard Woodward in the Wolcott Congregationalist Church in 1810. In his autobiography Alcott remarks that Beecher spoke with "a style of eloquence as unique as it was effective" and preached a sermon that "left a lively impression on my memory."[30] This was no wonder, since Beecher was one of the most zealous reformers of his time. Taking on the "Old Lights" of the Congregationalist establishment, who preferred the traditional forms of church worship practiced by Woodward, Beecher's "New Light" evangelicalism advanced a more ambitious agenda. He wrote that "the great aim of the Christian church in its relation to the present life is not only to renew the individual man, but also to reform human society."[31] Toward that end Beecher took advantage of the transportation revolution by preaching his religious and moral message all across the Northeast, focusing in particular on crusades against Sabbath breaking, profanity, and intemperance. At the same time, he exploited the techniques of the communication revolution by devising "new means of influencing public opinion outside of politics: education, literature, magazines, religious revivals, and organized reform."[32] Armed with the weapons of the printing press, "Beecher pioneered the mass distribution of religious tracts, established a magazine to spread the crypto-New-Light gospel, and recruited writers for an incessant pamphlet warfare on Unitarians, Episcopalians, and other foes."[33] In Beecher, Alcott thus met one of the "early psychologists of the techniques of persuasion," a revivalist whose job it was to discover not only the means by which souls could be saved but by which society could be reformed.[34] This reformist motive endured in Alcott for the rest of his life.

But what made Alcott a Transcendentalist and not simply one more of the huge number of "New Light" crusaders was his yearning for a truly creative and independent voice that was not bound to any theology, ideology, or creed. Although he spent a few months in 1814 studying under Pastor Keyes, attracted by the new humanitarianism of the Congregationalists, he found that he could not tolerate the "stifling moral legalism" that accompanied it.[35] For there was something in the adventurous, personal, and transformative spirit of Bunyan's *Pilgrim's Progress* that had touched him deeply when he first encountered it as child. Alcott remained unsatisfied by the organized reformist movements that began springing up all around him, such as the Beechers' Connecticut Society for the Promotion of Good Morals. Bunyan's book, written in late seventeenth-century England, was a dreamlike Christian allegory of one man's journey from the "City of Destruction" to the "Celestial City" on Mount Zion and "stressed an emotional reliance on the grace of God operating above any human power, a mystical faith in a sovereign deity."[36] The reformers shared this belief but downplayed the importance of the journey, believing instead that social transformation came not from individual striving but from organized revivals, state legislation, and carefully distributed propaganda. But Alcott had gained a different lesson from his careful and constant reading of the book; he came to believe that the world was not something to be chastised and disciplined but something to be experienced and interpreted. That is to say, he came to interpret the world allegorically, meaning that he developed the habit, in Shepard's words, of "seeing all things double—here the fact and there its significance; here the event and there its universal meaning; here the concrete temporal instance and there the everlasting law."[37] What Alcott yearned for, as he began to perceive the opportunities around him, was his own journey to Zion.

He got that journey, but in a curious way: as a Yankee peddler. Thus the third formative influence on Alcott was his extensive travels in the Virginia, South Carolina, and North Carolina selling door-to-door the products of New England factories to southern plantation owners between 1818 and 1823. Not only did this short-lived career give him the adventure he so craved, but it also exposed him to the revolutionary changes that accompanied the transformation of the United States from an agricultural to a manufacturing economy. He was by no means alone in adopting this trade. During the first half of the nineteenth century, "Western Connecticut, where the soil was thin and the waters were swift, was beginning to pour her surplus of young men into the trails in the tote-roads, turnpikes and highways of America."[38] In 1800 towns such as Wolcott could still survive through the kind of subsistence farming and minor trade in agricultural and artisan goods that kept communities stable, conservative, and tight-knit for most of the eighteenth century. But as the forces of the market revolution began to accelerate—forces catalyzed by the War of 1812, whose embargo devastated overseas markets for agricultural products and increased internal trade in manufactured goods—children of farming families such as Alcott found farming prospects in their small-town diminishing while opportunities for making money in manufacturing increased. In fact between the years 1790 and 1820, the only Connecticut towns that experienced population growth were those involved in manufacturing, with even the patriarchs of small farming towns picking up and heading elsewhere, "leaving the management of the farms to the less capable and the less ambitious."[39] For young men such as Alcott, the options were slim. One could either work in a factory—which he did for a short time, making clocks—or embark on what seemed to be an exciting and challenging career as a peddler, bringing the fruits of New England factory innovation across the growing nation along its increasingly efficient roads and waterways. Thus in less than a generation, family farms that had been handed down from generation to generation for more than a century were abandoned as families flung their children across the nation's countryside with suitcases, trunks, and carriages, hawking the newest trinkets.

By the time Alcott was a teenager, he had been given opportunities for personal freedom and growth that had been denied his parents and grandparents. Provided an early education and surrounded by books that stimulated his imagination, he experimented with various forms of religious affiliation before abandoning the established church—and the whole tradition of New England communal, agrarian life—to become a peddler. His peddling actually began at age fifteen; he traveled for a short time in Western Massachusetts with his cousin Thomas to sell articles door-to-door, and at age sixteen he expanded his reach into western New York, "hawking subscriptions" to John Flavel's *Treatise on Keeping the Heart,* a New Light, sentimental Christian handbook for good living that remains in print today.[40] But his 1818 journey to Norfolk, Virginia, was different. Finding a dealer in "fancy goods" by the name of J. J. Allen who sold him two tin trunks full largely of toiletries, such as razors, oils, soaps, and perfumes, as well as toys and puzzles for children, Alcott now had for his primary consumer market the plantation owners of the South, the only people with the interest in such fineries and the money to purchase them.[41] This was one of the ironic roots of Alcott's Transcendentalism. Although known for his idealism and honesty in later life, he actually developed persuasive skills as a young man by becoming identified with a group that had the reputation of being charlatans: "a virile lot, bold, carefree, and adventurous, the Yankee pedlars of one hundred and more years ago made up one of the most picturesque classes of men that America has ever produced. They stood halfway between the merchant and the gipsy, with a faint touch added of the mountebank."[42] The virtues of the Yankee peddler were thus opposite those of the dutiful, hard-working, community-oriented Puritan farmer. One did not diligently labor for the glory of God and family to be a successful peddler; he aggressively persuaded others for the sake of profit, pleasure, and self-advancement.

It was precisely during the years he spent peddling for profit off and on between 1815 and 1821 that Alcott clearly developed the methods of dialogic rhetoric that came to form the basis of his radical Transcendental pedagogy. The most important rhetorical tool he learned during his years as a peddler was the art of salesmanship. Learning that art must been the most difficult challenge for the earnest, idealistic, and at times haughty boy from Wolcott. Alcott had been accustomed to acting superior to those around him, cultivating an affected style in his writing that distinguished him from others, certainly no virtue for a salesman. But in the aristocratic houses of the South, he found himself addressing an audience to whom he could relate, an audience of learning, cultivation, and beauty. Alcott must have discovered in that moment of identification that good salesmanship required putting oneself in the shoes of another, discovering his or her own needs and desires, and crafting a message in which the commodity one is selling is perfectly adapted to the wants of the consumer. And perhaps most of all, he came to learn that being a good salesman meant believing in the quality of what one was selling. He came to believe that the goods he sold would improve his customers and indeed would make their already elegant lives more beautiful. Shepard concludes that in peddling, Alcott "was beginning a long public career in which the hope of doing some good to the world, a simple love of beauty, and the longing for a light reflected upon him from happy faces, were to be the main motives from first to last."[43] Peddling, that is to say, not only taught him the art of adapting messages to people, which is at the core of the rhetorical attitude, but adapting specific messages to specific people in private conversation within the intimate spaces of their homes.

It took a final act of transformation, however—undoubtedly reminiscent of one of the chapters of *Pilgrim's Progress*—to encourage Alcott to put this revelation to work as a teacher. This transformation would come as a result of another encounter with the Second Great Awakening, this time in the form of a meeting with the Quakers. After his first relatively successful southern peddling expedition to Virginia in 1818, the next few years found him in various levels of debt, at one point suffering from typhus as a result of drinking bad water. Aimless and adrift, in 1823 he came across a community of Friends in North Carolina, near Albemarle Sound, where he stayed for the spring and summer of that year. An entry in his autobiographical timeline summarizes his experience there: "*March and April, 1823. Have a good deal of intercourse with Friends in Chowan* and Perquimans County's. Read Pann's 'No Cross, No Crown,' Barclay's Apology, Fox's 'Journal,' Clarkson's 'Portraiture of Quakerism,' William Law's 'Devout Call,' and other serious books of like spirit. The moral sentiment now supersedes peddling, clearly and finally."[44] Alcott thus underwent a religious awakening that helped him overcome his guilt and rootlessness and showed him the possibility of a life dedicated to the spirit. With their sincerity, silent worship, disregard for formality and dissension, and most of all their belief that "the individual soul may be so illuminated by the divine spirit as to speak its word to men," the Quakers gave Alcott his first example of a religious community of individual freethinkers and became an inspiration for his own brand of transcendental community that he would seek to cultivate as a teacher.[45] Although he did not become a Quaker, his experience with the community of Friends was a crucial step in "Alcott's search for a moral and spiritual purpose that would help him make sense of the disorder of a changing environment and would enable him to turn change itself into an instrument for reform and this-worldly salvation."[46] The Quakers gave him confidence not only in expressing his own inner light, but also in cultivating the light of others through personal dialogue and the model of extemporaneous rhetoric given by the simple examples of Jesus.

By the time he returned home and took a job as master of a school district near Bristol, Connecticut, Alcott had in effect become a Transcendentalist without ever having met Emerson or having read Carlyle or Swedenborg. He was a Transcendentalist by experience, a sojourner like the character in *Pilgrim's Progress* who reached his own version of the Celestial City quite on his own. Raised in a tight-knit farming community whose fabric was quickly being eroded, Alcott idealized its egalitarian spirit at the same time that he came to disregard completely the authority of its traditions. Immersed in the world of books at a young age, he embraced the life of the mind in a way that was rare for his environment, at the same time that he came to appreciate the limits of books in giving him the experience and learning he craved. Exposed to both a culture of religious dissent and the reformist atmosphere of the Second Great Awakening, he came to embrace the transformative and emotional spirit of the New Light at the same time that he grew to distrust the conservatism and formalism of established religions, both new and old. And thrown into the currents of the market economy as a peddler, he quickly became infatuated with the enormous capacities for self-advancement and self-culture in the growing United States, at the same time that he sank deeply into debt and became gradually aware of the evils of slavery and the grotesque inequalities and inevitable vices that accompanied it. Alcott returned, in short, with an incredible optimism in the potentialities of a liberated human nature tempered by a worldly realism that taught him that there were many enemies to that liberation. His Transcendentalism came from a fighting faith that it was his calling to reveal to the members of coming generations the full nature of their innate power and virtue that a changing United States would finally let them express—at least if they could finally let the scales fall from their eyes.

Alcott returned a fighter. He accepted his first teaching job in Bristol, Connecticut, thus beginning a period between 1825 and 1828 when he began to develop the methods of his experimental classroom in Connecticut schools, including Cheshire and Wolcott. Soon the characteristics of his progressive pedagogy emerged—access to a library; a circular arrangement of movable desks; the use of portable slates and writing books, objects such as blocks, cubes, and beads used to aid in arithmetic; the breaking up of traditional textbook exercises with walks, games, storytelling, physical activities, and dialogues; and a reduced emphasis on strict discipline and corporal punishment. Alcott even introduced a system of classroom democracy in which students were able to vote on proper disciplinary actions and serve as a type of jury for other students who had been accused of misbehavior. In all of this, his pedagogy strove to achieve a "dynamic synthesis of enlightenment rationalism, which emphasized the infinite capacity of the human mind, and of an emotional religion of the heart, which perceived the imminence of God in the world working for human regeneration and salvation."[47] Prepared to dismiss and challenge tradition whenever it functioned as a constraint, Alcott channeled his adventurous spirit and applied his persuasive techniques to creating a classroom environment in which children actually became excited to buy what he was selling, which in this case was not perfume and razors but the love of wisdom.

It was not long before Alcott became aware not only of the politics of his idealistic pedagogy but also of the necessity of rhetoric to overcome opposition. By late 1826 he had run into his first formal opposition from a community that wanted only a traditional education at a minimum cost. When Alcott asked the people of Cheshire for an increase in salary and funds for classroom alterations and new books for a library, they responded with complaints about his innovations and eventually a public decision to establish a rival school with a traditional teacher who was paid a lower salary. In his September 22, 1826, entry of his journal, Alcott complained that "those who in modern times attempt in education anything different from the old established modes are by many regarded as publick innovators on the peace and order of society, as persons desirous of destroying the structure which secures present happiness, and of substituting in its place anarchy and confusion."[48] But this opposition only provoked Alcott's rhetorical passions. After learning of the decision by some of the townspeople to found a rival school, he gave his radical spirit of transcendence full voice in his journal, railing against those who could see no further than the dictates of some dry and dusty book handed down by generations:

Ideas, when vended in a book, carry with them a kind of dignity and certainty which awe many into implicit belief. They often impose the most radical and absurd conclusions on the fearful understanding. It dare not doubt. Fear keeps it ignorant. Authority lifts her head and commands instant belief. Reason, thus hushed into slumber, sleeps in secure repose. To dare to think, to think for oneself, is denominated pride and arrogance. And millions of human minds are in this state of slavery and tyranny.

How shall they escape?

Rebel! Think for themselves! Let others grumble; dare to be singular. Let others direct; follow Reason. Let others dwell in the land of enchantments; be Men. Let others prattle; practice. Let others profess; do good. Let others define goodness; act. Let others sleep; whatever thy hand findeth to do, that do with all my might, and let a gainsaying calumniating world speculate on your proceedings.[49]

In these passages are found the many of the traditional figures of the old god of rhetoric—most notably the use of antithesis and repetition—put to use to make a vigorous contrast between the dying world of tradition and the new age of reason. Alcott on the one hand hurls invective against the secure ignorance, illegitimate authority, blind imitation, and the idle workings of the fearful understanding that crumbles, prattles, and professes its goodness while never daring to reason, practice, or act, while on the other hand challenging the singular intellects and daring reformers to rebel, to think for themselves, and to exert force in the world without concern for the gainsaying rabble. Here was the voice of heroism and the self-reliance that became the mark of Transcendentalist eloquence.

With this newfound resolve, Alcott spent the next decade making a concerted effort to exploit the communication revolution to publicize his own educational ideals. In January 1826 the first issue of the *American Journal of Education* was published in Boston by William Russell, who "preached that the gospel of education is the surest hope for humanity."[50] Soon after his move to Boston in 1828, Alcott struck up a friendship with Russell, who not only helped him get a job teaching at the Infant School Society of Boston but also began printing Alcott's articles in the *American Journal of Education* that same year. Alcott's reading of Adam Smith's *Theory of Moral Sentiments* and John Locke's *Essay Concerning Human Understanding* "helped legitimate his personal rebelliousness against established customs and traditions, and it enhanced the greater and greater importance he was attaching to his chosen profession."[51] This confidence then resulted in his first major educational manifesto, *Observations on the Principles and Methods of Infant Instruction* (1830), a twenty-seven-page pamphlet, one thousand copies of which he published at his own expense with Carter and Hendee of Boston. By the 1830s, then, he had become fully committed to the art of self-promotion through the available means of the mass media to attract patrons from the rising bourgeois and professional class.

It soon paid dividends. After marrying his first teaching assistant, Abigail May, in Boston, Alcott moved the couple to Germantown, Pennsylvania, exploring the opportunity of opening a school near Philadelphia with the support of wealthy patron and Quaker philanthropist Reuben Haines. The years 1831–34 that he spent around Philadelphia were productive both intellectually and personally. At the same time that he delved deeper into the philosophical basis of his pedagogy, his wife gave birth to his two daughters, Anna Bronson and Louisa May. Yet financially he was having challenges. School enrollment began diminishing, and then Haines died and his support dried up. Alcott had to seek help from his friend Russell in Boston; Russell connected him with the influential Unitarian minister William Ellery Channing, who pledged support for a new school with twenty students. With a talented and supportive new assistant, thirty-year-old Elizabeth Palmer Peabody (a former secretary to Channing, tutor for his daughter, and assistant editor for the *American Journal of Education*), Alcott opened the Temple School in 1834, attracting patrons such as Massachusetts chief justice Lemuel Shaw and Boston's mayor, Josiah Quincy. Its students included the children of "lawyers, successful merchants, and philanthropists such as Samuel Tuckerman, Nathan Rice, Patrick Jackson, Robert Bartlett, C. B. Cary, John Ware, and James Savage."[52] They represented the cutting edge of northeastern bourgeois society, ambitious for their children to achieve success "through hard work and by reliance upon the self, rather than the result of a predestined social order."[53] These parents wanted not just inspired and creative teaching; they also wanted a good, rigorous discipline of self-culture that would produce future leaders and professionals capable of forethought, time management, temperance, and focus to succeed in an increasingly diversified, complex, international, and competitive market.

The early success of the Temple School was driven in large part by the promise that it would inspire the unique genius of each student. In the model of Sampson Reed, their parents wanted their children to become geniuses who could master their environment through the power of their minds. Evidence of this promise is apparent in Alcott's *Record of a School: Exemplifying the General Principles of Spiritual Culture* (1835), which was an edited version of Peabody's daily accounts of the school's activities translated into a dialogue between Alcott and his students. In her introduction to the book, Peabody made it clear that the Temple School was no ordinary school for ordinary children. In conventional schools, Peabody told readers, most instructors are unaware "how much the art of composition is kept from being developed in children, by petty criticism."

Concerned narrowly with making students write the proper letters and words in order, teachers were intolerant of original expression, and their students came to shrink at the threat of criticism "more than they would at a rude physical touch." What they did not understand was that "if left to a natural development, and unhindered by internal moral evil, the mind always works itself out to perfect forms; while premature criticism mildews the flour, and blasts the promised fruit." How different would it be if teachers understood the true method and art of teaching! In contradistinction, true "intellectual education, as an art, is an embodiment of all those laws and means, which the development of genius manifests to be the best atmosphere for the production of creative power" and in which "all minds are to be cherished by the same means by which genius is developed."[54] Here was the appeal of Alcott's school to the parents of would-be geniuses—it was a place in which their sons and daughters would be given an intellectual education geared toward the unfettered production of creative power.

But *Record of a School* was more than a description of a physical space and its inspired activities; it was also a document of the principles of dialogic rhetoric that Alcott had begun to develop as a method of inspiring genius. At this point it is useful to step out of the historical narrative and put Alcott into conversation with another modern theorist—in this case literary critic Mikhail Bakhtin. Bakhtin helps identify the tension between dialogue and rhetoric at the center of Alcott's pedagogical method. For Bakhtin the difference between rhetoric and dialogue is determined by how many "voices" are included in any narrative or discourse. He considered rhetoric a single-voiced utterance designed to evoke a specific, preferred, and final response in the listener. Thus "all rhetorical forms, monologic in their compositional structure, are oriented toward the listener and his answer."[55] By contrast dialogue is always a double-voiced exchange that uses any answer as a stimulus for further conversation and development in time. Living dialogue thus "provokes an answer, anticipates and structures itself in the answer's direction. Forming itself in an atmosphere of the already spoken, the word is at the same time determined by that which has not yet been said but which is needed and in fact anticipated by the answering word."[56] Or as he draws the contrast more sharply in his notes, "in rhetoric there is the unconditionally innocent and the unconditionally guilty; there is complete victory and destruction of the opponent. In dialogue the destruction of the opponent also destroys the very dialogic sphere where the word lives."[57] Given this difference, rhetoric and dialogue are seemingly at two opposite ends of the spectrum and cannot overlap. Rhetoric is a one-way dissemination tool by which the language of a single individual dominates the mind of a listener, whereas dialogue is a two-way exchange whereby a common language is developed through progressive questions and answers and thereby creates a new unity out of difference.

Yet if Bakhtin gives reason to set rhetoric and dialogue in opposition, he also provides resources for their reconciliation. This is what Zappen argues when he sees the possibility in Bakhtin of recognizing "the 'double-voicedness' of rhetorical discourse, its orientation both toward the listeners who answer and react to it and the prior speakers whose words it transmits and re-accentuates."[58] This recognition is only possible, however, by first taking into account that Bakhtin does not restrict dialogic utterances only to the context of oral exchange, a restriction that certainly would deny any dialogic character to a speech or written medium. Indeed his whole point in defining the nature of dialogue is to show how the modern polyphonic novel, such as those of Fyodor Dostoyevsky, can also be dialogic when it is "constructed not as the whole of a single consciousness, absorbing other consciousnesses as objects into itself, but as a whole formed by the interaction of several consciousnesses, none of which entirely becomes an object for the other."[59] Even though Dostoevsky's novels are products of his own creative imagination and printed as a unified text, they nonetheless each contain, in the expression of its many characters, a "plurality of independent and unmerged voices and consciousnesses, a genuine polyphony of fully valid voices . . . with equal rights and each with its own world."[60] To incorporate rhetoric into this model creates a tension between preserving the relative autonomy of each of the voices on the one hand while producing a unity that reflects the intentions and aims of the authorial consciousness that brought them together on the other.

The method Alcott developed in his Temple School and publicized in *Record of a School* reveals both the promise and the challenge of a dialogic rhetoric that attempts to reconcile the ethic of welcoming the speech of others with the rhetorical imperative to move an audience toward a certain answer preferred by the author. This challenge, while made explicit in Alcott, really pervaded all of the work of the Transcendentalists. This is because one of the aims of transcendental eloquence was precisely to challenge the single-voiced traditions of American religious, poetic, and political discourse by revealing it as only one part of a universal whole that encompasses a plurality of voices across geographic space and historical time. Alcott's desire to downplay his own voice while emphasizing the contributions of the children in his pedagogy was thus no different in kind than the Transcendentalist desire to dissolve the illusion of self by showing its inherent connectedness not only to all things but also to all words. For instance Eric G. Wilson describes the writing of Margaret Fuller as "tensely poly-vocal, a melding of numerous contrary forces. Not wishing to impose her voice on the fecundity of our own textual landscape, she selflessly becomes a vortex through which multiple forces flow, an organized cacophony of styles, speakers, stories, and digressions."[61] But the same could be said for Thoreau in *Walden* (the charm of which, according to Lawrence Buell, lies in its "heterogeneity and unpredictableness")[62] or Emerson in *Nature* (which Alan D. Hodder describes as "the creation of many voices").[63] The method of dialogic rhetoric in Alcott's classroom was thus paradigmatic of the dialogic nature of transcendental eloquence that sought to embody the multitudinousness of the world through polyvocality of the word.

More than simply creating a supportive environment, Alcott's classroom became a space for language to reveal itself as language. What comes through clearly in *Record of a School* is how this style of eloquence is contingent on the degree to which people recognize that their very being is implicated in the richness of language. One of the most remarkable aspects of Alcott's school is that he made the word a living thing to be cared for and cultivated rather than simply an instrumental vehicle for the transmission of thought. Peabody spends the considerable bulk of her observations, in fact, recording how Alcott taught the meaning of individual words through dialogue. A group of words were written on the board, then used in sentences, then explored through conversation about their origins, meetings, and applications. Just how freewheeling Alcott could be in these discussion is indicated by a short comment about teaching the word *nose*. Peabody writes: "The word *nose* led to a consideration of its uses; and its convenient situation in our own faces, and also in the heads of those animals, who need a still more perfect organ for their purposes. There was a long conversation about cultivating the senses, and on the abuse of the senses by cultivating them too much."[64] Typical of Alcott, any discussion of a physical object inevitably culminated in some moral or spiritual lesson, as indicated in this lengthier account of Alcott's discussion of the importance of words themselves:

> It was eleven o'clock, and they began to fidget; Mr. Alcott asked who was tired of explaining these words; and one of the boys held up his hand. Mr. Alcott asked another boy what a *word* was; he replied, something made out of letters. The next boy said, A word is a thought shaped out by letters. Mr. Alcott replied, Or a feeling; feeling may be denoted by inarticulate sounds also; as oh! ah! &c. Why do you come to school? To learn, said several. Yes, said he, to learn *words;* to learn to *word* your thoughts; this is a *word shop*. What do you come to school for, then? he repeated. To *buy* words, said one. I said, To *word your thoughts. Words,* then, are the signs of *thoughts.* What great things *words* are! a *word* has saved a life when spoken at the right time. Mary, said he, do you remember that it is said somewhere, In the beginning was the Word, and the Word was with God, and the Word was God;—What does Word mean there? It means God, said she. Yes, language is a representation of God in the world, said he: how important then are *words;* how sacred should

be our use of them; how carefully should we learn their meanings; how carefully should we express our thoughts in words.[65]

A purely "Yankee" reading of this passage might interpret him as admitting that he has become a peddler of words, the owner of a "word shop." But looking back on this passage in the wake of contemporary philosophy, it is hard not to recognize in Alcott's words a predecessor to Martin Heidegger's claim that "language is the house of Being."[66] That is to say, language does not *follow* users and their intentions, as if one merely had thoughts and intentions and reached out for a word as he or she would a hammer or a nail. As Heidegger writes, "what we speak of, language, is always ahead of us. Our speaking merely follows language constantly. Thus we are continually lagging behind what we first ought to have overtaken and taken up in order to speak about it."[67] Alcott refers to the Gospel of John, in which the beginning was the Word. But as Heidegger reminds readers, "the word is *logos*. It speaks simultaneously as the name for Being and for Saying."[68] Thus before someone can say anything, he or she must recognize that the words used to speak are also the words people use to exist as speaking beings. This is the starting place for the growth of a self-aware dialogic consciousness.

It was not until Alcott's follow-up to *Record of a School, Conversations with Children on the Gospels* (1836), that his more fully developed methods of dialogic rhetoric were recorded and publicized. Although following much the same form as the earlier book, *Conversations* showcased Alcott speaking specifically about religious topics drawn from biblical passages. Perhaps more significant, it showed him stressing the importance of interpreting scripture emblematically, which in Alcott meant the method of perceiving every image, word, act, or phenomenon as a sign of some larger spiritual or symbolic meaning. Thus emerged the tension between the dialogic form of his interaction with the children and the often blatant rhetorical motive he possessed in moving the children toward the answer that he had clearly believed to be the correct one. According to Barbara Packer, Alcott often had difficulty pulling this off with eloquence, the result being that he appeared clumsy, overbearing, and simplistic, while the children themselves were "sometimes charmed, frequently perplexed, and occasionally stoutly resistant to the things their peculiar teacher is trying to get them to say."[69] One is thus reminded of Bakhtin's warning that even when rhetoric seeks to be double-voiced and deeply connected with the forces of historical becoming, it exists "at best merely a distant echo of this becoming, narrowed down to an individual polemic."[70]

The method of dialogic rhetoric most explicitly employed was that of the collaborative interpretation of symbols in order to disclose some religious meaning that had a direct bearing on moral action and judgment. These were Alcott's "emblems." Emblems abound in *Conversations,* whether posited by Alcott or the children. Nature is an emblem of God, but so is Jesus. God's bosom is an emblem of God's love. The color blue is an emblem of faith. Doves are emblems of either a child's innocence or mother's love. Water is an emblem of purity. A lamb is an emblem of mildness. Circumcision is an emblem of self-sacrifice. At one point Alcott asks the children to provide an emblem for creation. The children reply: "A little child beginning to speak"; "A little bud beginning to open"; "A plant coming out of the ground"; "A little child beginning to exist."[71] Thus birth itself was an emblem. As he explained to his young audience, there are the physical facts of birth, as when one has "seen the rose opening from the seed with the assistance of the atmosphere; this is the birth of the rose." But this rose also is a sign of spiritual birth and "typifies the bringing forth of the spirit, by pain, and labor, and patience."[72] So too with the birth of human children, such as Jesus, which occurs when a mother "gives up her body to God, and he works upon it in a mysterious way and, with her aid, brings forth the child's Spirit in a little Body of its own." Not hiding from children the reality of physical birth, Alcott nonetheless interprets this phenomenon as an emblem, as a sign of some specific spiritual meaning.

Yet it was not always the case that Alcott had a particular rhetorical goal in mind. Some of the most fascinating dialogues have no clear endpoint and exist purely as a stream of voices whose aim is to generate a state of curiosity and experimentation. At these times he challenges students to interpret emblems concerning almost every subject, while at the same time providing space for them to explore their own interpretations—even if the occasional result was, as Packer describes it, a dialogue that "often sounds as if it had been written by a particularly relentless dramatist of the absurd."[73] One particular revealing conversation is about the meaning of Matthew 3:2, when John the Baptist mentions a coming baptism of fire. Peabody's narrative shows the children creatively struggling to come to the answer desired by their teacher, who in this case is content to sit and listen:

MR. ALCOTT:	What does the word *baptize* mean?
JOSIAH:	It means purify.
MR. ALCOTT:	Why do people purify—baptize with water?
JOSEPH:	To clean the body.
MR. ALCOTT:	What does purify with fire mean?
JOSEPH:	I don't know.
LEMUEL:	To baptize with fire means to purify with love, and baptizing with the Holy Ghost means preaching with love, and baptizing with water is an emblem of these.

JOSIAH: John did not mean Jesus would use outward fire, but he wanted to express how very powerful Jesus was over everything.

GEORGE K: Yes; John meant that Jesus had power like unquenchable fire.

EDWARD J: I think Jesus baptizing with fire meant the kind of punishment he would inflict.

FRANKLIN: Baptizing with water was an emblem, and baptizing with fire was punishment, and baptizing with the Holy Ghost was the miracles which he did.

FREDERICK: Baptizing with the Holy Ghost is the love of Jesus; baptizing with fire is the punishment of conscience.

NATHAN: Baptizing with fire means to make our spirits pure.

WELLES: Water is an emblem of spiritual purity. The fire that the tree is to be cast into, is our conscience when we have done something to repent of. Jesus, trying to make them better by talking and preaching, is baptizing them with the Holy Ghost.

JOHN D: Baptizing with fire is conscience. Baptizing with Holy Ghost is love.

MARTHA: Holy Ghost is love. Fire means the punishment of conscience. Water is an emblem, meaning to cleanse the spirits of people of their sins, so as to be ready for the love of Jesus.[74]

This discussion continues for another page, as the children eventually arrive at a consensus that "conscience is a fiery baptism," with one child adding for good measure that "very often there is a fiery baptism in my conscience." Notably, however, Alcott neither denies nor affirms this consensus about conscience but rather jumps to the summary conclusion that "the doctrines of repentance and purification were preached to introduce Jesus," because "no one could understand the subjects upon which Jesus was to preach, till his mind was purified."[75] The fine distinctions between a baptism of fire and a baptism of water are for the most part left open, just as what is an emblem and what is not remains unclear. But by leaving these questions unanswered, Alcott also indirectly validates the speculations of the children, giving them a sense that there remains more to discover than what has been said and that by continuing their own inquiry into the meaning of emblems, they might make those discoveries on their own. It is this effect on attitudes, rather than production of any specific belief, that is the most emancipatory product of the type of dialogic rhetoric one finds in transcendental eloquence.

Published along with *Conversations* was a copy of Alcott's 1836 pamphlet, *The Doctrine and Discipline of Human Culture*. In this work Alcott presents the most explicit articulation and defense of the methods and aims of Transcendentalist pedagogy. His vision of true education was in many ways a restatement of the optimistic Unitarian faith, first expressed by William Ellery Channing in 1828, that human beings were put on the earth not to bow to God as a sinner but to "approach God by the free and natural unfolding of our highest powers, of understanding, conscience, love, and moral will."[76] True education was thus directed toward the cultivation of power and virtue in creatures made in the likeness of God. "Man is the noblest of the Creator's works," Alcott declares, "the rightful Sovereign of the Earth, fitted to subdue all things to himself, and to know of no superior, save God," yet he nonetheless "enters upon the scene of his labors, a feeble and wailing Babe, at first unconscious of the place assigned him, and needs years of tutelage and discipline to fit him for the high and austere duties that await him."[77] Constrained neither by Calvinist piety nor scientific realism, Alcott painted for his audience the supreme image by which his pedagogy is guided:

> It is the mission of this Age, to revive [God's] Idea, give it currency, and reinstate it in the faith of men. By its quickening agency, it is to fructify our common nature, and reproduce its like. It is to unfold our being into the same divine likeness. It is to reproduce Perfect Men. The faded Image of Humanity is to be restored, and man appear in his original brightness. It is to mold anew our Institutions, our Manners, our Men. It is to restore Nature to its rightful use; purify Life; hallow the functions of the Human Body, and regenerate Philosophy, Literature, Art, Society. The Divine Idea of a Man is to be formed in the common consciousness of this age, and genius mould all its products in accordance with it.[78]

This "genius" is not merely synonymous with intellectual capacity. Genius is the expression of power. It is "the free and harmonious play of all the faculties of a human being," not simply in thought but in action. Genius is "the Whole Man—the central Will—working worthily, subordinating all else to itself; and reaching its end by the simplest and readiest means. It is human nature rising superior to things and events, and transfiguring these into the image of its own Spiritual Ideal."[79] Alcott prophesizes the development of what he calls a completely "self-subsistent" individual capable of using all organs and instruments to remake the world (and him- or herself) into the image of a divine idea.[80]

What makes Alcott's *Doctrine* so rhetorically rich, however, is that, having aroused a desire in his readers for their children to become geniuses, he satisfies it by articulating a vision of pedagogy thoroughly guided with the spirit of dialogic rhetoric. Because genius is something that can only unfold from within children naturally, as each discovers his or her own divine capacities and expresses them through acts of individual will, true education must be a persuasive drawing-out of the child rather than a forceful imposition from outside. As he explains, in any comprehensive idea of education, the best "agency is that of mind leaping to meet mind; not of force acting on opposing force. . . . A tingling influence goes forth to inspire; making the mind think; the heart feel; the pulse throb with his own. He arouses every faculty. He awakens the Godlike."[81] Here is the dialogic emphasis on cultivating the voice of the other in the faith that it has its own unique wisdom, virtue, and authority. Yet this dialogic ethic is balanced with an emphasis on the rhetorical skill of the teacher, who must craft a discourse capable of invoking a particular response. Employing the language of classical rhetoric, Alcott claims that a teacher "is to inform the understanding, by chastening the appetites, allaying the passions, softening the affections, vivifying the imagination, illuminating the reason, giving pliancy and force to the will; for a true understanding is the issue of these powers, working freely and in harmony with the Genius of the soul, conformed to the law of duty."[82] In this vision of education, the teacher uses all rhetorical means available to stimulate the affections and cognitions of students, appealing to their reason and imagination to bring them closer to the idea. Dialogic rhetoric attempts to balance both of these imperatives within a continuous discourse of becoming, the result being the production of eloquence in others: "The Genius of the soul is waked, and eloquence sits on her tuneful lip."[83] Eloquent teachers thus produce eloquent souls.

In a masterstroke of rhetoric, Alcott gives authority to his method by using as his model of imitation no less than the figure of Jesus. In Alcott's hands he appears not so much as the Son of God sent to die for the salvation of irredeemable sinners; he rather is reinterpreted as a teacher whose main contribution to humanity is to demonstrate what Alcott calls "the Art," namely the "art of revealing to a man the true idea of his being—his endowments—his possessions—and of fitting them to use these for the growth, renewal, and perfection of his spirit." In short it is not the art of attaining God's grace but rather "the art of completing a man."[84] Consequently, for Alcott, "the Gospels are not only a fit Textbook for the study of spirit, in its corporal relations, but they are a specimen also of the true method of imparting instruction. They give us the practice of Jesus himself. They unfold the means of addressing human nature."[85] In Alcott's classroom the Gospels offered teachers a perfect model for rhetorical imitation in the form of Jesus, whose speech was popular, bore the stamp of naturalness, force, and directness, and whose ideas were clothed in the simplest, yet most commanding, forms to make them come alive in the souls of his listeners.

In perhaps his clearest summary of this extemporaneous method, Alcott describes how, "from facts and objects the most familiar, he slid easily and simply into the highest and holiest themes, and, in this unimposing guise, disclosed the great Doctrines, and stated the Divine Ideas, that it was his mission to bequeath to the race."[86] "The true Teacher, like Jesus, must inspire in order to unfold";[87] and one inspires by using a dialogic rhetoric that draws from the experiences, voices, and language of the people to craft a discourse that inspires them to be perfect just as God in heaven is perfect. When this happens, genius is awakened: "Man faces his fellow man. He holds a living intercourse. He feels the quickening life and light. The social affections are addressed; and these bring all the faculties in train. Speech comes unbidden. Nature lends her images. Imagination sends abroad her winged words. We see thought as it springs from the soul, and in the very process of growth and utterance. Reason plays under the mellow light of fancy."[88] Pointing in particular to the moments when Jesus spoke "at the well side discoursing with the Samaritan woman, on the Idea of Worship; and at the night with Nicodemus, on Spiritual Renewal," Alcott celebrates those moments in which Jesus encounters individuals on their own terms and adapts his message to their lives and experiences.[89] Alcott thus sought to apply the art of Jesus to awakening the same powers of the imagination and reason in the students in his Temple School, encouraging them to have trust in their own individual genius while at the same time moving them gently toward the true revelation of the whole of which they were but a part.

The realities of politics soon interrupted Alcott's idealistic revelry. After the publication of *Conversations,* he found himself a target of those who worshiped the old god of tradition. Nathan Hale, editor of the *Boston Daily Advertiser,* summarized his "Art" this way: "the essence of the system appears to be, to select the most solemn of all subjects—the fundamental truths of religion as recorded in the Gospels of our Savior,—and after reading a chapter, instead of offering any illustration of what is there recorded, to invite the people to express, without discrimination or reserve, all their crude and undigested thoughts upon it—and especially on those points which are most difficult to be understood and not accepting those upon which inquisitiveness is useless, and often improper and mischievous."[90] Joseph T. Buckingham, taking special aim at the relatively open discussions of birth, intimacy, death, and love, concluded that it was "a more indecent and obscene book (we say nothing of its absurdity) than any other we ever saw exposed for sale on a bookseller's counter."[91] Representative of the opinions of the Unitarian establishment, Andrews Norton pronounced the book "one third absurd, one third blasphemous, and one third obscene."[92] Even Peabody, who otherwise sympathized with Alcott's goals, thought he had had pushed the children too far in giving them a false sense of authority, writing to him that "I think you are liable to injure the modesty and unconsciousness of good children by making them reflect too much on their actual superiority to others."[93] Correctly anticipating the firestorm that would result after its publication, Peabody resigned at the beginning of the third year of the Temple School. She was replaced by a twenty-six-year-old Margaret Fuller.

Although Alcott may not have practically lived up to the standards of genius that he set for the true teacher—a standard set by Socrates, Plato, and Jesus—he definitely accomplished his political goal of startling the public consciousness by making the true aims and methods of education a matter of controversy and debate. In an April 13, 1837, entry in his journal, he remarked that "an unusual degree of excitement has pervaded this metropolis regarding my book," noting that not only has he been "severely censured" in the press, but also "at one time the excitement threatened a mob" whose "plan was to make the assault at one of my Friday evening Conversations."[94] The assault did not happen, but the threat had an effect on Alcott—it made him even more dedicated to his reformist ends. He understood and accepted the necessity of resistance that would be provoked by any genuine effort "to unmake and reconstructs the consciousness of men."[95] In an 1837 journal entry, he articulates what is perhaps the most succinct expression of the reformist motivation behind Transcendentalism:

> Men will not be taken to pieces without some outcry. They fear the loss of their identity, placing this, as they usually do, in forms: in the associations of their terrestrial experience; in the images which they have assumed upon their intellectual being. They fear that all is going. Hence distrust, fear, and all manner of misapprehensions and forebodings. But every reform implies all this. It is an experiment on the common consciousness of the time. It is a demolition of an old, traditional, conventional form of consciousness, a substitution of a new, real, and true perception of things. It is a stripping off, from the intellects of men, of the outworn garb of associations and images in which they have been wrapped. It is taking all encumbrances from between their minds and things.[96]

True to a degree of all efforts at reform, it was even more true in Alcott's case. He was not simply out to change the minds of adults; his task was to alter the consciousness of a new generation of children. What Peabody feared was thus precisely what Alcott desired—to make them feel superior to the traditions of their elders and to encourage them to cast off the servile humility to and unconscious acceptance of their traditions and beliefs. No wonder, then, that Alcott's conversations with children may have incited a mob; for inside the walls of his school, he was demolishing the old, traditional, conventional form of consciousness that was already felt to be under assault by the other revolutionary changes in the nineteenth century.

Perhaps Alcott's most lasting political legacy, then, is the simple proposition that the most radical reformer in any society is the teacher—namely the teacher of genius, whose true art of dialogic rhetoric is to use words to arouse every faculty and awaken the godlike in children so that they, too, can eventually "word" their thoughts with eloquence and thereby remold the world in the image of their ideas. Whether Alcott himself lived up to this ideal is in many ways beside the point. His political task was to articulate through his eloquence a new calling for teachers in a way that, like Jesus near the tomb of Lazarus, breathed new life into their mission. Likewise, he concludes, "apprehending the Divine Significance of Jesus—yet filled with the assurance of coming Messiahs to meet the growing nature of Man—shall inspired Genius go forth to renovate his Era; casting out the unclean spirits and the demons that yet afflict the Soul. And then shall Humanity, leaving her infirmities, wrongs, her sufferings, and her sins, in the corrupting grave, reappear in the consciousness of Physical Purity; Inspired Genius; and Spotless Holiness."[97] And thus it is that the teacher becomes a new messiah, using the art of words to cast out the demons of recalcitrant tradition and bring new vitality and spirit to the coming generation who will unfold their powers into the fullness of God.

In the end the demons had the last word, casting out Alcott instead. Although many of his new Transcendentalist friends came to his public defense, most notably Emerson and Peabody, the relentless attacks in the press had done their work—by summer of 1837, only eleven pupils remained at Temple School. Forced to rent a smaller room in the temple, sell his prized library, and let Fuller go, Alcott struggled along through the next year with between five and eight students until he finally had to close the school in June 1838. Still undaunted, with the help of some friends he opened a day school for the poor in Boston's South End, accepting twenty students, including the son of his friend and patron William Russell. Yet the demons chased Alcott even here. One of the people he admitted was a black girl, Susan Robinson. When he refused the demand by his latest wealthy supporter, Dr. John Flint, to expel her immediately, his enrollment withered. By the next spring, the only students enrolled in his school were his own three daughters, the young William Russell, and Robinson. On June 22 he closed his school and ended his career as a teacher. "I closed my school today," he wrote in his journal. "It is quite obvious that labors like mine cannot take root in the community, and more especially in the city, until parents and adults are better instructed in the principles and methods of human culture."[98] Like his experience as a peddler, his experience peddling a new kind of transcendental pedagogy ended with his emotional and financial ruin.

Although one can narrate the collapse of Alcott's educational experiments in terms of his own failure as a businessman, it is fairer to judge the Temple School as an extraordinary, if short-lived, success. Alcott had been able to perceive more

astutely than any of his contemporaries the growing demand for a new education for "genius," a demand rising most quickly in the bourgeois classes of the
industrial Northeast, who, like Sampson Reed, had become enthralled by the new
possibilities of power that seemed within reach of individuals with the capacity
for genius. Yet at the same time, he had not merely catered to this need but had
maintained throughout a courageous idealism that saw genius as more than the
ability to found a joint-stock pharmaceutical company or any other number of
bourgeois accomplishments. Alcott had ridden the wave of the market revolution,
exploiting the freedom and power that it gave him once unshackled from the
agrarian life of a Connecticut farmer; but he had ridden the current to its natural
end, which was a vision of genius that also committed itself to the liberation of
all people, no matter their race, gender, religion, or social station. Thus the same
audience that was persuaded by Alcott's initial sales pitch came to reject it when
they realized he actually meant what he said. Abigail Alcott's brother, Samuel J.
May, summed up the problem with Alcott's teaching this way in a letter: "The
worldly, the great, the wise, the prudent will sneer at it because its tendency is
not to make good merchants, or lawyers, or civil engineers, or manufacturing
agents."[99] This audience wanted a genius that transcended both conventional
aristocratic and agrarian education, but only so long as it then stayed within the
strict limitations of a rising entrepreneurial middle-class that put class, profit, and
respectability first.

Alcott's impatience with the emerging limits of bourgeois respectability ultimately marked his rhetoric as Transcendentalist in a way in which Reed's was
not and could never be. Although both had certainly pronounced a new order
of things that bestowed spirit's blessings on genius, Reed championed a largely
bourgeois vision of genius that could be translated immediately into practical,
economic, and technological power and could remake both nature and man in
the name of growth—a vision that led him to be complicit in the Compromise of
1850, to the disappointment of Emerson. Alcott, perceiving the same tendencies
as Reed, arrived at a far more radical vision. In his ideal the purest form of power
was found in the innocence of a child, and genius represented the capacity for
a child to express her full capacities in virtue, art, expression, communion, and
language, thus seeking not to bind together a nation but to cultivate a beautiful
soul. For him, then, the grand ambitions of bourgeois heroes such as Reed were
constraints to his mission. As he wrote in the same journal entry in which he
lamented the closing of his school, there were rhetorical challenges ahead of him:
"I must address myself to adults in the spirit of the words of Jesus: 'Except ye be
converted, and become as little children, ye shall not apprehend the doctrines and
disciplines of the Kingdom of the Soul.'"[100] Here was the central challenge of all
Transcendentalist eloquence—not only to pronounce ideals that were continuous

with the tendencies of a changing era, but also to convince those attracted to these ideals that they must be as little children again to be able to enter a new age free of the burden of the past.

Alcott fully embraced this new prophetic identity as a Transcendentalist only after the time of his greatest rhetorical influence had already passed. On July 19, 1839, he attended the Harvard Divinity School to hear Emerson deliver his address that condemned the Unitarian faith as a slave to history and tradition while admonishing his listeners to "go alone; to refuse the good models, even those most sacred to the imagination of men, and dare to love God without mediator or veil."[101] Alcott was clearly in a receptive mood. A few weeks later, on August 5, he wrote in his journal that he "had an agreeable walk amidst Emerson's sylvan haunts this morning, discoursing with him on the great questions of the time." But on one point he challenged Emerson: "He, faithful to his own Genius, asserts the supremacy of the scholar's pen. I plead the omnipotence of the prophet's spoken over the written word, and the sovereignty of epic action over both."[102] Outdoing even Emerson, Alcott asserted that his acts of prophetic speech and epic action, here clearly meaning the dialogic rhetorical encounters with his students made possible by his ventures with his Temple School, were more important than any essay published by Emerson or any other oracle of the new school. But this assertion came at a point at which Alcott never again had such a captive audience of young minds to mold into the image of God.

To those who believe that rhetoric is a matter of quantity and magnitude and that truly great rhetoric is only that which impacts a mass audience in the moment of speaking, Alcott's pronouncements may seem indicative of a naive and fantastical mind, a man who never grew out of childhood and continued his whole life believing in dreams. Certainly this seems even more the case when looking at the course of the next few decades of his life, which included his short-lived and disastrous exercise in utopian living at the Fruitlands, the publication of absurd-sounding aphorisms in two collections of "Orphic Sayings" in the *Dial,* and his years of economic debt and mismanagement at his family farm. Yet proof of the rhetorical power of Alcott's prophetic speech can be found in the source of his own economic salvation in the 1860s—the literary success of his daughter, Louisa May Alcott, whose *Little Women* is based on her own experience growing up. Louisa became the type of genius whose arrival her father had prophesized— and no wonder, for in her words Bronson saw the workings of God. In a January 4, 1835, passage in his journal, Alcott recorded his high expectations for his calling as a father: "He who kindles the fire of genius on the altar of the young heart unites his own prayers for humanity with every ascending flame that is emitted from it through succeeding time. . . . But here come my two children to spend an hour with me in the study, and I resign my thoughts to their spirits whence, if I do my part, shall soon shoot forth branches to heal and bless the people. For genius is the endowment of every spirit, and parents are its supervisors while on its terrestrial mission. May I fulfill my divine behest!" Louisa, at that time just two years and two months old, took up her father's pencil to make scrawlings on the journal's pages. Alcott gazed upon these markings with awe, as a magus who saw a star in the sky:

> I have conversed with the little ones, whose imagings appear on the paper above—fit emblems of the essayings of an inapt skill on terrestrial things. These marks—who knoweth their meaning? Who shall divine the ideas that sought linear expression in the shaping? Within was a heavenly spirit, and it attempted to picture forth itself, even as the terrestrial father had been shaping forth the images of his own spirit on the same page. Look at the beginning! Behold the imitative strokes! These were *letters*, the Spirit's letters. They were types of ideas; and doubtless the mind had within it, while delineating them, a glad sense of the fellow-feeling, a temporary quality, a self-complacent skillfulness in the divine art of shaping forth the soul in emblems.[103]

Using the same language of his classroom pedagogy, Alcott gazed and wondered at his young daughter's effort—her irrepressible impulse—to shape and cultivate her soul, by mastery of emblems expressed through the word. In possessing this impulse, she was perhaps like almost all children; but unlike so many of them at this time, Louisa was raised by a father who sought to draw out this impulse with his own eloquent speech, using words in conversation to bring forth words in his child, not as a form of discipline but as a source of wonder. And perhaps the true power of transcendental eloquence can find no better evidence than this—the production of another genius.

CHAPTER 3

"To break the fetters of the bound"

Orestes Brownson and the Ideology of Democratic Radicalism

According to the Christianity of Christ no man can enter the kingdom of God, who does not labor with all zeal and diligence to establish the kingdom of God on the earth; who does not labor to bring down the high, and bring up the low; to break the fetters of the bound and set the captive free; to destroy all oppression, establish the reign of justice, which is the reign of equality, between man and man; to introduce new heavens and a new earth, wherein dwelleth righteousness, wherein all shall be as brothers, loving one another, and no one possessing what another lacketh. No man can be a Christian who does not labor to reform society, to mould it according to the will of God and the nature of man; so that free scope shall be given to every man to unfold himself in all beauty and power, and to grow up into the stature of a perfect man in Christ Jesus. No man can be a Christian who does not refrain from all practices by which the rich grow richer and the poor poorer, and who does not do all in his power to elevate the laboring classes, so that one man shall not be doomed to toil while another enjoys the fruits; so that each man shall be free and independent, sitting under "his own vine and fig-tree with none to molest or to make afraid."

Orestes Brownson, "The Laboring Classes," 1840

In 1837 Bronson Alcott was not the only one struggling to keep his head above water. In the spring, just before Alcott was forced to close his Temple School, the New York mercantile house of Arthur Tappan and Company collapsed, signaling the beginning of the Panic of 1837 in the United States. In what was to become a recognizable cycle, the "bust" had been preceded by a "boom" of land speculation and runaway development marked by "entrepreneurial frenzy for banking capital and internal improvements" that had pushed "states into extravagant debts and Congress into distribution."[1] But with the destruction of the Bank of the United States by Andrew Jackson, this increasing debt had to be financed by foreign money. As more and more projects began to be financed purely by credit without the backing of specie (or "hard money"), more American entrepreneurs had to rely on the guarantees of foreign banks—guarantees that in 1837 ran dry as the Bank of England abruptly cut off all credit to American institutions while raising interest rates as high as 24 percent. As one wealthy capitalist, George Templeton Strong, recorded in his diary, "The merchants going to the devil *en masse*. . . . Arthur Tappan has failed! . . . Workmen thrown out of employ by the hundreds daily. Business at a stand; the coal mines in Pennsylvania stopped and no fuel and prospect for next winter."[2] Everywhere people flocked to withdraw whatever money they could but found either the doors closed or the bank without any money left to give. On May 4 the president of a leading deposit bank was found dead. As Emerson wrote in his journal that spring, "Loud cracks in the social edifice.—Sixty thousand laborers, says rumor, to be presently thrown out of work, and these make a formidable mob to break open banks & rob the rich & brave the domestic government." It was, he wrote, a "cold April; hard times."[3]

One Transcendentalist, however, was not surprised by the suffering brought about by the waves of the market revolution—Alcott's distant cousin Orestes Brownson (1803–76). A self-taught farm boy from a rural New England town like Alcott, Brownson shared similar reformist ideals and the same dissatisfaction with establishment religion as he journeyed from Congregationalism to Presbyterianism to Universalism. In his 1834 essay "Social Evils and Their Remedy I," for instance, he had enthused, "EDUCATION! He who pronounces that word pronounces the remedy for the evils of man social condition."[4] But the bold, blunt, and not infrequently belligerent Brownson channeled his rhetorical energies in a dramatically different way than did his gentle and idealistic cousin. Brownson was after bigger game than simply pedagogical reform; he hoped to effect a wholesale reconstitution of a social system whose primary vice was the maintenance of the division between the realm of matter and spirit. In his 1836 manifesto, *New Views of Christianity, Society, and the Church* (published a few months after he temporarily moved in with Alcott on his arrival in Boston), Brownson called for a new church that would transcend all institutional and sectarian divisions and give form to a democratic order of justice in which "slavery will cease," "wars will fail," "education will destroy the empire of ignorance," "civil freedom will become universal," "industry will be holy," and "church and state will become one."[5] Until that time, however, there has only one thing to expect from the persistent antithesis between spiritualism and materialism: "perpetual and universal war."[6]

Brownson saw actual war coming if the American public, duped by a political spectacle of the 1840 "log cabin and hard cider" campaign of Whig presidential candidate William Henry Harrison, could not use the ballot to free themselves from economic oppression. To help avoid this war (or to prophesize its coming), Brownson launched a broadside attack, "The Laboring Classes," against the entire political, economic, and moral system of the United States. Although advertised as a review of Thomas Carlyle's *Chartism*, "The Laboring Classes" quickly moved into detailed polemic that traced the origins of contemporary economic oppression to a collusion between a corrupt, institutionalized priesthood and a rising bourgeois merchant class. His solution—destroy the priesthood, limit the power of the government, abolish inheritance of private property, and finally constitute a new fusion of church and state organized by mass public persuasion that disclosed the nature of justice to all and then compelled them to act in concert to attain that end. It is because of this sweeping vision that Arthur Schlesinger Jr. declared Brownson to be the nearest American forerunner to Karl Marx and judged that "The Laboring Classes" was perhaps "the best study of the workings of society written an American before the Civil War," and as such it "deserves a high place in revolutionary literature."[7] More than a typical campaign tract, it represented the most radical political application of Transcendentalist principles while at the same time exhibiting a rhetorical style that had more in common with the old god of rhetoric than the new god of eloquence.

Although often sidelined in the literature on Transcendentalism as a marginal figure, Brownson deserves a central place in its tradition precisely because he does not fit neatly into the mold of a Transcendentalist. On the one hand, he was arguably central to the formation of Transcendentalism as a self-conscious movement, a founding member of the Transcendental Club who engaged vigorously in the early Unitarian debates, became a Universalist minister, and founded a magazine, the *Boston Quarterly Review,* which published works by Margaret Fuller, George Ripley, and Elizabeth Peabody. On the other hand, Brownson's working-class upbringing made him highly critical of Emersonian individualism and dismissive of transcendental eloquence that seemed more suited for generating creative tropes for the literary elite than for advocating for social justice in the language of the common people. His support of the Jacksonian Democratic Party was indicative of his rejection of Whig elitism and his desire to align himself with the laboring classes rather than with entrepreneurs such as Sampson Reed. His eventual conversion to Catholicism and his subsequent condemnation of his earlier Transcendentalism proved that despite his early radicalism, he neither could cease his devotion to the god of rhetoric nor lose the god of tradition. There are thus good reasons to argue that Brownson should not be formally considered a member of the Transcendentalists, and certainly his later self would insist that he should not; but his tense and often contradictory relationship with Transcendentalism illuminates crucial aspects of the rhetoric and politics of the movement, whether by exhibiting them or contradicting them.

One thing Brownson's rhetoric illuminates about transcendentalism is the relationship between myth and ideology in its discourse. By myth and ideology, I refer to what Kenneth Burke sees as the distinction between, on the one hand, a language of poetry and image that narrates a relation between absolute origins and ultimate destinies and, on the other hand, a discourse of rhetoric and ideas that "constitute a political or social doctrine and inspires the acts of a government or party."[8] For Burke ideologies are always argumentative affairs that seek to unmask opponents and build up support for a new (or old) political system, but which themselves lack any warrant that transcends their own argumentative logic. Myth, by contrast, at its best always has "the effect of 'revelation.' And it takes us from the order of reason to the order of imagination."[9] In fact he recognizes "the highest purpose of poetry in the communication of 'transcendental feeling,' and we might define this technically, as the sense of oneness with the universe in which individual's being is grounded."[10] Myth thus allows a ground of ideology that transcends argumentative logic through the language of poetry, thus providing a poetic source of identification for those who might not yet accept certain ideological commitments.

Brownson was unique for recognizing this relationship and exploiting the mythic qualities of Transcendentalism for explicitly ideological purposes. When compared with the dialogic spirit of his cousin Alcott, he demonstrates what happened to Transcendentalism when it largely discarded its dialogic character and embraced the full-throated single-voicedness of a monologic rhetoric. Emerson records an incident in his journal that demonstrates the stark difference between the two men. Their friend Charles Lane, he wrote, "gives a very good account of his conversation with Brownson, who would drive him to an argument. He took his paper & pencil out of his pocket, & asked Brownson to give him the names of the profoundest men in America. Brownson stopped, & gave him one, and then another, & than his own for third. Brownson will never stop & listen, neither in conversation but what is more, not in solitude."[11] This characteristic was both a virtue and a vice. It gave Brownson the focus and courage it took to be the most prolific and outspoken individual associated with Transcendentalism, pouring his scathing criticisms and lofty ideals into the pages of his own magazine. Yet his single-minded political and rhetorical orientation often made him fail to live up to the poetic standards of transcendental eloquence and continually got him embroiled in controversies that would inevitably force him to abandon old positions and take up new ones as the circumstance demanded. Despite his limitations, however, Brownson remains a remarkable historical figure for his ability to construct an ideological criticism of the new capitalist order and to make a serious, if incomplete, effort to build a new vision of an egalitarian society on the foundations of a Transcendentalist myth. This vision he called democracy, and its articulation by Brownson represents one of the most radical political ideologies of the nineteenth century.

From the day of his birth, Orestes Brownson seemed destined for great things. Unusual for a child born to parents who eked out a living farming the poor soil of Stockbridge, Vermont, he was given a name not from the Bible but from Greek mythology. When a pair of fraternal twins were born in 1803 to Sylvester and Relief Brownson, they named the brother and sister Orestes Augustus and Daphne Augusta. Perhaps because of the proximity of Stockbridge to the Connecticut River, Daphne was named after a famous naiad, a nymph associated with fountains, wells, springs, and streams, who had been pursued by the god Apollo and, in order to escape, had prayed to Zeus, who changed her into a beautiful laurel tree. But the Brownsons must have seen something much different in their son's character. They gave him the name of the son of King Agamemnon and Queen Clytemnestra, who killed his mother out of vengeance for her own killing of his father, an act of matricide that violated the laws of the gods and condemned him to be pursued by the Furies. As the chorus of Aeschylus's *The Libation Bearers* says to Orestes after his act of violence, "There is no mortal man who shall turn/ unhurt his life's course to an end not marred./There is trouble here. There is more to come."[12] Whether or not his parents fully understood the significance of the name, one cannot know; but time ultimately revealed the name to be prophetic. Orestes Brownson and trouble would have a long history together.

The trouble began even before he was born. Although, like Alcott, his parents lived and worked in a New England farming community, they had a far more difficult life than the one Alcott endured on the moderately successful Spindle Hill farm. Sylvester Brownson had moved to Vermont sometime in the late eighteenth century looking for land and had settled in Stockbridge, which in 1803 had one hundred inhabitants. Although a beautiful setting near what is now the Green Mountain National Forest, with lush hills, forests, and countryside, Stockbridge promised only a hard life for its inhabitants. "The Stockbridge landscape was beautiful," writes Patrick Carey, "but the soil was stingy. Many Vermonters who tried to make the land yield fruit were frustrated in the early nineteenth century and eventually moved west for more fertile acreage."[13] Brownson tried to make a living, barely supporting his family as a sheepherder and working as a hired hand for wages. One can imagine that the birth of his children gave him hope that they would eventually provide him the labor that would enable him to acquire his own farm and establish himself as an important member of his small Vermont community.

This was not to be, however. Two years after the birth of Orestes, Brownson succumbed to a fatal case of pneumonia, leaving his twenty-nine-year-old wife,

Relief, and five children under the age of nine without a father and supporter. She tried to keep her family together, but without means to support them, around 1809 she had to send the children away to live with family and friends. Orestes was sent to live with James Huntington and his wife in the town of Royalton, about fifteen miles northeast along the White River, where he would stay until he was fifteen years old. The Huntingtons, like so many New Englanders, had inherited the ethics of New England Congregationalism, although Brownson remarked that while being "honest, upright, [and] strictly moral," they also "had no particular religion, and seldom went to meeting."[14] They did their best to teach Brownson to read and to make him conscientious and truthful. However, as Schlesinger observes, "their life gave little outlet to the exuberance usually spent in boyhood rough-and-tumble."[15] Furthermore they insisted that he work, first doing chores at the house and later making use of his considerable physical strength to work for wages, "all of which he saved towards his education."[16] As Brownson wrote later in his autobiography, *The Convert*, "properly speaking, I had no childhood. . . . Brought up with old people, and debarred from all the sports, plays, and amusements of children, I had the manners, the tone, and taste of an old man before I was a boy."[17] When Relief finally brought the family back together in 1817, moving to join her sister in Ballston Spa, New York, after the devastating famine of 1816 (called the "year without a summer" because of a sudden global decrease in temperatures), she encountered a son who was old beyond his years.

All the trouble that Brownson had endured had the constructive benefit of forming his character; it had "created in him a strong sense of personal independence, initiative, and self-reliance" at the same time that it "put him in a constant search for the communion, continuity, order, and stability that he did not enjoy."[18] To a considerable degree, the first of these effects can be attributed to living with the Huntingtons. Despite being stern and somber, they were not dogmatic, and they gave young Brownson considerable freedom to explore his own beliefs and faith without censure. He wrote that by eight years old he had already read a great deal of the scriptures on his own (and free from any sectarian dogma). Indeed his "greatest pleasure was in conversing or hearing others converse on the subject of religion."[19] In his autobiography he told a story of when, as a nine-year-old boy, he walked about four miles to witness a muster of a brigade of militia but was distracted by a discussion of two old men talking about religion: "The discussion, I remember, was on free will and election, and I actually took part in it, stoutly maintaining free will against Edwards, who confounds volition with judgment, and maintains that the will is necessarily determined by the state of the affections and the motives presented to the understanding." How his contribution was received by the old men, Brownson does not say. He remarks only that he was so interested in the discussion that "I almost forgot to eat my card of gingerbread."[20]

This episode shows the degree to which Brownson had been raised to think (and argue) for himself, an attitude exhibited by the fact that he later recounted this entire episode to his foster parents, without guilt or fear, on returning home.

No doubt the Huntingtons also contributed to his desire for communion because of their emotional distance and their lack of participation in any church; but Vermont itself also contributed to Brownson's desire for a community that promised more than sectarian dogmas and rigid boundaries. More so than Alcott's Connecticut, Brownson's Vermont was "dominated by an intense denominationalism," with even the small town of Stockbridge hosting "Congregationalists, Methodists, Baptists, Universalists, and a variety of lesser-known sects," with each proclaiming "its form of worship to be the one most pleasing to God."[21] Even considered a "hotbed of infidelity" by men such as Timothy Dwight, the Calvinist president of Yale, Vermont offered no clear and uncontested path to religious community to a young man without any sectarian commitments.[22] And when Brownson became interested for a time in the Methodist preachers who attempted to bring the evangelical spirit of the Second Great Awakening to this hotbed of infidelity, he found himself disappointed: "All I learned . . . was, that I must be born again or go to hell, get religion or be damned. The more I listened to them the more I feared hell, and the less I loved God. Love gave place to terror; and I became constantly afraid that the devil would come and carry me off bodily."[23] In the end, however, he did not get religion that way. He heeded the warnings of an elderly woman who had taken him aside after another Methodist revival and told him to "beware of sects and New Lights, they will make you fair promises, but in the end will deceive you to your own destruction."[24] By the time he had moved back in with his mother at Ballston Spa, Brownson was a man of faith without a church.

Brownson's journey to Transcendentalism (which in the end turned out to be a detour on his way to Catholicism) effectively began at his arrival in New York and continued for the next two decades. Reflecting back at this moment of origin from the perspective of a Catholic convert, Brownson could see in his younger self only naive cynicism. He writes: "after I was 14 years of age, I was thrown upon a new world, into the midst of new and strange scenes, and exposed to new and corrupting influences. I fell in with new sectaries, universalists, deists, atheists, and nothingarians, as they are called with us, who profess no particular religion."[25] Although he still held to his personal religious beliefs and enjoyed silent meditation, Brownson lamented that eventually "my young head became confused with the contradictory opinions I heard advanced, with the doubts and denials to which I listened, and for a time my mind was darkened, and I had persuaded myself that all religion was a delusion—the work of priestcraft or statecraft. I was in a labyrinth of doubt, with no Ariadne's thread to guide me out to the light of day."[26]

Yet the older man's judgment of his younger self is too harsh. Young Brownson clearly thought he had found Ariadne's thread, and in time he was more than ready to reveal to the world the pathway to the kingdom of God. As with Alcott, then, it is instructive for an understanding of the context of Transcendentalism to investigate the possible environmental influences that made him sympathetic to their new ideas and eventually made him one of the most vociferous defenders of their infidelities. For like Alcott, Brownson was largely self-educated and had pieced together his own version of Transcendentalism to serve a specific function. For Alcott it provided an emancipatory myth that could justify his radically new pedagogical method of dialogical rhetoric that would unfold the genius in each individual student. It gave Brownson the divine warrant to lash out against an economic system that he believed condemned many people (his mother and family not the least of them) to a life of struggle, poverty, humiliation, ignorance, and subservience. The language of Transcendentalism thus provided him what none of the traditional established religions could—a mythic foundation on which to build an ideological rhetoric that would finally expose the workings of naked power and inaugurate a new age of justice.

Of what Brownson called the "new and corrupting influences" that led his teenage self out of the labyrinth of cynicism, three stand out. Perhaps more new than corrupting, one of the most important influences was his enrollment in a nearby academy, which gave him the first and only experience with formal schooling he had in his life, an academy that was reflective of the new push for early education in which Alcott participated. The fact that the town of Ballston Spa was then a fashionable resort north of Albany with enough resources to support a good school was likely the reason Brownson's mother moved to New York. According to the biography written by his son, Henry, at the academy Brownson "acquired some Latin and less Greek, and attained to a fair knowledge, as it was then considered, of the usual branches of English education," including the classics.[27] Although it was a traditional school that taught by the standard method of rote memorization, it exposed Brownson to a world of classical learning and philosophy while honing his skills as a writer by drilling him in the arts of the rhetorical tradition. But perhaps equally important, Ballston Spa was where Brownson likely had his first real, direct, and long-term exposure to the increasing disparity of wealth in the United States. Whereas many of the other students were undoubtedly children of wealthy families, Brownson actually had to make use of savings from his own labor to pay for school while his mother and his family continued to struggle to make a living on wages while surrounded by luxury.

Brownson attended school until he was around nineteen (at least when he was not working) and thus acquired an elite education at the same time that he was continually reminded that he was not a member of the elite.

Second, Brownson participated in the communication revolution of the early nineteenth century in a way that would have a direct impact on his future profession as a writer and editor. Despite earning only a passing mention in his biography as a source of interruption to his studies, his training as a journeyman printer exposed him to the power of what was then new media to disseminate revolutionary ideas to the masses. Sometime around 1822, his son writes, "Orestes had left the academy and worked as an apprentice, and then as a journeyman, in James Comstock's printing office at Ballston Spa," where he remained until sometime in late 1823.[28] Although little is known about his time at the printing office, it is notable that Comstock was a Universalist and a publisher of Universalist tracts, most notably *Lectures on the Prophecies* and *The Three Woe-Trumpets,* works by Dr. Elhanan Winchester, one of the eighteenth-century founders of the Universalist Church of America.[29] In addition Comstock printed the first temperance tract ever published in New York State in 1814; a weekly newspaper, the *Ballston Spa Gazette;* and an antiwar book called *The Friend of Peace,* by one "Philo Pacifus" in 1822 (which Brownson likely had a direct hand in publishing). Having mastered the art of words in the classroom, Brownson thus saw this art translated directly into power through the technology of the printing press.

This brief experience as a journeyman printer left a lasting impact on him, as is evidenced by passages in his early writings that surround the printing press with a utopian, emancipatory aura. In his 1834 "Independence Day Address" at Dedham, Massachusetts, Brownson channeled the progressive spirit of Sampson Reed by praising the "creations of science, of industry, and genius," including such things as the mariner's compass, global navigation, steam engines, and free government, each of them demonstrating that there is "one law of our nature . . . IMPROVEMENT."[30] Special care was taken to praise what he called "that ART OF PRINTING, an art that electrifies the mass of mind, creates a universe of thought and opens a medium of intercourse between all nations and all ages."[31] Later, in his *New Views,* he credited "the art of printing, unknown to Greek and Roman civilization," with bringing about a remarkable "diffusion of knowledge." Whereas before "the masses were enveloped in thick darkness, . . . the millions, who then were in darkness, now behold light springing up."[32] No doubt inspired by his own direct experience as a printer, Brownson found in this technology the means by which the masses emancipated themselves from ignorance, inculcated virtue, and channeled power in its purest and least corruptible form—as the direct expression of justice.

The third influence was the content of the Universalist tracts, the message of which was reinforced at home by his aunt, herself a Universalist and avid supporter of Dr. Winchester. These works, he said, aided by his aunt's "brilliant and enthusiastic commentaries . . . had shaken my early belief in future rewards and punishments, and unsettled my mind on the most important points of Christian faith."[33] Distinct in its origins from Unitarianism, which had as its basis the rejection of the Trinity, Universalism was best understood as a reaction to Calvinist exclusivism or the sense that God had separated the world into sheep and goats, the elect and the damned. In fact Universalists such as Winchester could still accept the doctrine of Original Sin and even the mystery of the Trinity, both concepts that Unitarians rejected. Central to the Universalist faith was the belief that the defining characteristic of God and the saving power of Jesus was found not in judgment but in love, a love committed to the redemption and restoration of all humankind, quite irrespective of their virtues or vices (although, according to Winchester, vices would still be punished in the afterlife, but only for a short time, much like Catholic purgatory). David Robinson explains his logic this way: "If God can save me, Winchester suggested, you can save anyone; and if he can, surely he will: 'Has he taught us to do good to all? And will he not much more do good to all?'"[34] Thus, to be a Universalist one need not believe, as William Ellery Channing did, that the only way to know God is to become like God; one need only believe that God so loved all sinners in the world that he gave his son to redeem not just a few but everyone.

Although Brownson initially reacted against the Universalist message by embracing Presbyterianism, eventually he tired of the grim moralism of the Calvinists and joined the Universalist Church in 1826, immediately applying to the Universalist Association in Vermont for a license as a preacher. He was drawn to Universalism by the message of Hosea Ballou, who was, according to Brownson, "the patriarch of American Universalism, and at the time when I became a Universalist minister was its oracle, very nearly its Pope." Ballou, explained Brownson, had given a "new face to Universalism," going beyond the reformed Calvinism of Winchester to attack "the whole fabric of so-called Orthodox Christianity." In Brownson's system God demands no expiatory sacrifice for redemption, and grace becomes not a personal act by a personal god but simply a natural effect of God's decrees "irresistibly executing themselves in the government of the world." Sin, according to Ballou, is not a component of the soul but of the body and the flesh, and thus when the body dies the sin dies along with it, thus making punishment on earth reformatory rather than redemptive and punishment in the afterlife nonexistent. The entire idea of a personal relationship with God, from whom one requests an act of grace because of his or her individual virtue or faith, is thus effectively jettisoned. Ballou simply "demands the salvation of all men, not from the mercy, but from the justice of God, as a right, not as a favor."[35] Humanity's goal on earth is not to fret about the afterlife or worry about God's judgment but to create a life worth living (and a world worth living in) while still alive, trusting that God will reserve a place for all humankind in heaven. Perhaps after Brownson had married Sally Healy, the daughter of a prosperous farmer, he had begun to see the attraction of a form of faith that could help them build a better world for his family. With the concern for eternal damnation or God's vindictive punishment removed, "the best he could do at the moment was to use his ministry as a means of helping to make the earth more tolerable."[36]

At this point Brownson "began a long career as a writer, journalist, and public man."[37] He took advantage of the relatively light doctrinal obligations that allowed him to speak and associate with whomever he wished as well as the freedom to hold forth on all sorts of topics. These years cultivated in Brownson not a pious or deferential attitude toward his new faith but rather an ambitious and aggressive rhetorical voice. For the next three years, he preached his version of the Universalist message at several churches in the states of Vermont, New Hampshire, and New York while writing for and eventually editing the denominational magazine the *Gospel Advocate*. Because the church had rejected eternal punishment and the distinction between the saved and the damned, he felt free to challenge any scriptural interpretation that he found repugnant to reason and inconsistent with the creation of a good society. Yet this meant that his own version of reason, not that of any church or religious scholar, was the authority for correct biblical interpretation. Brownson drew the logical conclusion: "Natural reason thus became the measure of revealed truth; and if so, I had the right to reject every interpretation of Scripture that deduced from a doctrine which reason could not comprehend and approve."[38] This is the opposite attitude of the Catholicism he came to embrace; but as a young man, Brownson saw no other route to social justice than to strike out on his own rather than genuflect to the god of tradition.

The result of his developing ideas was an outpouring of increasingly radical writings in the *Gospel Advocate* during 1828 and 1829 that to many sounded like a dangerous turn toward atheism and socialism. Although continuing to profess a personal Christian faith in the afterlife, he forswore making any definitive pronouncements with respect to "a world I have never explored, and to a mode of existence of which I am totally ignorant."[39] In effect declaring himself an agnostic, Brownson rejected supernatural speculation as at best an exercise of the aesthetic imagination and at worst a distraction from consideration of "what amelioration the progress of Truth will make in the condition of human society below."[40] Brownson saw in human society the sorry state of humankind: "Robbed by the political despot of the right of pursuing happiness and enjoying the fruits of his labor—divested by the priest of the liberty of conscience and all the felicity of mental independence, he rises in gaudy ignorance or splendid poverty, in the most abject servitude and the most degrading superstition."[41] What was needed was not more sectarianism or supernaturalism but a complete reformation of the political and social order that "will be accomplished when men shall have recovered mental independence, and shall dare reason on the nature and propriety of existing institutions; when they shall acknowledge no law but *reason,* no religion but *justice,* no morality but *humanity* in all its forms."[42] Reason, justice, and humanity—these were the virtues that guided the construction of Brownson's political ideology of democracy.

Brownson at this point in his life was clearly more interested in ideology than he was about spreading the gospel of Universalism, as is perhaps most evident in the fact that he found support in one of the most controversial voices in American politics at the time—that of Scottish freethinker Frances ("Fanny") Wright. She, in turn, found in Brownson a kindred spirit: "We recognized him by his writings," Wright editorialized. "For an honest labourer in the same vineyard with ourselves; we saw that if nominally attached to a sect, he was neither in thought or feeling sectarian, we saw that he had dropped from the clouds upon the solid earth, and that he had renounced the chair of dogmatism to pursue enquiry into the field of nature and human life."[43] Self-confident, charming, passionate, and bold, Wright had first come to the United States in 1818, and after writing her first book, *Views of Society and Manners in America* (1820), she returned to the United States in 1824. Taking on almost every hot button issue of the day, Wright called for the end of slavery, liberalized divorce and marriage laws, birth control, the end of religious authority, universal secular education run by the state, and the political organization of the working classes. As Brownson summed up her position, Wright's ambition "was to rouse the American mind to a sense of its rights and dignity, to emancipate it from superstition, from its subjection to the clergy, and its fear of unseen powers,—to withdraw it from the contemplation of the stars or imaginary heaven after death, and fix it on the great and glorious work of promoting man's earthly well-being."[44] Clearly what drew the two together had little to nothing to do with his being "nominally attached to a sect" and everything to do with the fact that they both appeared committed to political ideologies that put reason before faith, justice before piety, and humanity before God. Thus after Brownson attended one of Wright's public lectures in New York, he developed a close relationship with her during 1829, reprinting some of her articles in the *Gospel Advocate* while she published his in her own magazine, the *Free Inquirer.*

His relationship with Wright is crucial to understanding the rhetoric and politics of Brownson, because she revealed to him, in actual practice, both the

potentialities and the limitations of her radical reformist vision. In stark contrast
to the idealism of Alcott, who placed great faith in the emancipatory power
of the word, Wright believed that the cause of evils such as Southern chattel
slavery or the Northern economic exploitation of wage labor was rooted mostly
in the material conditions that effectively educated people to tolerate injustice,
violence, oppression, poverty, and war. Consequently she believed that the only
way to achieve liberation was not through the gradualism of symbolic persuasion
but rather the wholesale remaking of material society. As Brownson explained
her position, "the act must be laid at the root of the tree, and slavery must be
abolished only as the result of a general emancipation and radical reform of the
American people themselves."[45] The key step in this radical reform was thus to
remake the environment, namely through state guardianship of education, "in
which all the children from two years old and upward should be fed, clothed, in
a word, maintained, instructed, and educated at the public expense."[46] By raising
an entirely new generation on the ground of firmly secular, egalitarian morality,
not only slavery but all social evils would be cured.

Wright also provided Brownson the opportunity to interact directly with
the Workingman's Party, which was the first labor-oriented political organization in the United States. Labeled as the "Fanny Wright Party" by its critics in
order to taint the party with her presumed atheism, the Workingman's Party
showed ideology in action. Founded in 1828 by Philadelphia shoemaker William
Heighton and soon established in New York City, the party reacted to the growing divide between capital and labor, between nonproducers and producers. The
"Workies" advocated for the concerns of craftsmen and journeymen, pressing for
protection from debtor prison and compulsory military service, shorter working
hours, greater financial security, equal education, and universal male suffrage.
But the party was a loose confederation with competing visions and only mini-
mal organization that had been cobbled together out of necessity. According to
Schlesinger "the depression of 1828–1829 drove the city workers of New York
into the companionship bred by misery; and the Workingmen's party staggered
blindly forth, not knowing what direction to take and catching at almost anyone
offering to serve as a guide."[47] In New York, for instance, some followed machinist
Thomas Skidmore, who advocated a "patriarchal utopia of free and independent
producers" and "exhorted the poor to force an equal division of property and
inheritance through a democratized political process."[48] But others were more
attracted to Wright's vision, in which education became the primary means
to reform, with changes such as higher wages and shorter working days being
seen as inevitable consequences. Despite their differences, however, the reformist
energy and optimism that pervaded the party energized Brownson and revealed

to him what he called the most "striking characteristic" of the nineteenth century: the "tendency to association" that threatened all earlier institutions with obsolescence.[49]

Yet the experience with Wright and the Workingman's Party also revealed the Brownson the limitations of a movement that did not undergird its ideology—however rational, just, and humane—with an energizing myth that could create a common identification despite political differences. Once the actual members of the party analyzed the competing proposals, they rejected Wright's leadership in large part because of "the bad odor of atheism and radicalism" attached to her name.[50] Without her leadership the party itself quickly splintered, "with Democrats co-opting their rhetoric and leaders while satisfying a few demands" and demonstrating in the process that "the American two-party system made an independent radical politics almost impossible to sustain."[51] Wright, realizing how her reputation had come to hurt the interests of the party, severed her connection with it and soon married and returned to France. Brownson also suffered consequences, as his association with Wright and public defense of her positions led many Universalists to accuse him of being an atheist and an infidel. Thus in 1830 Brownson broke off his relationship with both Wright and the *Free Inquirer* about the same time that he resigned from the Universalist Church in anticipation of being excommunicated from them. Trouble had found him again.

But even in trouble there was a lesson to be learned about politics—that any truly lasting and meaningful changes in American society could only be established on the firm ground of committed public opinion produced through mass public persuasion that used Christianity to construct a myth that could justify a radical ideology of social change. Brownson thus identified three problems with Wright and with the Workingman's Party. First, Wright failed to recognize that, in Brownson's words, "man must have religion." In rightly criticizing the corruption of the priesthood, she went too far and left "man destitute of all religious notions."[52] But this left people without a coherent myth to create a common bond of identification. Second, according to Schlesinger, the party targeted the interests of only one group and set it in opposition to a stronger group, an unfair competition from the start. Brownson concluded that "a party dedicated to the cause of labor would lead, not to victory, but the systematic oppression by mobilized business interests." Last and most important, he saw that an exclusive focus on policy goals distracted from the more important project of altering public opinion. Schlesinger writes that for Brownson, "the one hope seemed to lie in securing the cooperation of all classes, and this could be achieved only by moral suasion. Reform must come from within men before could come from without."[53] Unlike Wright's proposal of wholesale social reconstruction, he recognized that an enlightened minority cannot force a society to change its attitude by instituting state-run education systems before the population itself believes that such a change is necessary. Education was surely needed, Brownson wrote, but not simply formal education of the intellect in a state-run school; education was needed for all the masses everywhere in Christianity, "not as a system of belief, but as a grand, all-comprehending principle of moral and social action."[54] That is to say, they must be educated in Christianity as an energizing myth.

It is worth returning to Burke to look closer at the relationship between ideology and myth, as this relationship will be central to understanding what differentiates the rhetoric of Transcendentalism from the rhetoric of other nineteenth-century reformers who shared similar political aims. For certainly one cannot argue that the Transcendentalists were unique in arguing for the abolition of slavery, the emancipation of the working class, equality for women, or other causes of social justice that were prevalent in the early nineteenth century. Indeed the Transcendentalists often were latecomers to movements with well-established orators and writers. They were distinguished from their rhetorical peers by their persuasive strategies, which often directly contradicted established rhetorical patterns. In one of the earliest studies of transcendental eloquence in the field of rhetoric, Irving Rein argues that "the Transcendentalists' rhetoric poses a distinctive problem for rhetorical critics. Their discourse violates many of our common expectations: the Transcendentalists ignored facts; they avoided statistics and thought others' personal testimony a sham. Their lack of conventional proof and organization prompts the complaint that their discourse defies analysis, often seems patternless, and sometimes seems without purpose."[55] Brownson came in for particular criticism for the fact that, in his writings, "the audience was scathed relentlessly."[56] The result, for Rein, was rhetorical failure. Because of their use of strategies that relied so heavily on revelation and transcendence, the Transcendentalists "produced an anti-rhetorical rhetoric, a rhetoric that did not share and in fact rejected the commonly held linguistic symbols of his [the Transcdendentalists'] audience."[57] Although, as Philip K. Tompkins points out, Rein is "wrong in his assumptions about their rhetorical objectives and wrong in his assessment of their rhetorical effectiveness," his critical judgment of the Transcendentalists' rhetoric correctly identifies the challenge for contemporary rhetoricians to understand the nature of what often seems to be paradoxical methods of persuading an audience.[58]

To use Burke's terminology, the central aim of transcendental eloquence was not to alter particular beliefs or even to put forward a particular ideology; it was to alter attitudes toward history (and thereby people's role within history) by immersing listeners in the poetic imagery of a transcendental myth. This is the core of Rein's central misunderstanding—to assume, in Tompkin's words, that "their strategies were adapted to an overarching goal of organizational recruitment."[59] This would be the goal of any traditional social movement rhetoric, such as would be expressed by the Workingman's Party. But as Roberta K. Ray points out, in the philosophy of rhetoric of someone such as Emerson, "the primary role of the oratory is not to 'convert men to one's own faith,' but rather, to persuade men of their own innate worth."[60] For the Transcendentalists, in other words, the most political type of speech was one that made explicit political commitments secondary to the reconstitution of the self in history. As Burke put it, "in the face of anguish, injustice, disease, and death one adopts policies. One constructs his notion of the universe or history, and shapes attitudes in keeping."[61] The normal chain of consequences is thus reversed. Instead of first possessing attitudes and a notion of history and then applying those to the exigencies of anguish, injustice, disease, and war, one uses those exigencies as opportunities to develop new attitudes toward history and to form and reform identities and identifications capable of acting in an emerging historical drama.

Transcendental eloquence provided the rhetorical resources for what Burke calls this "reidentification" (or "transformation" or "rebirth") through myth.[62] Perhaps the most important function of this myth was to provide what Burke calls "mythical firsts," or those primordial origin events that provide principles and archetypes, such as the Fall of Adam and Eve that originated the principle of Original Sin. He explains that "to derive a culture from certain mythic ancestry, or ideal mythic type, is a way of stating that culture's essence in narrative terms."[63] At the core of the Transcendentalist myth, for instance, was thus a rejection of Original Sin and an acceptance of a more optimistic narrative that saw human beings created with all the powers of an impersonal god or world spirit—what Emerson called the "Over-Soul"—which one could use to pursue godlike perfection for oneself on earth while communicating this latent divinity to others through eloquence. As Lawrence Buell writes, Transcendentalism's "cardinal tenet" was that "the Oversoul is immanent in all persons and things, which are all thereby symbols of spirit and conjoined by analogy in an organic universe."[64] In the transcendental myth, the kingdom of God is not only immanent within each individual but within all of nature, and thus even the lowest still have the spark of divinity that could be unfolded in beauty and power as long as they were able to slay that part of themselves that kept them meek, guilty, fearful, and ignorant. As Burke writes, "the *killing* of something is the *changing* of it, and the statement of the thing's nature before and after the change is an *identifying* of it."[65] By encouraging others to accept the myth of Transcendentalism in place of that of Original Sin, Transcendentalists thus evoked in a new class of thinkers, poets, and reformers the virtue and courage to seek perfection in an imperfect world and the hope that the rest of the world might follow.

One thus finds in transcendental eloquence frequent detours into the language of myth that seem antirhetorical for those expecting only a narrowly focused forensic or deliberative argument about a current state of affairs. But the Transcendentalists were typically after bigger game, namely the reformation of the self. First, they tended to insert themselves into an immediate controversy or problem that gave them an opportunity to speak. Second, they then used this opportunity as an excuse to transcend to the realm of the mythic, the poetic, and the imaginative. But this detour served an important rhetorical function. On the one hand, it detached people from the limitations of their conventional myths, whether the religious mythologies that subordinated them to the authority of some doctrine or the political mythologies that subordinated them to established hierarchies of power, both of which created structures of identification that often constrained their freedom of thought and action; on the other hand, it immersed them in a new mythology in which their task was to accept and unfold the immanent spirit of the divine within them, even in the face of social stigma or political oppression. As Ray puts it, "the role of the oratory is to provoke men into breaking the chains of fear and dogma, so that they can walk like God through the world of ideas."[66] I would stress, however, that for the Transcendentalists ideas and actions are always unified; indeed the world itself is interpenetrated with ideas. Consequently the third general characteristic of transcendental eloquence was usually to return to the world of things and point in the direction of actions that would be consistent with their newfound principles, ideas, and powers—directions that often overlapped with those advanced by what were the political ideologies of the day without necessarily being consubstantial with them.

That said, the case of Brownson is instructive precisely because it demonstrates the degree to which ideology never fully subordinated itself to myth in the actual rhetorical practice of the Transcendentalists. Just as the dialogic and rhetorical tendencies in transcendental eloquence always remained in tension, so too did the mythic and ideological ones. In fact Brownson more than any other Transcendentalist demonstrates the degree to which the firm commitment to ideology can render the mythic component of rhetoric just another argumentative instrument to serve a proximate political end. Burke notes, for instance, that any "transcending of local political ideologies can itself be interpreted as an ideology," just as one might critique Plato's mythology as one more manifestation of his "aristocratic politics, conservatively opposed to the rising class of businessmen."[67] With Brownson, of course, the political motive was reversed. He used the mythic component of Transcendentalism to challenge and unmask the ideology of the rising bourgeois class and replace it with what he saw as a "democratic" ideology that placed not only political power but also economic capital in the hands of the laboring classes. Yet despite being something of an outlier in the tradition of transcendental eloquence, he nonetheless represented the tension between ideology and that recurred in the later political writings of Margaret Fuller and Henry David Thoreau.

Brownson began crafting his rhetorical public ethos in earnest after leaving the Universalist Church. In 1831 he founded his own small church in Ithaca, New York, while at the same time founding his first magazine, the *Philanthropist*. For Brownson the two went hand in hand, as the sermons he preached in his church were then subsequently published in his magazine. As Theodore Maynard observes, "he was much more of a journalist than a preacher; in fact his preaching and lecturing were only journalism."[68] Lost in the printed word however, was Brownson's presence: six foot, two inches tall and powerfully built, with black hair combed straight back, often a quid of tobacco in his mouth, and always a black swallowtail coat that flowed out behind him. He nonetheless tried to express his character through writing, using bold assertions and uncompromising judgments. According to Hutchinson, "in the pulpit he was a fiery and convincing orator, on the printed page a relentless logician."[69] Although the *Philanthropist* soon went out of print because his subscribers stopped paying him, it helped make a name for him to the degree that he was invited to lead a Unitarian congregation in Walpole, New Hampshire, about ninety miles from Boston. There he began sending articles "on the French philosophers and on the alliance between Christianity and social progress to the Unitarian journals such as the *Christian Register* and the *Unitarian,* and soon to the most dignified of them all, the *Christian Examiner.*"[70] By the time he started preaching at Lyceum Hall on Hanover Street in May 1836, he had "become a sought-after intellectual property in the city."[71] Soon after he was able to leave Walpole to form his own congregation, called the "Society for the Promotion of Christian Union and Progress," which (like his cousin's school) met in Boston's Masonic Temple, but often with five hundred or more attendees instead of just a handful of children. His rise to success ultimately inspired Brownson to publish his *New Views of Christianity, Society, and the Church* late in 1836. It appeared that he had finally outrun trouble after all.

Unitarianism provided Brownson with the key mythic components to his rhetoric that he felt were lacking in the reformist discourses of either traditional Christianity or the more secular orientation of the burgeoning labor movement. Unitarianism provided a mythic foundation that could help them promote an ideology of social change largely free from Christian orthodoxy and supernaturalism. To Brownson "Unitarianism elevates man; it preaches morality; it vindicates the rights of the mind, accepts and uses the reason, contends for civil freedom, and is social, charitable, and humane."[72] The basic premise of the Unitarians, as the name implies, was a rejection of the Trinitarian conception of God as Father,

Son, and Holy Spirit—a conception that emphasized the personal character of God, saw the Bible as a divinely inspired text, and emphasized the relationship among sin, forgiveness, and salvation. It then embraced a more impersonal Unitarian conception of God as the embodiment of divine reason that was disclosed through the teachings of Jesus and could be learned and perfected by human effort. Unitarianism thus "denied that people were born sinful, celebrated the potential greatness of human reason and conscience, and developed a spirituality of self-culture."[73] For Brownson, then, Unitarianism seemed to provide the mythic basis to preach a morality that was rational, social, charitable, and humane not only because it prodded individual geniuses to seek perfection, in the model of Reed, but also, and more important, because it mandated that people pursue policies that create the social conditions by which all can form themselves in the image of God free from the fetters of economic exploitation.

Yet even with Unitarianism, Brownson soon felt himself too limited. His final embrace of Transcendentalism was thus a way to cast off the remaining constraints of what Emerson famously called, in his "Divinity School Address," the dead hand of "historical Christianity." The last vestige of orthodoxy to which the Unitarians held was the belief that the Bible remained the single authoritative text of Christianity and that the logos of God, as articulated by Jesus and validated by his miracles, represented only those principles expressed in the Bible at that specific historical moment. As Brownson later summarized the Unitarian position in an 1839 refutation of Andrews Norton, "it refers us not to what we feel and know in ourselves, but to what was said or done in some remote age, by some special messenger from God; it refers us to some authorized teacher, and commands us to receive our faith on his word, and to adhere to it on peril of damnation."[74] But for Brownson this doctrine had deleterious effects: "It denies to man all inherent power of attaining to truth. . . . It therefore destroys all free action of the mind, all independent thought, all progress, and all living faith."[75] Cut off from the full resources of modern science, art, politics, and philosophy, Unitarianism for Brownson remained locked in the past, condemned to utter the same principles—however virtuous and true they might be—over and over unto eternity. In Transcendentalism he discovered a reinterpretation of the Christian myth that made it a living force of reform in the present and licensed the wholesale reconstruction of society based on the revelations of reason to the receptive soul.

The end result was a bold rewriting of the Christian myth that transformed humanity from a fallen being who requires God's forgiveness into what he called "the symbol of the God-Man" that seeks godlike perfection. This was the myth he articulated in *New Views*. He focuses on a passage from the Sermon on the Mount, interpreting Jesus as saying that "in ourselves are the elements of the Divinity. God then does not sustain a figurative resemblance to man. It is the resemblance of a parent to a child, THE LIKENESS OF A KINDRED NATURE." Here, he argues, is the sublime declaration that announces that "humanity, after so many years of vain search for a father, finds itself here openly proclaimed the true child of God." Yet although similar sentiments were made by Unitarians like Channing, Brownson in the symbol of the God-Man takes its conclusions to the ultimate limit. In this myth man not only pursues the perfection of God but also becomes a kind of god himself: "By asserting the Divinity of Humanity, it teaches us that we should not view that symbol as the symbol of two natures in one person, but of kindred natures in two persons. The God-Man indicates not the antithesis of God and man; nor does it stand for being alone of its kind; but it indicates the homogeneousness of the human and divine natures, and shows that they can dwell together in love and peace." Having provided an origin story for the God-Man, Brownson thus draws the natural conclusion for humanity's ultimate destiny. When humankind has finally cast off the burden of tradition and of all of the "reproachful epithets" that had made it "necessary to degrade him in order to exalt his creator," the full power of the God-Man will be made manifest: "The slave will become a son. Man is hereafter to stand erect before God as a child before his father. Human nature, at which we have pointed our wit and vented our spleen, will be clothed with a high and commanding worth."[76] Here is a myth capable of inspiring greatness and justifying a revolution.

In typical fashion Brownson threw himself fully into his latest passion. Having become friends with George Ripley, in the fall of 1836, he attended the first meeting of the Transcendentalist Club at Ripley's house along with Emerson, Alcott, F. H. Hedge, Convers Francis, and James Freeman Clarke. Although never fully feeling himself to be an intimate member of their group (in no small part because of his argumentative spirit and tendency to bang on the table and shout even in conversations with friends, Hedge later remarking that "Brownson met with us once or twice, but became unbearable and was not afterward invited"),[77] he shared many of their views and admired their willingness to critique Unitarian orthodoxy and take independent stands based on the independence of their own reason. But with Ripley he found a soulmate who seemed equally committed to active social change. Gura remarks that "in 1836, the two were the de facto field generals of the emergent Transcendentalist movement, popularizing Idealist thought through their seminal publications and applying it to pressing social needs."[78] Now feeling part of a coherent movement, Brownson felt empowered in his lifelong "attempt to realize a social harmony he had never been fortunate enough to know, and particularly to provide the laboring classes with the education and ministry they needed to better their lot."[79]

Brownson wasted no time in using this myth to advance a political ideology that he believed could accomplish his reformist ends. He called this ideology

"democracy." In direct opposition to conceptions of democracy grounded in legislation, voting, or parliamentary procedure, Brownson advocated a democracy
based on the universal capacity of all individuals to comprehend truth through
their inner light (and to recognize that truth when spoken) and then to put these
truths directly into practice. In his essay criticizing the conservative character of
Unitarianism, he gave perhaps his finest expression to how his transcendental
myth justified his ideological commitments:

> The doctrine, that truth comes to us from abroad, cannot coexist with
> true liberty. . . . The democrat is not he who only believes in the people's
> capacity of being taught, and therefore graciously condescends to be
> their instructor; but he who believes that reason, the light that shines
> out from God's throne, shines into the heart of every man, and that truth
> lights her torch in the inner temple of every man's soul, whether patri-
> cian or plebeian, a shepherd or a philosopher, a Croesus or a beggar. It is
> only on the reality of this inner light, and on the fact, that it is universal,
> and all men, and in every man, that you can found a democracy, which
> shall have a firm basis, and which shall be able to survive the storms of
> human passions.[80]

In this system, as he explains in *New Views,* all hierarchies and divisions, namely
those preserved in the institutional churches and the organs of government, will
be seen as holdovers of illegitimate authority grounded in the false Calvinist myth
of the sinfulness of humanity. In a true democracy, power grows out of the will
of the people, which is constituted by the collective revelation of the inner light
in each person. Consequently in a true democracy, church and state will become
one, just as the government and the people will become one: "The church will not
be then an outward visible power, coexisting with the state, sometimes control-
ling it and at other times controlled by it; but it will be within, a true spiritual
—not spiritualistic—church, regulating the heart, conscience and the life."[81] Making this democracy a reality required breaking down institutional barriers both of
church and the state, consolidating the people into a single spiritual and political
entity, and building up a mechanism to propagate the truth that would light the
inner temple of every patrician, plebeian, shepherd, philosopher, and beggar.

True to his faith, in 1838 Brownson achieved his lifelong goal of establishing his own independent medium that would give his new views their fullest
expression and widest breadth—the *Boston Quarterly Review.* Filled almost excessively by Brownson's own writing, it provided him "an outlet for his overflow-
ing energies, and the aggressiveness of printed polemical discourse suited his
temperament as well as the lecture platform's alternating current of seduction
and challenge suited Emerson's."[82] In his introductory marks on the first issue,

Brownson criticized the timidity and censorship of other publications that refused to print anything that has not first "been through the mint of public opinion." For a man such as himself, who refused to remain silent, such a restriction could not be tolerated: "I must and will speak. What I say may be worth something, or it may be worth nothing, yet say I will. But in order to be able to do this, I must have an organ of utterance at my own command, through which I may speak when and what I please. Hence, the Boston Review."[83] The first issue included an article titled "Christianity Not an Original Revelation with Jesus, nor a System of Theological Doctrines, Properly So Called," a review of a book of John Greenleaf Whittier's poems, a commentary on the relationship between John Locke and Transcendentalism, a defense of Emerson's 1837 Phi Beta Kappa address, and a reprint of an address Brownson delivered at the Democratic State Convention of Massachusetts held in Worcester on September 20, 1837, titled "Democracy."

In "Democracy" Brownson offered the political ideology that provided the foundation for his more incendiary "The Laboring Classes," published three years later. In this address he set out to articulate his own ideology of democracy and to undermine any competing democratic ideologies based on parliamentary procedure, partisan politics, or majority rule that supposedly represented the "sovereignty of the people."[84] The problem with all three notions is the same: they all legitimate a politics based on the will to power, whether it be the will of republican politicians, political factions, or the popular majority. That is to say, it grounds democracy in the pursuit of raw self-interest, whether of the individual or of the group. Naturally Brownson was particularly concerned to distinguish himself from a notion of majority rule, which on its face might sound similar to his own ideology. But for him they could not be more different. In current conceptions of majority rule, the people may hold power, but they do not necessarily hold truth. Consequently to move the majority to act requires (as one finds in Plato's critiques of the sophistical rhetoric) acts of base flattery. Brownson explains: "The effects of this doctrine, so far as believed and acted on, cannot be too earnestly deprecated. It creates a multitude of demagogues, pretending a world of love for the *dear* people, lauding the people's virtues, magnifying their sovereignty, and with mock humility professing their readiness ever to bow to the will of the majority." But it is all a ruse, "gross bribery and corruption."[85] Even as demagogues give lip service to truth, justice, and wisdom, they nearly always appeal to sheer force of numbers. The system thus "perverts inquiry from its legitimate objects, and asks, when it concerns a candidate for office, not, who is the most honest, the most capable? But, who will command the most votes? And, when it concerns a major policy, not, what is just what is for the public good? But, what can the majority be induced to support?"[86] To talk about the "sovereignty of the people" as a basis for democracy is thus to sanction the sovereignty of the demagogue who possesses the means of persuasion to constitute a majority of voters who do not know their own self-interest and care nothing for the good of others. It is simply the rich bankrolling propaganda to hoodwink the poor.

To see such demagoguery in action, Brownson argues, one need only look at the sudden ascendancy of what had become the dominant class not only in Europe but also in the United States—the bourgeoisie. As history has shown, he wrote, this class was composed of "merchants, bankers, manufacturers, lawyers, large farmers, in a word of the stirring, business part of the community" who ascended after the demise of the old aristocracy. Although at first it expressed the most vitriolic hatred against hereditary nobility and artificial hierarchies in the name of liberty for all, once in power it only wanted to take down those above it while retaining "an invincible aversion to leveling up to itself those who are below it." So even as it claimed to support equality and liberty for all, it nonetheless "demands a laboring class to be *exploited*."[87] But if this is the case, how is it that in every community (no matter how poor and destitute) the bourgeois class is the one that is "the most praised; and it is always accounted the most virtuous"? Clearly it is their capacity to express "love" for the people through the method of the demagoguery. Realizing that they need to "attend to the wants of the lower classes up to a certain point," it "will build them, if need be, churches, and establish ministries for the especial purpose of keeping them to be quiet; it will furnish them with the rudiments of education, see that they are fed, clothed, maintained in a good working condition, and supplied with work."[88] Having shown themselves to be lovers of the people, the bourgeoisie can then rely on the support of the laboring classes to institute policies that will keep those same people exploited with "order, peace, and quiet."[89]

For contemporary readers of Burke, all of Brownson's rhetorical strategy probably sounds familiar. It is the method of ideological criticism. In this approach the ideologies of one's opponents are treated as but "eulogistic coverings" or "figleaves of the mind," that is, as a verbal screen of attractive ideas that masks the true, selfish material interests of the authors. As an example Burke points to the use of the term "national interest" by people who might argue that some economic policy or military campaign must be done for the national interest, implying that everyone's interest is the same. Yet by unmasking the eulogistic coverings, an astute critic would see the working of the self-interest of a particular group of nationals, whether they be individual citizens or a corporate enterprise. A policy justified by appeal to the national interest might therefore in actual practice "be a loss to the nation as a whole which was a gain to the special body of nationals profiting by this loss."[90] In the case of Brownson, these nationals are clearly the banks and the bourgeoisie, who in modern parlance would have been said to be partners in a rising hegemony. As Barry Brummett summarizes the relationship between hegemony and ideology, "hegemony is a situation in which powerful groups and institutions create in those they dominate the belief that such domination is natural, commonsensical, and the way things ought to be," while ideology is a type of rhetorical discourse that "recruits the disempowered to participate in their own disempowerment by agreeing to the hegemonic domination of more empowered groups."[91] Part of Brownson's genius was to anticipate even Karl Marx's conceptualization of these strategies of power maintenance by elites and to develop a critical rhetoric designed to unmask them.

Yet while Brownson was explicit in his negative criticism of bourgeois hegemony, he was less clear about what was the substance of his "positive" ideology of democracy. In place of bourgeois hegemony justified by the ideology of "the sovereignty of the people," he advocated for what he called a "philosophical democracy, or democracy as it should be."[92] In this democracy there was only one sovereign to rule over all: "Justice the sovereign, the sovereign of sovereigns, the king of kings, lord of lords, the supreme law of the people, and of the individual." Consequently "the sovereignty of justice, in all cases whatsoever, is what we understand by the doctrine of democracy."[93] Brownson never explicitly defined justice, however, or made clear what were to be the means of its definition and implementation. By justice he seems to mean a sense of limits, of boundaries, of due proportions, by which each individual, group, and institution acted within its proper sphere and did not overreach, thus maintaining a sense of harmony and order. Justice was thus connected with a sense of bounded liberty, "which leaves every man free to do whatever it is just to do, and not free to do only what it is unjust to do."[94] Brownson was clearly more concerned with limiting injustice than with expressing liberty. For him, by asserting the sovereignty of justice and denying the sovereignty of people, "we need to deny to the body politic unlimited authority, or the right to act at all, in any way, or by any agent whatever, on any except certain specific objects, indispensable to the maintenance of the social order, and, if the phrase be taken strictly, the common weal."[95] The sovereignty of justice was thus a tragic concept insofar as it occurs when boundaries have been arrogantly crossed to the degree that it will bring retribution caused by hubris— much in the same sense as the Furies pursued the Greek hero Orestes.

How those boundaries were defined and enforced remained vague. In terms of practical politics, Brownson did not deny a place for the state or even for majority influence in the government; he called for a system of limited government in which the state was not an executive arm of the people but actually a restrictive force that prohibited any one interest from exerting total authority. On the one hand, then, Brownson's view appeared wholly consistent with that of the Democratic Party, who affirmed a reading of the Constitution as a defense of limited government. Here would be a "constitutional government in the worthiest sense of the word," meaning one whose task was to protect the rights of citizens and to define the natural boundaries of the state according to a written constitution.[96] On the other hand, Brownson's embrace of the mythic component of Transcendentalism always gave him recourse to a higher law that would supersede the Constitution. In this view the Constitution would have authority only insofar as it embodies the principles of justice, however imperfectly. His vision of democracy thus rendered the Constitution a mere written reminder of what were ultimately transcendent principles. Through a strained argumentative gymnastic, Brownson recognized the necessity of maintaining a stable constitutional state with access to the means of legal and physical coercion to limit the actions of hubris while at the same time arguing that the people could at any time overrule formal constitutional authority if they felt that it was in violation of the sovereignty of justice.

For those familiar with the language of Emersonian individualism, Brownson's appeal to the sovereignty of justice might appear its antithesis—a validation of the opinions of the masses against those of the individual genius. But Brownson makes use of the myth of Transcendentalism to reconcile this apparent contradiction in his political ideology. As it turns out, the source of enlightenment for the masses was the rhetorical eloquence of courageous geniuses whose "sole business is to inquire what truth and justice, wisdom and virtue demand at his hands, and to do it, whether the world be with him or against him." Explicitly channeling the reformist spirit of Plato, Brownson rejected the authority of public opinion simply because it was the opinion of the majority, placing his faith instead in the sovereignty of a transcendental virtue that existed apart from human experience and yet could be accessed by human reason and put into practice in their common world. Herein lies his iconoclastic individualism, even as he spoke on behalf of the laboring classes and the people: "There is within every man, who can lay any claim to correct moral feeling, that which looks with contempt on the puny creature who makes the opinions of the majority his rule of action. He who wants the moral courage to stand up 'in solitary grandeur,' like Socrates in the face of the Thirty Tyrants, and demand that right be respected, that justice be done, is unfit to be called a statesman, or even a man."[97] Sounding now like Emerson, Brownson challenged his readers: "Dare be a man, dare be yourself, to speak and act according to your own solid convictions, and in obedience to the voice of God calling out to you from the depths of your own being"![98] Ironically, then, only by resisting the sovereignty of the people could these lonely and courageous souls, speaking in "solitary grandeur," make real the promise of democracy by educating the people in the meaning of justice and then put these principles into action.

In a nod to the Aristotelian spirit, Brownson advocated for a vibrant and critical public sphere in which the free workings of transcendental eloquence

would not only unmask the ideological deceptions of the powerful but also identify and disclose the meaning of justice to all. To those who might turn his argument against him and claim that he was simply dressing up the sovereignty of
the people in new clothes, Brownson, like Aristotle, argued that rhetoric is useful
because it is the means by which truth may be set free and that time would reveal
the true nature of justice:

> Progress is always slow, and slow let it be; the slower it is the more speed
> it makes. So long as we find the thinkers busy canvassing all great mat-
> ters, discussing all topics of reform, and publishing freely to the world
> the results of their investigations, we have no fears for the individual,
> none for society. Truth is omnipotent. Let it be uttered; let it spread from
> mind to mind, from heart to heart, and in due season be assured that it
> will make to itself hands, erect itself a temple, and institute its worship.
> Set just ideas afloat in the community and feel no uneasiness about insti-
> tutions. Bad institutions, before you are aware of it, will crumble away,
> and new ones and good ones supply their places.[99]

According to Gregory Butler, Brownson's writing gave full voice to a gnosticism,
meaning faith that "ultimately nothing shall remain hidden or mysterious, for
the destiny of humanity is endless progress toward perfection, the inevitable
unfolding of the Divine Idea."[100] But if this is so, it is a gnosticism with a particular rhetorical spirit; for clearly the divine idea requires courageous rhetors
not simply to speak the truth but also to harness the power of the printing press
to disseminate that truth to the people and make justice a reality in their hearts
and minds. Truth may be omnipotent within its limits, but it requires thinkers to
publish freely to the world the results of their investigations in order to inspire
those hands to build new temples and institutions. That those temples had not yet
been constructed in history was not due to any fault in the people but to the fact
that truth had not yet been set free.

As the 1840 election drew closer, however, Brownson's gnostic faith that the
divine idea would unfold effortlessly on the heels of the dissemination of truth
began to be shaken. Having been fully convinced that truth and justice was on
the side of the Democratic Party, he had expected that their political ideology,
rooted firmly in a conception of limited government and promotion of the rights
of labor, would easily sweep away the feeble effort of the bourgeois Whig party
to maintain their hegemony, notwithstanding the latter's efforts to sell their
candidate by having him shed "crocodile tears over the deplorable condition of
the poor laborer, while he docks his wages, twenty-five percent."[101] How absurd,
after all, was it to watch "the Banks discount freely to build 'log cabins,' to purchase 'hard cider,' and to defray the expense of manufacturing enthusiasm for

a cause which is at war with the interest of the people."[102] Yet Brownson had to admit that the bourgeois party was resilient beyond his expectations: "That they will succeed, we do not for one moment believe; but that they could maintain the struggle so long, and be as strong as they now are, at the end of ten years' constant hostility, proves but all too well the power of the Banks, and their fatal influence on the political action of the community."[103] To prevent this catastrophe from happening, something had to be done: "The subject must be freely, boldly, and fully discussed, whatever may be the fate of those who discuss it."[104] For Brownson more was riding on the election than the determination of who was to be president; the selection of Democrat or Whig would determine whether or not the people could be trusted to be able to distinguish truth from falsity, justice from injustice.

The result of Brownson's anxiety was "The Laboring Classes," a tract so radical that it had the ironic effect of pleasing his enemies and horrifying his allies. Much of the argument was simply a more vigorous restatement of assertions he had been making for a decade, but in this essay he took two controversial stances that complicated his democratic gnosticism and its faith in the inevitable triumph of justice on the heels of its rhetorical propagation. First, in recognizing the recalcitrance of the bourgeois class to relinquish power, Brownson for the first time sanctioned (rather than simply predicting) the use of force and coercion as a means of social reform: "The rich, the business community, will never voluntarily consent to it, and we think we know too much of human nature to believe that it will ever be affected peaceably. It will be affected only by the strong arm of physical force."[105] Second, Brownson took an uncompromising stance on the scope of the reform to be brought about by physical force—nothing less than the total eradication of all monopolies and all privilege whatsoever. In short "the system must be destroyed."[106] Specifically he advocated for the eradication of hereditary property and its replacement through a process by which, after an owner's death, "his property must then become the property of the state, to be disposed of by some equitable law for the use of the generation which takes his place."[107] Three years prior Brownson had recommended simply setting ideas afloat in the community and letting justice work its will; but in 1840 he saw that justice required not only hands to build temples but arms, phalanxes, and weapons to wage war.

The result of his embrace of political radicalism thus accomplished an eventual reversal in the relationship between myth and ideology in his rhetoric. The two had never been comfortable partners, but during the 1830s the myth of Transcendentalism had given him the authority to reject established Christian doctrine, speak truth to power, and place trust in the innate wisdom of the laboring classes against the elite. By 1840, however, his embrace of an ideology that supported organized violence to enact a policy of property redistribution relegated the mythic elements of his thought to a mere shadow. Since his early writings, Brownson had sought to expose the nature of hegemonic ideology as propagated by the priestly class in collaboration first with feudal lords and then with bourgeois industrialists, but up until the late 1830s, he had held the optimistic view that emancipation would follow naturally from successful rhetorical persuasion. But the successful "log cabin and hard cider" campaign of the Whigs began to shake that faith. By 1840 he came to believe that a recalcitrant minority might actually be able to hang on to power through manipulating the procedures of democratic voting. There still remained in his thought a mythic component of Transcendentalism, namely in the faith in individual genius and the existence of transcendent principles of justice that could express the will of the people; but the more he concentrated on the practicalities of everyday politics, the less this faith became emphasized and the more he focused on the instrumental challenges of a policy of redistribution through force against a recalcitrant minority of bankers and bourgeois capitalists. It is thus illuminating to discern the method of social change embedded within "The Laboring Classes" to see how Brownson attempted to reconcile the mythic and ideological aspects of his thought as he implemented his vision of radical reconstruction.

None of this to say that Brownson had rejected the mythic component of Transcendentalism. Indeed he still made use of the myth in ways familiar to Emerson or Thoreau. He used the mythic narrative both of Christianity in general and of Transcendentalism in particular to celebrate the centrality of the individual prophetic voice in revealing divine truth to the people (although he clearly preferred prophets such as Amos who rose from the humble ranks of the laboring classes). Brownson thus launched into an encomium to those new prophets who would announce the coming of the kingdom of God:

> When God raises up a prophet, let that prophet prophesy as God gives him utterance. Let every man speak out of his own full heart, as he is moved by the Holy Ghost, but let us have none to prophesy for hire, to make preaching a profession, a means of gaining a livelihood. Whoever has a word pressing upon his heart for utterance, let him utter it, in the stable, the market-place, the street, in the grove, under the open canopy of heaven, in the lowly cottage, or the lordly hall. No matter who or what he is, whether a graduate of a college, a shepherd from the hill sides, or a rustic from the plough. If he feels himself called to go forth in the name of God, he will speak words of truth and power, for which Humanity shall fare the better.[108]

In this mythic narrative, Brownson gave eloquent expression to the love of the prophet that was shared by every Transcendentalist. These prophets would speak words of truth and power from the place from which they stood for no other motivation than the well-being of their brothers and sisters. While persecution might be inevitable in the short term, inevitably, in Bronson's view, the kingdom of God would be established on earth, the low would be made high, captives would be set free, equality would exist among men, and the reign of justice would endure. It is this shared prophetic faith that firmly links Brownson to the Transcendentalists.

Characteristic, too, of the prophetic character of transcendental eloquence is Brownson's attempt to balance what he called the "destructive" and "constructive" tendencies of his rhetoric. Destructively the Transcendentalist prophet must shock his or her audience out of complacency and reveal to it the structure of hegemony that kept it oppressed. Brownson does this in his criticism of the "Christianity of the Church," which he characterizes as having evolved from its humble origins into a system complicit with economic oppression, "jealous of power, and ambitious of confining it to as few hands as possible."[109] Brownson unmasks its ideology, which attained power by separating the world of spirit from the world of matter and then praising those who disdain material goods for spiritual asceticism (all the while supporting a church that profits off of material gain and establishes as lords and tyrants those who care only for the materialistic life). The result for the masses is that their world is turned into a prison in which one "cannot make one single free movement. The priest holds his conscience, fashion controls his tastes, and society with her forces invades the very sanctuary of his heart, and takes command of his love, that which is purest and best in his nature, which alone gives reality to his existence, and from which proceeds the only ray which pierces the gloom of his present house."[110] In the quest to emancipate the laboring classes, the first remedy must "be sought in the destruction of the priest" along with the entire ideological structure that provides the foundation for the authority of the Christianity of the Church.[111]

But engaging in destruction is not enough for the true prophet, who must promise a new covenant: "We are not mere destructives. We delight not in pulling down; but the bad must be removed before the good can be introduced. Conviction and repentance precede regeneration."[112] It thus remains for Brownson to open a window to the sanctuary and to give outlet to those rays of love that the priestly class and its industrial overlords have kept sealed up through awe of the gods, fear of divine displeasure, and dread of unforeseen chastisements. Despite the enduring power of ideological control, faith in the myth of Transcendentalism gives him hope for the future, for it promises that "the free soul can never be wholly subdued; the ethereal fire in man's nature may be smothered, but it cannot be extinguished. Down, down deep in the center of his heart it burns inextinguishable and forever, glowing intenser with the accumulating heat of centuries; and one day the whole mass of Humanity shall become ignited, and be full of fire within an all over, as a live coal."[113] It is thus the responsibility of the one who knows the nature of justice and can harness the power of persuasion to direct the energy of that fire, not simply for the purposes of consumption but also for the aims of creation, to create a new kind of faith that calls "every man to be a priest" and establishes a "religion of the new covenant, the religion written on the heart, of a law put within the soul."[114] This law, which in "Democracy" Brownson called justice, would then "arm every Christian with power to effect those changes and social arrangements, which shall secure to all men the equality of position in condition."[115]

Yet the mythic elements of his rhetoric that Brownson shared with other Transcendentalists soon came to be overwhelmed by ideological elements that departed significantly from the sublime type of eloquence called for by Reed and Emerson, whose audience was as elite as the orator. In his review of Emerson's "American Scholar," for instance, Brownson had rejected this suggestion that the reformer, in order to effect change in the world, "must be a solitary soul, living apart and himself alone; that he must shun the multitude and mingle never in the crowd"; rather he suggested that "he who would move the people, influence them for good or for evil, must have like passions with them; feel as they feel; crave what they crave; and resolve what they resolve. He must be their representative, their impersonation."[116] In perhaps the most direct challenge to the logic of transcendental eloquence, Brownson rejected any idealistic notions of social change that would alter history by unfolding the powers of the mind within a few extraordinary geniuses who might attain the heights of self-culture. "Self-culture is a good thing," he wrote; "but it cannot abolish inequality, nor restore men to their rights." In effect, whereas men such as Channing or Reed had seen self-culture not only as an end in itself but also as a means to producing change agents in history, Brownson relegated self-culture purely to the sphere of the private. The problem, he explained, is that "the evil we speak of is inherent in all our social arrangements, and cannot be cured without a radical change of those arrangements." For example, the structural demand for profit in any joint stock company overwhelms the idiosyncratic virtues of any particular individual. Even if one could convert all of the heads of the banks to Christianity through appeal to "self-culture," nothing would change: "Put your best men, your wisest, most moral, and most religious men, at the head of your paper money banks, and the evils of the present banking system will remain scarcely diminished. The only way to get rid of its evils is to change the system, not its managers." So who must be persuaded? Brownson explained: "The evil we have pointed out, we have said, is not of individual creation, and it is not to be removed by individual effort, saving so far as individual effort induces the combined effort of the mass."[117] In other words the only individual effort that matters is a rhetorical one that induces the combined effort of the masses—which is to say that they must be the ultimate audience.

Taken literally, this argument appears also to deny the utility of moral suasion entirely and to render Christian rhetoric completely useless for the purposes of social change. If Christian morality cannot alter the behavior of a powerful individual for good, then what use is it as a method of persuasion? Brownson's skepticism seems reaffirmed when he boldly stated that "could we convert all men to Christianity in both theory and practice, as held by the most enlightened sect of Christians among us, the evils of the social state would remain untouched."[118] However, on closer examination, he was only rejecting a type of Christian rhetoric, namely the Unitarian form of persuasion that emphasized the pursuit of self-culture over commitments to social justice. In fact Brownson retained an enormous faith in moral suasion when it delivered the right message to the right audience. As he made clear, "we deny not the power of Christianity. Should all men become good Christians, we deny not that all social evils would be cured. But we deny in the outset that a man, who seeks merely to save his own soul, merely to perfect his own individual nature, can be a good Christian."[119] The aim was not simply to convert everyone to Christianity but to convert everyone to *good* Christianity, meaning Christians committed to "making war on the mischievous social arrangements from which [their] brethren suffer."[120] In other words Brownson called for a type of rhetoric that spoke to the masses rather than to the elite and that used Christian ethics to advocate collective social action rather than encourage individual perfection.

To this rather conventional praise of the rhetoric of the Christian reformer—not unlike the language of Methodism—Brownson added an important qualification that marked him as a dangerous radical. Perhaps encouraged by his own transcendental myth that gave him warrant to supersede conventional laws and constitutions if they seemed to violate the sovereignty of justice, he asserted that if a recalcitrant minority resists reform by arming itself with money and influence, then the strong arm of physical force must be applied to break their hold on systemic power. Brownson's ideological commitments to total structural change strained the logic of his philosophical democracy to the utmost. He was by no means advocating armed rebellion or mob rule, as if democracy could be established through a kind of peasant revolt. Force must be channeled through the arm of government, even as government itself must remain limited. Thus he walked a fine line. He continued his call for government to enact "further limitation of itself" by "circumscribing within narrower limits its powers"—namely its collusion with the banks, its influence over the states, and its investments in national infrastructure.[121] At the same time, he insisted that the only way that the system will be destroyed is "by the action of society, that is, by government, for the action of society is government."[122] Paradoxically, while the government limits itself and its powers, it aggressively pursues policies that set out to destroy the banks, dismantle industrial interests, eradicate the hereditary descent of property, and redistribute resources from the rich of one generation to the poor of the next one. If it met resistance in its endeavors, it had license to use physical force to accomplish its social ends.

The political ideology expressed in "The Laboring Classes" thus comes close to affirming the authority of the "sovereignty of the people" that Brownson had rejected in "Democracy." It threatened to turn him into the very demagogue he condemned. In his 1837 essay, the government was conceptualized as constitutional body tasked with protecting the rights of citizens and minorities, even if that meant resisting the will of the majority. But by 1840 the government had become literally an arm of "society" and thereby the means by which the people expressed its will—even if that meant imposing its will on a recalcitrant minority, which in this case was the industrial, propertied, and priestly classes. As he writes, "government is instituted to be the agent of society, or more properly the organ through which society effects its will. Society has never to petition government; government is its servant, and subject to its commands."[123] Although ideally bound by the limits of Christian justice, this new government found itself awash in new powers and cloaked in a much greater aura of authority as it became the arm of society, which in turn was guided by justice, the meaning of which was explained to them through the rhetoric of one Orestes Brownson. For as Brownson wrote, before any such revolutionary measure could be brought before the legislature, there was much work to be done: "It must be canvassed in the public mind, and society prepared for acting on it."[124] Only when society at large has been brought into the fold of the Christianity of Christ through the bold but plain-speaking rhetoric of its prophets would the government fully come under its sway.

Nothing exemplifies more the triumph of ideology over myth in Brownson's rhetoric than his closing prophetic vision in "The Laboring Classes." Stripped away were any pretenses to eloquence, any rich natural imagery, any appeal to genius, or any optimistic faith in the capability of individuals of transcendence in search of perfection. In their place was the rigid either/or logic of an ideology committed to a total structural revision of the social order and spoken in the bold language of a demagogue in its literal meaning of "leader of the people." And to the people he had a simple message:

A man shall have all he honestly acquires, so long as he himself belongs to the world in which he acquires it. But his power over his property must cease with his life, and his property must then become the property of the state, to be disposed of by some equitable law for the use of the generation which takes his place. Here is the principle without any of its details, and this is the grand legislative measure to which we look forward. We see no means of elevating the laboring classes which can be effectual without this. And is this a measure to be easily carried? Not at all. It will cost infinitely more than it cost to abolish either hereditary monarchy or hereditary nobility. It is a great measure, and a startling [one]. The rich, the business community, will never voluntarily consent to it, and we think we know too much of human nature to believe that it will ever be effected peaceably. It will be effected only by the strong arm of physical force. It will come, if it ever come at all, only at the conclusion of war, the like of which the world as yet has never witnessed, and from which, however inevitable it may seem to the eye of philosophy, the heart of Humanity recoils with horror.[125]

There is no eloquence here. There is simply exposition and fact. But even with this bold statement, Brownson still held back: "We are not ready for this measure yet." But the time had come "for its free and full discussion." Here was the time when the prophets such as himself would have to speak words of truth and power that would guide all Christian believers to the kingdom of God and bring low all those who would resist. And those who would think that they could silence and resist these prophets should heed this warning: "Men have, for what they believed the cause of God of man, endured the dungeon, the scaffold, the stake, the cross, and they can do it again, if need be."[126] But this is not the language of Transcendentalism. It is the language of populist Christian radicalism harnessed for the defense of political revolution.

Once Whig critics got hold of "The Laboring Classes," they knew they had found the weapon to brand their Democratic opponents as French-style revolutionaries. John Quincy Adams, for instance, included in his memoirs "Brownson and the Marat democracy" on his list of dangerous elements, alongside phrenology, animal magnetism, and resistant abolitionism, each of which had contributed an "ingredient for the bubbling cauldron of religion and politics" that was ruining the country.[127] Publicly Brownson was given no rest. "On every side Brownson was denounced. His party repudiated him in an effort to undo the damage it caused. All in vain: the Whigs reprinted his article and distributed by the hundreds of thousands to show what it was the president and his party really held."[128]

In a brilliant strategy, they used his own arguments against him, claiming that his criticism of the virtues of Lowell factory girls and his claim that slaves were actually better off than laborers were both slanderous and insulting to the class he was attempting to support. Having finally captured the public's attention, Brownson discovered that he was not welcomed as a prophet but condemned as a heretic and sentenced to endure—at least proverbially—the dungeon, scaffold, stake, and cross.

In a last-ditch effort to justify his position before the 1840 election, the October issue of the *Boston Quarterly Review* included a follow-up to "The Laboring Classes" in which Brownson responded to his critics: "We have been accused of proposing to rob the rich of their estates, and of proposing to do it by physical force," he wrote. He protested that he advanced no such agenda. Reaffirming a more conventional commitment to political persuasion, he claimed that his party of reform "will use no arms but those of the intellect and the heart. It fixes its eye on Justice, and marches steadily toward its realization."[129] His observation of the need for physical force was not a desire for a policy but simply a scientific prediction and a warning. With a sober tone, he gave his last prophecy:

> If a general war should now break out, it will involve all quarters of the globe, and it will be in the end more than a war between nations. It will resolve itself into a social war, a war between two social elements; between the aristocracy and the democracy, between the people and their masters. It will be a terrible war! Already does it lower on the horizon, and, though the storm may be long in gathering, it will roll in massy folds over the whole heavens, and break in fury upon the earth. Stay it, ye who can. For ourselves, we merely stand on the watchtowers, and report what we see. Would that we had a different report. But the war, if it comes, will not be brought about by reformers, but by conservatives, in order to keep the people out of their rights; and on the heads of conservatives, then, must all the blame.[130]

Such nuances were lost on his readers, and the prophecy was ignored. Brownson remained a target of criticism, Martin Van Buren lost the election in a landslide to Harrison, and drunken mobs celebrated by chanting "Tippecanoe and Tyler too!" If the war was to come, the 1840 election was a harbinger that it would come quicker than Brownson feared.

The electoral defeat shattered Brownson. For two decades he had developed a religious and political philosophy grounded in a rhetorical faith in the power of truth, disseminated through lectures and the printed word, to illuminate the nature of justice to the masses and give them the social solidarity and political power to emancipate them from bourgeois hegemony. And just at the revolutionary moment where justice had a chance to be made real, the masses had been seduced by hard cider and log cabins to throw their support behind the ideology that kept them in chains. Schlesinger narratives the impact on Brownson:

> The flood of Whig votes washed away Brownson's faith in the people and left in its place two convictions that sharp and anguished disappointment fixed enduringly into his experience: that the people as a whole were incapable of seeking the good without more stimulation than their own natures provided; and that good government required stronger guarantees than popular suffrage and the popular virtue and intelligence. Fourth of July orations would continue, and America might roll on in its comfortable trust that *vox populi* was *vox dei;* but Orestes Brownson had put his soul into the people's cause; and in the people's defeats he lost a shining faith that did not return. The people had sold their birthright for a barrel of cider, and Brownson never forgave them.[131]

So low had he fallen, in fact, that the only place he could find comfort was in his growing friendship with John C. Calhoun, whose philosophy of states' rights in defense of slavery appealed to Brownson's earlier constitutionalism. "Only a rigorously constitutional system, Brownson decided, could the proper sort of democracy be achieved only within a rigorous constitutional system: else the government would always be the servant of special interests."[132] Conveniently ignoring the fact that slavery itself was a special interest of certain nationals, Brownson believed that only by severely restricting the federal government could anything close to justice be accomplished, for clearly the people themselves were incapable of comprehending it and acting upon it on their own.

At this point Brownson effectively ceased to be a Transcendentalist. Witnessing the gullibility of people and the ease by which they were seduced and turned toward what he considered evil, he had abandoned the key Transcendentalist faith in the capacity of individuals, by the power of their own reason and intuition, to transcend their social and political constraints in order to discern the nature of some higher law and virtue upon which they could act. Eventually Brownson argued that Transcendentalism, far from embodying the spirit of reason, "represents the irrational as superior to the rational, reverses all our common notions of things, declares the imperfect more perfect than the perfect, the less of a man one is the more of a man he is, the less he knows the more he knows, that the child is wiser than the adult, the madman more to be trusted than the sane man."[133] The sin of Transcendentalism, he felt that he now clearly saw, was its embrace of a myth that had denied the inherent fallenness and finitude of human beings and replaced it with an egoistic idealism that turns sinners into gods and placed the whims of children and madmen on equal level with the words of Christ and the apostles.

To the dismay of his former Transcendentalist friends, Brownson found a better myth in that the most apostolic of all religions, Catholicism. But his conversion in 1844 was really a logical consequence of the loss of his Transcendentalist faith. His earlier, relentless critique of the priesthood had been premised on the assumption that, without the constrictions and dogmas of the institutional church, the true nature of Christian truth and justice would well up naturally in the soul of every individual once they encountered the Gospel of Jesus. But after the 1840 campaign had completely invalidated that assumption, Brownson came to the exact opposite conclusion—that the priesthood, in fact, was the only way that a fickle and undisciplined populace could be brought slowly to see the light of God's reason through participating in the ancient sacraments of the one true church. Whereas before the ritual, trappings, and sacraments of the church struck him at best as distractions, at worst as a method of control, now he recognized them as necessary means of persuasion to appeal to an audience incapable of understanding the nature of truth and justice without careful instruction and institutional guidance. As Anne Rose observes, Brownson at this point had come to believe that "urban industrial society had reached a stage were idealism was not enough" and in fact had become "so complex and interdependent that only an institution with the authority of history could adequately direct its future."[134] Only the Catholic Church, with its ancient history and claim to universality, could fulfill this most awesome responsibility.

Thus it came to be that the same individual who, as a Transcendentalist, had called for a rhetorical organization of society to impose its will through the arm of government later, as a conservative Catholic, came to warn against any rhetorical movement that would challenge governmental legislation by rallying society to its side. In an 1851 defense of the Fugitive Slave Law, Brownson lashed out at socialism, radicalism, and Free Soilism, not because of their values but because of their means—which were rhetorical. By calling on groups of citizens to resist the Fugitive Slave Law and reject the legitimacy of any legislation that violated some abstract notion of justice, these movements in effect advocated despotism by replacing the rule of law with the tyranny of public opinion. He went on:

Tell us, ye wise ones, ye enlightened reformers of the nineteenth century, when you have succeeded in making way with government, what protection will ye have left for my individual and personal freedom? Whither, then, shall I be able to fly to save myself from being crushed beneath your huge, social despotism, rolling on under the impetus of lawless passion and irresponsible demagogues? . . . A cruel and despotic public opinion, variable and capricious as morbid feeling, will then become supreme, universal, all pervading, and overwhelm every individual who has the hardihood to hesitate for a moment to comply with its imperious demands. What now takes place on a small scale in your voluntary associations for reforming society, will then be exhibited on the large-scale. The capricious despotism will not stop with putting chains on the limbs, and a padlock on the hips, but it will enter into the soul, penetrate into the very interior of man; all free thought will be stifled in its conceptions, all manliness, all nobility of character, depart, virtue be unheard of, and men become a race of mean, cringing, cowardly slaves of an intangible despot, and wild and lawless passion revel in one universal and perpetual saturnalia.[135]

And so Brownson completed the circle. Whereas once he had complained that it was the priesthood that held his conscience, controlled his tastes, and invaded the sanctuary of his heart, now it was public opinion that penetrated into the interior of man to stifle his conceptions, his manliness, and nobility of character. Whereas once it had been the rhetoric of everyday prophets that would unmask this priesthood and release the common laborer from its prison house, now it was the priesthood that warned the people against falling for the rhetoric of everyday demagogues who called for things such as the abolition of slavery and the resistance to the Fugitive Slave Law. Brownson himself still made use of his own outlet for rhetorical dissemination, now called *Brownson's Quarterly Review,* but his aim was not to call society to arms but to warn it against the dangers of rhetorical hubris that came from believing that anything is possible and any law expendable when one speaks with truth and power.

Yet Brownson's legacy endures despite his flirtation with Calhoun and the slavocracy during the 1840s. His motive had been on the side of "unity," a commitment that made him see abolitionists as a threat, despite their good intentions. But after the Supreme Court's decision in the Dred Scott case of 1857, which effectively stripped all African Americans, free or slave, of their rights as citizens, Brownson drifted toward the new Republican Party and soon argued for the "unity of the races and the inherent dignity of each person, and he lambasted Southerners for trying to enlarge their political base." And even in opposition to many of his Catholic readers, after the beginning of the Civil War, "he continued to advocate the notion that the war was not only to preserve the Union but to effect full emancipation."[136] Perhaps this points to the lasting legacy of Brownson, despite his many contradictions. Throughout his life he continually expressed a desire for unity and equality across all religions, classes, races, and sects. His turn to Catholicism was thus a natural expression of his desire for a truly "catholic" union of church, state, and society. In his 1835 essay "Progress of Society," for instance, he had agonized over the fact that "the Christian world is now distracted, torn into contending sects, and exhibiting a spectacle saddening to the hearts of all real friends of humanity. These sects must be brought together, these alienated hearts must be united, and the scattered and inoperative elements be brought into one grand and complete whole." His journey through Universalism, Unitarianism, Transcendentalism, and Catholicism all represented his effort to find that "chord which shall vibrate alike to all moral nature." But in the end there was only one chord that he found to be consistent among all of those systems, which was "the law of love, a law that requires us to love one another as Christ loved us, that is, well enough, if need be, to die for our fellow beings as Christ died for us."[137] Brownson often had difficulty effectively and consistently applying the law of love to matters of justice for all who suffer, particularly when he interpreted the world so thoroughly through the lens of ideology. But in his efforts to achieve that long-sought unity, he left a rhetorical legacy that retains its prophetic character for the laboring classes still untouched by the blessings of capital.

CHAPTER 4

"The transformation of genius into practical power"

Ralph Waldo Emerson and the Power of Eloquence

If the whole history is in one man, it is all to be explained from individual experience. There is a relation between the hours of our life and the centuries of time. As the air I breathe is drawn from the great repositories of nature, as the light on my book is yielded by a star a hundred millions of miles distant, as the poise of my body depends on the equilibrium of centrifugal and centripetal forces, so the hours should be instructed by the ages, and the ages explained by the hours. Of the universal mind each individual mind is one more incarnation. All its properties consist in him. Each new fact in his private experience flashes a light on what great bodies of men have done, and the crises of his life refer to national crises. Every revolution was first a thought in one man's mind, and when the same thought occurs to another man, it is the key to that era. Every reform was once a private opinion, and when it shall be a private opinion again, it will solve the problem of the age.

Ralph Waldo Emerson, "History," 1841

The year in which the remains of Brownson's Transcendentalist faith collapsed after the crushing defeat of Van Buren by the Whig Party's campaign machinery was also the year of the ascendancy of the Transcendentalism of Ralph Waldo Emerson. Five years after the Transcendentalist annus mirabilis of 1836, in which Emerson's short book *Nature,* George Ripley's *Discourses on the Philosophy of Religion,* Brownson's *New Views of Christianity, Society, and Church,* and Amos Bronson Alcott's *Record of Conversations on the Gospels* were published, Emerson solidified his position as the movement's prophet, spokesperson, and celebrity by publishing his *Essays.* Characterized by Albert Von Frank as "a manual of self-defense for young persons against the tyranny and authority of age," *Essays* had been cobbled together from passages of his journal and the many lectures that he had tested on the lyceum circuit, culminating in a style that was a distinctive fusion of the oral and the written, the aphoristic and the prosaic.[1] The result was an encomium to the calling of the self-reliant hero, whose maxim was "To believe your own thought, to believe that what is true for you in your private heart, is true for all men,—that is genius."[2] This mantra made Emerson unfazed by the sorry spectacle of American presidential politics and made him a celebrity. By the time he published *Essays: Second Series* in 1844, he had "moved from being a little-known lightning rod for the movement's religious eccentricity to center stage as his chief proselytizer for an imperial self."[3] If Brownson had used print to become infamous by 1840, Emerson had used the rediscovered art of oratory to become perhaps the most recognizable and celebrated American literary figure of the early nineteenth century.

But more is at stake in the comparison between Emerson and Brownson than a popularity contest. Indeed, for Emerson, his own status as a celebrity intellectual was irrelevant to his historical significance, just as Brownson found in his suffering proof that he was a genuine prophet. What mattered more was that they represented opposite ends of the rhetorical spectrum within Transcendentalism. Whereas Brownson was an argumentative polemicist and relentless logician who attempted a direct reform of public opinion, Emerson was an orator-poet who often sounded like he was speaking to his audience from a star a hundred million miles distant. Gura describes his appearance at the speaker's platform: "Six feet tall, long-necked, with sloping soldiers, he had dark brown hair, blue eyes, and a Roman nose which was his most prominent feature. At the podium he appeared oracular, revealing truth in finely chiseled sentences, each of which might be infinitely expanded but which he instead treated like the pieces of an artfully constructed mosaic that comprised his topic. One went to listen to Emerson, not to be entertained. If not all in attendance captured his full meaning, they still believed that they were in the presence of genius."[4]

These differences in rhetorical style grew out of substantial philosophical disagreements about the method and pace of social change. To Brownson in the period leading up to "The Laboring Classes," social change was a rapid, catastrophic affair that occurred as soon as "the sovereignty of justice," spoken in the argumentative language of populism, was made apparent to the inner light of the masses by being disseminated in print. In contradistinction Emerson was always dismissive of public opinion, noting in his journal that it will always "bear a great deal of nonsense."[5] For him public opinion was not a leader but a follower. However public opinion did eventually follow—as evidenced by Emerson's own popularity. As long as the eloquence of genius had the freedom to be heard, most powerfully through particular acts of oratory, then its truths would percolate slowly through culture. In this way Emerson was both more skeptical and more ambitious than Brownson—more skeptical because he never expected more than a few souls to recognize the value of those ideas in his lifetime, but more ambitious because over time he expected those ideas to solve the problems of the age without any recourse to violence. Whereas Brownson wagered all of his confidence on the results of a single election and warned of a war if those results were not favorable, Emerson was more content to wait for the laws of the universal mind, once discovered and articulated, to work their way gradually from individual mind to individual mind until that private opinion would become the spark of a revolution and the key to the reform of an era. Indeed the way that private revelations of genius work their way into the public opinion over time is the meaning of history. And the way they get expressed is eloquence. For Emerson, then, the meaning of eloquence can be found in history and represents the art of what he called "the transformation of genius into practical power."[6] From Emerson's perspective, then, it was Brownson's impatience with this process that led to his populist style and eventually to his embrace of violence, just as for Brownson it was Emerson's naïveté that led him to believe that the keys of power were found in obscure orations comprehensible only to the bourgeois elite.

Emerson's *Essays* is best understood, when taken as a whole, as an exposition of this gradualist model of social change and a rigorous defense of what may be called a "philosophy of eloquence." That is, in place of traditional philosophies of rhetoric stemming from Aristotle—philosophies that focused on defining speech genres, classifying arguments, and categorizing tropes and figures in order to help an orator speak with appropriateness so that they might have immediate and measurable effects on a situated audience—Emerson proposed a philosophy of eloquence that justified a form of speech that violated any and all rhetorical constraint in order to articulate a higher truth that spoke to a universal audience of history. In other words the entirety of *Essays* is written to define the various aspects of the method of the orator-poet, that rare genius who produces not arguments but eloquence. The poet, Emerson wrote, "smites and arouses me with his shrill tones, breaks up my whole chain of habits, and I open my eye on my own possibilities. He claps wings to the sides of all the solid old lumber of the world, and I am capable once more of choosing a straight path in theory and practice."[7] Against Brownson's criticism that such a poet is not only incomprehensible but also impotent, Emerson suggests it is only through the eloquence of the poet that genuine change is possible. Traditional philosophies of rhetoric, constrained by the demands of an audience, largely leave that audience in the same place as where it began; but by breaking up all chains of habits, illuminating real possibilities, and clapping wings to the solid old lumber of the world, eloquence is able to navigate a long path to the different future.

Although it is easy to dismiss Emerson's defense of eloquence in *Essays* as mere idealistic fantasy, a serious consideration of his position leads to one of the central questions in contemporary rhetorical theory—how does one critically evaluate rhetorical discourse? This was the question that Edwin Black famously tackled in his foundational study, his 1965 *Rhetorical Criticism: A Study in Method.* In that work Black sought to undermine the foundations of neo-Aristotelian criticism, which was based on the assumption that any rhetorical "discourse is discrete and its relevant effects are immediate."[8] In other words rhetoric is to be judged by the same criteria that one judges a marketing campaign—how many units were sold, how many votes were tallied, how many bodies were moved from one place to another. Such is precisely the criteria that Brownson used to judge the rhetoric of the 1840 presidential campaign and that caused him largely to throw Transcendentalism overboard. For Black, however, there is another way to judge rhetorical criticism. Using John Jay Chapman's 1912 "Coatesville address" as an example—an address initially delivered to only three people—he argues that its power must be evaluated by expanding the notion of rhetorical context. Its context "must be measured by a continent and [its] time must be reckoned in centuries. Its direct audience has been and is all of those who are interested in a meaningful interpretation of the history and moral status of this country, and indirectly its audience is all of those who are influenced by the direct audience."[9] The speech, that is, still lives within an ongoing historical dialogue: "The passage of time, therefore, can only enable the audiences to the speech to apprehend its ramifications, to discern the range of its applicability, to explicate its complexities and absorb its overtones."[10] One hears the narrow view of neo-Aristotelianism in Rein's sweeping dismissal of the rhetoric of the Transcendentalists as having "made no effort to find areas of agreement between rhetor and auditor" and thus producing an "anti-rhetorical rhetoric."[11] But the enduring legacy of the Transcendentalists, and the fact that they still capture the contemporary imagination, bears out Black's central thesis—which is also Emerson's—that the capacity for eloquence to transform genius into practical power must be judged not in the moment but in the light of historical time.

Essays, I suggest, represents Emerson's most successful work that charted a "straight path in theory and practice" for eloquence. This does not deny that the collection resists any attempt to read into it a single, foundational message. There is an element of truth behind the kind of critique of it one finds in Brownson's review: "To most persons, who read the essays, they will seem to be wanting in unity and coherence. They will always strike as beautiful, often as just, and sometimes as profound: but the reader will be puzzled to round their teachings into a whole, to discover their practical bearing on life or thought."[12] At the same time, however, there is a thread (one among many) that runs through all of the essays and unites them in common theme and purpose. Barbara Packer has suggested a philosophical one, namely to urge the reader on every page to "grasp the underlying principle of unity that binds together both the internal laws and the phenomena that manifest them."[13] I would suggest a rhetorical one: to orient the reader to different aspects of that principle of unity in order to present opportunities for rhetorical invention and practice. Continuous with Bloom's notion of a "strong reading," there is good reason to read *Essays* as a work written to inspire a new generation of poets by constructing for them a philosophy of eloquence built on the foundations of Transcendentalism and designed to exert power in the context of history.

This chapter reintroduces Emerson to contemporary readers not as a poet, philosopher, or reformer but as a rhetorical theorist. Specifically I argue that one of Emerson's lasting legacies is to provide a philosophy of eloquence that challenged—and still challenges—the neo-Aristotelian "god of rhetoric" and suggests a process and a method whereby a work of genius that breaks all the rules of rhetoric can, when judged within a wider circumference of space and time, become a means of influencing the course of history. As Emerson wrote in his journal, if words "awaken you to think—if they lift you from your feet with the great voice of eloquence—then their effect is to be wide, slow, permanent over the minds of men: but if they instruct you not, they will die like flies in the hour."[14] Whereas traditional rhetoric challenges and transforms public opinion about a pressing state of affairs, eloquence achieves its influence by immortalizing great words and great deeds in such a way that creates a new understanding of the common world to which everyone belongs. As Hannah Arendt writes, "the task and potential greatness of mortals lie in their ability to produce things—works and deeds and words—which would deserve to be and, at least to a degree, are at home in everlastingness, so that through them mortals could find their place in a cosmos where everything is immortal except themselves."[15] The task of eloquence is thus to alter humanity's conception of this immortal cosmos and thereby change their understanding of themselves. For Emerson eloquence possesses the keys to power because it immortalizes those works, deeds, and words worthy of praise, articulates the possibilities that shatter and challenge existing habits, and keeps alive that promise of immortality that inspires greatness in all those capable of new beginnings.

On January 25, 1820, Emerson, then a sixteen-year-old junior at Harvard College, started his first journal. He called it affectionately "Wide World" and wrote that its pages were "intended at this their commencement to contain a record of new thoughts (when they occur)" and to serve as a "receptacle of all the old ideas that partial but peculiar peeping at antiquity can furnish or furbish." Less than a week later, his voice is characteristically Emersonian. He begins by contemplating "the bold Genius of ancient Rome all splendor & majesty" but then pauses to consider how often human beings fail to live up to the heroic ideals of the past in light of the pressures of present society: "I may admire, I fear I cannot obey, & there is an apology which every man make for himself when his independence is put to the test that by nature we are social beings & it is utterly against the order of things for a single man to presume to encounter all the prejudices & violence & power & war of the world, invidious & alone." However, Emerson takes heart from the accomplishment of those rare individuals who can meet the challenge and achieve immortality: "But there are on earth great men who disdainfully alike of the multitude's scorn & the multitude's applause elevate themselves by their own exertion to heights of human exaltation where the storm of varying opinion cannot hurt them & the levin-bolts of furious envy & disappointed passion will not reach or harm them." His conclusion: "Every man of talents & application has it in his power to be one of these."[16]

What is striking about these early passages is the degree to which they encapsulate the spirit of Emersonian eloquence that later formed the basis of his *Essays*. They are not just expressions of youthful boasting—although undoubtedly they are that, too. More important, the journal shows Emerson steeling himself to transcend the constraints of his social environment by expanding the circumference of his world to include all the great works and deeds of the past—hence the title "Wide World." By erasing the distance of time and space that separated him from greatness, Emerson first widened his world to include infinity and then condensed it into a point—the point he calls his own individuality. A lesser man, he wrote in that same early passage in his journal, "worms himself into good opinion & patronage of men & secures himself present peace by the sacrifice of his high honour."[17] But a true individual finds his individuality by associating with better company—with the mind that penetrates the vast, interminable universe and all of the immortal geniuses who have expressed aspects of that mind in what they have written, said, and done in history. As he wrote in a journal entry a few months later, in June 1820, it is the existence of these immortals and their accomplishments that proves, against that evidence of the whole history of human degradation, that "the soul hath appetites & capacities by which when well guided she soars & climbs continually towards perfection & is backed by the omnipotence of her magnificent career."[18] The product of eloquence is this striving toward perfection brought about by interpreting oneself in terms of what one is not yet but can and should become.

To understand the root of the rhetorical power of this form of eloquence, it is necessary to turn to Kenneth Burke's concept of "identification," especially since, for him, "identification in itself is a kind of transcendence." Burke argues that persuasion is not to be understood simply as a manipulation of beliefs or ideas, as if changing judgments were an affair of rearranging loose pieces on the blank slate of a person's mind. Rather people act in certain ways because those actions follow from the kind of person they believe themselves to be—and how they define themselves by identifying the substances of their being that they share with others. As he explains, "identification ranges from the politician who, addressing an audience of farmers, says, 'I was a farm boy myself,' through the mysteries of social status, to the mystic's devout identification with the source of all being." For any particular group of people, substance refers to any number of "common sensations, concepts, images, ideas, attitudes that make them *consubstantial,*" or of the same common substance that allows an "*acting-together.*"[19] But as his examples indicate—which brings the discussion closer to Emerson—identification need not only be concerned with the commonalities of people who live side by side. When a mystic identifies with the source of all being, that individual finds common substance with a universal soul that often serves to create a division between the mystic and the particular souls who populate ordinary society. Similarly when Emerson identified with the bold geniuses of ancient Greece and Rome, he elevated himself to the height of human exaltation while at the same time exhibiting scorn and disdain for the multitude in their applause.

When Burke thus defines transcendence as an active stretching forth of hands through love of the farther shore, thereby defining something here in terms of something there, he is also describing a process of reidentification, of defining oneself in a new way by casting off old substance and taking on a more perfect one. What is particularly significant in the strategy of Emersonian eloquence in this regard is the importance of what Burke describes as widening the circumference that determines identity—again returning to the title of Emerson's first journals. For Burke circumference is a way of defining an act or an agent by situating itself within a context of varying scope, such as how one might define oneself as a friend, a citizen, or a *Homo sapiens* depending on the scene that determines one's substance. Burke explains, for instance, that "a man is not only in the situation peculiar to his era or to his particular place in that era. . . . He is also in a situation extending through centuries; he is in a 'generically human' situation; and he is in a 'universal' situation."[20] Viewed from this perspective transcendence often takes the form of a rapid expansion of the scene in which people find themselves, such that they achieve what Burke calls a "higher synthesis" that redefines all of their actions as more virtuous because they are performed on a larger and grander stage.[21] In his early journal entry, for instance, Emerson wrote that "we can imagine the shadow of the incomprehensibly large, glorious mass blackening the infinity behind it; we can send Conjecture forth to ride on the wings that are bearing the worlds forward & sit & explore & discover what is to occur when the wheels stop & the wings fall in the immediate presence of the source of light which for ages past & ages to come they have been & will be advancing." Emerson was expanding the circumference of his scene to include the end of the universe as he knew it—yet finding grandeur nonetheless in the sublime. As he remarks: "But what matters it? We can talk & write & think it out."[22] For him the end of the universe was not a frightening prospect as long as it produced eloquence in those yet living.

Just what led Emerson to such majestic contemplations and heroic conclusions at such a young age is almost impossible to explain by any cause other than his own innate character. As Rose remarks, "in no other case does one feel so strongly that here was a Transcendentalist by nature."[23] Unlike with Alcott or Brownson, for instance, Emerson did not struggle with extreme poverty, make a pilgrimage to Unitarianism, or emancipate himself from small-town agrarian life. His early life was so unspectacular that Robert Richardson's six-hundred-page biography, *Emerson: The Mind on Fire,* begins with its subject at Harvard University and dedicates less than five pages to his life prior to starting his journal in 1820. It is as if, like Athena, Emerson sprung full-grown from the mind of Zeus to exclaim (as he did in his first journal entry): "O ye witches assist me! enliven or horrify some midnight lucubration or dream (whichever may be found most convenient) to supply this reservoir when other resources fail. Pardon me Fairy Land! rich region of fancy & gnomery, elvery, sylphery, & Queen Mab! Pardon me for presenting my first petition to your enemies but there is probably one in the chamber who maliciously influenced me to what is irrevocable; pardon and favor me!"[24] No amount of historical context or biographical events can sufficiently explain how this string of words was produced by a sixteen-year-old's pen, or why a week later that same young man would feel it necessary to harden himself to do battle alone against all the prejudices, violence, power, and war of the world.

Certainly, however, there were important enabling conditions for the flourishing of Emerson's extraordinary intellectual gifts, the most important of which was being raised in a literate household that prized ideas and held education and self-culture in the highest regard. He was born on May 25, 1803, in a rural part of Boston to William and Ruth Emerson, the second of five sons who lived to adulthood. William Emerson was a Unitarian minister of the First Church in Boston and the latest in a line of four generations of New England clergymen (Emerson was eventually the fifth). A deist in the tradition of Thomas Jefferson, he kept a library filled with literature and science, helped found the *Christian Monitor* and the *Monthly Analogy,* and wrote *A Historical Sketch of the First Church in Boston.* Emerson's mother, Ruth, was a devout, if undogmatic, believer who preferred more popular self-help-oriented Christian books (she owned a copy of John Flavel's *Treatise on Keeping the Heart,* the same book once peddled by Alcott), which emphasized "religious self-knowledge and religious self-cultivation."[25] If his father embodied the perfection of eighteenth-century rationalism (Richardson notes that his writing always had "a bland, correct, rational tone"), his mother channeled the nineteenth-century spirit of the New Lights with their "intense interest in religious thought and feeling, in personal, immediate religious experience."[26] But despite their differences, both were dedicated to giving their children the best education possible in what was then the center of intellectual activity in the United States.

But the person who would have the single most important impact on the young Emerson was his father's sister, Mary Moody Emerson, who often stayed with the Emerson family and corresponded extensively with them in letters. Although standing only four foot three inches tall, Mary had a powerful personality that far exceeded her physical presence. A brilliant, self-educated visionary who balanced an intense Puritan piety with a passion for philosophy, poetry, and the clash of ideas, she not only exposed Emerson and his brothers at an early age to the works of Plato, Samuel Taylor Coleridge, John Locke, Lord Byron, Jean-Jacques Rousseau, Wolfgang Goethe, Benedict Spinoza, and Mary Wollstonecraft, but also "debated with them the meaning of what they had read."[27] In his journal entry of February 7, 1821, Emerson wrote that "the religion of my aunt is the purest & most sublime of any I can conceive," a religion "independent of forms & ceremonies" that allowed her the freedom "to walk in narrow but exalted paths which lead onward to interminable regions of rapturous & sublime glory."[28] Phyllis Cole speculates that when Emerson appeals to the powers of Queen Mab in his journal, "Mary seems to be that creatively witchlike influence, herself a model of journal writing and a spinner of dark fancies."[29] Whereas William and Ruth had given him a stable home life and had demonstrated the moral standards of respectable Bostonian Federalists, Mary—who never married—slept in a coffin-shaped bed, went around wearing a burial shroud, and exemplified an extraordinary kind of self-reliance that made her disdainful of any convention that contradicted her high intellectual and religious standards. Consequently "her hunger for personal experience of the strongest, most direct kind must have pushed Waldo to settle for nothing less authentic, less direct, or less original in his own life."[30]

The influence of Mary and his mother only increased after the occurrence of the one tragedy of his childhood—the death of his father from stomach cancer in 1811, when Emerson was eight. Care of the children fell to his mother, who supported the family by taking in boarders. At that point forward, Ruth dedicated herself to giving each of her children a good formal education. The year his father died, Emerson enrolled at public grammar school, and two years later he entered the Latin School, a public school for the Boston elite that put knowledge of the classics in high regard. From this point until his entry into Harvard, Emerson's life was one of common routine: "He rose at six, made the fire, set the table for prayers, and joined the other children in a spelling lesson before breakfast; Latin School followed till eleven, writing school till one, dinner, Latin School at two, errands after school and chores, supper, hymns and chapters, and reading round in turn Rollin's history; then private devotions at eight, ending the day. This was a scheme of work and duty fitted to boyish years and quite in the manner of the common life of the old time in homes of family religion."[31] By the time he entered Harvard—which at that time had only 250 students and was "a small, nondescript place, half boys school, half center for advanced study"—Emerson did not particularly stand out among his peers as someone of significance.[32] Upon graduating in 1821, he was inspired by Sampson Reed's oration "Genius" to do great deeds and create great things; but having no money and no clear profession, he moved back in with his mother and worked for his brother William, who ran a school for girls out of her home.

Compared with the adventurous early adult years of Reed, Alcott, and Brownson, those of Emerson hardly narrate the life of a future genius. The 1820s were years in which he lived a passionate life of the mind in his journals but outwardly could hardly be distinguished as a man of extraordinary significance. His entry of October 25, 1820, records him saying that "I find myself often idle, vagrant, stupid, & hollow. This is somewhat appalling & if I do not discipline myself with diligent care I shall suffer severely from remorse & the sense of inferiority hereafter. All around me are industrious & will be great, I am indolent & shall be insignificant. Avert it heaven! Avert it virtue! I need excitement."[33] But there was not much excitement to be had. In the years between 1825 and 1828 he battled eye illness, rheumatism, and a generally weak constitution—traveling at one point to Florida to avoid the New England winter—as he studied intermittently at the Harvard Divinity School while also teaching in Roxbury and Cambridge. Following a traditional pattern of genteel life, in 1828 he become engaged to the beautiful Ellen Tucker and in 1829 was invited to become the junior pastor of Boston's Second Church and later the chaplain to the Massachusetts state legislature. Richardson remarks, with knowing irony, that at this time "Emerson the private person became more or less overnight a complete institutional person."[34] Grateful for a well-paying, respectable position and a loving future wife, Emerson wrote in his journal of 1829, with characteristic humility, an expression of thankfulness for the bounty of God: "I throw myself with humble gratitude upon his goodness. I feel my total dependence. O God direct & guard & bless me, & those, & especially *her,* in whom I am blessed."[35]

As mundane it seems, this early pious life of Emerson was actually essential to developing the unique nature of his eloquence. Although outwardly the young Emerson seemed to be a paradigmatic institutional person, his journals reveal an inward life that seemed more comfortable dwelling in the sphere of the infinite.

For unlike Brownson, who dealt with specific challenges in his life and focused his energies on the struggles of a particular class, Emerson faced no discrete challenges other than having to conform to the expectations of a conservative social environment that wanted nothing more of him than to be a genteel minister. Consequently, as long as his outward life was satisfactory, Emerson seemed content to live a double existence. But when that life no longer satisfied him, the energies he had poured into his private journal became channeled into public eloquence of a type never seen before. This is because Emerson targeted no specific social injustice, condemned no particular law, and sought no specific reform; rather he lashed out against the entirety of the conservative social structure that he felt constrained the never-ending unfolding of genius that represented for him the true meaning of power. The mundane existence of his early life was important because it represented for him the key problem of his age—how an individual with such potential for power and genius as himself could be so easily silenced and domesticated by the god of tradition.

If Emerson had a conception of social injustice, it was the injustice that pervaded the entire body of society itself, of which evils such as slavery, poverty, and greed were but its most grotesque symptoms. The true social injustice was that which society did to the individual by stifling his or her power, forcing the individual to conform to predefined social categories—capitalist, slave, wife, laborer, citizen, minister. For this reason Harold Bloom attributes to Emerson what he calls an "amoral dialectics of power." For Bloom he remains "*the* American theoretician of power—be it political, literary, spiritual, economic—because he took the risk of exalting transition from one activity or state of mind or kind of spiritual being to another, for its own sake." Whereas great works such as the Bible or Shakespeare's plays always show characters being caught in a psychic conflict in which "we need to be everything in ourselves while we go on fearing that we are nothing in ourselves," Emerson "dismisses the fear, and insists upon the necessity of the single self achieving a total autonomy, of becoming its own cosmos without first having to ingest either nature or other selves." Emerson's constant provocation is thus to call attention to people's complicity in being dominated by society, of conforming to some expectation and limiting power for the sake of maintaining some traditional hierarchy instituted not by any divine spirit but by men. Against this system Emerson insisted that that the spirit "called you forth only to your own self, and not to any cause whatsoever."[36] One's first duty was to become self-reliant, because for Emerson the only lasting change is brought about by changing the nature of identity.

At the same time, it is important to recognize that Emersonian eloquence never fully emancipated itself from the traditions of Enlightenment liberalism. Against Bloom's celebration of Emerson as a proto-Nietzschean moralist, Neal

Dolan finds that his work is "structured by an Enlightenment-Platonic hierarchy of values in which experience, observation, and independent critical reason are given preference over authority and tradition as guides to basic truths about the world." Not simply celebrating a continual reinvention of the self for the sake of power, Emerson admits the existence of an "objectively intelligible moral law" in which "virtue is achieved by bringing one's actions into conformity with the dictates of this law." Moreover Dolan criticizes Richard Poirier for reading into Emerson a postmodern linguistic skepticism. In Dolan's words Poirier argues that Emerson turns "to complex rhetorical strategies of punning, troping, and playing one type of discourse against another in the hopes of occasionally finding seams in the entangling net of language, knowing all the while that the most such breakthroughs can provide is a momentary and unstable self-enhancement." Against this view, Dolan suggests that "Emerson's work tries everywhere to inspire precisely the sort of exaltation in shared (liberal) values that Poirier dismisses."[37] Rather than using his eloquence to revel in the act of troping, Emerson used language to celebrate the formation of the traditional liberal self that strives to achieve objective excellence within an environment characterized by free-market economics and limited government.

Dolan's position is an important corrective to the tendency to abstract Emerson's eloquence from the context of his age in order to revel in the playfulness of his tropes. Both Bloom and Poirier are correct to find in Emerson resources for acts of self-creation of the type identified by Richard Rorty. In fact this effect of his eloquence is precisely what has given it its enduring power. At the same time, there are other ways to encounter Emerson's eloquence than just as a consumer of his tropes. He can also be read through the eyes of a rhetorician—that is, of someone who seeks to understand the theory and practice of eloquence. From this perspective acknowledging Emerson's liberalism is an essential step precisely because it encourages readers to find in Emerson an acknowledgment of certain objectively intelligible laws that regulate human thought, feeling, and action. Although Emerson's explicit political liberalism was complex, sometimes criticizing bourgeois ambitions and the pursuit of wealth and other times sounding like a prophet of laissez-faire capitalism, he never wavered in the classically liberal ambition to grasp the laws of persuasion that would function as the keys of power in an age that increasingly bestowed power on those who could command the word.

The event that set Emerson on this path to power was one of suffering, death, and loss. In June 1829 his fiancée started coughing up blood—a sure sign of tuberculosis. The best treatment at the time was thought to be fresh air and "jolting," meaning that "Ellen rode all over New England trying to shake the tuberculosis out of her" through bumpy carriage rides.[38] The young couple optimistically married on September 30, 1829, but Ellen's condition gradually worsened, until Emerson recorded a single entry in his journal in early 1831: "Ellen Tucker Emerson died 8th of February. Tuesday morning 9 o'clock."[39] Her death shattered the stability of his outward life and transformed what had been a comfortable existence into a rigid and empty list of formal duties demanded by society. By April he was being worn down: "The days go by, griefs, & simpers, & sloth & disappointments. The dead do not return, & sometimes we are negligent of their image. Not of yours Ellen—I know too well who is gone from me. And here come on the formal duties which are to be formally discharged, and in our sluggish mind no sentiment rises to quicken them, they seem."[40] By the next year he was despairing of his career. He recorded in his journal on January 10, 1832: "It is the best part of the man, I sometimes think, that revolts most against his being the minister. . . . The difficulty is that we do not make a world of our own but fall into institutions already made & have to accommodate ourselves to them to be useful at all. & this accommodation is, I say, a loss of so much integrity & of course so much power."[41]

In September of that year he resigned from the church. He had chosen power. It is important to emphasize that in the context of the 1830s, Emerson's choice to pursue power was not an abstraction. On December 10, 1832, he decided to sell his house and sail for southern Europe, an impulsive act that completed his transformation into a Transcendentalist. In many ways this decision was the embodiment of the Emersonian conception of power, which had its origins in the revolutionary changes in the nineteenth century. He was able to dispose of his property and, on Christmas Day, 1832, he departed for Malta on the 236-ton brig *Jasper*, which reached its destination just over a month later on February 2, 1833. Released from his sheltered life in Boston and whisked away to Europe by a product of the transportation revolution, Emerson traveled from Sicily all the way up through Italy to Paris and then across the Channel to England and up to Scotland, more freely than any member of the eighteenth-century ruling class had ever dreamed. While he was there he met many of the literary geniuses of his age, notably, William Wordsworth, Coleridge, and Thomas Carlyle, as well as touring of two of the embodiments of nineteenth-century science, the Cabinet of Natural History and the botanical gardens at the Jardin des Plates in the old King's Garden in Paris. These experiences taught him the true meaning of power—the capacity for human innovation and effort continually to overcome obstacles, strive toward new horizons, and refashion one's identities even as one transforms the world through knowledge, technology, politics, and art.

His experience touring the Cabinet of Natural History bears specific mention because in many ways it functions as a metaphor for his method of eloquence. As indicated by its name, the cabinet attempted to compress all of the diversity of nature into a manageable size and was part of the "larger movement, beginning in the second quarter of the nineteenth century, to make all branches of knowledge, and especially the natural sciences, accessible to the layman."[42] Made possible by the triumphs of technology, colonialism, and science—the first allowing for extended research journeys across the oceans, the second giving European naturalists uninhibited access to the flora and fauna of foreign lands, and the third allowing for these collections to be carefully analyzed, catalogued, and exhibited according to Georges Cuvier's classification system, the Cabinet of Natural History was the embodiment of the nineteenth-century effort to turn the entire world into a microcosm that could be not only displayed but also comprehended and controlled. For Emerson, seeing the fruits of this effort was revelatory. According to Elizabeth A. Dant, "the cabinet above all acted as a coherent representational and epistemological model—an object lesson on the uses and power of eclecticism in building your own world."[43] In other words it showed him how gathering together a multiplicity of artifacts, ideas, memories, words, and images could disclose a whole that was greater than its parts.

This method is precisely representative of what Lawrence Buell called Transcendentalist "catalogue rhetoric," which on its face appears as "a cluster of images, placed in loose apposition, with a bit of moralizing at the end." One often finds the list in Emerson, to the point where they seem tedious and formless. Yet Buell argues that the cataloging of phenomena in this way serves a rhetorical purpose: "to overwhelm us with a multiplicity of instances but at the same time impress us with the design inherent in these."[44] Emerson's response to the cabinet that he recorded in his journal is representative of this type of catalogue rhetoric:

> Here we are impressed with the inexhaustible riches of nature. The universe is a more amazing puzzle than ever as you glance along this bewildering series of animated forms,—the hazy butterflies, the carved shells, the birds, beasts, fishes, insects, snakes,—& the upheaving principle of life everywhere incipient in the very rock aping organized forms. Not a form so grotesque, so savage, nor so beautiful but is an expression of some property inherent in the observer,—an occult relation between the very scorpions and man. I feel the centipede in me—cayman, carp, eagle, & fox. I am moved by strange sympathies, I say continually, "I will be a naturalist."[45]

As indicated by his description of his experience, Emerson did not equate being a naturalist with practicing natural science on the model of Charles Darwin. Rather he meant rather that, from this point forward, observing and experiencing nature would be an inspiration for his speech and thoughts, seeking in their physical forms expressions of those upheaving principles of life that are common to both scorpion and man and bind them together in common sympathy. He would use the power of language to compress the inexhaustible unity and diversity of nature (and thereby of God) into a single work of art in order to expand the circumference of the audience's world and by so doing change the substance of its identity. Emerson's assertion that he will be a naturalist because of his "strange sympathies" with nature represents the type of reidentification through consubstantiality that he would seek to inspire in others through eloquence.

His decision to become a naturalist turned out to be a stroke of genius, not only because nature became the source of his eloquence but also because it became, on his return, the most immediate route to practical power as a lyceum lecturer. Part lecture series, part dramatic theater, part instructional school, and part town fair, the lyceum movement was founded in the 1820s by Josiah Holbrook to promote the "universal diffusion of knowledge." According to Sellers, on the lyceum stage, "Emerson found his secular pulpit for this doctrine of spiritual self-making in the new role of paid lecturer to bourgeois/middle-class self-improvers."[46] It was thus in the lyceum that Emerson began to make a public name for himself and in fact "shaped many of the lecture circuit's fundamental practices," such as hiring speakers to "deliver a series of connected lectures—sometimes as many as five or six, usually at least three—on consecutive nights, allowing for broader development of a topic."[47] Emerson delivered his first public lecture, "The Uses of Natural History" on November 5, 1833, before the Natural History Society. Soon he was the most recognized face on the lyceum circuit and America's first professional lecturer. By the time he published his *Essays* in 1841, he was giving almost thirty lectures a year in cities such as Boston, Providence, New York, and Philadelphia.[48] Traveling by train, steamboat, and carriage and promoted by the new methods of publicity, "Emerson is the first intellectual to benefit from dramatically changing technologies that shape the distribution of knowledge, and he is one of the first to fully exploit the newfound possibility of celebrity and culture."[49]

But more important to Emerson's rhetorical legacy is that in nature he had found a new source for both rhetorical invention and rhetorical authority. He had come to realize by this time is that the god of tradition and the god of rhetoric both conspired to limit the horizons of thought and speech in the same way—namely by restricting both what can be said and how it can be said to what has already been said and recorded in books. The god of tradition maintained authority by sanctioning and censoring certain ideas preserved in canonical texts, while the god of rhetoric limited the expression of those ideas to the predictable patterns and forms that had been taught for centuries. In nature, however, Emerson located a source of unlimited invention in the phenomena of the living, growing world and a source of absolute authority in the laws, principles, and virtues disclosed in those phenomena. Susan Roberson aptly describes both of these functions that nature served for Emerson. In terms of authority, "seeing the natural or material world as another spiritual text, as additional evidence of God's omnipotence and divine plan not only undermined the sole authority of the Bible but also indicated the correspondences or connections between the material and spiritual realms." In terms of invention, "such an understanding prompted a symbolic reading of nature to get at larger truths, an attempt to unpack the hiero-glyphics of the natural world by the reader, again putting a degree of power in the hands (or eyes) of the perceptive individual."[50] Whereas the young Emerson still clung to the models established by the texts of antiquity to inspire him, upon his return from Europe he turned his eyes to all of nature for resources to construct a new spiritual authority on which to build self-reliant individuals.

However, as he announced in his first Transcendentalist manifesto of 1836, this new form of authority had a confounding irony about it. On the one hand, *Nature* at first glance seemed to be a conventional poetic effort to develop a richer perspective toward the natural world by seeing it in one of four ways. Nature is a commodity that in its material form is a resource for the useful arts; a medium by which the forms of beauty make themselves known to the senses and the intel-lect; a discipline by which the laws of physics, astronomy, and magnetism, among many others, are learned; and the phenomenological disclosure of *Spirit*, which is Emerson's gnostic reinterpretation of the Christian God. On the other hand, on closer reading the book seems to be misnamed. Harold Bloom writes that rather than a treatise on nature, Emerson's first book is "a blandly disassociative apoca-lypse, in which everything is cheerful error, indeed a misreading, starting with the title, which says 'Nature' but means 'Man.'"[51] More complicated still, *Nature* seems to call into question whether nature or man can really be represented at all through language. According to Richard Poirier, Emerson in *Nature* confronts readers with the radical possibility that "there is no such thing as natural lan-guage, any more than there is a natural literature. It is all *made up*."[52] Thus a book titled *Nature* is not about nature and rejects the possibility that such a book could ever be composed as anything more than a series of tropes.

Yet even in its impossibility of being expressed through words, there was an authority that Emerson gestured toward that was sovereign over all things and called all traditional authorities into question. He announced this authority most dramatically in one famous passage: "Standing on the bare ground,—my head bathed by the blithe air, and uplifted into infinite space,—all mean egotism van-ishes. I becoming a transparent eye-ball. I am nothing. I see all. The currents of the Universal Being circulate through me; I am part or parcel of God."[53] The effect of this experience is described by Donald Pease as being simultaneously alienat-ing and sublime—alienating because it detaches readers from a naive belief in the autonomy and independence of individual existence as an "ego" but sublime because it confronts them with a sphere of being that cannot be represented in language but whose sovereign influence nonetheless penetrates all things. Pease writes that in defining the eyeball as transparent, "Emerson wanted to provide an image for the impossible act of sight seeing itself," of being simultaneously dissolved into nothing and yet seeing everything—including one's own nothingness. Yet unlike the traditional mystical experiences of religion, the encountered thing in this experience is "undefinable as either subject or object, God or nature," and thus "seems more like a living glance exchanged when God and Nature look face-to-face." It is a moment in which one cheerfully lets go of all of the stable meanings and opens oneself up to a sphere of pure possibility, "a field of play where every conception approaches the inconceivable."[54] The paradox of this authority is that it can be located in no one source, and yet its influence is sovereign over all things and demands only one thing—that people keep playing.

At the same time, Pease's reading of Emerson is largely a Derridean one that seems content to revel in the play of signifiers; it does not draw the rhetorical conclusion that this experience of alienation and sublimity is a process not only of losing oneself but also of continually finding oneself. This process of transformation is at the heart of what Alan Hodder calls Emerson's rhetoric of revelation. For him *Nature* recapitulates the structure of apocalypse in the Bible, which anticipates the destruction of the old order and "rests in the faith that only when such perfect vision dawns will be 'new heaven and earth' be realized." Consequently Emerson's rhetoric is designed neither to delight nor to instruct but rather to galvanize: "Provocation, not edification is its concern. . . . What he meant was to provoke in the root sense of calling forth—to stimulate in others what was productive in oneself." His troping thus had an explicit rhetorical purpose to shock readers out of their comfortable beliefs and predispositions in order that they might seek new identities that have new powers. As Hodder explains, "as readers we are brought back to ourselves fully only when we are willing to sacrifice our prior understandings. Emerson believed this and knew that the reader's revelation is dependent therefore on the author's own voluntary deliberate self-negation."[55] But the self-negation was a prelude to its reconstitution in power, or what Burke calls an act of slaying prior to an act of reidentification.

The primary "creation" that Emerson strove to produce through his own eloquence was another self who was capable of eloquence. This follows a line of argument from Stanley Cavell, who argued that one of the key foundations of Emersonian self-reliance is an understanding of the full meaning of what it is to write—that is, "how it is that one writes better than one knows (as well as worse) and that one may be understood better by someone other than oneself (as well as understood worse)."[56] Unfortunately the worse possibilities of writing and understanding are derived from a common vice, which is the assumption that people are always in control of their words and that their language should be judged by how it channels some private inner motive or belief. This is the kind of "self" so loved by the god of tradition, who exalts convention and thereby limits thought, action, and speech to readily understood arguments, maxims, and figures. For Emerson, however, true eloquence requires awareness that one is never fully in control of one's words and that all of these constraints that the god of rhetoric places upon humanity are, as Poirier says, "made up." Yet this does not condemn people to passivity, ennui, or pure play. For Emerson eloquence grows out of an attitude of power, a willingness to write the world (and oneself) into being in full knowledge of its impossibility. Eloquence thus requires people to pass through a stage in which they are but transparent eyeballs in order to reconstitute themselves as highly visible eloquent orators and writers.

Returning to the text of *Nature*, it is not difficult to see how the basic structure of the book is designed to transform readers' attitude toward language in a way that is productive of eloquence. Reworking the ideas of Swedenborg that had inspired Reed, Emerson argues that "1. Words are signs of natural facts. 2. Particular natural facts are symbols of particular spiritual facts. 3. Nature is the symbol of spirit."[57] The first proposition is etymological. It reports that "every word which is used to express a moral or intellectual fact, if traced to its roots, is found to be borrowed from some material appearance." The word "*right* originally means *straight*," for example, thus showing how all words began as indications of natural forms that eventually took on greater symbolic meaning. The second proposition expresses his theory of correspondence. It states that "every appearance in nature corresponds to some state of mind, and that state of mind can only be described by presenting the natural appearance as its picture." Here is the language of metaphor and allegory, exemplified by the fact that "light and darkness are our familiar expression for knowledge and ignorance; and heat for love." The last proposition is Transcendentalist. It proclaims that the allegories we perceive are not merely symbolic but actual, namely because "the world is emblematic. Parts of speech are metaphors because the whole of nature is a metaphor of the human mind. The laws of moral nature answer to those of matter as face-to-face in a glass."[58] In sum words not only originate by imitating natural objects, but in their capacity as symbols they also point to nature again, constructing images of natural forms in the imagination that correspond to states of mind in the particular and in the general disclose the universal laws of spirit that interpenetrate all things. Eloquence, then, represents the capacity to identify those words that most vividly convey those natural facts, which in turn allow people to see the moral laws of nature as in a mirror—albeit a darkened one.

If one were to look for clear and simple rules of eloquence in *Nature* (or what Emerson calls methods of producing "good writing and brilliant discourse"), three stand out. First, a true orator must purge him- or herself of the "corruption of language," the residue of a long process that occurs when "new imagery ceases to be created, and old words are perverted to stand for things which they are not; a paper currency is employed when there is no bouillon in the vaults." Severed from nature, language becomes artificial, frozen, and conventional, a collection of dead symbols preserved in books that no longer carries any true authority. Here is an emancipatory attitude that allows readers to cast aside tradition and convention and lifts them into the sphere of the purely creative. Second, the true orator must positively embrace a language of trope and thereby "pierce this rotten diction and fasten words again to visible things so that picturesque language is at once a commanding certificate that he who employs it, is a man in alliance with truth and God."[59] Once again reflecting the importance of identification to Emerson's understanding of eloquence, it is the use of language that proves (or establishes) humankind's common substance with truth and with God—just as calcified speech that relies on nearly paper currency reaffirms people's base identification with mere society.

Perhaps the most explicit exposition on rhetorical method, however, is found when Emerson turns his attention to the traditional rhetorical concerns of revolution and reform. As if he crafted this passage as a direct critique of the method of Brownson, for whom nature was irrelevant to the suffering of the laboring classes, Emerson gives the keys of power to the individual genius communing with nature rather than to the social reformer doing battle in the political agon. Put simply, he suggests that that any orator or poet who seeks to direct the course of history through eloquence must ironically immerse oneself in nonhuman nature in order to acquire the power of influence.

> The poet, the orator, bred in the woods, whose senses have been nourished by the fair and appeasing changes, year after year, without design and without heed,—shall not lose their lesson altogether, in the roar of cities or the broil of politics. Long hereafter, amidst agitation and terror in national councils,—in the hour of revolution,—the solemn images shall reappear in their morning luster, as fit symbols and words of the thoughts which the passing events shall awaken. At the call of a noble sentiment, again the woods wave, the pines murmur, the river rolls and shines, and the cattle low upon the mountains, as he saw and heard them in his infancy. And with these forms, the spells of persuasion, the keys of power are put into his hands.[60]

Notable of these passages is their pragmatic character. There is no transcendental eyeball here, although the memories of that sublime experience remain salient. What matters in the hour of revolution is that those transcendental revelations come rushing back with a newfound relevance in an act of speech that moves thought and action in the moment. Here the pure naturalist becomes a reformer, and nature becomes an instrument for rhetorical invention, a resource for creating those natural images that can cast the spells of persuasion and put the keys of power into his or her hands during a time of revolution, when the course of history hangs in balance.

It is important, however, not to read this statement about persuasion too instrumentally—as if a completely self-conscious rhetor could simply stroll through the woods and find the spells of persuasion. The keys of power are only put into the hands of those individuals willing to lose themselves in order to embrace a life of continual growth and becoming. To be able to express symbols and words fitting to passing events is merely a happy side effect of the more primary activity of continual self-creation that occurs once one becomes truly open to the emblematic language of nature. Eloquence thus represents the creation of symbolic objects that compress and contain some aspect of spirit as revealed through nature. Emerson writes, "A new interest surprises us, whilst, under the view now suggested, we contemplate the fearful extent and multitude of objects: since 'every object rightly seen, unlocks a new faculty of the soul.' That which was unconscious truth, becomes, when interpreted and defined in an object, a part of the domain of knowledge,—a new amount to the magazine of power."[61] In this way power is the outcome of the poetic (and rhetorical) construction of symbolic objects that occurs only when one can truly contemplate the sublimity of nature and absorb within people identities the new faculties of the soul, which this experience awakens and activates.

Emerson quickly found himself practicing what he preached. Having made a name on the lyceum circuit, published a successful book, surrounded himself with the leading members of the Boston intelligentsia, reestablished himself as a respectable family man by marrying Lidia Jackson in 1835, and given his Phi Beta Kappa address, Emerson now had the public standing to be thought a suitable choice to address the small but prestigious group of six graduates of the Harvard Divinity School, along with their families, friends, and teachers on July 15, 1838—this despite the fact that Emerson had earlier rejected Unitarianism and quit the ministry. On its face his Divinity School Address was, as Barbara Packer notes, "intended as a provocative attack on what he regarded as the current corruptions of preaching and religious life."[62] In short Emerson accepted the invitation in order to deliver a scathing Transcendentalist critique of what he called "historical Christianity," a Christianity that binds itself to the study of the life of Jesus as recorded in the Bible. This approach, Emerson complained, has two errors: it focuses too much on the "*person* of Jesus," meaning a reconstruction of every detail of his life and works for the purpose of admiration and imitation, and it speaks of "revelation as somewhat long ago given and done, as if God were dead."[63] Consistent with the critical method of eloquence, which seeks to emancipate by unmasking the corruption of language, Emerson condemns a form of preaching that limits itself to the dead language of the past: "The imitator dooms himself to hopeless mediocrity."[64] Thus Emerson's advice to the new graduates of the Harvard Divinity School, who had been trained to become gentlemen ministers of the Unitarian pulpit, was this: "Let me admonish you, first of all, to go alone; to refuse the good models, even those most sacred in the imagination of men, and dare to love God without mediator or veil."[65] In other words, alienation from every model of goodness they had ever known was merely a step to the encounter with the sublime.

But Emerson's critique of historical Christianity was once again merely a means to unlocking the power of eloquence in his particular audience. As Richardson explains, he used the address less as an assault on Unitarianism than as an opportunity to announce that "the religious impulse in human nature demands not only expression but communication with others. Great truths demand great utterance."[66] And great utterance came not from the dry repetition of what was in books but from the poetic expression of what nature disclosed to the individual in the solitude of his or her own soul. The opening lines of his address announce this new celebration of nature: "In the refulgent summer it has been a luxury to draw the breath of life. The grass grows, the buds burst, the meadow is spotted with fire and gold in the tint of flowers."[67] But nature is not there simply for human sensual gratification; nature is revelatory. There occurs the moment when "the mind opens, and reveals the laws which traverse the universe, and make things what they are, then shrinks the great world at once into a mere illustration and fable of this mind."[68] The true office of the preacher is to communicate the universal moral laws to others through the language of nature, which sees the whole through the part, the macrocosm through the microcosm, and ultimately to "speak the very truth, as your life and conscience teach it, and cheer the waiting, fainting hearts of men with new hope and new revelation."[69] It was Emerson's hope to give an exhibition of the type of speech he was calling for—that is, the type of speech that communicates a "life passed through the fire of thought."[70] The result of the speech would be creation of a new breed of eloquent geniuses.

The reaction to Emerson's address was, by early nineteenth-century standards, almost immediate. Five weeks later Andrews Norton published an uncharacteristically violent, abusive, and dismissive assault on it, using it as the most "extraordinary and ill boding evidence" that there existed a "new school in literature and religion" whose "obscure intimations, ambiguous words, and false and mischievous speculations" would have a "disastrous effect upon the religion and moral state of the community." The members of this new school, he writes, boldly "announce themselves as the prophets and priests of a new future, in which all is to be changed, all old opinions done away, and all present forms of society abolished." And yet "by what process this joyful revolution is to be affected we are not told." Instead the writer "floats about magnificently on bladders, which he would have it believed are swelling with ideas," and "to produce a more striking effect, our common language is abused; antic tricks are played with it; inversions, exclamations, anomalous combinations of words, unmeaning, but coarse and violent, metaphors abound, and withal a strong infusion of German barbarisms." Worst of all, for Norton, was the fact that—in Emerson's case at least—the community saw fit to give this sort of oration on audience: "what *his* opinion may be is a matter of minor concern; the main question is how it has happened, that religion has been insulted by the delivery of these opinions in the Chapel of the Divinity College of Cambridge, as the last instruction which those who were to receive, who were going forth from it, bearing the name of Christian preachers."[71]

Although Norton's public censure and the flurry of attacks and defenses that followed clearly shook Emerson, the controversy soon died out and left no lasting damage to his public reputation; if anything it gave him more publicity. By the time he began a new lecture series in late 1838, his audience attendance remained high and continued to grow. In fact Norton's critique of his speech and writing seemed to make him ever more committed to defending his conception of eloquence as the key to power. In October he reflected on his experience being the target of public criticism and came away galvanized:

> How soon the sunk spirits rise again, how quick the little wounds of fortune skin over & are forgotten. I am sensitive as a leaf to impressions from abroad. And under this night's beautiful heaven I have forgotten that I ever was *reviewed*. It is strange how superficial are our views of these matters, seeing we are all writers & philosophers. A man thinks it of importance what the great sheet or pamphlet of today proclaims of him to all the reading town; and if he sees graceful compliments, he relishes his dinner; & if he sees threatening paragraphs & odious nicknames, it becomes a solemn depressing fact & sables his whole thoughts until bedtime. But in truth the effect of these paragraphs is mathematically measurable by their depth of thought. How much water do they draw? If they awaken you to think—if they lift you from your feet with the great voice of eloquence—then their effect is to be wide, slow, permanent over the minds of men: but if they instruct you not, they will die like flies in hour.[72]

Emerson was playing the long game, he assured himself, and his words would win the war even if he may have been wounded in battle. This conclusion was more than simply a momentary rationalization to justify his actions and heal his damaged pride. It was the validation of his entire theory of social change, which identified "the great voice of eloquence" and not the shallow but spectacular blowups of the daily press, as the prime mover of history.

His experience of the Divinity School Address and its aftermath is central to understanding Emerson's attitudes as he began composing his first volume of *Essays* published a few years later in 1841. In one way the structure and tone of *Essays* harkens back to an ancient tradition. According to Von Frank, Emerson "writes in the tradition of the wisdom literature of the Old Testament, of Proverbs and Ecclesiastes," concerned, "as the prophets were, with the relation of spirit and human behavior, of right seeing and right living, the perfection of justice, and the power that comes into human beings when they yield to the truth."[73] With titles that encompass sweeping aspects of the human condition, including in order "History," "Self-Reliance," "Compensation," "Spiritual Laws," "Love," "Friendship," "Prudence," "Heroism," "The Over-Soul," "Circles," "Intellect," and "Art," the essays of his collection indicate an author who wished to present, in the words of David Robinson, "a guidebook for the culture of the soul."[74] The essays are both of these things: a literature of wisdom and a guidebook directed toward the production of eloquence as its ultimate aim. Furthermore, they represent Emerson's most thorough defense of eloquence as an art of power whose influence far surpasses the kind of speech that masks its impotence with mere rhetoric.

A journal entry of May 12, 1830, offers insight into the motivation behind the essays. In this passage Emerson sought the secret of how to speak with authority and expressed his disdain for the practices of the god of rhetoric that remained pervasive in nineteenth-century society. Like Alcott he looked back to the figure of Jesus and interpreted him as an orator: "It was said of Jesus that 'he taught as one having authority'—a distinction most palpable." For Emerson, though, Jesus attained his authority through the possession of eloquence rather than being the Son of God. Not only did he give recent examples of this type of authority in Sampson Reed, but he also turned his critical eye toward the current state of rhetoric in society. "There is nevertheless a foolish belief among teachers that the multitude are not wise enough to discern good manner & good matter. And that voice & rhetorick will stand instead of truth." The consequence of this pervasive belief among both teachers and the multitude itself pointed in the direction of the sorry state of political oratory: "The multitude suppose often that great talents are necessary to produce the elaborate arrangements which they hear without emotion or consequence. & so they say what a fine speaker, what a good discourse but they will not leave any agreeable employment to go again & never will do a single thing in consequence of having heard the discourse." In contradistinction the effects of eloquence were far-reaching: "But let them hear one of these Godtaught teachers & they surrender to him. They leave their work to come again. They go home & think & talk and act as he said. Men know truth as quick as they see it." The key lesson Emerson takes away from this is that "a tone of authority cannot be taken without truths of authority."[75] The one who would be eloquent must thus first obtain these truths of authority (through direct encounter with nature) and then speak the truth without condescending to the expectations of the multitude and their love of elaborate harangue.

The entire structure of *Essays* grows out of this basic impulse in Emerson to articulate a form of eloquence that speaks with authority and expresses power. To be sure the great bulk of the text of the essays does not specifically address questions of eloquence but rather fits into that model of wisdom literature and a guidebook for self-culture. But I believe that most of the tendencies of the key passages point in a single direction, namely toward the final essay, "Art," which in effect is the culmination of all of the prior chapters. In other words the art of the poet is the new form of identification that results from having moved progressively through all that came before it. In the language of Kenneth Burke, the essays follow a psychology of form, which is the "creation of an appetite in the mind of the auditor, and the adequate satisfying of that appetite."[76] Lawrence Buell argues that despite the apparent formlessness of individual essays, "the appearance of formlessness is to a large extent a strategy on Emerson's part calculated to render his thoughts more faithfully and forcefully than direct statement would permit."[77] What holds for individual essays also holds for *Essays* as a whole. In fact this apparent formlessness gives them their eloquence. For instance, from a Burkean perspective, form "at times involves a temporary set of frustrations, but in the end these frustrations proved to be simply a more involved kind of satisfaction, and furthermore serve to make the satisfaction of fulfillment more intense." Consistent with Emerson's own understanding, Burke contends that eloquence itself represents a kind of "formal excellence" that occurs, for instance, in great works of tragedy or comedy in which the satisfaction only comes after a long period of frustration.[78] In *Essays,* in other words, Emerson uses the form of eloquence to inspire and justify it.

The remainder of this chapter traces the development and progress of form in the essays that would be produced from a reader with an appetite for eloquence. This is not the only possible form one can derive from *Essays,* particularly since Burke's notion of form is not simply a product of the text but results from the active participation of an audience with its own psychological needs and desires. However, a case can be made that Emerson composed *Essays* with this type of form in mind and had as its ultimate aim the creation of the symbol of the poet. Once again, however, a symbol should not be interpreted merely as a representation of an idea or emotion. For Burke a symbol is what he calls a "verbal parallel to a pattern of experience," in which a pattern of experience represents adjustments made by an individual in relationship to a specific type of environment. For instance "the protest of a Byron, the passive resistance of a Gandhi, the hopefulness of a Browning, the satirical torment of a Swift, the primness of a Jane Austen—these are all patterns of experience."[79] In the case of Emerson's *Essays,* the overriding symbol is the poet.

The topic of the first essay, "History" is a natural starting place for Emerson, because it is only in relationship to the sweeping environment of history that eloquence functions as an adaptation. History, properly understood, shatters the boundaries of limited horizons and situates humanity within a circumference of global space in which universal ideas become manifest through infinite time. This is the proper stage for eloquence. "History" challenges the small-minded view of history as a mere sequence of facts and events of which individual lives are but one more detail. This materialist view of history creates an army of what Emerson calls "the man of routine, the men of *sense,* in whom a literal obedience to the facts has extinguished every spark of that light by which man is truly man." These are the sorts of men who worship the god of rhetoric and find it their duty to speak sensibly—that is, to speak only of the facts of the matter and limit the scope of their speech to the circumference of their immediate life. But for Emerson history is not a progress of facts but a progressive unfolding and expression of the laws of the universal mind in different circumstances and through different individuals. Facts are but partial expressions of universals given objective form that appeal to the human senses. The course of history is thereby not determined by the causal agency of facts but by the revelatory power of the ideas behind them. Thus he makes the expression of eloquence the key to an era, for it is through eloquence that those ideas that remake the self into a powerful agency for change are encountered. As he concludes the essay: "Who knows himself before he has been thrilled with indignation at an outrage, or has heard an eloquent tongue, or has shared the throb of thousands in a national exultation or alarm? No man can antedate his experience, or guess what faculty or feeling a new object shall unlock, any more than he can draw to-day the face of a person who he shall see to-morrow for the first time."[80] Eloquence is the remaking of the self through symbols in a way that reveals new powers and determines the course of revolutions.

Given the caricature of Emerson as a "transparent eyeball" completely detached from the exigencies of his surroundings, it is important to emphasize that "History" does not simply dissolve the historical self or historical circumstances into a vaguely defined universal idea that is impotent to effect change. Quite the opposite, Emerson argues for a dialectical understanding of history that leads to a specific theory of power. History, that is to say, is the product of the dialectical interaction over time between universal ideals and particular circumstances, while for Emerson power is the force produced from that interaction within the lives of individual actors. For instance, "Columbus needs a planet to shape his course upon";[81] transport Napoleon "to large countries, dense population, complex interests, and antagonist power, and you shall see that the man Napoleon, bounded, that is, by such a profile and outline, is not the virtual Napoleon."[82] Both of these examples show that, for any individual, "power consists in the multitude of his affinities, and the fact that his life is intertwined with the whole chain of organic and inorganic being." Power is thus like the public network of roads in old Rome that stretched in every direction and related the center to the periphery, the organism to its environment, the city to its empire. Without those roads the power of Rome is nothing. Similarly Emerson writes that "a man is a bundle of relations, a knot of roots, whose flower and fruitage is the world. His faculties refer to natures out of him, and predict the world he is to inhabit as the fins of the fish foreshadow that water exists, or the wings of an eagle in the egg presuppose air. He cannot live without a world."[83] It is no use, then, to imitate heroes in one's own time and expect the same result. Each circumstance demands a different set of faculties, just as different sets of faculties demand a different environment for their unfolding. The challenge for eloquence is thus not to mimic thoughtlessly the great works of the past but to be able to discern in a particular historical situation the unique relationship between universal ideas and particular circumstances that unlocks faculties of power.

To move from "History" to "Self-Reliance" is thus to explore the relationship between the orator and his or her environment in the context of the early nineteenth century. It is to articulate the method by which power is accrued and expressed in the world in which Emerson and his readers find themselves. That power is the central concern to self-reliance, he reminds readers in his famous definition. For Emerson power is not the possession of a "new thousand eyes and arms"—that is, a quantitative measure of pure force, whether expressed in a battalion of soldiers or a mob of voters. Rather power represents a capacity of overcoming, acting, and becoming: "Power ceases in the instant of repose; it resides in the moment of transition from a past to a new state, in the shooting of the gulf, in the darting to an aim." The masses thus possess a great deal of force but no power, for power requires the ability of the soul to become something other than it was, even if it means violating what seems to be virtue. Hence in "Self-Reliance" Emerson identifies the central exigence that motivates his entire *Essays,* which is the growing constraints that a modern mass society places upon the expression of individual power. "This one fact the world hates, that the soul *becomes;* for that forever degrades the past, turns all riches the poverty, all reputation to a shame, confounds the saint with the rogue, shoves Jesus and Judas equally aside."[84] But this one fact is also the central problem confronting Emerson in his essays—how to overcome the hatred of the world for a soul that becomes by giving that soul the tools of eloquence by which to transition both self and other from a past to a new state.

To understand Emersonian self-reliance, one must see it as a challenge to the rise of a new form of social organization in the nineteenth century—that of mass society characterized by a "slavish respect for numbers." What is the nature of this mass society? First, it holds to a utilitarian ethic that asserts that the desires of the few should be sacrificed for the interests of the many. Hence "society is a joint-stock company in which the members agree for the better securing of his bread to each shareholder." Second, mass society demands conformity and adherence to names and customs in order to ensure the smooth and effective operation of this joint-stock company, thus meaning that its members, in order for each to secure his bread, must "surrender the liberty and culture of the eater."[85] Third, mass society directs its displeasure at those who reject its opinions and is capable of quickly arousing the "indignation of the people" and then mobilizing "the unintelligent brute force that lies at the bottom of society" against them.[86] Fourth, mass society, in addition to demanding conformity in action, creates a fetish for a "foolish consistency" in our thoughts and speech such that they always move within familiar patterns that are easily recognized and communicated.[87] But last, and quite ironically, mass society is characterized by an incredible fickleness that allows it to change its opinion almost at will, a result of its being essentially constituted by the whims of the mass media: "The sour faces of the multitude, like their sweet faces, have no deep cause, but are put on and off as the wind blows, and a newspaper directs."[88] Reminiscent of his earlier complaint about "elaborate harangue," he pronounces that the multitude's superficial love of consistency (which in reality is simply a desire for sameness) is made possible only by its extreme forgetfulness and utter shallowness, such that when a movement or political party changes its position and demands a new conformity, the multitude immediately switches to a new mind-set and continues on as if nothing had changed.

Self-reliance thus identifies the first and most foundational pattern of experience that must be developed in those who would seek to alter the course of history through eloquence. Five attitudes embody the virtue of self-reliance for Emerson. The first is an attitude toward history: "We lie in the lap of immense intelligence, which makes us receivers of its truth and organs of its activity." The second is an attitude toward oneself: "To believe your own heart, to believe that what is true for you in your private heart, is true for all men,—that is genius." The third is an attitude toward one's audience: "What I must do, is all that concerns me, not what the people think." The fourth is an attitude toward speech: "Go upright and vital, and speak the rude truth in all ways." The first three attitudes mean nothing without the fourth. For power to be expressed, it must be expressed in action, and the highest form of action for Emerson is speech and writing. In one of his boldest commitments to the vocation of eloquence, he writes: "I shun father and mother and wife and brother when my genius calls me. I would write on the lintels the doorpost, *Whim.* I hope it is better than whim at last, but we cannot spend the day in explanation."[89] For Stanley Cavell this passage more than any other shows how the essay, despite its fame for preaching individualism, "is a study of writing, as if one's wish to write simply *Whim* already took upon oneself the full-blown burden of writing." For such an act asserts a kind of authority that defies any effort at explanation and provides "no justification for language apart from language."[90] What proves eloquence true is not rhetorical justification in the present but the effect of ideas over time in history. Hence the fifth and most important attitude of self-reliance, which expresses confidence in the power of one's eloquence: "Speak your latent conviction and it shall be the universal sense; for the inmost in due time becomes the outmost,—and our first thought is rendered back to us by the trumpets of the Last Judgment."[91]

There is a discernible irony in Emerson's use of the "Last Judgment" as a warrant for acts of self-reliant speech, as his essay "Compensation" makes readily clear. The entire thrust of that essay is to set forth a completely worldly standard of justice by which to evaluate one's actions, rejecting entirely traditional Platonic or Christian conceptions of justice rooted in the belief "that judgment is not executed in this world" but the next one.[92] Emerson has no use for this otherworldly kind of measure. In his philosophy of the act, "justice is not postponed. A perfect equity adjusts its balance in all parts of life." Thus "every excess causes a defect; every defect an excess."[93] This quote is misleading, however, if it is taken to mean that Emerson believed that justice is done to an individual and is immediately apparent in the moment. He admits, for instance, that "a fever, and mutilation, a cruel disappointment, a loss of wealth, a loss of friends seems at the moment unpaid loss, and unpayable." Certainly it is unpayable to those people who have suffered and died. In removing faith in a Last Judgment that rewards goodness after death, Emerson did not deny he had removed an important source of solace. Yet his concern was not with justice for the individual but with the nature of justice as it plays out in history. The compensation appears not in another world but in this world as it moves into the future. Despite humanity's present sufferings, then, "the compensations of calamity are made apparent to the understanding also, after long intervals of time." The tendency of justice cannot be denied, but its appearance may be postponed. Thus it is that "the death of a dear friend, wife, brother, lover, which seems nothing but privation, somewhat later assumes the aspect of a guide for genius; for it commonly operates revolutions in our way of life, terminates an epoch of infancy or of youth which was waiting to be closed, breaks up a wonted occupation, or a household, or style of living, and allows the formation of new ones more friendly to the growth of character."[94] In other words compensation is grounded in what one might today call an ecological notion in which actions and events are never judged within a single, bounded context but within a complex and holistic system that often only reveals the consequences of those actions and events over many years and by unexpected outcomes.

There is, however, one important exception to this rule of compensation that is central to understanding its relevance to eloquence. Emerson writes that although compensation punishes vice and loads suffering upon those who would hoard riches, goods, or political power, there "is no penalty to virtue; no penalty to wisdom; they are proper additions to being." That is, if one speaks the truth with courage and beauty, it is a pure positive to the world—even if its benefits might not be revealed until after a long interval of time. Here is that same confidence Emerson expressed in self-reliance, such that even in persecution, "every burned book or house enlightens the world; every suppressed or expunged word reverberates through the earth from side to side." Yet if persecuted eloquence returns with power, the case is much different when one adopts a method of partisan harangue and rhetorical demagoguery that targets a mob to do the work of history. For no matter their intent, "a mob is a society of bodies voluntarily bereaving themselves of reason and traversing its work. The mob is man voluntarily descending to the nature of the beast." The history of those who would seek the key to history by activating the mob to some persecution—no matter the victim—is thus "a history of endeavors to cheat nature, to make our run uphill, to twist a rope of sand."[95] The doctrine of compensation thus assures that the populist rhetoric that boasts of its power is in fact the weakest form of persuasion, while true power is held by those who hold to principle even though their bodies are tarred and feathered, lashed with the whip, or burned alive in their own houses.

Had Emerson stopped at "Compensation," he would indeed have written a collection of essays firmly in the genre of Old Testament wisdom literature continuous with the voice of Isaiah and Jeremiah. This is a voice, according to von Frank, that speaks not just to inspire but to judge and condemn: "*Essays* is a book for a world in which history is arid, men are washed-out images of deferred or absent authority, virtue is held to be disadvantageous, laws are disbelieved and dishonored, love is personal aggrandizement, friends are appurtenances, prudence is mere Yankee shrewdness, and nothing quite means enough to make life worth persisting in."[96] Like Brownson, Emerson saw himself as a modern-day prophet tasked with sweeping away corruption and calling people to a new covenant, even if it meant rousing the scorn of the multitude. But Emerson did not stop there. His efforts to redefine the purpose and the scene of action ("History"), the virtues of the actor ("Self-Reliance"), and the nature of the act itself

("Compensation") were necessary steps in the progression of form as it moved toward its ultimate satisfaction in eloquence. With the exceptions of "Love" and "Friendship," the remaining essays can be said to be a rhetorical inquiry into the nature of agency, or the means by which a self-reliant actor accrues and then wields power.

"Spiritual Laws" introduces this inquiry by turning readers' attention to the psychological (that is, "spiritual") laws that determine human motivation and action. It is, in other words, a study of audience. This fact is often missed by those who interpret the essays as a philosophical treatise. Packer, for instance, argues that "Spiritual Laws" looks "at truth from truth itself, an effort that leads Emerson to write proverbs of the pure Reason."[97] Robinson, meanwhile, claims that the point of the essay is to "call for conformity to the universal laws."[98] But despite occasional passages that sound, as Packer observes, "like fragments of Eastern wisdom," much of the essay is explicitly concerned with defining the ordinary laws that define human thought, motivation, and action.[99] From a rhetorical perspective, the essential spiritual law Emerson defines is this: "A man is a method, a progressive arrangement; a selecting principle, gathering his like to him, wherever he goes."[100] The argumentative purpose of stating this law is to reject Lockean notions of the tabula rasa, which makes the human consciousness into a blank slate that is passively imprinted on by external forces. Following Kant, Emerson makes human consciousness active in determining what aspects of the world are important to consider, leaving the rest in shadow. A person thus "takes only his own, out of the multiplicity that sweeps and circles around him. He is like one of those booms which are set out from the shore on rivers to catch driftwood, or the lodestone among splinters of steel."[101] The point of spiritual laws is thus to help people to understand, predict, and ultimately constitute human attitudes by recognizing the degree to which the a priori faculties of reason and understanding, combined with consciously adopted ideas and principles, make human beings active rather than passive agents in constructing and forming their world in their own image.

The richness of "Spiritual Laws" as a study of human motivation can be seen by tracing three distinct rhetorical consequences of this Kantian position. The first is reminiscent of Plato's advice in the *Phaedrus*—to adapt one's message to the unique character of each soul. Just as every person is born with a different "boom" or "lodestone," so too do different people have different standards of goodness that conform to the world they gather around them. For Emerson, that which "I call right or goodness, is the choice of my constitution; and that which I call heaven, and inwardly aspire after, is the state or circumstance desirable to my constitution; and the action which I in all my years tend to do, is a work for my faculties."[102] The same is true for every other individual. So although this could be read as yet another assertion of personal self-reliance, it is more fruitful to read it as a method by which one can evoke the self-reliance of others in eloquence. The second rhetorical consequence is to understand that power is a result not simply of the expression of what is inside a person but of how those inner faculties interact with outside circumstances. Emerson explains this through two of his favorite historical examples: "There is less intention in history than we ascribe to it. We impute the deep-laid, far-sighted plans to Caesar and Napoleon; but the best of their power was in nature, not in them. Men of an extraordinary success, in their honest moments, have always sung, 'not unto us, not unto us.'" Echoing what he had earlier said in "History," the great figures of history more often than not happen to be in the right place at the right time: "Their success lay in their parallelism to the course of thought, which found in them an unobstructed channel; and the wonders of which they were the visible conductors seemed to the eye their deed."[103] To unlock the powers not only of the self but also of the other thus requires an ability to discern the proper relationship between individual faculties and particular circumstances such that an act of eloquence can inspire an audience to pursue its own definition of "goodness" with force and effectiveness.

That all of these principles have to do with eloquence is made clear when Emerson defines one of the key virtues of the orator—abandonment. Although this recommendation on its face seems to be ironic, namely because his understanding of spiritual laws seem to be moving toward audience identification and adaptation, it actually is central to Emerson's understanding of the unique power of eloquence. This is because those that would presume to know the inner secret of others almost always fall short of the mark and underestimate their true potential, falling back instead on social convention and stereotypes. As he explains, "it is the vice of our public speaking that it has not abandonment. . . . The common experience is, that the man fits himself as well as he can to the customary details of that work or trade he falls into, and tends it as a dog turns a spit. Then is he a part of the machine he moves; the man is lost." But more than the man is lost; the situation is also. In losing the man, one also loses the message that might unlock the latent power of some audience. What should happen is that "not only every orator but every man should let out all the length of all the reins; should find or make a frank and hearty expression of what force and meaning is in him." The result of this act is not only to increase the self-reliance of the orator but also to increase the power in the audience. For "by doing his work, he makes the need felt which he can supply, and creates the taste by which he is enjoyed." In other words only abandonment allows full expression of one's own understanding of goodness in such a way that it can evoke the same appetite in others, or what Emerson terms "taste." As he concludes, "to make habitually a new estimate,—that is elevation."[104] Eloquence thus represents a capacity continually to elevate the tastes of an audience by establishing for them new "selecting principles" that literally remake their worlds and establish in others new aims and desires.

From the study of motives in "Spiritual Laws," Emerson turns toward the study and expression of natural laws in "Prudence." On first impression this essay seems the most explicitly connected with concerns of the classical rhetorical tradition: Emerson begins by defining prudence as "the virtue of the senses," the "science of appearances," and "the outmost action of the inward life."[105] This attention to appearances, as Thomas Farrell has argued, is distantly rhetorical insofar as the primary function of rhetoric at its origin was to give form and make "sense of appearances by expressing them as proposed themes and arguments, inviting decision, action, and judgment."[106] Rhetoric, like prudence, thus shares a mutual concern with, in Emerson's words, "the present time, persons, property, and existing forms" and represents "the art of securing a present well-being."[107] At the same time, he wished to move beyond the typical concerns of rhetoric, which limit themselves to trivial affairs or the latest controversy, focusing attention on those parts of life that are pressing in the moment but not significant in the long term. In this he criticizes what he calls a "base prudence," which represents a "a devotion to matter, as if we possessed no other faculties than the palate, the nose, the touch, the eye and ear," and asks "but one question of any project—Will it bake bread?"[108] Prudence is lifted out of the traditional concerns of rhetoric and into the affairs of eloquence when an orator aspires to a "highest prudence" that "unfolds the beauty of laws within the narrow scope of the senses." Here is found a type of prudence worthy of incorporation into a philosophy of eloquence.[109]

In many ways reminiscent of the "Discipline" chapter of *Nature,* "Prudence" calls for systematic inquiry into the laws of nature in order that these insights can be integrated within eloquence and conveyed to the public so that they might adapt their perceptions and behaviors to the true rhythms of the natural world. In base prudence the immediate data of the senses are taken as the ultimate authorities. This is the reason why sense perception is "the god of sots and cowards, and is the subject of all comedy." True prudence, by contrast, "limits this sensualism by admitting the knowledge of an internal and real world." Rather than dividing up existence into disconnected moments of pleasure and pain, as in base prudence, true prudence does not speculate on the origin and purpose of the world but rather studies "the laws of the world whereby man's being is conditioned, as they are, and keeps these laws, that it may enjoy their proper good." In effect Emerson uses the contrast between base and higher prudence in order to condemn the small-mindedness and superstition of traditional practices and urge their replacement by a more scientific mind-set that demands that everyone "learn that everything in nature, even motes and feathers, go by law and not by luck, and that what he sows, he reaps." The duty of eloquence is to take this knowledge of nature and express it through poetic form so that the laws of nature can be comprehended and acted upon by those otherwise ignorant of the law. In short, "poets should be lawgivers; that is, the boldest lyrical inspiration should not chide and insult, but should announce and lead the civil code, and the day's work."[110] Indicative of the ethos of the nineteenth century, with its market economy, its expanding nationalism, and its empirical science, Emerson's vision of "higher prudence" gives to eloquence the task of delegating the laws that would regulate human health, labor, and household in conformity with the laws of nature.

Whereas "Prudence" had given rhetorical guidance to those reformers who would improve society by bringing its habits in conformity to natural laws, in "Heroism" Emerson steps outside of that ethic to give rhetorical resources to those radicals who would violate the written law in the name of a higher justice. He acknowledges that there are times when one must act even without full knowledge when faced with gross injustice. In its rhetorical character, heroism "speaks the truth, and it is just, generous, hospitable, temperate, scornful of petty calculations, and scornful of being scorned."[111] The character of the hero, Emerson asserts, is thus the opposite of the sober rationalism and self-discipline that characterize bourgeois culture. Heroism thus "feels and never reasons, and is therefore always right"; it shows a "contempt for safety and ease, which makes the attractiveness of war"; it expresses a "self-trust which slights the restraints of prudence in the plenitude of its energy and power to repair the harm that may suffer"; and finally it "works in contradiction to the voice of mankind, and in contradiction, for a time, the voice of the great and the good." In short heroism is the ultimate expression of self-reliance in action, for "heroism is an obedience to a secret impulse of an individual's character." It is "the state of the soul at war, and its ultimate objects are the last defiance of falsehood and wrong, and the power to bear all that can be inflicted by evil agents."[112] In one of the only passages in which Emerson names a contemporary reformer, he holds up the example of Elijah Lovejoy, an abolitionist editor who died defending his press against a mob in Alton, Illinois as an exemplar of heroism: "Human virtue demands her champions and martyrs, and the trial of persecution always proceeds," Emerson writes. "It is but the other day, that the brave Lovejoy gave his breast to the bullets of the mob, for the rights of free speech and opinion, and died when it was better not to live."[113] Prudence thus reaches its limits when the mob comes knocking at the door. Such a situation demands the eloquence that arises in the field of battle when the enemy is joined.

The language of the hero only has power, however, when it speaks with the authority of revelation. This is the central purpose of "The Over-Soul"—to establish a new form of authority for transcendent acts of eloquence. As a substance Emerson disposes of the Over-Soul in one succinct passage. The Over-Soul is that unity "within which every man's particular being is contained and made one with all other; that common heart, of which all sincere conversation is the worship, to which all right action is submission."[114] Despite the title, however, Emerson is less concerned with describing the substance of the Over-Soul than with analyzing it as a communicative encounter with a sublime authority. His essay investigates the value of those rare moments of faith that stand apart from our habitual life, for "there is a depth in those brief moments which constrains us to ascribe more reality to them than to all other experiences."[115] The experiences in which the Over-Soul reveals itself are consequently those times when one is finally able to "go behind nature" to discover the origin of prudent appearances and, perhaps more important, to see the light that inspires impulses of heroism. As Emerson explains, "from within or from behind, a light shines through us upon things, and makes us aware that we are nothing, but the light is all," a light that "is not the intellect or the will, but the master of the intellect and will."[116] Authority thus accrues to eloquence that channels the light of revelation to an audience with ears to hear and eyes to see. For "only by the vision of that Wisdom can the horoscope of the ages be read, and by falling back on our better thoughts, by yielding to the spirit of prophecy which is innate in every man, we can know what it saith. . . . Only itself can inspire whom it will, and behold! their speech shall be lyrical, and sweet, and universal as the rising of the wind."[117] Exemplified by the trances of Socrates, the conversion of Paul, the convulsions of the Quakers, the illumination of Swedenborg, the revival of the Calvinists, and the experiences of the Methodists, this is a kind of speech that communicates the "shudder of awe and delight with which the individual soul always mingles with the universal soul."[118]

If the central chapters of *Essays* can be said to have elliptically provided resources for eloquence by defining human motivation and identifying the situations that call for applied science, courageous resistance, and sublime revelation, the final three essays turn to a more explicit study of the process by which eloquence expresses its power in history. From this reading "Circles" represents his clearest contribution to the understanding of social change, for in this essay Emerson explained what he meant in "History" when he argued that a revolution in one man's thought could be the key to an era: "The key to every man is his thought. Sturdy and defying though he looked, he has a helm which he obeys, which is the idea, after which all his facts are classified. You can only be reformed by showing him a new idea which commands his own. The life of man is a self-evolving circle, which, from a ring imperceptibly small, rushes in all sides outward to new and larger circles and that without end."[119] Here are the insights of "Spiritual Laws" and "History" combined to articulate two of the foundational principles of persuasion—first that genuine reform does not come by attacking the facts and beliefs of the periphery but by reconstituting the selecting principle at the helm of a person's thought; and second that there are no limits to the human capacity for growth, because the possible circumference of thought is as infinite as the universal mind. For against the god of tradition that places limits on all things, the god of rhetoric asserts that "every action admits of being outdone" and that "around every circle another can be drawn; that there is no end in nature, but every end of the beginning; that there is always another dawn risen on mid-noon, and under every deep a lower deep opens."[120] "Circles" thus articulates a progressive view of social change suggested in "History" by which an idea revealed to a single individual gradually spread from mind to mind until they become the source of revolution and the key to an era.

To be sure this pragmatic reading of "Circles" departs from conventional readings of the essay, which focus more on how it articulates Emerson's philosophy of life and self-culture. Bloom, for instance, calls the essay the key to "the glory and sorrow of Emerson, and of our American Romanticism."[121] "Circles" for Bloom celebrates the constant outflow of energy and newness, unconstrained by necessity and always desirous of breaking toward a new horizon and expanding the circumference of one's being. One finds in this essay perhaps the most exemplary expression of that American romanticism that is ready to disregard the past and break into the future: "I am only an experimenter. Do not set the least value on what I do, or the least discredit on what I do not, as if I pretended to settle anything as true or false. I unsettle all things. No facts are to be sacred; none are profane; I simply experiment, an endless seeker, with no Past at my back."[122] Here is that familiar celebration of the self as a source of constant becoming. According to Robinson, "unbounded by the past or by attitude that might tie us to any particular interpretation of the facts before us, this experimenter approaches the world as a series of trials, the results of which are primarily valuable as moments of education."[123] "Circles" can thus be read as a sort of manifesto for Rorty-style acts of constant self-creation, presenting what Emerson calls the "power and courage to make a new road to new and better goals."[124]

The romantic reading of "Circles" overlooks the explicit rhetorical and political orientations of the essay. Its politics, for instance, clearly stands on the side of radical social change. Emerson notes, for instance, the way that the god of tradition constantly reestablishes himself by transforming a live idea into an inert one: "It is the inert effort of each thought, having formed itself into a circular wave of circumstance,—as, for instance, an empire, rules of an art, a local usage, a religious rite,—to heap itself on that ridge, and to solidify and hem." This solidity comes in the form of habits, values, virtues, and expectations, along with its accompanying set of vices, to maintain the boundaries of the negative. In these circumstances new statements are always met with resistance: "The new statement is always hated by the old, and, to those dwelling in the old, comes like an abyss of skepticism." But the force of a new statement, if backed by the authority of truth, inevitably works its way into the social order and forms cracks in the ridges until all resistance "pales and dwindles before the revelation of the new hour." At that point the terrifying realization dawns that "there is no virtue which is final; all are initial." This is what Emerson calls "the terror of reform," a necessary step to the reconstitution of society on the basis of a new revelation: "The terror of reform is the discovery that we must cast away our virtues, or what we have always esteemed such, into the same pit that has consumed our grosser vices."[125] The politics of "Circles" is thus on the side of radicalism, of sweeping away the vestiges of inert ideas and creating a social order that would celebrate rather than fear the birth of a new generalization.

Rhetorically it is the art of generalization that Emerson puts forth as the medium of power that brings forth the terror of reform. "Circles" in this way refers to the circumferences of a generalization. Generalization, he writes, "is always a new influx of the divinity into the mind." True, circles are not necessarily argumentative. Emerson calls the eye a circle, just as the horizon that forms in the mind. The boundaries of property are circles, as are continents and the globe. Nature itself is a series of circles. But for the most part, Emerson describes a circle in logical terms as a way the mind draws boundaries around percepts and concepts that are more or less inclusive. For instance he writes that "conversation is a game of circles." Argumentation is a competitive process whereby a debater "draws a circle outside of his antagonist." Literature is a circle that affords "us a platform whence we make commanding view of our present life, a purchase by which we may move it." And the works of the greatest poet represent a circle that "smites and arouses me with his shrill tones, breaks up my whole chain of habits, and I open my eye on my own possibilities." The most persuasive circle thus represents a communicative generalization that encompasses within its circumference "the very hopes of man, the thoughts of his heart, the religion of nations, [and] the manners and morals of mankind." The lessons for eloquence are thus clear: "The one thing we seek with insatiable desire, is to forget ourselves, to be surprised out of our propriety, to lose our sempiternal memory, and to do something without knowing how or why; in short, to draw a new circle."[126]

"Intellect" naturally follows on the heels of "Circles," because it represents Emerson's analytical treatment of the art of drawing new circles. Although Emerson notes there are two forms of the intellect, "intellect receptive" and "intellect constructive," it is primarily the latter with which he is concerned in this essay, having explored the first already in his discussion of revelation in "The Over-Soul." The intellect constructive is thus the more conscious, deliberative, scientific, and methodological component of intellect that "produces thoughts, sentences, poems, plans, designs, systems." As a result of this methodological emphasis, one does not find in "Intellect" what one would expect from a Transcendentalist, which would be a vague paean to the intuitive faculties much as one finds in "The Over-Soul." Instead one hears the language of Aristotelian rhetoric, which finds in the method of the constructive intellect "a conversion of all nature into the rhetoric of thought, under the eye of judgment, with the strenuous exercise of choice."[127] Yet it is important that the two forms of intellect are not opposed to one another. The receptive intellect is the primary resource for those revelations that provide the principles, values, and ideas on which to build poems, plans, and systems. The constructive intellect is its necessary secondary faculty that builds a symbolic structure on top of the authoritative foundations of revelation and makes them communicable to others.

In classically Aristotelian fashion, Emerson identifies five steps of the method that the constructive intellect employs in creating powerful generalizations —what we might label *detachment, observation, reduction, naming,* and *vigilance.* Detachment provides that freedom from "the considerations of time and place, of you and me, of profit and hurt, [that] tyrannize over most men's minds." It puts one in a state that is "void of affection" and "sees an object as it stands in the light of science, cool and disengaged"; it thus "separates the fact considered from *you,* from all local and personal reference, and discerns it as if it existed for its own sake."[128] By allowing people to step back from what is closest to them, detachment thus allows them to take more in, thus allowing them to expand the circumference of their vision without blindness or bias. Observation then collects and arranges the phenomenon that they are able to include within their field of vision. Observation is no mere looking but systematic inquiry that occurs when people "take pains to observe; when we of set purpose sit down to consider an abstract truth; when we keep the mind's eye open, whilst we converse, whilst we read, whilst we act, intent to learn the secret law of some class of facts."[129] Following acts of observation, reduction then collects all that is observed and "detects intrinsic likeness between remote things, and reduces all things to a few principles."[130] Naming then symbolizes this principle in a word, for truth is impotent without a name: "To make it available, it needs a vehicle or art by which it is conveyed to men. To be communicable, it must become picture or sensible object. We must learn the language of facts."[131] Lastly "neither by detachment, nor by aggregation, is the integrity of intellect transmitted to its works, but by a vigilance which brings the intellect in its greatness and best state to operate every moment." Vigilance thus represents the enduring commitment to give to one's own intellect "the same wholeness which nature has."[132] The method of the constructive intellect is thus not merely a capacity but a way of life, specifically a life dedicated to the discovery and communication of truth by which the universe might reappear in miniature through the vehicle of the word.

If all of the essays thus far have been circling around the question of rhetoric, "Art" finally turns all of their energies in its direction, revealing that the goal all along has been the transformation of genius into practical power through the medium of eloquence. There is more to art than the concise expression of intellectual truth; it must also be imaginative, practical, moral, exhilarating, and creative:

> Art has not yet come to its maturity, if it do not put itself abreast with the most potent influences of the world, if it is not practical and moral, if it do not stand in connection with the conscience, if it do not make the poor and uncultivated feel that it addresses them with a voice of lofty cheer. There is higher work for Art than the arts. . . . Nothing less than the creation of man and nature is its end. A man should find in it an outlet for his whole energy. He may paint and carve only as long as he can do that. Art should exhilarate, and throw down the walls of circumstance on every side, awakening in the beholder the same sense of universal relation and power which the work evinced in the artist, and its highest effect is to make new artists.[133]

There is no longer any need for complex interpretation to show the consequences and relevance of Emerson's conception of art—indeed of his entire philosophy—to eloquence. For the true artist (which he calls the poet) is revealed as a rhetorician of the highest order, an artist who can only become so by having absorbed and put into practice every aspect of Emerson's philosophy. To view one's actions in the light of universal history, to perceive a morality that transcends the limits of prudence, to have a heroic self-reliance to throw down circumstance at every side, to communicate the practical significance of an idea with such eloquence that even the poor and uncultivated receive it with lofty cheer, and to inspire new artists so that one work is carried on with power by members of the next generation—all of these are functions of rhetorical eloquence and represent the consummation of lifelong intellectual and poetic labor. The poet is thus Emerson's symbol of symbols, the emblem of that pattern of experience he believes to be the highest accomplishment of human effort and genius.

To embody fully the pattern of experience of the poet, Emerson relates, requires really only one added skill—that ability "to convey a larger sense by simpler symbols."[134] By no means does this mean using simple words or ideas. It means neither adapting oneself to the beliefs of the time nor speaking to people as if they were children. It means that "the artist must employ the symbols in use in his day and nation, to convey his enlarged sense to his fellow men."[135] Tracing out more fully the consequences of the theory of language he had articulated in *Nature*, Emerson in effect recommends to artists to find the symbols that refer to the everyday objects and experience of a nation, most notably those natural phenomena that themselves correspond to a wider meaning and significance. In this way the new idea can take on the clothing of something older and familiar such that its novelty will not make it appear as a monster. Thus "the new in art is always formed out of the old. The Genius of the Hour sets his ineffaceable seal on the work, and gives it an inexpressible charm for the imagination."[136] The poet thus uses the old as a vehicle for the expression of the new and appeals not only to the intellect but also to the imagination of an audience so that they might witness the beauty and comprehend the possibility of circumstances they might never have truly considered.

Yet Emerson adds a qualification to this strategy for those who would try, literally, to squeeze all of the world's complexity into a single work of art. Even the greatest genius cannot accomplish such a task. In yet another application of spiritual laws, Emerson reminds readers that the mind only expresses power through selectivity, not totality. Humanity is "immersed in beauty, but our eyes have no clear vision." That does not mean that one can reveal the entirety of beauty with one eloquent gesture. The revelation of the world's beauty is progressive and incremental: "Until one thing comes out from the connection of things, there can be enjoyment, contemplation, but no thought. Our happiness and unhappiness are unproductive. The infant lies in a pleasing trance, but his individual character and his practical power depend on his daily progress in the separation of things, and dealing with one at a time."[137] Just as one gives power to an infant by exposing him or her to one thing at a time, so too does one empower citizens in the public: "it is a habit of certain minds to give all excluding fulness to the object, the thought, the word, they alight upon, and to make that for the time the deputy of the world. These are the artists, the orators, the leaders of society."[138] To be able to discern and communicate the truth is one thing; to be able to communicate it with power and make it the deputy of the world is quite another.

The true orator thus not only conveys a larger sense through simple symbols, but also does so with the right symbol at the right time when people are capable of comprehending it and acting upon it with the full force of their character. Thus Emerson arrives at the conclusion, in which he sums up the aim at which he had been driving at for the whole collection of essays. In "Self-Reliance" he had mentioned that "the voyage of the best ship is a zigzag line of a hundred tacks. See the line from a sufficient distance, and it straightens itself to the average tendency."[139] *Essays* follows this same rule, but as Emerson reaches the end, he lets the tendency be known. What is the key to power? "The power to detach, and to magnify by detaching, is the essence of rhetoric in the hands of the orator and the poet. This rhetoric, or power to fix the momentary eminency of an object,—so remarkable in Burke, in Byron, in Carlyle,—the painter and sculptor exhibit in color and in stone. The power depends on the depth of the artist's insight of that object he contemplates. For every object has its roots in central nature, and may of course be so exhibited to us as to represent the world. Therefore, each work of genius is the tyrant of the hour, and concentrates attention on itself."[140]

Rhetorical power for Emerson is thus tyrannical without being totalistic; it dominates attention in an hour, drawing everything to itself for that time. With each new work of genius, "for the time, it is the only thing worth naming, to do that,—be it a sonnet, an opera, a landscape, a statue, and oration, the plan of a temple, of a campaign, or of a voyage of discovery. . . . For it is the right and property of all natural objects, of all genuine talents, of all native properties whatsoever, to be for their moment the top of the world." Yet no sooner had someone thought an object or property to be supreme, prepared to throw themselves wholly into some project or campaign, when it is overthrown by a new tyrant: "presently we pass to some other object, which rounds itself into a whole, as did the first."[141] The key to power is thus being able to seize the *kairos* of the moment and concentrate attention on one part of the whole, content with the fact that it is but a part but nonetheless confident that, over time, "from this succession of excellent objects, we learn at last the immensity of the world, the opulence of human nature, which can run out to infinity in any direction."[142] The essays conclude back where they began—trusting that eloquence over time will progressively disclose the universal laws of history and thus continually unlock the keys to the era that will culminate in the unending pursuit of power.

When *Essays* was published, even his consistent critic Brownson praised the work. Writing in the *Boston Quarterly Review,* he declared that "he who reads it will find, that he is no longer what he was. A new and higher life has quickened in him, and he can never again feel, that he is merely a child of time and space, but that he is transcendent and immortal."[143] This was precisely the experience Emerson wished to produce—a transcendent experience of reidentification that detaches readers from their connection with the ordinary and makes them consubstantial with the infinite. But while Brownson praised the mythic component of *Essays,* he also was an astute enough critic to identify the underlying ideological commitments that pervaded the work. His one complaint about the essays was "the little importance they assigned to the state, and the low rank they allow to patriotism as a virtue." Emerson had heroically defended eloquence as a medium of power often neglected by the multitude, but at the same time he had implied that eloquence was enough. For Brownson, however, it was not. The perfection of society also "depends on the right organization of the commonwealth," which means that "the science of politics, when rightly viewed, is a grand and an essential science, and needs always to be held in honor."[144] In *Essays* Emerson had offered only disdain at the workings of government and partisan politics, suggesting instead that the organization of the commonwealth would follow naturally the leadings of eloquence. His politics amounted to a rejection of government and its replacement by the leadership of genius.

Brownson's review is notable because at the same time that he praises Emerson, he also sees past his mythic narrative and reveals the ideology of nineteenth-century liberalism that ran like a current through his writing. At the heart of this ideology, writes Dolan, is a tendency to "pit freedom against equality," particularly when a call for equality was used by reformers such as Brownson to advocate aggressive leveling policies of property redistribution. Echoed in other nineteenth-century authors such as Alexis de Tocqueville and John Stuart Mill, "liberal political thought and practice was increasingly pervaded by profound anxiety about equality and a compensatory emphasis on freedom as a value that would provide a bulwark against the leveling tendencies of mass democracy."[145] According to George Kateb, "Emerson's guiding sense [was] that society is a means for the end of individuals" and that "democracy is the set of political arrangements that provide the protections and encouragements to become individuals, rather than servants of society."[146] Consequently, as Brownson correctly noted, Emerson's ideal liberal culture was to minimize the influence of both society and government so as to support the flourishing of the individual—even if it came at the expense of increasing social inequality. Yet Emerson appealed to Brownson because his liberalism was rarely made explicit and in fact was often expressed with the voice of radicalism and dissent. As Sacvan Bercovitch observes, "the appeal of Emersonian dissent lies in an extraordinary conjunction of forces: its capacity to absorb the radical communitarian vision it renounces, and its capacity to be nourished by the liberal structure it resists."[147] Unlike Brownson, whose ideology suffocated his mythic voice, Emerson always kept his liberalism at bay so that the power of his mythic vision could do its work.

Yet there is one passage in which his liberal ideology was given full voice. It occurs at the end of *Essays* when he turns his attention to the specific circumstances of the United States as it moved toward the middle of the nineteenth century, a nation whose technological and organizational innovations were preparing it to become the greatest power the world had ever seen. A poet was required who was able to create those symbols that could truly harness all of the latent power not only of the people but also of their tools and techniques. Echoing the Whig vision of the nation as a continually expanding organism driven by capitalistic entrepreneurialism, Emerson thus concludes *Essays* on this final prophetic sentiment in "Art":

It is in vain that we look for genius to reiterate its miracles in the old arts; it is its instinct to find beauty and holiness in new and necessary facts, in the field and road-side, in the shop and mill. Proceeding from a religious heart it will raise to a divine use the railroad, the insurance office, the joint-stock company, our law, our primary assemblies, our commerce, the galvanic battery, the electric jar, the prism, and the chemist's retort, in which we seek now only an economical use. Is not the selfish and even cruel aspect which belongs to our great mechanical works,—to mills, railways, and machinery,—the effect of the mercenary impulses which these works obey? When its errands are noble and adequate, a steamboat bridging the Atlantic between Old and New England, and arriving at its ports with the punctuality of a planet, is a step of man into harmony with nature. The boat at St. Petersburgh, which plies along the Lena by magnetism, needs little to make it sublime. When science is learned in love, and its powers are wielded by love, they will appear the supplements and continuations of the material creation.[148]

In the end, then, Emerson transcended the politics of his Whig allies just as Brownson had done with the Democrats. The Whigs, inspired by Henry Clay's "American System," had endeavored to use the power of the federal government to expand the vibrancy of the market economy through enhanced communication and transportation networks built by joint stock companies funded by loans from a national bank. To this endeavor Emerson threw his support, but with the caveat that the goal was not simply the enhancement of profit, but also the constitution of a unified nation inspired by love and motivated by possibilities of beauty and power. This was a timely message, as the Whigs had just taken the White House in 1840. Perhaps now was the moment, Emerson thought, when the tides would turn against conservatism and the nation would finally recognize its own Transcendentalist calling as the pioneer of a new age.

Yet the lasting impact of Emerson's eloquence transcends the expression of this provincial ideology. *Essays* has endured as a work of art because the experience of reading it is exemplary of the rhetorical impact of the type of eloquence he holds up as an ideal. Against the conformity of mass society, the determinism of cynical religion, the materialism of physical science, and the sheer nihilism of contemporary politics, Emerson evokes in his readers a belief in what Arendt calls "the fact of natality, through which the human world is constantly invaded by strangers, newcomers whose actions and reactions cannot be foreseen by those who are already there and are going to leave in a short while." Emerson, despite all of his talk of history and the Over-Soul, does not posit a universe that is already formed; rather, as in "Circles," he throws readers into a universe of constant becoming in which action, in the sense of beginning a new story, is always possible. Emerson thus reminds readers that, in Arendt's words, "each new generation, indeed every new human being as he inserts himself between an infinite past and an infinite future, must discover and ploddingly pave it anew." But as was intimated at the beginning of this chapter, what truly inspires acts of greatness is a constant striving for a kind of immortality, for "immortality is what nature possesses without effort and without anybody's assistance, and immortality is what the mortals therefore must try to achieve if they want to live up to the world into which they were born, to live up to the things which surround them and in whose company they are needed for a short while."[149] Emersonian eloquence makes a symbol out of nature to inspire readers to its perfection, daring to resist those merely human voices that remind of human finitude by proclaiming the possibility of immortality in history.

CHAPTER 5

"The cause of tyranny and wrong everywhere the same"

The Revolutionary Nationalism of Margaret Fuller

Could we succeed, really succeed, combine a deep religious love with practical development, the achievements of Genius with the happiness of the multitude, we might believe Man had now reached a commanding point in his ascent, and would stumble and faint no more. Then there is this horrible cancer of Slavery, and the wicked War, that has grown out of it. How dare I speak of these things here? I listen to the same arguments against the emancipation of Italy, that are used against the emancipation of our blacks; the same arguments in favor of the spoliation of Poland as for the conquest of Mexico. I find the cause of tyranny and wrong everywhere the same,—and lo! My Country the darkest offender, because with the least excuse, foresworn to the high calling with which she was called,—no champion of the rights of men, but a robber and a jailor; the scourge hid behind her banner; her eyes fixed, not on the stars, but on the possessions of other men.

Margaret Fuller, "New and Old World Democracy," 1847

Sometime toward the end of 1847—the same year Emerson began his second trip to England—Margaret Fuller sent a dispatch to Horace Greeley's *New-York Daily Tribune* from Rome to offer "a few New-Year's reflections." These reflections were not intended to flatter her American readership. Even before accusing the United States of being the darkest offender of tyranny and wrong, she had taken the time to divide Americans abroad into three different species, two of which stood out for their utter depravity. There was the "servile American—a being utterly shallow, thoughtless, worthless," who "comes abroad to spend his money and indulge his tastes"; and then there was "the conceited American, instinctively bristling and proud of—he knows not what." Only the "thinking American" comes in for praise, the one who recognizes "the immense advantage of being born to a new world and on a virgin soil, yet does not wish one seed from the past to be lost," and so becomes "anxious to gather and carry back with him all that will bear a new climate in new culture." Such Americans were few and far between; as scarce, perhaps, as any thinking individual in Western history. For even if one has the capacity to think, what motive do events give for the one who would seek reason, meaning, and value in history? Time and again history narrates "a crashing of the mass of men beneath the feet of a few, and these, too, of the least worthy," such that with "so little achieved for Humanity as a whole, such tides of war and pestilence intervening to blot out the traces of each triumph, that no wonder the strongest soul sometimes pauses aghast!"[1] So too would Fuller eventually stand aghast as 1848 approached, when the whole of Europe would be torn by revolution and her own country would disappoint her yet again.

Fuller remained a Transcendentalist to the end. She never lost faith that the achievements of individual genius, motivated by a deep religious love would inspire practical development and culminate in the happiness of the multitude. Looking around her, she had every right to despair: "See this hollow England, with its monstrous wealth and cruel poverty, its conventional life, and low, practical aims! see this poor France, so full of talent, so adroit, yet so shallow and glossy still, which could not escape from a false position with all its baptism of blood! see that lost Poland, and this Italy bound down by treacherous hands in all the force of genius! see Russia with its brutal Czar and innumerable slaves! see Austria and its royalty that represents nothing, and its people, who, as people, are and have nothing!" Yet even in the face of so much brutality, cowardice, and suffering, Fuller found reason for optimism: "Still Europe toils and struggles with her idea, and, at this moment, all things bode and declare a new outbreak of the fire, to destroy old palaces of crime! May it fertilize also many vineyards!" Typical of the Transcendentalists, she finds the motivating force for such a new era in youth: "It is to the youth that Hope addresses itself, to those who yet burn with aspiration, who are not hardened in their sins." She wrote not to the mass of servile and conceited Americans but to the "thinking" youth of America: "To these, the heart of my country, a Happy New Year!"[2] Such was the voice that readers back in the United States heard in what Packer has called "one of the most absorbing, brilliant, and far-ranging of all texts written by the Transcendentalists."[3]

To follow the rhetorical development of Margaret Fuller is to challenge at every point the conventional portrayal of the Transcendentalists as dreamy idealists writing opaque encomiums to their private experiences in pastoral Massachusetts. In her dispatches from Italy during the Italian revolution of 1848, Fuller placed transcendental eloquence on the global stage, lashing out against the cause of tyranny and wrong that was everywhere the same, criticizing the United States for the same barbarity that she saw in Europe, and championing the rights of all people—not only individuals but entire nations—to pursue self-determination and tap into the sources of their own unique genius that would give them both beauty and power. According to Jeffrey Steele, Fuller's dispatches exhibit a voice completely distinct among the Transcendentalists for realizing that "imaginary pathways of illumination could be utilized for national, not just personal, transformation." To be sure, in her early years, under the influence of Emerson, she pursued a similar ideal of individual self-culture, although she soon endeavored to extend "the promise of personal liberation to women," most notably in her 1845 book *Woman in the Nineteenth Century*. But as the circumference of her world expanded through her work as a journalist for Greeley's *Tribune*, she soon began to imagine "a new, revitalized nation that might extend the promise of democracy to its forgotten and silenced inhabitants." By the time she was writing from Italy, this promise of democracy had expanded to all peoples and all nations. For Steele this shift in "Fuller's vision cannot be overemphasized, for it represented a pivotal displacement from an ideal of personal transformation, modeled in part on Emersonian self-reliance, to a revolutionary model of national transformation that was unique among her American contemporaries."[4] In short Fuller demonstrated how the discourse of Transcendentalism could be used to develop a rhetoric of revolutionary nationalism that critiqued the structures of domination and constituted power through collective action.

Fuller's later writings demonstrate how Emersonian-style eloquence evolved as the world of the writer became not only broader in circumference in the abstract but also more attuned to the actual complexities, challenges, and struggles of present historical circumstances. As a woman facing the constraints of the growing "Cult of True Womanhood" in the nineteenth century, Fuller had from her youth already "learned the painful lesson that self-development could be facilitated or hindered by others."[5] From the beginning she developed a critical perspective that attuned her to the way power was diffused throughout society and complicated Emerson's call for a genius of pure and uninhibited creativity. The result was her first major work, "The Great Lawsuit," which used eloquence to map the specific challenges faced by women in a world that wished to constrain them within a narrow domestic sphere. But as Fuller's world expanded, so did the scope and form of her writing. The narrative of her journey across the upper Midwest, *Summer on the Lakes*, demonstrated such a careful eye for detail that she was soon recruited by Greeley to be a reporter and then an editor for the *Tribune*. Exposed now to the tumultuous urban landscape of New York, including not only its beautiful works of art but it prisons, workhouses, and asylums, Fuller began to drift away from Emersonian eloquence and develop a more journalistic form of rhetorical advocacy that spoke the language of fact of which Emerson often seemed so contemptuous. By the time she was writing from Italy, Fuller developed a powerful rhetorical voice that addressed not the ages but the age.

Fuller's writing integrates within transcendental eloquence the strategies of critique now associated with Michel Foucault. According to Raymie McKerrow, these strategies represent a kind of "critical rhetoric" whose "aim is to understand the integration of power/knowledge in society—what possibilities for change the integration invites or inhibits and what integration strategies might be considered appropriate to effect social change." Foucault is useful in interpreting Fuller's rhetoric because he introduced a more structural conception of power than the one offered by Emerson. For Foucault power is always relational, regulated by forms of knowledge and conceptions of truth, and is not simply localized in a sovereign authority but distributed throughout society. Power exists neither as an expression of individual capacity nor a direct action of domination or resistance; rather it "is a set of actions brought to bear upon possible actions; it incites, it induces, it seduces, it makes easier or more difficult; it releases or contrives, makes more probable or less; in the extreme, it constrains or forbids absolutely, but it is always a way of acting upon one or more acting subjects by virtue of their acting or being capable of action. A set of actions upon other actions."[6] To critique power is thus not simply to condemn it or even to resist it; it means to reveal the complex relationship among truth, power, and the subject, between established facts, principles, procedures, and the practical systems of encouragement and constraint that establish accepted forms of subjectivity. Critique, then, "is the movement by which the subject gives himself the right to question truth on its effects of power and question power on its discourses of truth." Critique forces truth and power to make an account of itself while at the same time opening up a "field of possibles, of openings, indecisions, reversals, and possible dislocations" that foster expressions of power as Emerson understood it—only not simply as individual overcoming but as the continual growth of a collective.[7]

Fuller thus created a multilayered rhetorical performance that simultaneously critiqued the dominant social structure of power and articulated possibilities for new individual and collective identities. This rhetorical strategy was similar to that of Brownson, but substantively it was completely different. Whereas Brownson concentrated on the concerns of only one class and had difficulty seeing beyond the narrow circumference of his own experience and ideological commitments, Fuller possessed, like Alcott, a thoroughly dialogical imagination that integrated multiple voices while at the same time endeavoring to construct a form of identification inclusive enough for all and yet which preserved the liberty of the individual. This was an ambitious and arguably impossible goal, and yet one she pursued with passionate intensity. The result, according to Christina Zwarg, was that she anticipated the trends of modern cultural criticism that trace "the radical dispersion of power in the variety of discourses through which we make our daily negotiations." For her "Fuller's critical writings reveal an awareness of the complex overlay of ideological frames through which we are forced to read our lives, as well as a willingness to shift those frames in order to make some conversation or translation between them possible."[8] By continually juxtaposing the real against the ideal, the present against the past, the individual against the social, the marginal against the dominant, the local against the universal, and the conflicted against the transcendent, Fuller constructed a rhetoric that used a strategy of "double vision" by which life was measured against a "vision of idealized alternatives" and thereby generated in her audience that combination of dissatisfaction and desire necessary for a politics of transcendence.[9]

On December 25, 1819, nine-year-old Sarah Margaret Fuller wrote a letter to her father, Timothy Fuller, who was then beginning his second term as a US congressman from Massachusetts. Although forced to live away from home for half the year when Congress was in session, he had told his daughter that he expected regular correspondence updating him on the "diligence" with which she pursued her studies and the "considerable progress" she was making on her work.[10] Fuller proudly complied. "I enclose you my composition and specimen of writing," she boasted. "I assure you I wrote the former off much better and made *almost* as many corrections as your critical self would were you at home." Yet despite her triumph on her composition, she confessed that all had not been accomplished that she had wished: "Write My Deserted Village goes on slowly. I have only translated a page and a half. However I am determined to finish it before New Years day which is about six days from this time." Still she had been keeping up with her reading and had started "a novel of the name of Hesitation. Do not let the name novel make you think it is either trifling or silly. A great deal of sentiment a great deal of reasoning is contained in it. In other words it is a moral-novel." After some description of the plot and a few updates about what her brothers wanted for Christmas, she signed off, "I am your affectionate daughter. SARAH-MARGARET FULLER."[11]

Of what she wrote to her father, the most telling about her life was her lament about the slow work on her translation. Before he left, her father had given her a copy of a popular eighteenth-century pastoral elegy by the Irish poet Oliver Goldsmith called "The Deserted Village." Written in 1770, the 430-line poem narrates the decline and eventual disappearance of the culture of the rural countryside, as independent small farmers were either moved off their land or had their property absorbed within large landowning estates by the process of enclosure. A scathing critique of the pursuit of wealth, international trade, urban corruption, and consumerism, the poem presented a stark contrast between agrarian virtue and industrial vice.

> Ill fares the land, to hastening ills a prey,
> Where wealth accumulates, and men decay:
> Princes and lords may flourish, or may fade;
> A breath can make them, as a breath has made;
> But a bold peasantry, their country's pride,
> When once destroyed, can never be supplied.

Even though virtually the entire poem functions as a kind of dirge, the poet does not lose faith; at the end he reveals "the power of the poet to defend truth." Thus all it not lost:

> Still let thy voice, prevailing over time,
> Redress the rigours of the inclement clime;
> Aid slighted truth with thy persuasive strain,
> Teach erring man to spurn the rage of gain.[12]

The rage of gain may destroy a village, a people, or an empire, but it can never silence truth when poets aid it with persuasive strain and bestow upon it a self-dependent power that can resist the decay of time. Whether or not the message resonated with young Fuller is impossible to know, but the spirit of the closing lines reappeared in her own writings decades later.

At nine years old, however, she was perhaps more concerned with the task at hand—translating "The Deserted Village" into Latin. This was not an unusual request. As the first child of Timothy and Margarett Crane Fuller, born on March 23, 1810, she was their only surviving child until the birth of her brother, Eugene, in 1815. Consequently she received the full force and attention of her ambitious and disciplined father during these years, during which (according to Fuller's autobiographical sketch) "he helped to make me the heir of all he knew." By age three he had taught her to read, and soon after, she reflected, she was "put at once under discipline of considerable severity, and, at the same time, had a more than ordinary high standard presented to me. . . . Thus I had tasks given me, as many and various as the hours would allow, and on subjects beyond my age; with the additional disadvantage of reciting to him in the evening, after he returned from his office." The reading list was rigorous and extensive. She was explicitly forbidden from reading popular novels or plays (such as *Hesitation*), which Timothy thought were distracting and frivolous. Fuller recalled her father's hostile reaction, for instance, one Sunday when she found a volume of Shakespeare: "Shakespeare,—that won't do; that's no book for Sunday; put it away and take another." By age six she had begun to read Latin: "I was expected to understand the mechanism of the language thoroughly, and in translating to give the thoughts in as few well-arranged words as possible, and without breaks or hesitation,—for with these my father had aptly no patience." Timothy Fuller's tutelage continued even after his election to Congress. For years thereafter he would continue to instruct his daughter and request update on her progress. In a letter to him in May 1824, Fuller complained that she had been reading Warren Colburn's arithmetic and felt herself "rather degraded from Cicero's Oratory to One and two are how many. It *is* a change is it not?"[13] Having spent so much time with her imagination in Ancient Rome with its orators, it was always difficult for Fuller to attend to such incidental matters as the sum of one and two.

Of all the Transcendentalists, Fuller stands out for having been the only one whose primary influence on her intellectual life was her father. Both Brownson's and Emerson's fathers had died young, and Alcott's father was quiet, mild-tempered, and loving but hardly a source of intellectual stimulation. Fuller thus received from Timothy Fuller what Emerson had gotten from his aunt—an intense early education in literature, philosophy, and the classics—but without the passionate, eclectic, argumentative style of Mary Moody. Timothy Fuller was not a Puritan mystic but a Unitarian lawyer and a believer in Thomas Jefferson's "natural aristocracy." The key to public success was not spiritual nonconformity but strict Armenian self-discipline. According to Joan von Mehren, "as a convinced Jeffersonian, Timothy Fuller believed that for the first time in history virtue and talent were to be rewarded and sanctioned by a national government." His rigid self-discipline had, by the time of his daughter's birth, been rewarded with public office, and so "to qualify Margaret to continue in the high rank he had earned for her as a daughter of the republic, she was to be carefully trained from early childhood."[14] Rare for fathers of his age, he thus showed his love for his daughter by measuring her by the same standards as he would if she were his son and heir, holding her to account for meeting those standards at the price of his censure and disapproval. A note to Fuller when she was ten years old made his attitude explicit. He had offered to buy her a piano, but only if she would promise to dedicate herself to its mastery: "To excel in all things should be your constant aim," he wrote; "mediocrity is obscurity."[15]

The high expectations of her father came at a price, however. Fuller's father was, she recounted, a "severe teacher" and would often rouse her from sleep after he returned from work—sometimes after ten o'clock at night—at which point they would spend hours going over her reading and writing. The consequence, Fuller reflected, "was a premature development of the brain, that made me a 'youthful prodigy' by day, and by night a victim of spectral allusions, nightmare, and somnambulism, which at the time prevented the harmonious development of my bodily powers and checked my growth, while, later, they induced continual headaches, weakness and nervous affections, of all kinds."[16] The house of Timothy Fuller was not a place of freedom. Despite his apparently emancipated spirit, he habitually treated women either as objects or subjects—objects of sexual interest in his public relationships (namely with the wives of other congressmen) and subjects of his command in his private relationships with his wife and children within his patriarchal household. Meg McGavran Murray observes that "Timothy Fuller's pattern of conduct with women seem to have been to demand that they comply with his demands—which were not always honorable—and then to lecture them if they defied him."[17] His wife's protestations that he talked excessively about the women he met in Washington thus inevitably sparked a lecture about her needing to be a more "agreeable, dutiful wife"—a demand that Margarett Crane seemed willing to accommodate by playing the submissive and supportive role celebrated in the nineteenth century.[18] What made Fuller special was that she became both subject and object to her father, subject to his rigid discipline and perfectionist ideals while also being an object of his affections in a way that had elements of sexual flirtation. According to Murray Fuller's father "aroused in her strong feelings, some of which were no doubt erotic in the polymorphous way a child experiences sexual desire as a generalized craving that can be excited and gratified in a number of ways."[19] The challenge for Fuller was to transcend the limits of being a subject or an object and become an agent with her own judgments, will, and desires.

That Fuller did eventually craft one of the most distinctive individual personalities of the nineteenth century does not necessarily validate the methods of her father; certainly she never fully accepted them. But it cannot be denied that the tensions with which Fuller wrestled within the family household were central to her understanding of the tensions inherent in the nineteenth century itself. For at the core of Timothy Fuller's attitude toward his daughter was a central contradiction characteristic of his age—the tension between individual power and social role. On the one hand, being a Unitarian and a believer in Jefferson's natural aristocracy, he strove to cultivate in his daughter all of the Armenian virtues of self-reliance, self-discipline, wisdom, independence, and ambition that would outfit her to be a member of the new intellectual and moral elite. On the other hand, being an upholder of an emerging system of patriarchal values suited to a rising market economy, he demanded that even his precocious daughter limit herself to the confinements of her gender while at the same time enforcing a rigid chastity that made discussions of her sexuality taboo. For many years the result was a vigorous intellectual training that had as its primary function not to fit her for any particular profession or to give her a meaningful and intimate social life but rather to allow her to write flattering letters to her father while he was away in Washington.

To understand the unique pressures that Margaret was under, it is important to acknowledge the degree to which Timothy Fuller's attitudes toward sexuality was in line with the conventions of the nineteenth century, conventions that stood in stark contrast to those of the prior century's more dominant agrarian subsistence culture. The patriarchal family, of course, was nothing new, nor were limitations on women's political, social, and sexual freedom. But the patriarchal family of the rural United States was made up of a large family living and working together on a farm and usually socializing with other families in the same community. With respect to labor, the women were as necessary as the men to the operation of the farm, since the sphere of domestic life was included within the larger sphere of economic production. But the market revolution had begun to transform these norms in radical ways by the time Margaret Fuller was coming of age. As exemplified by the lifestyle of her father, whose profession as a lawyer made him spend long hours away from home while at the office, the defining social characteristic of the market economy was a clear separation between the household and the workplace, a separation that "created a male public world of competitive production sundered from a female domestic world of altruistic reproduction."[20] To maximize their efficiency in the market, men had to be effectively atomized and then reorganized according to the rules of the market dictated by the logic of profit. Women were thus deprived of their "autonomous sphere of authority and respect in household production," while at the same time they were "called upon to provide the love, tranquility, and socially invisible domestic labor needed by men pushing themselves to the limit of effort."[21] In other words women went from being junior partners in the management of the family farm to being obedient supporters of the autonomous labor of a husband who made the solitary domestic sphere their sole responsibility.

Out of this situation arose the twin cults of the true man and the true woman that radically redefined gender roles during the 1820s and 1830s. On the one hand, the intense pressures of conforming to the demands of the market economy created the new ideal of the businessman that embodied middle-class ideology, which promised to reward "each according to effort."[22] True manhood was thus no longer associated with physical strength, sexual prowess, or even property, name, or title; it became synonymous instead with self-repressive norms that "pushed egoism to extremes of aggression, calculation, self-control, and unremitting effort." The true man, in other words, was one who could control his urges and channel all of his energies toward maximizing productivity and profit. On the other hand, the demands placed upon the true man produced an image of true womanhood as its necessary counterpart, for "True Men could sustain this gender-wrenching only by wrenching True Women to opposite extremes of altruism and submission. Buffeted by the world's fierce competition, they could brook no competition at home. A masculinity tested daily by competitive males required a domestic domain of unquestioned mastery."[23] The true woman was thus seen as "weak, selfless, and pure," a figure made by God to support men in their labors, to embody ideals of purity, and to be contented within the confined walls of domestic isolation and male authority.[24]

The household in which Fuller was raised represented a perfect example of what Foucault later described as the process of "transforming sex into discourse" and thereby into a phenomenon to be carefully regulated through the workings of power. Against the notion that this kind of nineteenth-century discourse about sexuality was primarily repressive, Foucault suggests that in fact sex was talked about more than ever before and became the subject of sermons, scientific tracts, legal restrictions, and home medical manuals. This is because sexuality now had become a subject and expression of power that had to be regulated and controlled to serve the needs of the rising bourgeoisie. On the one hand, frivolous or self-gratifying practices of sexuality in men became a vice primarily because the pressures of the marketplace demanded that one "avoid any useless 'expenditure,' any wasted energy, so that all forces were reduced to labor capacity alone." On the other hand, female sexuality became almost entirely harnessed for the purposes of reproduction, including "conjugality" and the "regulated fabrication of children." In short "the primary concern was not repression of the sex of the classes to be exploited, but rather the body, vigor, longevity, progeniture, and descent of the classes that 'ruled.' This was the purpose for which the deployment of sexuality was first established, as a new distribution of pleasures, discourses, truths, and powers."[25] As Sellers sums it up in the context of nineteenth-century America, "through a new sexual politics of erotic guilt and asexual love, families reconstructed themselves for self-repressive effort."[26]

Those looking to Fuller's early life to understand the origins of her conceptions of gender and the power should thus avoid placing too much emphasis on the sovereignty of her father. Although she would never have become the person she was without his influence, in terms of his attitudes toward sexuality, Timothy Fuller was simply the most visible manifestation of an entire network of power that constituted and regulated sexuality in the early nineteenth century. According to Foucault this type of power does not emanate from a single point but rather existed as the "multiplicity of force relations immanent in the sphere in which they operate and which constitute their own organization." Fuller was a subject of power not only to her father and the state, but also to the actions of her mother and siblings, the physical design of the household, the clothes she wore, the books she read and was restricted from reading, the way she was taught to understand her own body, the school she had access to, and the speech patterns that were acceptable in mixed company. Power, being everywhere, can thus be interpreted for Foucault in four interconnected ways: "as the process which, through ceaseless struggles and confrontations, transforms, strengthens, or reverses them; as the support which these force relations find in one another, thus forming a chain or a system, or on the contrary, the disjunctions and contradictions which isolate them from one another; as the strategies in which they take effect, whose general design or institutional crystallization is embodied in the state apparatus, in the formation of the law, and the various social hegemonies; and lastly, as the multiplicity of force relations immanent in the sphere in which they operate and which constitute their own organization."[27] Most important, power should be seen as something organized and structured by discourse; for it is only in discourse that a multiplicity of individual actors within a society can coordinate and authorize a network of practices of the complexity and scope of sexuality. Fuller's education in power of came from her ability to discern the pressures and confrontations, the combinations and contradictions, the strategies and weaknesses of a system of power and knowledge that sought to cultivate her as a strong woman while restricting her firmly to a narrow sphere of action.

The contradictions within this system of power readily became apparent to Fuller. As tidy as this gender division seemed on the surface—in which "men were supposed to be active, autonomous, intellectual, and hence masculine, and women passive, family oriented, sentimental, and hence feminine"—Fuller began to cross these lines at a young age in part because of the contradictions inherent in her father's attitudes.[28] Timothy Fuller was a quintessential nineteenth-century man who enforced rigid obedience at home from his women in order to help strengthen himself for enduring the competitive environment of law and then of governance—all the while talking obsessively about his own sexuality and that of other women he associated with in public. Yet at the same time, he instilled in his daughter the virtues of intellectual rigor and personal autonomy that he felt were necessary for her to carry on the family legacy as the first child. So even after Fuller began her formal schooling at the elite Boston Lyceum for Young Ladies, where she received one of the best educations available to women at the time, her father "continued to insist that his daughter excel not only in her studies, a pursuit then seen by society as masculine, but also in her feminine deportment."[29] He reconciled this tension in his mind by believing that her intellectual powers could be put to use helping "homeschool her younger siblings, in particular her brothers," thus maximizing the family's resources to advance its prosperity.[30] But Fuller quickly came to chafe at the limits placed upon women in the nineteenth century, seeking full expression of those so-called masculine characteristics that her father had helped cultivate in her in recognition of her unique intellectual gifts.

Early evidence that Fuller was not fit for the feminine role she was being asked to play came in the form of an exaggerated "air of bravado" that she took on as she entered her teenage years.[31] Tall for her age, heavyset, and suffering from a skin condition that caused her face to break out, she decided to overemphasize that part of her personality that clearly superseded all of her peers in excellence —her intellectual exuberance. As she later recalled, "my parents were much mortified to see the fineness of my complexion destroyed. My own vanity was for a time severely wounded, but I recovered and made up my mind to be bright and ugly."[32] Soon nicknamed "Germanicus" by her friend Henry Hedge because of the breadth of her knowledge of European literature and philosophy, Fuller took to mixing with college students and "flaunting her ready wit and mental attainments" in mixed company of adults whenever possible—to the extent that her family began "complaining that Margaret was making a spectacle of herself."[33] Indeed her belief in her own importance was so high that, when the Marquis de Lafayette made a triumphant return to the United States and attended a ceremony at Bunker Hill to which the Fullers were invited, fifteen-year-old Fuller wrote him a personal letter, concluding on this note: "Sir the contemplation of a character such as yours fills the soul with a noble ambition. Should we both live, and it is possible to a female, to whom the avenues of glory are seldom accessible, I shall recall my name to your recollection."[34] Clearly a humble domestic life of a true woman was not in the cards for Fuller. As an early teen she had already formed an identity for herself that was consubstantial with a French military hero.

What finally solidified her ambition to be more than the precocious daughter of Timothy Fuller, however, was her admission into the circle of the young Boston intelligentsia that would be associated with the Transcendentalist movement a decade later. After a few years at Prescott's Young Ladies' Seminary at Groton, Connecticut, Fuller was called back home to assist her mother in the domestic sphere while finishing her studies in Greek and Latin at the Port School in Boston. When she had time to study between tutoring her brothers and assisting her mother around their new, more luxurious home her father had purchased, called "Dana Mansion," she set for herself a rigorous plan of study. Relying on her network of friends to acquire books (as women could not have an Athenaeum reading card), Fuller read voraciously and "presided over her own salon in the Dana Mansion," which included discussions of works by Voltaire, Austen, Dante, Petrarch, Benjamin Disraeli, Thomas Carlyle, Friedrich Schiller, and Wolfgang von Goethe.[35] For the next seven years, she developed close relationships with some of the rising stars of the Harvard intelligentsia—in particular Frederick Henry Hedge (eventually to become a minister in West Cambridge and author of numerous Transcendentalist-leaning essays in the *Christian Examiner*) and James Freeman Clarke (future editor of the *Western Messenger*). Recognizing in Fuller a fellow traveler, her circle of Cambridge friends praised her talents and encouraged her to write and publish. Here was a discourse of power that was less interested in disciplining the self than in translating it into a work of art.

But Fuller's confrontation with and emancipation from the nineteenth-century practices of domination did not come until the death of her father. Despite the opportunities that seemed to be opening to her to pursue possibilities of individual growth, by 1833 it seemed likely that Fuller's potential would be restricted to the sphere of her father's new domestic ideal. In April of that year, Timothy Fuller had purchased a farmhouse in Groton to "imitate Thomas Jefferson by becoming a farmer-scholar and writing a history of the United States."[36] Having retired from Congress in 1825 and failing to get appointed to a federal position by John Quincy Adams, he had decided to abandon the bourgeois life of a lawyer and return to the Jeffersonian ideal of the eighteenth century. At age twenty-three Fuller found herself back in the rural countryside of Groton, where she "ran the homeschool, served as the family seamstress, and helped her mother in the dairy."[37] Without any serious prospects for a husband beyond unrequited flirtations with James Clarke, Fuller found herself largely confined to a household that played host to the "bizarre routines that Timothy subjected himself and his sons to in his perverse effort to teach them Spartan endurance and the value of hard work."[38] Not only did he insist on simple meals of bread and milk, but he also would wake his sons before dawn (at the price of receiving a beating if they were not alert within a minute) and would force upon himself and others a regimen of ice baths every two days, to be followed by drying off with "rough towels" to teach endurance.[39] Fuller was spared the abuse given to her brothers, yet she had her own stresses to deal with at home. Circumstances "had forced her to promise her father that she would teach her younger siblings five days a week for five to eight hours a day."[40] Her father's household had become a sphere of constant labor and absurd degrees of self-repression as he struggled to purge all natural joy, affection, and spontaneity out of the vestiges of Jefferson's rural ideal.

Had Timothy Fuller's vision for his life come to fruition, Fuller might have never fully emancipated herself from her father's dominance. However, just two and a half years after moving to Groton, her father fell ill with cholera after draining lowlands on his farm and died on the morning of October 1, 1835. Being the oldest and most educated of all the children, Fuller "moved into the power vacuum left by her father's death" and became the de facto head of the family.[41] But de facto did not mean de jure. After his death it was discovered that the elder Fuller had written no will and kept no records of his holdings. Not trusting his widow to be able to administer the estate, and with Fuller's not having the equivalent rights of an eldest son, Timothy's brother Abraham Fuller immediately took control over all of the finances and effectively treated the women as his dependents, occasionally giving them stipends while insisting that they sell parts of the farm and cut down on their expenses. Perhaps worse still, he found that his brother had almost no cash on hand, only modest investments tied up in notes or in land, and the income coming only from rents on the old house in Cambridge and two relatively unprofitable farms.[42] Fuller thus became the head of the family over which, as a woman, she had neither financial control nor legal authority.

In the face of complete domination by her environment, Fuller exploited the contradictions within power to pursue a practice of freedom—or what Foucault calls "an exercise of the self on the self by which one attempts to develop and transform oneself, and to attain a certain mode of being."[43] What made this practice possible was the same context that had also facilitated the practices of Reed, Alcott, Brownson, and Emerson—the market and communication revolutions that provided public intellectuals a new route to both economic independence and public influence. Paradoxically, at the same time that the bourgeois cult of true womanhood attempted to discipline Fuller as a subject, the equally bourgeois ideal of genius authorized and supported her ambitions as a writer. So even as she toiled on the farm to pay down the family debt, she found time to write and publish three reviews in the New York–based *American Monthly Magazine* and received an invitation by Emerson to stay at his house for three weeks in July 1836, where she met her future employer, Bronson Alcott. Buoyed by her success, in autumn of 1836 Fuller said goodbye to Groton and moved to Boston, where she catered to the women of the upper class who wanted personal tutoring in German, Italian, and French literature at the considerable cost of fifteen dollars per student for a twelve-week course of twenty-four lessons. Soon she had more than twenty adolescent girls and young women in her classes, almost all from "wealthy and highly literate Boston families," including daughters of a state supreme court justice, the cofounder of the Boston Manufacturing Company, several bankers and merchants, and the owner of the firm Bryant and Sturgis, which "controlled over half of the American trade with the Pacific coast in China."[44] In less than two years after her father's death, she had replaced Elizabeth Peabody for the spring 1837 semester at Alcott's Temple School and had made a name for herself as the premier educator of elite young women in Boston.

During this time in Boston, Fuller began actively developing the critical rhetorical skills that she believed were necessary to help others cultivate their own practices of freedom. Although there is no record of her activity in Alcott's school, there is documentation—believed to have been recorded by Peabody—of what Fuller referred to as a series of "conversations," each of which functioned as a "conscious-raising seminar for educated women who sought to continue their education and paths trod most often by their fathers and brothers."[45] Held in Peabody's house in Boston, these conversations involved two-hour meetings of between twenty-five and thirty women (at ten dollars apiece for a thirteen-week session, enough to bring in the considerable sum of five hundred dollars a year), who included "Fuller's close friends, young women who were married to Transcendentalists or social reformers, and women who were themselves social activists, as well as older women from Boston's traditional Unitarian elite."[46] They came to hear her "brilliant opening monologues, then to be coaxed out of their reticence by Fuller's kind yet insistent questioning."[47] Her goal, as she wrote to a participant in 1839, was to "systematize thought and give the precision in which our sex are so deficient, chiefly, I think because they have so few inducements to test and classify what they receive."[48] Rhetorically the five years of conversations gave Fuller the first real, immediate experience with how the art of words, especially in the context of dialogical exchange, could be used to shatter constraints and emancipate the latent powers of others—in this case other women.

One rhetorical strategy that becomes clear from the documentation of the conversations is that form of critique Foucault calls "eventalization." According to him "eventalization means rediscovering the connections, encounters, supports, blockages, plays of forces, strategies, and so on, that at a given moment establish what subsequently counts as being self-evident, universal, and necessary."[49] It means taking a condition that seemed to be natural and turning it into a contingent event made possible by a conscious or unconscious network of practices and techniques. Although Peabody does not record Fuller's specific rhetorical strategies, the general attitude that emerges from her notes is consistent with this method of critique. In one conversation, for instance, the issue came up of whether the action of Brutus against Caesar could have been performed by a woman. Peabody continues: "A great deal of talk arose here—and Margaret repelled the sentimentalism that took away woman's moral power performing a stern duty. In answer to one thing she said that as soon as we began to calculate our condition & make allowances for it, we sank into the depths of sentimentalism. And again—Nothing I hate to hear so much as *woman's lot*. I wish I could never hear that word *lot*. Something must be wrong where there is a universal lamentation. You ought not to be mourned—for it ought to be replaced with something better."[50] Particularly notable in this description is not only that Fuller aspires to greater things for women, although that is significant enough in the context of her time; more significant is how she calls into question the whole idea of "woman's lot" as being self-evident, universal, and necessary. For Fuller the first and most important function of a feminist rhetoric is to call into question everything that had been naturalized and to make a condition that might otherwise have been lamented over into something to be calculated, critiqued, and ultimately replaced.

If the changes wrought by the market revolution had provided the clientele for Fuller's emancipatory conversations, the impact of the communication revolution provided her a unique opportunity to cultivate a powerful rhetorical style in writing—becoming the editor of what was to be the vehicle for Transcendentalist eloquence, the *Dial*. The Transcendentalists had imagined the *Dial* to be what Susan Belasco characterized as "a magazine that would overturn conventions and offer the reading public dissenting views in religion, philosophy, and literature," and they turned to Fuller to be the editor in acknowledgment of her reputation as an extraordinary intellect and commanding personality.[51] The magazine published its first issue in July 1840 and continued for two years under Fuller's editorship and another two years with Emerson at the helm until it ceased publication in April 1844. The *Dial* came to represent what Charles Capper refers to as "America's first and, until the next century, only avant-garde intellectual journal," expressing, "as did no other journal, the idealistic, anti-institutional, 'come-outer' spirit of the era."[52] Although the journal was never financially stable, it did have a respectable readership and lasted longer than most other comparable periodicals of the time, making it "the most widely read intellectual journal in the country."[53] Not only did it help define Transcendentalism as a movement and give a public forum to its members, but it also set the standard for the more radical magazine publications of the twentieth century insofar as "it eschewed academic affiliation, disregarded commercial demands, promoted experimental writing, offended middlebrow tastes, and critically engaged the major reform ideas of its time."[54]

Although Fuller did not use her own editorship to publish much of her own writing, upon her departure from the *Dial* she handed to Emerson a radical piece of writing that was decisive in establishing her prominence as a public intellectual: "The Great Lawsuit: Man *versus* Men, Woman *versus* Women." In characteristic Transcendentalist fashion, the cryptic title was meant to dramatize a kind of prosecution of historical men and women by the representatives of the ideal Man and Woman. As she explained later, "I meant by that title to intimate the fact that, while it is the destiny of Man, in the course of the ages, to ascertain and fulfil the law of his being, so that his life shall be seen, as a whole, to be that of an angel or messenger, the action of prejudices and passions which attend, in the day, the growth of the individual, is continually obstructing the holy work that is to make earth a part of heaven." She added the important caveat that "by Man I mean both man and woman: these are two halves of one thought."[55] The implications of this caveat represented her most radical critique of the power and knowledge in society that organized the complex network of sexual practices, social norms, and legal restrictions through a discourse grounded in a dualistic conception of gender as distinctly masculine and feminine. According to Murray this was a position "far more radical than that forwarded by Emerson, who wrote and spoke in behalf only of men's soul liberty."[56] As von Mehren observes, "the heart of the program that Fuller recommended to activate a richer development of women's nature was the theory of sexual identity that sprang from her conception of the completely developed soul as without gender."[57] Once liberated from this constraint, women could thus be free to pursue that overarching aim of all the Transcendentalists, the development and deployment of power. Murray sums up Fuller's position this way: "Only after women have explored the groundwork of being, only after they have tapped into this gender-free core of power and converted their 'material' energies into spiritual vision . . . will women be able to redeem men and bring peace to a world now in chaos and disarray."[58] Here was Fuller's politics of transcendence.

In addition to its title, which places the essay squarely within a forensic genre, there is considerable warrant for reading "The Great Lawsuit" rhetorically because of Fuller's thorough study and knowledge of the rhetorical tradition. Annette Kolodny, for instance, places significant emphasis on the fact that during the eighteen months she taught senior girls at the Greene Street School in Boston from 1837 to 1939, she designed a course in rhetoric in which she assigned Richard Whately's *Elements of Rhetoric.* Yet this course was not designed simply to reproduce traditionally masculine forms of rhetoric, such as that of Brownson, that focused heavily on argumentation. According to Kolodny, Fuller adapted Whately's text to her own purposes in an effort to "fashion a set of rhetorical strategies appropriate to the emerging feminist consciousness of her era." She recognized that "as a *woman* speaking for women, she needed to put forward a treatise that would not simply replicate the strategies that might have been employed by any of her well-intentioned male contemporaries." Consequently while she clearly incorporated many of the strategies and methods outlined by Whately, she favored the development of a dialogical and open-ended voice over Whately's tendency toward monological argumentation. "In inventing a discourse appropriate to feminism, Fuller rejected alike the authoritarianism of coercion and the manipulative strategies of the disempowered, endeavoring instead to create a collaborative process of assertion and response in which multiple voices could—and did—find a place."[59] Her rhetoric was thus as much a hybrid as her conception of gender, refusing easy classification and challenging all preconceived model and standards.

That Fuller was nonetheless a master of traditional rhetorical argumentation is made clear in the explicitly forensic component of "The Great Lawsuit." Here she speaks a language consistent with other women reformers of her day, such as Mary Wollstonecraft, Angelina Grimké, and Abigail Kelly Foster. Having established the basis of the "lawsuit"—that is to say, the prosecution of men and women in history by the idealized Man and Woman for not living up to their high ideals—Fuller specifically targets men for having created a system of domination to exploit labor and inhibit the growth of women throughout history. The charges run as follows: (1) Women are denied property rights, "so that, if a husband dies without a will, the wife, instead of stepping at once into his place as head of the family, inherits only a part of his fortune, as if she were a child, or ward only, not an equal partner." (2) Women have little financial independence, such that "profligate or idle men live upon the earnings of industrious wives." (3) Women have no legal protection, such that those who flee their husbands and take their children with them are hounded by their spouses, who "threaten to rob them of the children, if deprived of the rights of a husband, as they call them, placing themselves in their poor lodgings, frightening them into paying tribute by taking from them the children, running into debt at the expense of these otherwise so overtasked helots." (4) Women are placed on the same level as slaves and children, such that it is thought "better for them to be engaged in active labor, which is to be furnished and directed by those better able to think." (5) Women are restricted to the domestic sphere, to be under the control of their husbands, based on the cult of true womanhood and justified by the male maxim "I am the head and she the heart." (6) Women are denied access to the public sphere, such that there is as much opposition to them "seizing on the rostrum or the desk" as there used to be about their learning "use of the pen" in learning how to write. (7) Women who do have talents are exposed to social criticism and mockery, discouraged "with school-boy brag; Girls cant do that, girls cant play ball." (8) Finally, women who do succeed in the face of all this are perceived as a threat, so that "let anyone defy their taunts, break through, and be brave and secure, they render the air with shouts." In short Fuller lays out all the ways in which men have sought "to mark out with due precision the limits of woman's sphere, and woman's mission, and to prevent other than the rightful shepherd from climbing the wall, or the flock from using any chance gap to run astray."[60] Such an effort in practice is not the pious labor of the good shepherd but the paranoid work of a prison warden.

Familiar, too, was Fuller's explicit appeal to the ideology of liberalism, which, taken to its extreme, encourages the development of all individual capacities within a free system of competition. This occurs in her vision of an ideal marriage bond as the marriage between equals rather than merely a household partnership or mutual idolatry. As she argues, quoting one of Emerson's favorite aphorisms, "union is only possible to those who are units."[61] Any other form of relationship is not a true companionship but either a business contract or a negotiation between authority and obedience, however benign. For women to establish truly loving relationships in marriage thus requires not self-sacrifice but self-development and self-reliance: "give the soul free course, let the organization be freely developed, and the being will be fit for any and every relation to which it may be called. The intellect, no more than the sense of hearing, is to be cultivated, that she may be a more valuable companion to man, but because the Power who gave a power by its mere existence signifies that it must be brought out towards perfection."[62] Against the view that women's ambitions for self-cultivation are a form of corruption or even sin, Fuller argues that God would not have given women the power to think, create, and initiate if that power had not been meant to be perfected. Consistent with the rhetoric of women's rights at the time, Fuller applied the tenets of liberal individualism to women and argued that they, too, should have access to all the same rights and privileges of men not only in public but also in the context of the private sphere of marriage.

Fuller's rhetorical style departs from conventional patterns, however, when she begins to critique the discursive foundations that authorize and constitute these practices of domination. Here Fuller offers her definition of a "self-conscious female identity defined by both its divine humanity and its dynamic androgyny," and by doing so "offered a new American protofeminist ideology encompassed by neither the pathbreaking but one-sided rationalist-utilitarian Wollstonecraft tradition nor the galvanizing but intellectually parochial one of the moral rights abolitionists."[63] More than just offering a new ideology, Fuller set an example for a new kind of criticism that would transcend the merely argumentative. To return to the language of Foucault, Fuller's essay exemplifies that kind of criticism he called for "that would try not to judge but to bring an oeuvre, a book, a sentence, an idea to life; it would light fires, watch the grass grow, listen to the wind, and catch the sea foam in the breeze and scatter it. It would multiply not judgments but signs of existence; it would summon them, drag them from their sleep. Perhaps it would invent them sometimes—all the better." This would be a criticism "of scintillating leaps of the imagination. It would not be sovereign or dressed in red. It would bear the lightning of possible storms."[64] This is the kind of criticism that transcends the maxims of the god of rhetoric in order to call into question the most dearly held basic truths and replace them with possibilities never before imagined. It is a form of criticism that seeks not to alter power piecemeal but to reenvision it as a totality.

The target of Fuller's critique was the conventional duality of gender, an unassailable truth grounded not only in obvious physiological differences but also, more important, in that maxim that the man is the "the head" and the woman is "the heart." This maxim formed the entire base of discursive knowledge that restricted women's power to that of emotional sympathy and limited her sphere of action to the household (the cult of true womanhood) while celebrating men's capacity for intellectual rigor and competitive vigor that made him suited to the public world of action—the cult of true manhood. As long as this psychological dualism remained accepted by men and women alike, the appeal for women's self-development would remain confined to that sphere of the heart for which she was made, quite irrespective of any superficial commitment to liberalism. But Fuller knew that such a truth was unassailable by using only the weapons of conventional argumentation. Its citadel was too well defended, particularly by the Judeo-Christian tradition, "which taught that the happiness of the race was forfeited to the fault of a woman, and showed its thought of what sort of regard man owed her, by making him accuse her on the first question to his God, who gave her to the patriarch as a handmaid, and, by Mosaic Law, bound her to allegiance like a serf."[65] Onto this truth was built the practices that penetrated into the intimate lives of men and women and structured their relationships to themselves and to each other. These practices would not be dislodged merely through forensic wrangling.

At this point in her development as a writer, Fuller found her greatest resource within the language of history and myth. Her experience still largely restricted to the boundaries by which most women were confined in the early nineteenth century, Fuller relied largely on her wealth of knowledge taken from books. From these resources she was able to weave many stories and images together to challenge the established gender hierarchy. Of the Judeo-Christian tradition, she notes that despite their condemnation of women, they "greeted, with solemn rapture, all great and holy women as heroines, prophetesses, nay judges in Israel; and, if they made Eve listen to the serpent, gave Mary to the Holy Spirit."[66] This contradiction, she believes, runs through all of history, in which even the most patriarchal societies who held to the inferiority of women somehow managed to recognize Semiramis, Sappho, Aspasia, Elizabeth I of England, Isabella of Castile, Catherine of Russia, or Héloïse when they combined wit, genius, and strength. Similar fractures emerge within the patriarchal cultures of Greece and Rome. Thus "whatever may have been the domestic manners of the ancient nations, the idea of women was nobly manifested in their mythologies and poems." Even in Greece, in which women "occupied there a very subordinate position in actual life," one finds "the poets producing such ideals as Cassandra, Iphigenia, Antigone, Macaria." The gods, too, appear in feminine form, such as Sita in the Ramayana, the Egyptian Isis, and the Greek Ceres, Proserpine, Diana, Minerva, and Vesta. Thus against the imperfections and inequities of any particular social system, including those in which they arose, the mythical images of women contrast an ideal realm in which "male and female heads are distinct in expression, but equal in beauty, strength, and calmness."[67] Fuller thus does not merely confront one discourse with another but works within a dominant discourse to find resources for resistance within its reversals, dislocations, openings, and indecisions.

She makes her boldest rhetorical move in the closing paragraphs of the essay. There Fuller suggests that the stark division between male and female be replaced with a fluid conception of gender reconstituted as a balance of two powers that are immanent within all individuals regardless of their physiology. In other words there is no such thing as a pure man as distinct from a pure woman, but rather different mixtures of masculine and feminine energies that are manifested in a variety of physical forms. What was then characterized as a strict gender dichotomy was actually a shorthand for two competing tendencies. Consequently "it is no more the order of nature that it should be incarnated pure in any form, than that the masculine energy should exist unmingled with it in any form. Male and female represent the two sides of a great radical dualism. But, in fact, they are perpetually passing into one another. Fluid hardens to solid, solid rushes to fluid. There is no wholly masculine man, no purely feminine woman." Physiologists have attempted to create hard and fast laws that distinguish men from women, but history "jeers" at their attempts: "they make a rule; they say from observation what can and cannot be. In vain! Nature provides exceptions to every rule. She sends women to battle, and sets Hercules spinning; she enables women to bare immense burdens, cold, and frost; she enables the man, who feels maternal love, to nourish his infant like a mother."[68] According to Steele, by using the language of myth, Fuller "decentered her society's dominant ideologies by connecting masculinized god-language with images of female power that called their terms into question."[69] Here the mythic and the dialogical elements of her rhetoric cooperate together to construct a new drama of origins and destinies.

Her final critique came in the form of an articulation of a new possibility for power constructed on a new image of truth. This truth was not put forward as if to supplant one form of sovereignty with another, however. It was a metaphorical truth, a vision of possibility that combined within its form a dialogic relationship between two tendencies of power. These were not powers in the traditional sense, however, representing the difference between the head and the heart, between intellectual development and emotional sensitivity. To redefine the substance of human nature, Fuller goes back to Greek mythology to identify the two forms of power "expressed by the ancients as Muse and Minerva." On the one hand, the muse is that part of the soul that expresses its power in beginnings, connections, and transitions; it is "electrical in movement, intuitive in function, spiritual in tendency." On the other hand, Minerva represents that part of the soul concerned with endings, productions, and conclusions; it is expressed in the "selecting or energizing of art" and knows how to "turn all dross to gold."[70] The muse and Minerva thus are not synonymous with the head and the heart, which represent "faculties," or distinct mental processes. Rather they represent the relationship between those faculties (for both the muse and Minerva think and feel equally, albeit in different ways) and external forms of action or of making, of praxis or of poiesis. The muse represents the acts not only of intuiting but also of active expressing and prophesizing, while Minerva stands not only for reasoning and ordering but also of the accomplishment of poise and individualism. This is what makes them powers in a more active sense than just the power to think or to feel; they are also their outward manifestation.

Women's particular calling of the nineteenth century, then, was to compensate for an often overdeveloped muse element by cultivating a greater appreciation for their Minerva potential. Historically, that is, it has been "especial genius of woman" to channel the muse, and Fuller acknowledges that in the past women have excelled less "in classification, or re-creation, as in an instinctive seizure of causes, and a simple breathing out of what she receives that has the singleness of life."[71] Here, for instance, is the root of the sudden visions of Cassandra or the genius of the Prophetess of Delphi. Fuller's vision for the new age was to "grant her then for a while the armor and the javelin. Let her put from her the press of other minds and meditate in virgin loneliness."[72] Only then could she emerge into society with complete self-reliance, prepared to act and create in a public world. As von Mehren sums up her program, "to harmonize the intellect and the affections, she recommended a program of self-discipline, intellectual rigor, critical reasoning, and self-awareness that included periods of isolation so as to check the harmful effects of too much emotional involvement, the common plight of the many 'incarcerated souls' she knew who could be freed by greater self-reliance."[73] Should this program be followed, Fuller believed, an era of freedom would arise: "new individualities shall be developed in the actual world, which shall advance upon it as gently as the figures come out upon the canvas."[74] This was the culmination of her rhetorical vision after having articulated the ideal, criticized the constraints of the actual, analyzed the emergent possibilities in human relationships, and provided a new framework of self-understanding and power that would produce radically new individualities. To the men and women reading Fuller's essay in the nineteenth century, here was a form of criticism that clearly bore the lightning of possible storms.

"The Great Lawsuit" turned out to be a great success for Fuller. Emerson declared it "proper and noble" and "quite an important fact in the history of Woman; good for its wit, excellent for its character." Her bad writing habits lingered, though, and even her supporters found the work characteristically verbose. Sarah Ripley mentioned that "Margaret's article is the cream of herself, a little rambling, but rich in all good things."[75] Fuller's work was regularly criticized for its verbosity and tendency to ramble in years to come. But as Kolodny has argued, this vice was the other side of her virtue. Whereas many disciples of the god of rhetoric found it easy to dismiss Fuller's rhetoric as "the byproduct of stereotypically uncontrolled female talkativeness transferred to the printed page," those who were willing to be carried away by her eloquence could appreciate the "sheer revolutionary daring of her attempt both to question existing gender hierarchies and to disrupt accepted sexual practices."[76] To be sure, the rhetorical vice was real, but in the coming decade see developed a rhetorical style that relied less on mythic sweep and more on narrative precision that channeled her power of eloquence in new revolutionary forms.

This new rhetorical voice emerged on the heels of the publication of her essayistic travel narrative *Summer on the Lakes* in June 1844. A product of her journey by train and then by steamer to Chicago with Sarah and James Clarke, her first major work was a "meandering, fragmentary, subjective book, almost a diary," filled with a chronological recounting of experiences, personal reflections, anecdotes, dialogues, poems, mythologies, and observations.[77] But it was also her first experiment in the critical analysis of the social conditions of an expanding nation based on a combination of immersive experience and direct observation. According to Steele, "while 'The Great Lawsuit' (and later *Woman in the Nineteenth Century*) became sites where Fuller began to find a public habitation for mythical power, *Summer on the Lakes* turned more to the question of diagnosis."[78] Thus what began largely as an endeavor to write a picturesque travelogue of her journeys out West was punctuated by moments of critique that laid bare the networks of power of the American upper Midwest. Although Chicago was by no means "the wild lands of the barely pioneer-invaded Far West," it was nonetheless the center of a rapidly developing area of the nation dominated by "hordes of farmers, peasants, and tradesmen" both from the Northeast and from Europe: "driven by hard times, cheap land, and the previous decade's removal of the last of the area's once numerous Indian tribes, this mass migration was forging America's now biggest and most kaleidoscopic frontier." Responding to this environment, Fuller sought not only to entertain her readers with lyrical descriptions of nature and renditions of poetry, but also to challenge them with vivid accounts of the difficult lives of women on the frontier and tragic dramatizations of the lives of the Native Americans who still lived there. It was during her experience out west that "she discovered that the aesthetic and discursive pressures limiting her own expression were linked to the larger social forces that had silenced creative women and treated Indians as nonhuman aliens."[79] The rhetorical challenge was to find a way to convey this realization to her readers while communicating a breadth of critical vision through the language of the symbol.

To understand the course of Fuller's rapid rhetorical development in just a few short years—that is, from *Summer on the Lakes* to her final dispatches from Italy in 1849—it is useful to turn to Kenneth Burke and his concept of synecdoche, for it was Fuller's mastery of this persuasive strategy that distinguished her later from her early writings. According to Burke a synecdoche functions as a representation of a larger whole, much as a map represents a nation or a politician represents a constituency. It is distinct from metaphor, metonymy, or irony in that one ideally can understand everything about what is represented by getting inside the symbol, as if one might unfold the laws of nature by interrogating a blade of grass. The other master tropes always involve somehow getting outside of the symbol, whether to gain perspective (as with metaphor), to reduce something to an underlying material essence (as with metonymy), or to contrast a thing with his opposite (as with irony). But in an ideal synecdoche, there is a relationship between microcosm and macrocosm, where "the individual is treated as a replica of the universe" and the "part can represent the whole." For this reason Burke sees much artistic representation itself as synecdochic, both internally and externally. Externally a work of art functions as a synecdoche insofar as "certain relations within the medium 'stand for' corresponding relations outside it." Internally there is also a sense in which a part of a work of art can be synecdochic "as the beginning of a drama contains its close or the close sums up the beginning, the parts all thus being consubstantially related."[80] A perfect work of art would thus contain not only a representation of the whole work in one of its parts but also the relations outside of that work, just as one might think of the phrase "Et tu, Brute?" as internally representing the entire drama of Shakespeare's *Julius Caesar* and externally representing the political turmoil of the late Roman Republic. To master the art of synecdoche thus requires both a scientific awareness of the complex environment to be represented as well as a symbolic artistry by which this circumference can be compressed into a simple and dramatic formula and then conveyed in a phrase, story, or image.

A perfect example of synecdoche in Fuller's work is her description of the bay in Milwaukee along the shores of Lake Michigan. She had spent an afternoon in a lighthouse, situated atop a bluff, overlooking a bay where great boats came in. There she reflected on the people she had met in the city, "drawn together from all parts of the world" and lured by the prospects of the West, including such character types as "the enthusiast and the cunning man; the naturalist, and the lover." Yet from the perspective of the lighthouse, she could also see how they still remained linked through networks of communication to the rest of the nation.

> Approaching the Milwaukie pier, they made a bend, and seemed to do obeisance in the heavy style of some dowager duchess entering a circle she wishes to treat with especial respect. These boats came in and out every day, and still afford a cause for general excitement. The people swarm down to greet them, to receive and send away their packages and letters. To me they seemed such mighty messengers, to give, by their noble motion, such an idea of the power and fullness of life, that they were worthy to carry despatches from king to king. It must be very

pleasant for those who have an active share in carrying on the affairs of this great and growing world to see them come in. It must be very pleasant to those who have dearly loved friends at the next station. To those who have neither business nor friends, it sometimes gives a desolating sense of insignificance.[81]

The Milwaukee pier thus stands as a representation of the city's entire social structure. From her position atop the lighthouse, she can obviously see more than simply the goings-on of the pier as her vision sweeps the circumference of the horizon; yet she chooses to focus on this one part because it represents a complex nexus of relationships. The boats on the pier represent the ties of communication between Milwaukee and the rest of the nation, just as the way that different individuals react to their arrival represents the various demographics of the city—the entrepreneurs and politicians, the pioneers and their families, the adventurers and the wanderers. One gets the impression that if Fuller sat long enough she would see the face of every citizen in Milwaukee and know each of their intimate lives.

Throughout the narrative of *Summer on the Lakes,* she turns her gaze away from the picturesque to focus on specific objects, events, or images that she feels to be representative of a broader social condition and then affirms their rhetorical power by concluding with a forceful aphorism. She describes her first impression of the prairie as "the very desolation of dullness," but on reflection she learns a on different lesson: "It is always thus with the new form of life: we must learn to look at it by its own standard."[82] She paints a comic image of upper-class women following their husbands out West but refusing to adapt to the rugged circumstances they face: "Accustomed to the pavement of Broadway, they dare not tread the wildwood paths for fear of rattlesnakes!"[83] She retells one of her encounters with a pioneer who looked contemptuously upon Indians as children and drunkards: "This gentleman, though in other respects of most kindly and liberal heart, showed the aversion that the white man soon learns the feel for the Indian on whom he encroaches, the aversion of the injurer for him he has degraded."[84] She describes the tragic fate of the "enthusiast" who fled the city to seek a pastoral ideal that did not exist: "He has escaped from the heartlessness of courts, to encounter the vulgarity of the mob; he has secured solitude, but it is a lonely, a deserted solitude."[85] She encounters French Catholics and stern Presbyterians who exploited the natives and then forced them to listen to sermons in praise of purity: "Yes! slave-drivers and Indian traders are called Christians, and the Indian is to be deemed less like the Son of Mary than they! Wonderful is the deceit of man's heart!"[86] She describes the futility of the Chippewas in their effort to be admitted as citizens to the state of Michigan, as they remained inferior in the eyes of whites: "'Might makes right.' All that civilization does for the generality, is to cover up this with a veil of subtle evasions and chicane, and here and there to rouse the individual mind to appeal to heaven against it."[87] In each case Fuller not only constructed a symbolic representation but then made explicit what the synecdoche represents through a formula. The result is a wandering and lyrical travelogue punctuated with striking images and sweeping social critique.

This capacity to communicate the complexity of a new environment through the language of synecdoche that attracted the eye of the man at the forefront of the communication revolution in journalism—Horace Greeley, the editor of the *New-York Tribune.* Fuller had hardly been unknown to Greeley prior to its publication; he had republished some of her pieces from the *Dial,* and his wife, Mary, had attended some of her conversations. But *Summer on the Lakes* demonstrated a capacity not just for literary form and philosophical depth but also for journalistic style and sociological insight, and "Greeley was impressed with Fuller's ability to look beneath the surface appearances of American life to uncover troubling areas of concern."[88] As Capper notes, Greeley later touted the book's "socialistic promise, [and] would hail it as 'one of the clearest and most graphic delineations, ever given,' of the Middle West's great unequal contests between 'receding barbarism' and the 'rapidly advancing, but rude, repulsive semi-civilization.'"[89] Greeley recognized in Fuller the kind of voice he needed (at least once properly trained) at his newspaper, and by the end of the summer of 1844 he offered her a job as literary editor at a generous salary of five hundred dollars a year, her job being to "review the important new books, to keep the public informed on new trends in European literature, and to cover cultural events in New York."[90] After some deliberation Fuller accepted the offer and became the first woman to edit a section of a major newspaper in the United States.

Fuller's position at the *Tribune* gave Transcendentalism its widest platform, far exceeding the *Dial* or Brownson's *Review.* Founded in 1841 by Greeley, the *Tribune* became, according to Adam Tuchinsky, "the most important newspaper in antebellum America," achieving a circulation of a quarter million by the beginning of the Civil War.[91] At the time of Fuller's hiring, circulation was in the tens of thousands, but that was tens of thousands more than she had reached through the *Dial* or even the popular publication of *Summer on the Lakes,* which sold around seven hundred copies in its first printing. Perhaps even more important, it was a newspaper with a particular social mission. Greeley was a Whig and thus committed to "individual self-improvement and national economic development"; but he was also a socialist who wanted to use his paper to advance "a distinctly progressive version of free labor, becoming arguably the first popular forum where opposition to market values was vented in a developed way."[92] Deeply suspicious of the innate goodness of people and yet concerned with improving their social welfare, he used the paper to expose the problems with the growing market economy in order that those in authority might remedy the tensions in order to stave off the kind of war predicted by Brownson. The *Tribune* thus found an audience with the growing body of middle-class reformers who wished to confront social injustice while also preserving the independence of the individual to compete freely in the market economy. According to Tuchinsky, "at bottom, Transcendentalism, socialism, and even the *Tribune* itself were united by a shared commitment to a philosophy of liberal self-culture that aimed to institutionalize democratic access to ideas and self-expression. All pleaded for more intimate and harmonious union between the mind and the body, between the scholarly and the laboring classes."[93] Fuller's task was to be both a critical and philanthropic voice for the paper, exposing the abuses of the rising capitalistic order while encouraging the moderate forms and policies that might ease the transition to market economy.

So confident was Greeley in Fuller's potential that he placed her columns on the first page. Also, to give further publicity to his new star editor and reporter, prior to her starting the job, he encouraged her to expand "The Great Lawsuit" into book, the result of which was *Woman in the Nineteenth Century.* Substantially the original text remained basically unaltered, but it was now broken up with added sections on myths, historical figures, literary excursions, and references to present-day circumstances. Stylistically "it proceeded as before, marked by unexpected leaps, digressive eruptions, provocative juxtapositions, loose associations, and a disruptive multiplicity of voices."[94] At Greeley's urging she did add one burst of rhetorical advocacy that gave concreteness to her often abstract theorizing about the rights of women: "But if you ask me what offices they may fill; I reply—any. I do not care what case you put; let them be sea captains, if you will."[95] Greeley repeated this line whenever he wrote about Fuller's work. More important to her career, however, was the medium of its publication. Her book benefited from the development of paperback book publishing, with its debut edition of February 1845 selling at fifty cents a copy as part of a Greeley's new paperback series, "Cheerful Books for the People." Within a week of its publication, it sold out its entire edition of fifteen hundred copies on its way to being reissued by the London publisher Wiley and Putnam in the series "Library of Choice Reading."[96]

As successful as was *Women in the Nineteenth Century,* it was her work at the newspaper that finally pushed Fuller to develop a more explicitly rhetorical style adapted to the constraints of the newspaper column and its public readership. Greeley later remarked that her writing came to be characterized "by a directness, terseness, and practicality, which are wanting in some of her earlier publications."[97] And her influence grew in proportion. According to von Mehren, "after more than a year at the *Tribune,* Fuller had become a moral voice in the city of New York."[98] For instance, a visit to Sing Sing prison awakened in her an interest in prison reform, and "with Greeley's encouragement, she began to publicize conditions in the city's charitable institutions, not only the prisons but the almshouses, insane asylums, and homes for the blind and the deaf."[99] A perfect example of her moral voice is her article about a visit to an asylum for discharged female conflicts. Trying to improve their circumstances, she wrote: "To all we appeal. To the poor, who will know how to sympathize with those who are not only poor but degraded, diseased, likely to be hurried onward to a shameful, hopeless death. To the rich, to equalize the advantages of which they have received more than their share. To men, to atone for the wrongs inflicted by men on that 'weaker sex,' who should, they say, be soft, confiding, dependent on them for protection. To women, to feel for those who have not been guarded either by social influence or inward strength from that first mistake which the opinion of the world makes irrevocable for women alone."[100] Fuller was not departing from nineteenth-century journalistic standards by making explicit rhetorical appeals within a news article. In contradistinction to twentieth-century journalistic conventions, most news stories of this age were not fact-based summaries but "advocacy illustrated with on-scene reports."[101] In her *Tribune* articles, Fuller was refining the standard rhetorical style of the nineteenth-century moralistic journalist, whereby a writer would combine personal observation with enough background research to define a present exigency that public opinion, constituted by the press, could remedy by collective political action.

However, the emergence of Fuller's rhetoric of revolutionary nationalism awaited one last, ultimately tragic turn of events that thrust her into the center of radical thought and action in the nineteenth century—Rome during the revolutionary year of 1848. It happened quite by chance. In the summer of 1846, Quaker friends of Greeley's, Marcus and Rebecca Spring, were planning to go to Europe and invited Fuller to accompany them, paying part of her expenses in exchange for tutoring their nine-year-old son. With Greeley's additional promise to pay for any articles she sent back to the *Tribune,* she had enough money finally to take her European tour that was denied to her after her father's death. Arriving in August 1846 in Liverpool, Fuller toured Scotland and England, meeting Thomas and Jane Carlyle in their home and also enjoying the acquaintance Jane's friend Giuseppe Mazzini, the exiled leader of the Italian democratic republican movement, whom Fuller promised to deliver letters containing "secret instructions" to Mazzini's mother in Genoa on her arrival. By December of that year, she was in Paris, and in spring of 1847 she traveled south through Lyons, Avignon, and Genoa to arrive in Rome for Easter week, where she was struck with the beauty and grandeur of the city. Italy was everything she had dreamed it would be, and her only lament was that "there is very little that I can like to write about Italy.

Italy is beautiful, worthy to be loved and embraced, not talked about." But at the end of her May 1847 dispatch, she did note that "at this moment there is great excitement in Italy" and that "all things seem to announce that some important change is inevitable here, but what?"[102] Two years later she had her answer. Glorious Rome was stained with the blood of Italian revolutionaries, and Fuller fled Europe on a steamship with her young Italian husband and her one-year-old son conceived out of wedlock.

Fuller experienced three revolutions in Italy—one personal, one political, and one rhetorical. The revolution in her personal life was perhaps the most unexpected and immediate. After going to hear vespers at St. Peter's on Holy Thursday, April 1, 1847, she lost track of her hosts, the Springs, in the dense crowd, until she was approached by a handsome Italian man who offered to walk her back to her hotel. This was Giovanni Angelo Ossoli, the youngest son of an aristocratic family that, despite recent hard times, still maintained a palazzo on the Via Tor de Specchi. At twenty-six Ossoli was ten years younger than Fuller and also lacked her formal education or rigorous ethics of self-discipline; he was content to live at the palazzo and care for his invalid father. But he was "courteous, gentle, and responsible" and soon came to love and dedicate himself to Fuller completely.[103] So taken was Fuller with the romance that she transcended decades of sexual inhibition. By the new year in 1848 she was pregnant. To keep it a secret, she withdrew to Rieti—using her legitimate desire to write a book on Italy as cover—until her son, Angelo Eugene Philip Ossoli, was born around October. By that time Fuller and Ossoli had been secretly married in order to avoid the scandal of an Italian Catholic marrying a "notorious American Protestant radical Republican."[104] But by that time it may not have mattered for Ossoli, as with Fuller's support he had joined the newly organized civic guard in 1847 and by 1848 was actively supporting the Republican cause.

Perhaps it was the political revolution Fuller experienced that transformed her even more deeply than becoming a wife and mother. For 1848, the year of Angelo's birth, was the year of revolution across Europe, where "with an astounding rapidity, crowds of working-class radicals and middle-class liberals in Paris, Milan, Venice, Naples, Palermo, Vienna, Prague, Budapest, Kraków and Berlin toppled the old regimes and began the task of forging a new, liberal order."[105] In each case conservative autocratic regimes with striking suddenness either collapsed or made significant concessions in the face of mass protests and barricade street fighting—the most dramatic cases being the establishment of the Second Republic in France after the expulsion of King Louis Philippe and then, in the Austrian Empire, the appointment of a new, more liberal government by King Ferdinand after the conservative state chancellor and foreign minister Klemens von Metternich fled the country. The latter news was of particular importance to the Italians, as the regions of Lombardy, Venetia, Parma, Modena, and the Papal States were under Austrian control and the de facto rule of Metternich, who in July 1847 had occupied Ferrara under the guise of maintaining order "to provoke hostilities which could justify military suppression of the reform movement in central Italy."[106] After news of the Austrian upheavals and Metternich's exile reached the Italians on March 17, thousands of Milanese crowded the streets the following day and expelled the Austrians from the city after five days of street fighting, marking the formal beginning of the Italian revolution. Fuller pithily summarized events this way in the pages of the *Tribune:* "And Metternich, too, is crushed; the seed of the Woman has had his foot on the serpent. I have seen the Austrian arms dragged through the streets of Rome and burned in the Piazza del Popolo.—The Italians embraced one another and cried *Miracolo, Providenza!*"[107]

As in the United States, all of Europe was undergoing a rapid transition in the wake of the communication, transportation, and market revolutions. But in Europe it was occurring in an "Old World" context grounded on centuries-old feudal traditions and institutions. Jonathan Sperber, for instance, argues that the revolutions across the continent were the effect of changes "involving a replacement of an old regime society of orders with a post-revolutionary civil society of property owners." In the old society of orders, "different social groups, membership of which would was usually set at birth, and typically was connected to membership of an established church, had different legal rights and privileges that both set the pattern of their ways of making a living and also determined their possible participation in public life." Yet as in the United States, the reliable conservatism of this old regime was being attacked on all sides by new possibilities and patterns of life associated with a rising bourgeois middle class. Thus "in the post-revolutionary public order all citizens (male citizens, anyway; women had a subordinate position in both forms of society), regardless of their status at birth or their religion, were equal under the law, and equally entitled to pursue the acquisition of property." In hindsight, at least, the 1848 revolutions could be seen as a culmination a decades-long "movement towards expanded industrial production and a market-oriented agriculture," even though in the moment it also allowed people to express utopian political ideals and vent pent-up nationalistic frustrations that far exceeded a merely economic motivation.[108]

Particularly in the wake of the crop disasters and food riots that swept across Europe between 1845 and 1847, many of the old regimes rapidly collapsed when the rising middle class of professionals and entrepreneurs who were denied access to political power grew tired of propping up a dying society of orders. From this group, according to Peter Stearns, came three distinct ideologies that helped propel the revolutions: liberalism, radicalism, and nationalism. A direct outgrowth of the rise of the professional class, liberalism advocated for a "genuinely representative government, based on limited suffrage . . . protection for freedoms of thought, speech, publication, and assembly . . . [and] efficient government, run by men chosen for their talents, not their birth or status." From the liberal perspective, the economic crisis was in part brought about because the old ruling class did not understand how to manage the complexities of a new economy. Radicalism differed from liberalism mainly by including more voices and considering more interests. Instead of limited suffrage, they wanted a republic with wide or universal suffrage and were more "concerned about economic injustice and talked of the need for social reform to protect the working classes." Nationalism, by contrast, tended to subordinate economic interest to questions of identity and political autonomy. Nationalists "sought to promote the national culture, defined primarily in terms of language and historical heritage, and to equate political culture with this culture." Whereas liberals and radicals looked to change the way government was structured and administered, nationalists sought to redefine the boundaries of the state and to reconceptualize the entire meaning of what it meant to be a citizen.[109]

The language of nationalism—most notably as advocated by Giuseppe Mazzini—captured Fuller's imagination along with that of the Italian people. This was because unlike other Europeans, Italians did not actually belong to a nation but rather lived in one of seven distinct regions controlled by different political powers, the northernmost over which Austria still held control. Nationalism in this case thus became a means by which both liberals and radicals could expel the last remaining obstacle to Italian unification and political and economic reform. Movements such as Mazzini's "Young Italy" (Giovine Italia) thus transcended merely economic rationality to articulate a romantic vision of new generations of Europeans casting off the old order and creating (with the blessing of a nonsectarian, Universalist-style God) a new form of democratic republicanism founded on the principle of association inspired by the French Revolution. As Harry Hearder explains, Mazzini believed that the French Revolution "had established and won recognition for the rights of the individual. What was now needed was a recognition of the duties which individuals owed to each other and to society."[110] To create that recognition, Mazzini published revolutionary materials from Marseille and Geneva that were then smuggled into Italy as a means to "spread propaganda to which urban artisans and idealistic intellectuals and professionals were especially susceptible."[111] When the new pope, Pius IX (aka "Pope Nono"), moved to release political prisoners, liberalize the press, and create a "civic guard," it seemed to signal Vatican support for Mazzini's vision for the "Risorgimento," or the political Italian resurgence. All signs were pointing toward Italy's liberation.

Fuller became a convert to the nationalist cause almost as soon as she arrived in Italy, celebrating what she called a movement of "human mutuality and national unity."[112] Her early dispatches still retained the voice of a travel guide, as she commented on her encounters with nature, public art, and culture, but by October a more aggressive rhetorical voice was edging into her writings. A dispatch from October 1847, for instance, began with a lengthy summary of her experience visiting Italian lakes (complete with a romantic poem) and ended with a scathing critique of Austrian influence and an appeal for the cause of revolution. Almost without transition from her praise of the beauty of Lake Garda, Fuller upon return to Milan proclaimed that "Austrian rule is always equally hated, and time, instead of melting away differences, only makes them more glaring" (such as when Austrian police, breaking up a rally in support of the pope, "rushed upon a defenseless crowd that had no share in what excited their displeasure, except by sympathy, and, driving them like sheep, wounded them *in the backs*"). But while "the Austrian race have no faculties that can ever enable them to understand the Italian character," their "policy, so well contrived to palsy and repress for a time, cannot kill, and there is always a force at work underneath which shall yet, and I think now before long, shake off the incubus." In the meantime the Italians with a revolutionary spirit were "obliged to hold their breath while their poor, ignorant sovereigns skulk in corners, hoping to hide from the coming storm." She closed her dispatch: "Of all this more in my next."[113]

There was actually much more to come beyond the next dispatch. As indicated by the language she used to describe the political conflict not in terms of armies, policies, or states but rather the "Austrian race" and the "Italian character," Fuller had also undergone a revolution in her rhetorical style. She had, in short, adopted the rhetoric of revolutionary nationalism. To understand the nature of this rhetoric, one can look to how Benedict Anderson understands modern nationalism in terms of the production of an "imagined community," imagined because it exists primarily as an image in the minds of its members and a community because "regardless of the actual inequality and exploitation that may prevail in each, the nation is always conceived as a deep, horizontal comradeship." Nationalism is not indicative simply of a group of people who happen to live within a particular geographic area and are subject to the power of the state; the sovereignty of a modern nation resides within the imagined consubstantiality of the people who see themselves as sharing one history, one lineage, one character, and, most important, one language. Benedict places particular importance on language in the formation of a nation and credits the rise of print capitalism—particularly in the form of the newspaper—for having "made it possible for rapidly growing numbers of people to think about themselves, and to relate themselves to others, in profoundly new ways." However, characteristic of what Burke explains is the inextricable relationship between identification and division, nationalism not only inspired great acts of "love, and often profoundly self-sacrificing love," but also had its roots in "fear and hatred of the Other."[114] Thus when Fuller sings encomiums to the "Italian character" while hurling epithets at the "Austrian race," all in the service of constituting a new imagined community that is sovereign and limited, she uses the strategies of identification and division so central to the rhetoric of nationalism.

Consequently when the later dispatches are situated within the tradition of Transcendentalist rhetoric of reform, they appear in stark contradistinction to the ideal of Emersonian eloquence that saw the individual in possession of an idea as the key to an era. Resonant more with Brownson's emphasis on the importance of association over solitude, her rhetoric in Italy celebrated the potential for collective action that could emerge once the Italian people came to see themselves as an imagined community striving toward autonomy and independence. According to Steele, "in Italy, a concern with collective social movements, not with Transcendentalist individualism, oriented her writing," for "throughout her Italian dispatches, she expressed a deep commitment to radical social transformation."[115] This included social transformation in her home country as well. The more she became aligned with the cause of Italian nationalism, she more she looked back to the United States to criticize it for its failure to live up to the best of its nationalistic ideals. The result was a discourse that spoke simultaneously to two audiences that she believed could make common cause. In Steele's words, "attempting to restructure the physical relations that had created a vast web of social injustice both in America and in Europe, her final texts attended by necessity to the process of changing her readers' minds."[116] Her dispatches but did not address individual geniuses in their solitude but the consciences and character of entire nations whose commitment to collective action could push back the tides of tyranny. As she told her readers, "this cause is OURS, above all others; we ought to show that we feel it to be so."[117]

It is important to emphasize, however, that Fuller's rhetoric of revolutionary nationalism did not contradict but was built upon her previous rhetorical strategies. Her skill at critiquing the complex networks of power allowed her to criticize the strategies of domination and make visible the gaps and contradictions within power that created openings for new practices and identities. Her classical knowledge and familiarity with the language of myth were uniquely suited to constituting a sense of the "Italian character" rooted in a story of common origins of the type that was so central to the formation of national identities. And her growing mastery of the art of synecdoche, both in narrative and in aphorism, provided a key persuasive strategy for representing both the conditions of tyranny and the possibilities of freedom grounded in new forms of association. Thus whenever Fuller found Italians acting in concert and celebrating their shared characteristics in opposition to a foreign power, she had nothing but praise. At one point she wrote: "It is astonishing to see the clear understanding which animated the crowd as one man, and the decision with which they acted to effect their purpose. Wonderfully has this people been developed within a year!"[118] Abandoning the heroic individualism of Emerson, she began to celebrate not resistance to the power of society but its active constitution such that the Italian people might fulfill their destiny as "the advanced guard of Humanity, the herald of all Progress."[119] In short Fuller transformed the vertical structure of Transcendentalist individualism, which emphasized a sublime experience of being lifted out of oneself to a higher realm of ideas, into a horizontal structure of revolutionary nationalism, which called a nation into being based on an identification of common origin, character, and destiny that bound them together through systems of representations and practices. In her words, she would "penetrate beyond the cheats of tradesmen and the cunning of a mob corrupted by centuries of slavery, to know the real mind, the vital blood, of Italy."[120]

To accomplish this goal of nationalistic identification, however, required the people first to throw off the shackles of foreign power, which required a necessary act of mortification through which they had to acknowledge complicity in their domination. As with all old regimes, the Austrian Empire could endure only by placating the population so that it feared change more than it despised its own suffering. Fuller wrote that the Austrians, as with so many of the European powers still grounded in an alliance between the old aristocracy and the priestly class, had developed an effective way of maintaining domination: "the censure of the press prevents all easy, natural ways of instructing them; there are no public meetings, no free access to them by more instructed and aspiring minds:—the Austrian policy is to allow them a degree of material well-being, and though so much wealth is drained from the country for the service of the foreigner, enough must remain on these rich plains comfortably to feed and clothe the inhabitants." Through this arrangement Austria divided the population against itself at all levels. As she explains: "Her policy is, indeed, too thoroughly organized to change except by revolution; its scope is to serve, first, a reigning family instead of the people; second, with the people to seek a physical in preference to an intellectual good; and third, to prefer a seeming outward peace to an inward life."[121] Consequently revolution would occur when a people recognized itself as such and searched for a rewarding inward life that aimed toward a collective, intellectual good, then ousted its reigning families, suspended its physical wants, and chose active revolution over a superficial peace.

Having critiqued the structure of power that sought to keep Italians bound to a dominated subjectivity, Fuller then used her skills at synecdoche to represent a model for revolutionary liberation. Drawing from the assassination of Julius Caesar, she narrated the assassination of Count Pellegrino Rossi in her dispatch of December 2, 1848. Much had changed since the "Five Glorious Days" in the spring—namely the Austrians had retaken Milan after Italian troops had retreated. The pope, meanwhile, once the symbolic inspiration for Italian independence, now stood in opposition to war and sought conciliation with foreign powers. To try to stem the rising tide of radicalism in Rome, he had appointed Rossi as papal minister because of the latter's reputation as a moderate liberal who promoted constitutional reforms within a traditional monarchist framework that preserved the pope's authority and autonomy. His tenure turned out to be short-lived, however. On November 15 he drove to the opening of the Chamber of Deputies. Fuller recounted what followed:

> The chamber was awaiting the entrance of Rossi. Had he lived to enter, he would have found the assembly, without a single exception, ranged upon the Opposition benches. His carriage approached, attended by a howling, hissing multitude. He smiled, affected unconcern, but must have felt relieved when his horses entered the courtyard gate of the Cancelleria. He did not know he was entering the place of his execution. The horses stopped; he alighted in the midst of the crowd; it jostled him as if for the purpose of insult; he turned abruptly and received as he did so the fatal blow. It was dealt by a resolute, perhaps experienced, hand; he fell and spoke no word more.[122]

The people, however, were not struck with grief in her dramatization. The following day, at a rally of ten thousand demonstrators, including much of the civic guard, nationalist democrats rallied "to demand Pius's agreement to support a patriotic war against Austria and a new Democratic ministry."[123] During the rally Monsignor Giovanni Battista Palma, the pope's secretary, was shot and killed. A week later, fearing for his own life and realizing that his hold on power was collapsing, Pius fled Rome, leaving the city fully in the hands of the republican opposition.

The entire episode became for Fuller a representation of how the methods of violence—even of assassination—could be exploited to serve the revolutionary cause. Notably she actually made use of a dialogic form to solidify her case, but now it was dialogic in a way that was more consistent with the spirit of Plato than with Mikhail Bakhtin. Fuller narrated her encounter with an "old Patrona" on a street at night who told her Rossi had been killed. The patrona was troubled: "A wicked man, surely, but is that the way to punish CHRISTIANS?" An anonymous philosopher responds, "I cannot sympathize under any circumstances with so immoral deed; but surely the manner of doing it was *grandiose*." Meanwhile the soldiers and the populace sing out, "Blessed the hand that rids the earth of a tyrant." Having laid out the *dissoi logoi* of the case, Fuller did not make explicit her own judgment, but one could hardly misunderstand her position. After the assassination, she observed, "the soldiers in whom Rossi had trusted, whom he had hoped to flatter and bribe, stood at their posts and said not a word.—Neither they nor anyone asked 'Who did this? Where is he gone?' The sense of the people certainly was that it was an act of summary justice on an offender laws could not reach." The last she mentioned of Rossi was that the Romans "took a very pagan view of this act, and the piece represented on the occasion at the theaters was 'The Death of Nero.'" The next paragraph went on to note that there was a funeral service the next day—not for Rossi, but "in honor of the victims of Vienna."[124]

The entire event—to which Fuller herself was not present—is thus cloaked in what Capper calls "an impersonal, dreamlike narrative with all the trappings of a classical tragedy."[125] Drawing from her extensive knowledge of Greek and Roman literature, she used tragic narrative to lay blame for Rossi's assassination not on the assassin but on his character, as if it were not an assassination at all but a divine judgment of the gods. In this way Fuller effectively celebrated an act of violence—and, more important, encouraged her readership to celebrate it as well—while remaining firmly on the side of good. As she wrote to her mother the day after Rossi's assassination: "For me, I never thought to have heard of a violent death with satisfaction, but this act affected me as one of terrible justice."[126] It was through her narration of episodes such as Rossi's assassination that a "new hard-hitting tone found its way into her correspondence" as she became "more militant, more Italian, more certain than ever that her hopes were bound up with the fate of the revolutionary cause in Europe." In effect Fuller evolved over months into a revolutionary propagandist in support of Mazzini's vision, and in her writing "she began to assume the persona of Liberty in that figure's martial aspect—stoic, uncompromising, willing to shed blood if the cause demanded it."[127]

Having captured the judgment and attention of her audience through the synecdochic representation of a specific event, Fuller then used the panoramic language of myth to place this event within a broader historical narrative populated with heroes and villains. Here Fuller returned to the mythic foundations of Christian Rome, to Saint Peter, who, although denying his master three times, "returned to Rome to offer his life in attestation of his faith." The successors of Peter, Fuller writes, are honored by effigies throughout Rome, martyrs who "could be done to death in boiling oil, roasted on coals, or cut to pieces; but they could not say what they did not mean." Clearly, Fuller implies, those who rallies to the defense of Rome stood in this long tradition. But what of the pope? He denied his master but did not return, fleeing instead to the protection of the enemy. "Poor Pope!" Fuller writes, sarcastically. "How has his mind been torn to pieces in the later days. It moves compassion. . . . I believe he really thinks now the Progress movement tends to anarchy, blood, all that looked worst in the first

French Revolution." But there is good that comes of his flight (disguised as an ordinary priest), because he revealed himself not to be "the head of the Church" but merely "the Prince of the State, bound to maintain all the selfish prerogative of bygone days for the benefit of his successors." With a knowing wink at just who this "prince" represents, Fuller casually brushed him off the stage of history: "No more of him! His day is over." A new day is dawning, which "requires radical measures, clear-sighted, resolute men" who shall lead Rome to its "final triumph."[128] The cause of Italian nationalism became identified with the triumph of the kingdom of God, and its heroes and martyrs became consubstantial with the spirit of Christ and the apostles in their acts of courage and faith.

Fuller never lost sight of the practical deliberative aims of her rhetoric. Knowing she still had the ears of many influential American readers, she urged them to action in order to support the cause of Italian independence. Italy at that moment stood on the razor's edge, "and she must either advance with decision and force, or fall—since to stand still is impossible." That Italy would advance with decision, Fuller had no doubt; but whether it had sufficient force to assert its will remained in question. Thus it was contingent on American citizens to leverage their influence at home and bolster the revolutionary cause with the full support of the U.S. government (this despite the embarrassment that their nation had chosen, over the Whig candidate Henry Clay, "a new president from a Slave State, representative of the Mexican War"—Zachary Taylor). "Pray send here a good ambassador—one that has experienced the foreign life, that he may act with good judgment; and, if possible, a man that has knowledge and views which extend beyond the cause of party politics in the United States; a man of unity and principles, but capable of understanding variety in forms." Fuller was willing to take on this task herself, but "woman's day has not come yet," and she had grown "very tired of the battle with giant wrongs, and would like to have some one younger and stronger arise to say what ought to be said, still more to do what ought to be done." Just what ought to be done Fuller did not make explicit, but it was hardly unclear. She concluded her dispatch by wishing "a happy New-Year to my country! May she be worthy of the privileges she possesses, while others are lavishing their blood to win them—that is all that needs to be wished for her at present."[129] But what might have been wished for in the future would perhaps have put more burden on American lives and arms.

Fuller remained hopeful, to the end, that the lasting effects of this effort—not just by her, but by leaders such as Giuseppe Garibaldi or Mazzini—would fulfill the destiny of history, when the democratic revolution would come, like Christ, with authority and power. But it would not fulfill its destiny at that moment in 1850; the revolution was, for the time, over. In an ironic turn of events, the successful revolution in France, which brought the Second Republic to power, ended up being the demise of the revolution in Italy. The French elected as president Louis-Napoléon Bonaparte, who saw political gain in supporting the return of the pope to power as a means of rallying the support of French Catholics. After the French siege of Rome, the revolution was crushed and Austrian rule reinstated. Yet Fuller, in her final dispatch, still saw hope:

> The New Era is no longer an embryo; it is born; it begins to walk—this very year sees its first giant steps, and can no longer mistake its features. Men have long been talking of a transition state—it is over—the power of positive, determinant effort is begun. A faith is offered—men are everywhere embracing it; the film is hourly falling from their eyes and they see, not only near but far, duties worthy to be done. God be praised! It was a dark period of that sceptical endeavor and work, only worthy as helping to educate the next generation, was watered with much blood and tears. God be praised! that time is ended, and the noble band of teachers who have passed this last ordeal of the furnace and den of lions, are now ready to enter their followers for the elementary class.

Of course, she admits, that in the defeat of revolutions across Europe, "all the worst men are in power" and "all the falsities, the abuses of the old political forms, the old social compact, seem confirmed." But one misread the signs if that was their conclusion; "the struggle that is now to begin will be fearful, but even from the first hours not doubtful. . . . That advent called EMMANUEL begins to be understood, and shall no more so foully be blasphemed." The conservative editor of the *Times,* the Roman cardinal, or an Austrian officer might laugh, but in the new era that was coming, "soon you, all of you, shall '*believe* and tremble.'"[130]

The body of "Nino," Angelo Eugene Phillip Ossoli, washed up on the shore of Fire Island, New York, on July 19, 1850. He was not yet two years old. Just a few hundred yards offshore, the hull of the brig the *Elizabeth,* having crashed into a sandbar, was breaking up under the punishing force of the surf, driven by hurricane-strength winds. Rescuers had earlier tried in vain to reach the ship or at least attach to it a lifeline. Onshore, the few surviving crewmembers stumbled dazed along the beach as more bodies of the passengers accumulated along the banks and hordes of scavengers had scurried away with booty of loose cargo. Fuller and Giovanni Ossoli had remained behind until the end, hoping for rescue, she still dressed in a white nightdress as she clung to the fallen foremast. One of the surviving crewmembers, the cook, reported her last words after the steward had made a last effort to save Nino by jumping into the waves with the boy in his arms: "I see nothing but death before me—I shall never reach the shore." Just then a wave had crashed over her, and, as the cook recalled, she "was at once plunged into the sea & never rose."[131] Neither Fuller's nor Ossoli's body was ever recovered. Having endured years of war and risked everything for a cause, it was ultimately nature—that extension of the divine that had sent the young Fuller into raptures—that killed them.

At Emerson's request Henry David Thoreau was dispatched to the site of the wreck after news reached Concord three days later, to "obtain on the wrecking ground all the intelligence, and, if possible, any fragments of manuscript or other property." Of particular interest was a book manuscript Fuller had in her possession on the history of the Italian revolution. By the time Thoreau arrived by train five days after the wreck, however, little was left to find. Although two trunks had been found belonging to the Ossolis, they contained little of importance. The only thing of value Thoreau found was Ossoli's coat, from which he took a button. The manuscript was never discovered. Thoreau dutifully wrote back to Emerson what he had pieced together: "The ship struck at 10 minutes after 4 and all hands, being mostly in their night clothes made haste to the forecastle—the water coming in at once. There they remained, the passengers *in* the forecastle, the crew *above* it doing what they could. Every wave lifted the forecastle roof and washed over those within. The first man got ashore at 9. Many from 9 to noon. At floodtide about 3½ o'clock when the ship broke up entirely—they came out of the forecastle and Margaret sat with her back to the foremast with her hands over her knees—her husband and child already drowned—a great wave came and washed her off."[132]

As tragic an end it was for Fuller, she could not have asked for a more fitting conclusion to her life. Her death was not simply tragic in a colloquial sense of the word but in the original Greek context—as a divine compensation for an act of hubris, or the overstepping of conventional limits or boundary lines. At age forty Fuller had transcended almost every constraint ever put upon her by her family, her society, or her government to become arguably the most recognizable, influential, and controversial American woman of her age. On hearing of her death, Emerson wrote in his journal that "she was the largest woman; & not a woman who wished to be a man." But at the same time he lamented that "to the last her country proves inhospitable to her; brave, eloquent, subtle, accomplished, devoted, constant soul! If nature availed in America to give birth to many such as she, freedom & honour & letters & art too were safe in this new world."[133] But such is the nature of tragedy, that those who push too far beyond the limits allowed by their environment bring suffering and death upon their heads and those around them, not necessarily because they are unjust but because they are, to use Emerson's word, too large. In Italy the revolution had allowed Fuller to shatter whatever constraints remained upon her mind and body.

It is important to keep in mind that as much as Fuller became, literally, a revolutionary in Italian politics, she was also developing political opinions that placed her in even more direct opposition to the mainstream of public opinion at home. What she wrote to a friend in August 1849 she could have written as an open letter to the United States: "But will you have patience with my democracy, —my revolutionary spirit? Believe that in thought I am more radical than ever."[134] Fuller was not only a feminist but also an abolitionist, a socialist, and a revolutionary republican. Being outside of the bounds of her home country, she had been able to gain perspective on it and had not liked what she had found: "I find the cause of tyranny and wrong everywhere the same,—and lo! My Country the darkest offender, because with the least excuse, foresworn to the high calling with which she was called,—no champion of the rights of men, but a robber and a jailor; the scourge hid behind her banner; her eyes fixed, not on the stars, but on the possession of other men."[135] Going her longtime antagonist Brownson one better, Fuller saw fit to deliver to her country this message: "To you, people of America, it may perhaps be given to look on and learn in time for a preventive wisdom. You may learn the real meaning of the words FRATERNITY, EQUALITY: you may, despite the apes of the Past, who strive to tutor you, learn the needs of a true Democracy. You may in time learn to reverence, learn to guard, the true aristocracy of a nation, the only really nobles,—the LABORING CLASSES."[136] No wonder, then, that her friend Cary Sturgis Tappan speculated that perhaps Fuller had willingly allowed herself to be carried overboard: "The waves do not seem so difficult to brave as the prejudices she would have encountered if she arrived here safely."[137]

As reasonable as this conclusion sounds, it draws the wrong lesson from her death. The party who been relieved of suffering was not so much Fuller as the country to which she was returning. In Italy she had condemned the pope in the heart of Italy, called out the cowardice and brutality of the Austrians and the French, had given birth to her first child in secret and left it in the care of a nurse in order to support the republican cause, had married her lover against the explicit wishes of his Catholic family, and during the siege of Rome had accepted an assignment to nurse the wounded at the Hospital of Fate Bene Fratelli. To think that she would have been intimidated by a pack of "miserable, thoughtless Esaus" (Sad But Glorious Days, 154) eager to put a woman in her place and cease her talk about the rights of women, Native Americans, slaves, and laborers is hardly realistic. It was precisely these Esaus who likely breathed a sigh of relief on hearing of her death. Fuller had been able to perceive, with the clarity unmatched by few of her contemporaries, that the cause of tyranny and wrong was everywhere the same, and that the United States would not be spared the judgment that came to all who willfully denied the existence of a higher justice. That she had in the process gotten swept up into the fervor of the Italian revolution that led her to a dangerously romanticized support for violence in the cause of nationalism cannot be denied. But she also, in Steele's words, "modeled for her generation and those that followed the example of the politically engaged individual willing, if necessary, to accept great personal sacrifice in the service of her ideals."[138] Her life thus stands as a synecdoche not only for what was possible for a woman of the nineteenth century but what remains possible for any man and woman who would call others to their higher selves.

CHAPTER 6

"The perception and the performance of right"

Henry David Thoreau and the Rhetoric of Action

"All is quiet at Harper's Ferry," say the journals. What is the character of that calm which follows when the law and the slaveholder prevail? I regard this event as a touchstone designed to bring out, with glaring distinctness, the character of this government. We needed to be thus assisted to see it by the light of history. It needed to see itself. When a government puts forth its strength on the side of injustice, as ours to maintain slavery and kill the liberators of the slave, it reveals itself a merely brute force, or worse, a demoniacal force. It is the head of the Plug-Uglies. It is more manifest than ever that tyranny rules. I see this government to be effectually allied with France and Austria in oppressing mankind. There sits a tyrant holding fettered four millions of slaves; here comes their heroic liberator. This most hypocritical and diabolical government looks up from its seat on the gasping four millions, and inquires with an assumption of innocence: "What do you assault me for? Am I not an honest man? Cease agitation on this subject, or I will make a slave of you, too, or else hang you."

Henry David Thoreau, "A Plea for Captain John Brown," 1859

It had been just ten days since news had reached Concord, Massachusetts, of John Brown's failed raid on the armory at Harpers Ferry, Virginia. It had not taken long for public opinion to harden against Brown, whether for his aim of liberating the slaves, his method of using guerrilla tactics to achieve it, or the apparent incompetence and sheer fantastical nature of his plan. Even William Lloyd Garrison's abolitionist paper, the *Liberator,* called it "a misguided, wild, and apparently insane . . . effort."[1] But at least one citizen of Concord, forty-two-year-old Henry David Thoreau, held a much different evaluation of Brown's actions. The day he learned the news, on October 19, 1859, he wrote in his journal the following: "It galls me to listen to the remarks of craven-hearted neighbors who speak disparagingly of John Brown because he resorted to violence, resisted the government, threw his life away!—what way would they have thrown their lives, pray?—neighbors who would praise a man for attacking singly an ordinary band of thieves or murderers. Such minds are not equal to the occasion. They preserve the so-called peace of their community by deeds of petty violence every day."[2] Thoreau clearly felt that his mind—perhaps alone among his peers—*was* equal to the occasion. On October 30 he spread the news that he would be delivering a speech at the town hall that would come to be titled "A Plea for Captain John Brown." The Republican town committee refused to ring the bell to announce the event, so he rang it himself.

The crowd in attendance that day, whether to support or to jeer Thoreau, witnessed one of the most incendiary addresses by any Transcendentalist. In a clear nod to Fuller's dispatches, he aligned the United States with the imperial states of Austria and France, only worse in its hypocrisy—especially when one saw that its grand ideals were being used to rationalize its oppression of four million slaves and the execution of their would-be liberator. Using a reference now lost on most contemporary readers, he compared government leaders to the Plug-Uglies, which refers to the most prominent of the gangs in Baltimore who used violence, assassination, and intimidation to elect nativist candidates of the Know-Nothing Party to office and who gained national prominence when one member of the gang shot dead a Baltimore police officer in 1858. Like that gang member, the U.S. government now simply chose to execute any that opposed it, revealing itself as merely an expression of brute, demoniacal force whose only aim was to maintain a state of oppression. But, Thoreau concludes, "such a government is losing its power and respectability as surely as water runs out of a leaky vessel."[3]

In the face of such pervasive force, enacted not only upon but also through everyday citizens by petty acts of violence, only one course was open to those who felt themselves equal to the occasion—to be a Transcendentalist. But this was a different type of person than the poetical genius defined by Emerson. The true Transcendentalist was a man of action like Brown. As Thoreau explained, Brown was "a man of rare common sense and directness of speech, as of action; a transcendentalist above all, a man of ideas and principles,—that was what distinguished him. Not yielding to a whim or transient impulse, but carrying out the purpose of the life."[4] In the climactic statement at the end of his lecture, Thoreau transformed Brown from a flawed human being—indeed, a man who not only attacked Harpers Ferry and held sixty citizens hostages at gunpoint but also led a raid in Pottawatomi Creek, Kansas, in which five proslavery settlers were hacked to death with broadswords—into a divine symbol: "Some eighteen hundred years ago Christ was crucified; this morning, perchance, Captain Brown was hung. These are the two ends of a chain which is not without its links. He is not old

Brown any longer; he is an Angel of Light."[5] Thus he translated Brown's heroic pattern of experience of principled violent resistance to slavery into a symbol that he believed contained the key to his era.

Reading Thoreau's encomium to Brown today, in full knowledge of the latter's fanatical megalomania and aware of the years of carnage that soon engulfed the nation in civil war, it is easy to find fault with it both stylistically and ethically. Stripped of the beauty of its prose, it emerges as an exercise in adolescent hero-worship and a dangerous flirtation with terroristic violence. Even an admirer such as Lewis Hyde admits that reading "Plea" makes him reinterpret some of Thoreau's early essays with a more critical eye: "I pause more now when Thoreau proclaims his love of heroes. I am cautious before his grandiosity, his mythmaking, his manliness. His solitude and his refusal still stir me, but I am more aware of the political registers that they exclude." Thoreau had cultivated over many years what Hyde calls a uniquely prophetic voice that "speaks of things that will be true in the future because they are true in all time" and thus "juxtaposes today and eternity to make it clear that the latter may inform the former." Defined in this way, transcendental eloquence cannot but help make use of the prophetic voice insofar as it remains Transcendentalist. But the case of Brown, for Hyde, offers a reminder that prophesies "have an uncanny way of revealing a darker side when we finally embody them in action."[6] It is easy to applaud calls for heroic action against injustice when these actions exist only in the imagination; it is quite another thing to celebrate over the bodies of the dead who were killed by a so-called Angel of Light.

Rhetorically Thoreau's encomium of Brown also presents a challenge to those who look for an overarching style of eloquence that pervades all of his writing. Richard Dillman, for instance, has argued that "in addition to his importance as a stylist, a naturalist, and an apostle of self-reliance, Henry David Thoreau was also a philosopher of rhetoric." According to Dillman, Thoreau adapted the insights of nineteenth-century rhetoricians such as Hugh Blair, Richard Whately, and George Campbell to develop a style of truth-speaking that directly challenged an audience by use of vivacious images; "terse, aphoristic sentences; cumulative ones; and rhetorical questions." While true, this stylistic approach to Thoreau's rhetoric does little to inform the understanding of his two lectures on Brown, leaving readers with only the dissatisfying conclusion that both were "energetically presented and effective with their audiences."[7] Henry Golemba and Robert Milder, meanwhile, have gone beyond Dillman's neo-Aristotelian approach to offer more philosophical readings to Thoreau's rhetoric. Resonant with how Bloom, Poirier, and Pease approach Emerson, Golemba finds in Thoreau a "wild rhetoric" modeled on the complexity, contradiction, and never-ending mystery that he found in nature. Against the traditional uses of rhetoric to persuade, he uses a "language that speaks in riddles, a tormenting language that threatens to devour those who fail to decode its mysteries but laughs at those who believe they have solved its enigmas, a teasing language that baffles its readers but will not let them go."[8] Milder, meanwhile, describes how Thoreau used a "rhetoric of ascent" to reimagine himself continually in his own writing as one who was climbing a ladder to higher modes of living, with his constant self-mythologizing functioning rhetorically as a "Burkean act of bridge-building designed to lead his audience from a brutish to a semi-divine life."[9] It is notable that both Golemba and Milder focus almost exclusively on *Walden* and mention his more explicit political essays largely as biographical details. For despite clearly making use of these two genres of rhetoric in *Walden* and other essays, Thoreau's defense of Brown neither speaks in riddles nor mythologizes him as a model of imitation; instead he explicitly holds up Brown's violent resistance as an ideal to be followed by others without equivocation, justified by a clearly defined ethics of political resistance.

Despite clear differences, however, the attitude and style of his "Plea for John Brown" are for the most part remarkably consistent with his previous works in two significant ways. First, the moral and strategic logic of his plea is an extension of the same economy of power that he had developed throughout his life and applied both in his political and his nature writings. The phrase "economy of power" comes from Foucault, specifically when he called for a "new economy of power relations" that was more empirical and took "the forms of resistance against different forms of power as a starting point." Rather than interpret power as a preconceived whole with its own internal rationality to which people are subjected, this new economy of power consisted of "using this resistance as a chemical catalyst so as to bring to light power relations, locate their position, find out their point of application and the methods used."[10] In other words the economy of power understands power relations as an antagonism of different strategies and forces rather than a total coherent system, and it discerns the social economy of power—the complex interconnectedness by which it exerts force with more or less efficiency—by the ways it responds to particular acts of resistance. But in Thoreau the economy of power encompassed more than social critique; it also applied to the economy of nature, or "all of the living organisms of the earth as an interactive whole," of which the economy of one's own life was but a part.[11] The economy of nature established a transcendent ideal or standard by which the economy of one's life could be judged and modeled upon in order to maximize simplicity, self-reliance, and joy. Thoreau's transcendental economy of power operated on two levels. The first investigated the laws of nature and used them to regulate the patterns of one's life; the second used precise and targeted forms of action as a means to measure, criticize, and reimagine the power of both self and society so that through shock and reform each could progress toward a perfectionist ideal. In this sense encomium to Brown was just one more way of juxtaposing the ideal with the actual.

Second, we can see in "Plea" another manifestation of the rhetoric of action most powerfully articulated most in "Resistance to Civil Government." The rhetoric of action is an extension of the economy of power—it is a strategic publication of deeds that not only reveals the virtues of the actor but, more important, exposes the nature of corruption and domination inherent in a social network of power. The apparent contradiction between the nonviolent tenor of "Resistance" and the praise of Brown's violence in "Plea" is thus resolved when it is seen that Thoreau largely (although not entirely) interpreted both as symbolic actions whose aim was not to accomplish a specific instrumental end but to challenge the conscience of a nation. Moreover seeing in Thoreau a continuous commitment to the rhetoric of action responds to Hannah Arendt's criticism that he does not represent an ideal of civil disobedience because he placed solitary acts of conscience over collective political action. Arendt's critique of Thoreau is that "arguments raised in defense of individual conscience or individual acts, that is, moral imperatives and appeals to a 'higher law,' be it secular or transcendent, are inadequate when applied to civil disobedience."[12] But Arendt can make this claim only by ignoring the rhetorical character of Thoreau's lectures and writings that gave those individual acts of conscience publicity. Shannon L. Mariotti, for instance, argues that what she calls Thoreau's practices of withdrawal were "not apolitical retreats but ways of confronting particular objects that stimulate dissonant, rupturing, negative critiques of modern society and allow him to recuperate capacities that define truly democratic citizens." But whereas Mariotti focuses on the importance of "inglorious and inconspicuous acts" (such as huckleberrying) to the development of the self, I wish to emphasize the centrality of rhetorical performance for dramatizing them within the public sphere so that they might inspire the kind of civil disobedience celebrated by Arendt.[13]

In fact it is recognizing the absolute necessity of rhetoric to Thoreau's method of civil disobedience that makes it a complete and wholly realistic mode of resistance. Only by rhetoric one can realistically interpret the central claim of his earlier essay "Resistance to Civil Government": "Action from principle, the perception and the performance of right, changes things and relations; it is essentially revolutionary, and does not consist wholly with anything which was. It not only divides states and churches, it divides families; ay, it divides the *individual,* separating the diabolical in him from the divine."[14] This passage, so frequently quoted as to appear virtually mundane, does not simply argue, as Christopher Lyle Johnstone suggests, that civil disobedience "will nurture the growth of a just society by altering the consciousness of the individual who employs it."[15] Of course it does do that as well. Action from principle that is complete (rather than partial) forces the individual who performs it to make a total commitment that does not tolerate compromise with the diabolical. However, these individual effects do not explain how Thoreau can make the claim that if "*one* HONEST man, in this State of Massachusetts, *ceasing to hold slaves*, were actually to withdraw from this copartnership, and be locked up in the county jail therefor, it would be the abolition of slavery in America."[16] This example says nothing about the effect of this act on that individual's conscience; what is important are the effects that his or her act would have on the political landscape of the entire nation. But these effects are fundamentally rhetorical consequences. They are the consequences that followed in the wake of Brown's raid and subsequent execution.

Ironically what helped transform Brown's raid into the rhetoric of action was the phenomenon that Thoreau so famously criticized throughout his works—the rise of the telegraph press and the arrival of what Marshall McLuhan has called the "electric age." Thoreau, being younger than the other Transcendentalists, matured during the 1840s when the first telegraph lines were being laid in the United States and the possibility of instantaneous communication across great distances became possible. According to McLuhan the most immediate effect of this change was the rise of the "human interest story" in the telegraph press, namely because "the 'human interest' dimension is simply that of immediacy of participation in the experience of others that occurs with instant information." In short the electric media of the telegraph abolished the divisive spatial dimension and began to "resume person-to-person relations as if on the smallest village scale."[17] By exploiting the qualities of the communication revolution he so frequently disparaged, Thoreau was able to bridge the gap between his private perfectionist ideals of goodness and his political commitments to social justice. By calculating the potential persuasive influence of private actions that gain publicity through the new media of his day, he was able to integrate into his transcendental economy of power the political importance of individual acts of conscience once eloquence translated them into symbols. In this sense Thoreau was far from an example of Transcendentalist naïveté; he was in fact the most modern thinker of them all and the one who practiced and theorized a rhetoric of action whose power to shock and divide a nation was recognized and developed in the wake of the telegraph press and has continued unabated into the digital age.

Henry David Thoreau was not yet four years old when Sampson Reed delivered his oration "Genius" at Harvard in 1821. Born to Cynthia and John Thoreau on July 12, 1817, he was really of another generation than Reed, Alcott, Brownson, Emerson, or even Fuller, all of whom were born prior to the War of 1812 and the ascendancy of the United States to the position of international power. Thoreau was an inheritor of that power. His father had served faithfully as commissary at

194 | THE KEYS OF POWER

Fort Independence in Boston Harbor and had received 160 acres of land in return. However, despite the generous payment, the land did little to raise the standard of living of his family.[18] Throughout Thoreau's childhood there was no sudden rise in his family's fortunes. At the same time that he took for granted that the United States was a powerful nation, he also came to expect that this power would almost never translate into economic prosperity for himself or his family. Being of a naturally stoic demeanor, he thus turned his attention to other things. As one story goes, one night his mother found him awake in bed, staring out the window: "Why, Henry dear, don't you go to sleep?" "Mother," he replied, "I have been looking to the stars to see if I could see God behind them."[19]

As this anecdote indicates, there is a sense in which Thoreau almost belongs to no time. It is as if his body was simply a vehicle by which the mind of some universal observer took notes on the present. Emerson wrote, for instance, that Thoreau "knew how to sit immovable, a part of the rock he rested on, until the bird, the reptile, the fish, which had retired from him, should come back and resume its habits, nay, moved by curiosity, should come to him and watch him."[20] But Thoreau had the unnerving habit of applying his same method of patient, detached observation to human activities as well. One of the few reminiscences of Thoreau by a former classmate captures his impact on others: "No profane or vulgar words did I ever hear, or know, to come from his mouth, and in all his intercourse with his mates he was always gentle and obliging. He never engaged in any of the sports or games that the boys of his age delighted in, but preferred to stand still and look on, which he did with an indifference that to us boys was perfectly unaccountable and disgusting."[21] For the boys, no doubt, it was as if they were being spied on by some omniscient, judging eye, only in the form of an awkward and large-nosed boy from a poor merchant's family who lived down the road. There is no historical context that would account for Thoreau's stoical habits—particularly given the gregarious personality of his older brother, John Jr. It is just how nature had put him together.

But what Thoreau observed, and the judgments he came to make about those observations, can be directly attributed to the influences of his mother and father. In *Walden* he had observed that "the mass of men lead lives of quiet desperation."[22] Whether or not this statement remains true for the actual mass of men may be debated, but it is certainly true of the life of John Thoreau Sr. According to Thoreau's biographer Walter Harding, his father was "a quiet mousey sort of man," fond of music and reading classical literature, whose "favorite occupation was to sit by the stove in his little shop and chat by the hour."[23] Had John Sr. been contented in this life, perhaps his easygoing ways might have appeared a virtue; but he was not. Thoreau's father was a middling businessman at best and at times a failure. Neighbors described him as "an amiable and most lovable gentlemen, but far too honest and scarcely sufficiently energetic for this exacting yet not over scrupulous world of ours."[24] Before the birth of his children, he had already opened and closed his own store in Concord, had spent time in Bangor, Maine, selling goods to Native Americans, and then had taken over management of another man's store in Concord. After Henry's birth, John would try and fail at owning his own store in Chelmsford and teaching school in Boston before finally returning to Concord after his vagabond entrepreneur of a brother-in-law, Charles Dunbar, managed to get the mineral rights to a graphite mine and asked him to establish a business in manufacturing pencils in 1823. The income from the business was just enough to keep the family above the poverty line. Thus even after constantly moving his family, struggling against competition, experimenting with new ventures, and fretting over debt, John Sr. could never attain the autonomy he desired. In the end Cynthia Thoreau had to take in boarders to pay for food and the children's tuition.[25]

Although he observed in his father the kind of bourgeois striving he judged to be a sign of quiet desperation, Thoreau's mother provided him his first and perhaps greatest model of what he referred to in *Walden* as "that economy of living which is synonymous with philosophy."[26] Cynthia Thoreau was in many ways the opposite of her husband—tall, outspoken, moralistic, thrifty, and charismatic. Having been born just thirty days before the death of her father in 1787, she had been raised by her mother, who had made a living operating a tavern out of her home before remarrying in 1798. Having grown up without a patriarchal figure in the house, she quite naturally took to asserting power—not only in her own household but in the public sphere. Inside her home she applied a rigorous economics of living to their own affairs, dividing what little food they had with absolute equality, making the children wear hand-me-down or homemade clothes, and almost always going without "tea, coffee, sugar, and other luxuries, so that Mrs. Thoreau could spend a little money they could spare on music lessons." But she was equally active outside the home. A born reformer, she forcefully expressed her opinions about political affairs in social conversations and was a member of the Concord Female Charitable Society and founder of the Concord Women's Anti-Slavery Society. Harding points out that, "poor as they were, each year at both Thanksgiving and Christmas she invited her poorer neighbors in for dinner. Throughout her life she showed compassion for the downtrodden, whether Negro, Indian, or white."[27] If his father seemed concerned only with making pencils and chatting with his customers around the stove, his mother demonstrated a kind of life that sought to apply in every action, however small, some principle of justice.

Yet despite their differences, both John and Cynthia worked together to instill in their son what came to be his most important attitude—his love of nature.

In the early days of their marriage, "they could often be found in their spare time, at almost any season of the year, exploring the banks of the Assabet, the Cliffs at Fairhaven, or the shores of Walden Pond. One of their children, it is said, narrowly escaped being born on Lee's Hill, the site of one of their favorite rambles."[28] These habits continued into parenthood, particularly with Cynthia. Often she would take the children out into the woods to hear the songs of wild birds: "On bright afternoons she would gather them together and walk out to Nashawtuc Hull, the Cliffs at Fairhaven, or the 'little woods' between the river and Main Street, and there, after building a rough fireplace, would cook their supper while they enjoyed the flowers and bird songs. A chowder boiled on the Walden Pond sandbar when he was seven stood out particularly in her son's mind."[29] Given the fact that so few luxuries were offered Thoreau in his everyday life—not even the taste of sugar, for example—the pleasures of nature must have stood out that much more prominently for someone with such keen senses. Amid a growing market economy in which all worthwhile goods seemed to come with a price tag, nature was not only free but promised to deliver the greatest good of understanding and wisdom. It cost him nothing to gaze at the stars.

But it did cost something for him to learn about the science and symbolism of the stars. Thoreau was fortunate to have come of school age during the time when educational reformers, primarily Unitarians, were founding schools across New England. In Concord four prominent citizens, led by Phineas Allen, had founded the Concord Academy in 1822 as a college preparatory school, going well beyond the routine education in reading, writing, and arithmetic. They taught instead "Virgil, Sallust, Cicero, Caesar, Euripides, Homer, Xenophon, Voltaire, Molière, and Racine in the original languages as well as geography, history, grammar, spelling, astronomy, botany, algebra, trigonometry, geometry, natural philosophy, and natural history."[30] Recognizing the opportunity that such an education would provide her sons, in 1828 (the year that Bronson Alcott finished the first three years of teaching in Connecticut) Cynthia Thoreau enrolled John Jr. and an eleven-year-old Henry in the school in 1828 at the cost of five dollars per student per quarter, a cost absorbed by the boarders in her house. Soon her son would be able not only to see God behind the stars, but also to chart the stars, recognize the constellations, and tell stories of their Namesalces.

The Concord Academy also gave Thoreau his first rhetorical training. At the end of each twelve-week quarter, Allen would make the students engage in classical declamatory exercises. Thoreau recited such texts as Croly's "The Death of Leonidas," Shakespeare's "Prince Henry and Falstaff," and Bonaparte's "Address to His Army" and was only one of three students to receive a "good" recommendation. Less impressive but equally significant in terms of his exposure to rhetoric was his participation in the Concord Academic Debating Society, also organized by Allen. Thoreau participated several times during the end of the year in 1829, although in one case he and his disputant came so unprepared that the secretary lashed out at them in his notes: "Such a debate, if it may be called so, as we have had, this evening, I hope never again will be witnessed in this house or recorded in this book. It is not only a waste of *time,* but of paper to record such proceedings, of wood and oil." Yet the secretary would be spared such a torture; the debating society was dissolved that year as emphasis shifted to the newly formed Concord Lyceum. There, too, Thoreau eagerly participated, although as a member of an audience, hearing orations from some of the most eloquent public intellectuals of his day. For a young man who spent most of his free time walking through the woods or boating along Walden Pond, Thoreau received a remarkably thorough rhetorical education; and despite his reputation for shyness in seclusion, it was "reported that the boys used to assemble about Thoreau as he sat on the school fence to hear him talk."[31] Perhaps it was simply that he preferred to speak only when he had prepared an oration beforehand.

It was not until 1837, however, that he was finally given his chance to shine from the rostrum. In 1833 his family decided it would be Henry, because of his intellectual abilities, who would be sent to Harvard at a cost of $179 a year—John and their sister Helen, being content with becoming teachers to help support the family. There Thoreau experienced almost the exact same curriculum as did Emerson, with courses in the Greek and Roman classics, mathematics, English (including rhetoric, forensics, and elocution), languages, natural philosophy, natural history, and Western philosophy. In fact Emerson himself participated in this curriculum by invitation, and it was in this capacity that Thoreau first encountered him; in 1835 he examined Thoreau and a group of other students on rhetoric.[32] Presumably Thoreau passed. Yet the Emersonian spirit was hardly the norm. Although impressive in scope, the curriculum was taught largely through mechanical drilling, and the stagnant atmosphere created by President Josiah Quincy made Thoreau express "an unconcealed distaste for the system."[33] Still, due to his sheer intellectual capacities, he graduated in 1837 with a high enough rank to allow him to be part of the commencement exercises, where he delivered part of an oration, along with two other graduates, on the theme of "The Commercial Spirit of Modern Times, Considered in Its Influence on the Political, Moral, and Literary Character of a Nation."[34] In attendance as commencement speaker was his former examiner of rhetoric, who was just a few months away from becoming Thoreau's friend and mentor.

Yet the inspiration for Thoreau's first rhetorical oration was likely not as much from Emerson, whose *Nature* he had eagerly read that spring, as from a more unexpected, radical voice—Orestes Brownson. The meeting was quite by chance. In 1835 Harvard had instituted a policy by which students could take up to thirteen weeks' leave to teach school to finance their education. Thoreau had taken advantage of this opportunity to apply for a position in Canton, Massachusetts, for spring 1836, where he was interviewed by a member of the school board, then Unitarian minister Reverend Brownson. As later recollected by William Ellery Channing, on learning that Thoreau knew German, Brownson "sat up until midnight talking with him," after which they "struck heartily to studying German, and getting all they could of the time together, like old friends."[35] In exchange for being taught German, Thoreau helped tutor Brownson's children. Later Thoreau sent Brownson a letter of gratitude: "I have never ceased to look back with interest, not to say satisfaction, upon the six short weeks I passed with you. They were an era in my life—the morning of a new *Lebenstag*. They are to me as a dream that it dreamt, which returns from time to time in all its original freshness. Such a one I would dream a second or third time, and then tell it before breakfast."[36] Although little is known of the nature of their relationship beyond these passages, it is clear that "the six weeks gave young Thoreau his first continuous association with a mature and provocative intelligence."[37]

The second continuous association had a much more lasting and dramatic impact on Thoreau. After a brief and disastrous stint as a public school teacher (which he quit after refusing to administer corporal punishment), Thoreau had been temporarily freed to read, write, think, go on walks—and, most important, strike up a relationship with Emerson. By the next year, Emerson was referring to the younger man as "my brave Henry Thoreau" in his journal, often recounting stories Thoreau told him on their long walks together.[38] For example, an entry from February 11, 1838, reads as follows: "I delight much in my young friend, who seems to have as free & erect a mind as any I have ever met. He told as we walked this afternoon a good story about a boy who went to school with him, Wentworth, who resisted the school mistress' command that the children should bow to Dr Heywood & other gentlemen as they went by. And when Dr Heywood stood waiting & cleared his throat with a Hem! Wentworth said, 'you need not hem, Doctor; I shan't bow.'"[39] The story was clearly tailor-made for Emerson's ears, a story of youthful rebellion against staid tradition, the celebration of nonconformist individuality in adolescence. But more important, it shows the spirit that Emerson brought out in his admirer. As Richardson concludes, whereas Thoreau's life up until this point "can be seen as the unsurprising result of familiar and conventional shaping forces such as Concord, Harvard, and his immediate family," through the "extraordinary, catalytic, almost providential friendship of Emerson, Thoreau's life changed from the passive to the active mood. Emerson taught Thoreau that he could—indeed he must—shape his own life and pursue his own ends."[40] Emerson cultivated in Thoreau that same confidence, as it were, not to bow but to stand free and erect and speak the truth to the waiting world.

The effect on Thoreau was immediate. Perhaps in the whole history of American letters, no single remark was ever so influential on a future author than what Emerson suggested to Thoreau that fall: "'What are you doing now?' he asked. 'Do you keep a journal?' So I make my first entry to-day.'"[41] This was Thoreau's first entry, made on October 22, 1837, in a journal he was to keep throughout his entire life, by the end representing roughly seven thousand pages and two million words. One can already hear the same voice of *Walden* in just the second entry, made on October 24. Titled "The Mould Our Deeds Leave," it reads:

> Every part of nature teaches that the passing away of one life is the making room for another. The oak dies down to the ground, leaving within its rind a rich virgin mould, which will impart a vigorous life to an infant forest. The pine leaves a sandy and sterile soil, the harder woods a strong and fruitful mould.
>
> So this constant abrasion and decay makes the soil of my future growth. As I live now so I shall reap. If I grow pines and birches, my virgin mould will not sustain the oak; but pines and birches, or, perchance, weeds and brambles, will constitute my second growth.[42]

Distinctive about these passages is not necessarily how Thoreau draws analogies from the natural world to create maxims for living—a technique common to classical rhetoric and mastered by Emerson—but rather the level of detail, and familiarity with fact, that he brings to his analogies. Anyone who observes or labors in nature is familiar with the cycle of generation, decay, and rebirth; but not all know the differences in the molds left behind by oak, pine, and birch trees. Thoreau's journal was a method not only of making increasingly precise measurements and observations of nature, but also of finding a way of crafting ever more precise metaphors and analogies by which to interpret human existence.

One also sees in these early entries the strong urge in Thoreau to withdraw from society into his own private conscience. Anticipating the kind of antisocial attitude that Arendt later saw as antithetical to genuine methods of civil disobedience, his first entry provided the metaphor for the place that he could use to escape not only social pressures but his own ego. Titled "Solitude," the entry reads: "To be alone I find it necessary to escape the present,—I avoid myself. How could I be alone in the Roman emperor's chamber of mirrors? I seek a garret. The spiders must not be disturbed, nor the floor swept, nor the lumber arranged." The image of the garret returned on April 8, 1840, when he asked: "How shall I help myself? By withdrawing into the garret, and associating with spiders and mice, determining to meet myself face-to-face sooner or later. Completely silent and attentive I will be this hour, and the next, and forever. The most positive life that history notices has been a constant retiring out of life, a wiping one's hands of it, seeing how mean it is, and having nothing to do with it."[43] Thoreau preferred spiders to men, it seems. The ideal of the garret continually appealed to him throughout his life, tempting him with Emersonian retirement that would allow him to meet himself face-to-face in complete disregard for the rest of the world.

At the same time, however, Thoreau offered an appropriate metaphor for the counterimpulse toward public action in an entry of December 23, 1841—that of Robin Hood. He writes: "A forest is in all mythologies a sacred place, as the oaks among the druids and the grove of Egeria; and even in more familiar and common life a celebrated wood is spoken of with respect, as 'Barnsdale Wood' and 'Sherwood.' Had Robin Hood no Sherwood to resort to, it would be difficult to invest his story with the charms it has got. It is always the tale that is untold, the deeds done and the life lived in the unexpected secrecy of the wood, that charm and make us children again,—to read his ballads, and hear of the greenwood tree."[44] Much in the image of Robin Hood is consistent with Thoreau's garret, notably the fact that he chose to live in "the unexplored secrecy of the wood" apart from the utter poverty, both real and symbolic, of the social world everyone else inhabits. Yet Robin Hood only exists as a symbol of a hero who periodically emerged from his wood to shock and reform the political culture of his time. The purity of the wood thus functioned rhetorically as a standard by which to judge the corruption and decadence of society, with the juxtaposition made possible only through the heroic actions of Robin Hood, whose effect was more symbolic than practical. His raids from Sherwood Forest were not frontal assaults to topple the regime of Prince John but rather symbolic actions meant to provoke a response and thereby expose the nature of its domination to the people.

By his subsequent practice, it is clear that Thoreau sought to step into the role of Transcendentalist Robin Hood, only using eloquence instead of arrows. Just a few months after meeting Emerson and being encouraged to write out "the history of his college life," he produced a lecture titled "Society," which he delivered at the Concord Lyceum in the spring of 1838 (of which he then became the curator for the next two years).[45] Although the lecture does not survive, fragments indicate that Thoreau was not out to condemn or reject all of society but rather to establish within it "a truer association of people, not just people and crowds, but groups of individuals who are friends."[46] Not soon after his inaugural lecture, he was encouraged by Emerson to submit a short essay to the *Dial* in 1840, which Margaret Fuller politely rejected. Titled simply "The Service," it was a rambling treatise on the distinction between the courageous and the cowardly man, fraught with martial metaphors that anticipated his famous image of marching to the beat of a different drummer: "A man's life should be a stately march to an unheard music; and when to his fellows it may seem irregular and inharmonious, he will be stepping to a livelier measure, which only his nicer ear can detect.

There will be no halt, ever, but at most a marching on his post."[47] But despite the initial rejection, Thoreau nonetheless see another essay, "Aulus Persius Flaccus," appear in the inaugural issue of the *Dial,* and many essays in subsequent editions. From the moment he graduated college, Thoreau was firmly dedicated to honing the art of publicity.

As with Emerson and Fuller before him, the tragic death of someone close to him that provided the release that allowed him to embrace fully the militant lifestyle of the naturalist poet. Despite his ideal of working only on the Sabbath, the demands of life and his family forced him to find a job after graduation. After failing to land another established teaching job (at one point going in search of one all the way up to Maine, where he saw his first glimpse of a true wilderness and became acquainted with a Native American guide), he established his own academy in Concord with four paying students. Soon his older brother, John, joined him. Not only did the school thrive, but so did the relationship between the brothers. Despite John's physical frailty—he weighed only 117 pounds—they often spent time together when school was out, at one point in 1839 spending two weeks together sailing up the Concord and Merrimack Rivers with the goal to climb Mount Washington in New Hampshire. The time teaching with his brother was, according to Robinson, "one of Thoreau's more rewarding vocational experiences"; if all had gone well, it is highly likely that "Thoreau might have settled into the life of a schoolmaster."[48]

Then, on New Year's Day, 1842, John cut his finger with a razor. Eight days later his body was convulsed with spasms from lockjaw so violent that his head almost touched his heels. Thoreau nursed his brother as best he could, but two days later John died in his arms. "The cup that my Father gives me, shall I not drink it?" John was recorded as saying during his last hours.[49] Thoreau was so traumatized that a week later he suffered the same symptoms of lockjaw, only in his case psychosomatically. To make matters worse, the day he recovered, Emerson's son Waldo developed scarlet fever. Three days later the little boy, too, was dead. On March 1 Thoreau recorded in his journal: "My life, my life! why will you linger? Are the years short and the months of no account? How often has long delay quenched my aspirations! Can God afford that I should forget him? Is he so indifferent to my career? Can heaven be postponed with no more ado?"[50] Heaven could not. Richardson concludes: "It is almost as though John's death freed him. The final effect on him of such terrible losses was to confirm, by the very starkness of the contrast, his own continuing life, the vitality of which was now increasingly urgent, increasingly less something to be complacently taken for granted."[51] After this moment in 1842, Thoreau threw himself into the art of living.

It was fortunate that he embarked on his new journey having secured for himself his own kind of garret that allowed him a remarkable degree of freedom to think, walk, and write. From 1841 until 1843, this garret consisted of a room in Emerson's house, having been hired by his mentor to take "care of Emerson's children, his carpentry, his yard work, his gardening, all the while doing other chores for other people around the village, the Transcendental handyman."[52] It also gave Thoreau access to Emerson's library, opportunity for conversation with Emerson and his numerous guests, and a quiet place to retreat for intellectual work and reflection. After the death of John, Emerson's house also became a site for new creation. Identifying in Thoreau a rush of energy in the months after the loss of his brother, Emerson "picked up in Boston a stack of scientific surveys on the flora, fauna, and natural resources of Massachusetts" and in April set for Thoreau a task more suited to his personality than neoclassical criticisms of Roman poets such as Persius—he was to write a naturalistic survey of the region.[53] After months of work, the result appeared in the July edition of the *Dial*, now under the editorship of Emerson.

"The Natural History of Massachusetts," along with two essays published in 1843, "A Walk to Wachusett" (published in *Boston Miscellany of Literature and Fashion*) and "A Winter Walk" (published in the *Dial*), vaulted Thoreau from a poor imitator of Emerson to a master of a an emergent genre that Buell calls "literary naturism," or the effort to use literature to represent the nonhuman environment to a popular readership. For Buell there are four ingredients that comprise the text of literary naturism. First, "the nonhuman environment is present not merely as a framing device but as a presence that begins to suggest that human history is implicated in natural history." Second, "the human interest is not understood to be the only legitimate interest." This leads naturally to the third aspect, which is that "human accountability to the environment is part of the text's ethical orientation." Lastly, "some sense of the environment as a process rather than a constant or a given is at least implicit in the text." But these were not dry scientific treatises or moralistic lectures; they were also exercises in "romantic literary sublimity" of the type that were "consumed with relish in many a Victorian parlor."[54] According to Steven Fink, they "conformed to the current vogue for picturesque travel narratives and for work contributing to the spirit of literary nationalism." Although occasionally punctuated by Thoreau's paradoxical statements, militant judgments, and Transcendentalist imagery, these works "remained within the conventions of the romantic excursion quite familiar in the magazine literature of the day: a fairly detailed account of the sights and scenes of the tour, peppered with the thoughtful observations and reflections of the sensitive and literate traveler." Particularly in the case of the short-lived *Boston Miscellany*, the audience for this genre was "both New England gentility and those aspire to that class, with the deliberate emphasis on female readers."[55]

The reclusive and often caustic Thoreau won praise from an audience of young women for his delicate and poetic descriptions of nature.

It is indicative of Thoreau's literary ambitions that he did not use this opportunity to retire deeper into Sherwood Forest to commune with nature but to journey, of all places, to New York City to pursue his aims as a writer. In May 1843 he left for Staten Island (notably just a month after the Boston and Fitchburg Railroad, which was to stretch all the way to Albany, had been contracted to pass through Concord). Staten Island offered him a jumping-off place to visit the city in order to break into the literary marketplace (much in the way that Margaret Fuller did the following year). But despite numerous visits to the city (each of which fascinated him with new experiences of what he called "the crowd," which he said is "something new and to be attended to"), he found that the market was saturated with eager writers willing to sell their material for almost nothing. He wrote to Emerson: "Literature comes to a poor market here, and even the little that I write is more than will sell. I have tried the Democratic Review, the New Mirror, and Brother Jonathan. The last two, as well as the New World, are overwhelmed with contributions which cost nothing, and are worth no more. The Knickerbocker is too poor, and only the Ladies' Companion pays."[56] In the end he was only able to publish two pieces in the *Democratic Review:* a review essay called "Paradise (to Be) Regained" and a light sketch he consciously wrote for a broad audience called "The Landlord," in which "Thoreau facetiously celebrates the Tavern and its Landlord as epitomizing the true spirit of hospitality."[57] But realizing he could not make a living in New York, he returned to Concord at the end of the year to move back into his family's house and make pencils. But the trip had not been a total loss. He had met many people, including Albert Brisbane, Henry James Sr., and newspaperman Horace Greeley, who in time became "a tireless and loyal promoter of Thoreau's work."[58] More important, his failure had not quenched his desire to make a name for himself as a writer.

Although Thoreau had not been gone long, it is almost as if he had returned to a different world. On May 22, 1844, Concord heard the news that a new telegraph line had been built between Washington, D.C., and Baltimore. The next month saw the Fitchburg Railroad open, allowing anyone for fifty cents to take an hour train ride and arrive in Boston a full three hours before any stagecoach. What McLuhan would call the "message" of the medium was clear—Concord was soon integrated within the expanding transportation and communication network of the nation, dramatically increasing the scale of action and the pace of life while disrupting eighteenth-century patterns of agrarian life. According to McLuhan, by dramatically reducing the distance between center and margin, the railway "accelerated and enlarged the scale of previous human functions, creating totally new kind of cities and new kinds of work and leisure," while the telegraph, by eliminating the distance between minds, introduced the "simultaneity of electric communication," which "makes each of us present and accessible to every other person in the world."[59] In *Walden* Thoreau remarked that the result was a nation that "lived too fast. Men think that it is essential that the *Nation* have commerce, and export ice, and talk about a telegraph, and ride 30 miles an hour," as if all of these things can be accomplished as mere means to an end. They forget the important fact that the embrace of a new medium changes people's nature. In his words, "we do not ride on the railroad; it rides upon us." It lays tracks over the bodies of thinking, feeling, and acting individuals for the sake of establishing a leviathan called the "nation" that always has but one question on its lips when it wakes its sleepy head: "What's the news?"[60]

Yet as much as Thoreau complained about these changes, he could not help also being a part of them. Along with these technological changes, there was also a dramatic shift in the rhetorical tenor of Transcendentalism toward reform of the "nation" that Thoreau seemed to care so little about. The 1840s witnessed an "expanding and increasingly public sphere of the transcendentalists," as many of those directly or indirectly connected with the movement became "committed to testing their convictions by actual experiment and by writing and publishing."[61] Members of the once relatively close-knit group "found themselves being drawn into one of the practical reform movements of the day—association, prison reform, opposition to the Mexican war, antislavery."[62] Earlier in 1844 Emerson had delivered his lecture on New England reformers, noting that "it is easy to see the progress of dissent. The country is full of rebellion; the country is full of kings."[63] Even Emerson himself tried on the crown, delivering in August 1844—at the encouragement of his wife, Lidian, and Thoreau's mother, Cynthia, both of whom belonged to the Concord Women's Anti-Slavery Society—a lecture to celebrate the tenth anniversary of the abolition of slavery in the British West Indies. In his first statement on abolitionism, Emerson turned from a historical account of the emancipation to take aim at slavery in the United States, deriding the kidnapping of citizens, the cowardice of legislators, and the bullying of Southern states, concluding that "the Union already is at an end when the first citizen of Massachusetts is thus outraged."[64] Anticipating the provocative nature of the occasion, held at the First Parish Church, the sexton refused to ring the bell for the meeting— so Thoreau "rushed to the church, grasped the rope vigorously in his hands, and set the bell to ringing merrily until it had gathered a whole crowd for Emerson's speech."[65] Apparently Thoreau was more than happy to make news when it suited his own purposes.

Given all of these rapid changes, one might expect the ringing of the bell to signal Thoreau's newfound commitment to public action. Yet the opposite happened. Perhaps nothing reveals his love of paradox more than the fact that, within this cauldron of dissent and surge of association, he would choose to pursue his own opposite experiment—to shun politics and disassociate himself from society by building his own cabin in the woods along Walden Pond, about two miles from the center of Concord and five hundred yards from the Fitchburg railway. The idea of living alone by a pond to write and study nature had been with him for some time, but only after helping his father build a house did he acquire the skills to do so, and only after Emerson purchased (and then offered use of) fifteen acres of land around the north shore of the pond did he have a place to build it. On March 1, 1845, President John Tyler signed the bill annexing Texas, which Mexico claimed would be cause for war; that same month Thoreau began building his cabin. On July 4, 1845, he left his father's house to move into his own. Thoreau had finally found his garret in which to commune with mice and spiders.

Fittingly, however, the garret served as a means not only to study nature (and himself) in solitude, but also to craft his literary and rhetorical skills. As William E. Cain observes, "he was at Walden less as a sojourner in nature than he was a maker of books, an indefatigable writer who was *always* writing."[66] Not only did Thoreau work on a draft of *Walden* while at the cabin, but he also crafted an essay on Thomas Carlyle, an account of his experience in the Maine woods, and most important, a book-length project inspired by a boat trip he took with his brother before John's death, *A Week on the Concord and Merrimack Rivers*. The latter represented his first major treatise on the art of living, which would "defy all generic conventions, mingling poetry and prose, narrative and meditation, natural history and local lore, a lofty essay on friendship, commentaries on writers and writing, and fierce polemics on the injustices of contemporary social institutions."[67] Unfortunately, when *Week* was published at his own expense in 1849, it suffered terrible reviews, and he sold only two hundred of the thousand copies Thoreau had printed, leaving him with a debt of three hundred dollars and a wagonload of unsold copies. But portions of the book nonetheless represented some of the finest prose he had written up until that point.

Of particular rhetorical significance is the paradoxical notion of eloquence that he proposes in *Week*. In stark contrast with the chatter of contemporary politics and noise of the daily press, Thoreau posits a model of eloquence whose core virtue is silence. Silence was already a chief virtue of friendship, for after too much talk, "silence is the ambrosial night in the intercourse of Friends, in which their sincerity is recruited and takes deeper root."[68] The justification for this claim is that silence is not simply the absence of talk; it is the active listening to the subtle music of nature, for in nature's "music is the sound of the universal laws promulgated."[69] In the case of friends, being silent together allows them to better attune themselves to the rhythms of nature and to encounter each other on a level of perfect equality and mutual understanding. But what applies to friends also applies to society; and what applies to society affects the speech of those who would seek to reform it. In short, "as the true society approaches always near to solitude, so the most excellent speech finally falls into Silence." At that moment "the orator puts off his individuality, and is then most eloquent when most silent. He listens while he speaks, and is a hearer along with his audience."[70] The orator, in other words, aims not to change opinions through words but seeks to allow nature to speak with "harmony and purest melody."[71] The height of eloquence is consciously listening together to the harmony of nature's moral laws.

Yet if the perfect manifestation of silent eloquence seems almost wholly contained within one's private conscience, Thoreau also acknowledges that a more vigorous, vocal, and explicitly rhetorical kind of speech is required to make this kind of silent listening possible. The goal of the rhetorical style is to make oneself and others aware of and dissatisfied with the presence of injustice in their lives and societies, which pollutes lives and distracts from communion with the melodies of nature. And the greatest source of pollution Thoreau identified in *Week* was the state, which represented for him what he called "the institutions of the dead" and buried its citizens in "the grave of custom."[72] Custom blinds its members—no matter how noble their personal virtues—to the corruption with which they become complicit whenever they lend themselves to the state as instruments: "Herein lies the tragedy; that men doing outrage to their proper natures, even those called wise and good, lend themselves to perform the office of inferior and brutal ones. Here come war and slavery in; and what else may not come in by this opening? But certainly there are modes by which a man may put bread into his mouth which will not prejudice him as a companion and a neighbor."[73] The persuasive goal remains, as always, the change in personal habits and conscience rather than any sweeping reform; "the reform which you talk about can be undertaken any morning before unbarring our doors."[74] But clearly, as exemplified by his rhetorical practice in *Week,* even such personal reform still required a public rhetoric initially to raise the dead out of the grave of custom.

This dialectic between eloquence and rhetoric characterizes much of Thoreau's writing. On the one hand, eloquence was the style he preferred in the best of his nature writing. For Thoreau eloquence was not only an act of conscious listening to nature but also a form of poetic speech that turned listeners' attention less to the words themselves than to the nature that inspired them and expressed through its being the universal moral law. This is the type of speech that Golemba calls a "language of desire," whose "meaning seems to evaporate as the reader's eye follows Thoreau's words, enticing the reader to fill the gaps with his or her own meaning, transforming the reader into a co-author of the text."[75] To take an example from the essay "A Winter Walk," Thoreau narrates the experience of waking early on a winter morning: "Silently we unlatch the door, letting the drifts fall in, and step abroad to face the cutting air. Already the stars have lost some of their sparkle, and a dull, leaden mist skirts the horizon. A lurid brazen light in the east proclaims the approach of day, while the western landscape is dim and spectral still, enclosed in a somber Tartarean light, like the shadowy realms."[76] Here is the language of desire that immerses readers in a silent landscape covered with snow and reminiscent of the Homeric underworld, drawing them into nature and the depth of meaning that reside there.

On the other hand, Thoreau employed more traditional modes of rhetoric to shock and awaken the public and call them to a higher existence. His rhetoric was addressed to and spoke the language of the public. It also required considerable publicity to reach their eyes and ears, which were so often distracted by the clutter and detritus of society. Thoreau's rhetoric more often than not took a prophetic form, speaking as one of those whose office is to "announce, bear witness, and warn, to address and incite the constitutive and fateful choices of the community they 'serve' by their opposition."[77] Consequently the prophetic voice of Thoreau emerges in his explicit political writing when he directs his attention not to nature but to society, which for him largely functions to obstruct and conceal nature. In "Natural History of Massachusetts," for instance, he complains that "the merely political aspect of the land is never very cheering; men are degraded when considered as members of a political organization. On this side all lands present only the symptoms of decay. I see but Bunker Hill and Sing-Sing, the District of Columbia and Sullivan's Island, with a few avenues connecting them. But paltry are they all beside one blast of the east or the south wind which blows over them."[78] The rhetoric of prophecy thus acts as a kind of east or south wind that blasts away the corrupt veneer of society in order to let the eloquence of nature do its work.

Thoreau's experiment at Walden Pond suggested to him a third rhetorical possibility that might synthesize the methods of eloquence and rhetoric; this was the rhetoric of action, or the strategic and publicized performance of right. In other words the rhetoric of action neither described a nature outside oneself nor functioned as a purely instrumental behavior to accomplish a task, nor relied purely on words to prophetically pass judgment on society; it understood human action as itself a part of nature and thus made use of the human body, consciously guided by principle, as both a form of resistance to power and a method of communicating the law of justice. The rhetoric of action is eloquent because, in its character as a natural event, it has the potential to embody the harmony of the universal moral law as much as any other aspect of nature that can be contemplated in silence. However the rhetoric of action is also explicitly rhetorical because its effectiveness requires publicity in order to challenge and provoke a wider public prophetically.

The logic of the rhetoric of action can be heard in *Walden,* for instance, when Thoreau justifies his hoeing of beans "as some must work in fields if only for the sake of tropes and expression, to serve as a parable maker one day." Another example is when he boasts that his intent in writing about his experiences at the pond is "to brag as lustily as chanticleer in the morning, standing on his roost, if only to wake my neighbors up."[79] In both cases Thoreau makes his own deliberate action the subject of his discourse much in the way that he would describe an encounter with any natural phenomenon that might open eyes to new possibilities. And his most famous performance of right that Thoreau translated into the rhetoric of action occurred on July 23, 1846, when he was arrested in Concord and spent the night in jail for failure to pay his poll tax for the previous four years. This experience became the inspiration for "Resistance to Civil Government" in 1849 and also appears both in *Week* and in *Walden.* Thoreau framed his action as principled resistance to a government that legalized slavery, annexed Texas, and instigated a war with Mexico—a war that had been formally declared that May.

To interpret the persuasive power of Thoreau's rhetoric of action, it is useful to return to the work of the person who critiqued his method—Hannah Arendt. Specifically her concept of action is central to understanding Thoreau. For her the "revelatory" quality of action, unique to beings with the capacity for speech, is central. According to Arendt, action does not refer simply to any physical movement, of which any biological being is capable; it specifically refers to the freedom to begin something new within a condition of human plurality, or the sense in which one is surrounded by beings who share enough to understand each other and yet are distinct enough to appreciate difference and uniqueness. The specifically revelatory quality of action thus refers to the sense in which actions performed within a plurality of speaking beings discloses some aspect of themselves that makes them distinct: "In acting and speaking, men show who they are, reveal actively their unique personal identities and thus make their appearance in the human world." The prerequisite for action is thus publicity, or the ability to appear in public and have those actions potentially memorialized in speech: "Because of its inherent tendency to disclose the agent together with the act, action needs for its full appearance the shining brightness we once called glory, and which is only possible in the public realm." Action for her is thus always symbolic action, which represents in large part the capacity to set in motion a new story the meaning of which becomes clear only "to the storyteller, that is, to the backward glance of the historian."[80] Action, to use Burke's terms, is always dramatistic—it is rooted in the human impulse to conceptualize events as a drama.

Action thus takes on an explicitly political quality for Arendt when words and deeds appear in a specifically public realm of fellow citizens and clash with other perspectives in the effort to constitute power, which for her represents the capacity to act in concert. Arendt takes as a model for politics the ancient Greek polis, "the place where free men assembled and conversed," which existed for the Greeks "under the sign of the divine *Peithō,* the power to persuade and influence, which reigned among equals and determined all things without force or coercion." Arendt rejects an instrumentalist view of politics as the attainment of specific ends through manipulation or force. Politics for her had more to do with the sheer act of appearing in public and presenting one's views with an agonistic spirit. For this reason she attributes the ancient Greek Sophists with the invention of the political realm: "The crucial factor is not that one could now turn arguments around and stand propositions on their heads, but rather that one gained the ability to truly see topics from various sides—that is, politically—with the result that people understood how to assume the many possible perspectives provided by the real world, from which one and the same topic can be regarded and in which each topic, despite his oneness, appears in a great diversity of views."[81]

Actions that were, by their nature, hidden or secret could thus not appear in public and be properly "political"—even if they might have instrumental effects. Arendt uses the "doer of good works" and the "criminal" as examples of "lonely figures" who perform their deeds in complete anonymity and secrecy and thus "remain outside the pale of human intercourse."[82] For her Thoreau is just such an individual: "there is all the difference in the world between the criminal's avoiding the public eye and the civil disobedient's taking the law into his own hands in open defiance."[83] To be political meant to translate an action into speech and thereby into a unique perspective that could be taken up by others, stood on its head, refuted, or embraced.

Despite Arendt's passing reference to Thoreau as an example of the kind of "lonely figure" whose private acts of conscience stand outside the political, it is clear that she was referring more to the mythic Thoreau than the historical one. One needs only to contextualize Thoreau's actions within the larger context of his rhetorical performance that brought his deeds into the light of the public. Cavell does this in his reading of *Walden* and "Resistance." In both works Thoreau's problem, Cavell argues, is not only philosophical, religious, and literary but also "political—[it] is to get us to ask the questions, and then to show us that we do not know what we are asking, and then to show us that we have the answer." His acts of literary withdrawal are rhetorical in the sense that they function to "perform an experiment, a public demonstration of a truth." From this perspective *Walden* becomes "a tract of political education, education for membership in the polis," which "locates authority in the citizens and it identifies citizens—those with whom one is in membership—as 'neighbors.'" With respect to his night spent in the Concord jail, those who "complain of the pettiness of that one night forget that the completion of the act was the writing of the essay which depicts it."[84] As Arendt says of the nature of action, its meaning becomes clear only in the backward glance of the storyteller. Thoreau simply had the good fortune to be able to tell his story with a rare degree of poetic eloquence and rhetorical force.

But *Walden* and "Resistance," despite both being rhetorics of action, were guided by two different economies of power that culminated in contrasting rhetorical strategies. As Cavell points out, Thoreau in *Walden* followed in the old Puritan tradition of being a "visible saint."[85] Moreover, as Milder argues, his rhetoric was based on setting his own action as an ideal to follow, as from his semidivine height he would then weave "a rope ladder for his audience's spiritual ascent."[86] Thoreau's normative definition of economy in *Walden* refers to "that economy of living which is synonymous with philosophy."[87] According to Leonard Neufeldt, "in this context *economy* often referred to the inner righteous kingdom or the personal republic of higher law" and thus referenced a kind of "spiritual or divine government."[88] The art of personal economy thus dealt with understanding "what are the gross necessaries of life and what methods have been taken to obtain them" and then applying this knowledge to use one's free time and energy to seek the higher ends of life.[89] As Thoreau sums up the logic of the economy, it dealt with the relationship between benefits and costs, where the "cost of a thing is the amount of what I will call life which is required to be exchanged for it, immediately or in the long run."[90] Only by knowing how to exert the least amount of energy to attain these gross necessities (which he reduces to four: food, shelter, clothing, and fuel) can one be truly free "to love wisdom and to live according to its dictates" and "to solve some of the problems of life, not only theoretically, but practically."[91] In other words economy in Thoreau's normative sense requires a considerable exertion of forethought and rigorous self-discipline in order that one might, through careful management, reduce one's costs to its absolute minimum in order to gain the maximum reward of a meaningful existence. The reward was thus to free up the time and mental energy to listen to the eloquence of nature and attune one's thoughts and habits to its harmonies, rhythms, and laws. The economy of power in *Walden* was a positive and emancipatory one, an economy that guided one's behavior and helped facilitate joy as the condition of life.

In contradistinction "Resistance" was Thoreau's first and most extensive effort to set forth a rhetoric of action focused more on a negative critique of the economy of power, here understood in Foucault's sense as the complex structure by which society and the state disciplined subjectivities. Here one finds the Robin Hood nature of his action, designed explicitly to target some gap or disjunction in the system and thereby disrupt its functioning and publicize its injustice. This it does by exposing the poverty of what Thoreau calls society's "rule of expediency" (which can be summarized as the rule by which maximum public benefit, understood in purely tangible terms, that can be derived with the least amount of "danger and grievance") by contrasting it with the "law of justice" (that demands "a people, as well as an individual, must do justice, cost what it may").[92] The rhetoric of action in this case was not used so much to hold oneself up as an ideal as it was to provoke an aggressive response in another. It juxtaposed the virtuous act of resistance against the ignominious response by an organized system of power to create a sense of conflict and contradiction in an audience that is the precondition for an act of transcendence. "Resistance" thus turned attention away from the eloquence of nature to focus on a rhetorical critique of slavery, exploitation, and war, all of which were consequences of a social economy of power that treated both human beings and nature as mere commodities to be traded, exploited, and manipulated according to the rule of expediency. At the same time, however, it is important to keep in mind that these different emphases are but two means to the same end—namely trying to live a good life not only by positively satisfying one's higher spiritual aims but also by freeing oneself from complicity in the oppression of others. The critique of domination is simply a necessary step on the way to a critique of freedom.

It took two years for Thoreau to deliver his first lecture about his experience in jail. He delivered it in January 1848 before publishing it under the title of "Resistance to Civil Government" in 1849 in the first and only edition of Elizabeth Peabody's magazine, *Aesthetic Papers*. By that time his act of protest had taken on significance far beyond its original performance. In the passing of two years, the rule of expediency had run roughshod over the law of justice. A few months after Thoreau's arrest in 1846, a slave had arrived in Boston, stowed away on the sailing ship *Ottoman;* instead of freeing him, the ship's owner, in cooperation with the state of Massachusetts, immediately sent him back to his master in Louisiana out of fear of economic reprisals, thus proving that "mercantile concerns now clearly weighed more than morality in the scale of things, not only in South Carolina, but also Massachusetts."[93] Furthermore, by the time Thoreau delivered his lecture in 1848, the Treaty of Guadalupe Hidalgo had been signed, ending the Mexican-American War and awarding all the land north of the Rio Grande to United States in exchange for a pittance of fifteen million dollars. But despite being hundreds of miles away, Thoreau, and the entire nation, had been given a front-row seat to war. "By the end of the war the telegraph reached as far south as Charleston, and New Orleans news had been brought within three days of Washington." Meanwhile the newspaper industry had evolved to satisfy readers' demands for sensational news from the front, and in "1848 six New York City papers formed the first wire service, the Associated Press."[94] By the time Peabody published Thoreau's essay in 1849, these newspapers were reporting on the Gold Rush that sent thousands of Americans into the new land to seek their fortunes, instituting various forms of "mob law" while heedlessly denuding "the mountainsides of trees to get wood for their shantytowns, mines, and fuel."[95] As the United States pursued its manifest destiny, it seemed to carry with it waste, exploitation, and greed.

The metaphor that Thoreau used to capture the economy of power of the rising nation, constructed as it was out of steel rails and steel wires, is that of a machine. On its face this metaphor is not necessarily a departure from eighteenth-century revolutionary thought insofar as it is understood in a neutral sense as describing the government as a tool to accomplish the ends of "the people." But Thoreau did not intend the metaphor to be neutral. In the eighteenth century, critique of British rule tended to use the language of tyranny and treat British oppression as if it was an effect of the personal whim of the king. But in Thoreau this medieval notion of sovereignty is replaced by a nineteenth-century understanding of mechanism. The government is no longer to be understood as the embodiment of public reason, shared virtues, or sovereign rule but rather as a complex system of interlocking parts (such as "a spring, or a pulley, or a rope, or a crank"), each doing its part to maintain its proper functioning according to the rule of expediency. What is therefore central about this metaphor, for Thoreau, is that it makes clear that people are the parts and that power is everywhere. The power of the government thus no longer emanates from a single point of sovereignty but rather is dispersed throughout the system in every relationship between a pulley and a rope, a crank and a spring. The result is that "the mass of men serve the state thus, not as men mainly, but as machines, with their bodies," thus putting "themselves on a level with wood and earth and stones."[96] Just as people do not ride on the railroad but the railroad rides upon them, so too does the machinery of the state, once thought of as a means to an end, become a means unto itself, of which men and women are but parts.

The tragedy inherent within this new economy of power is that the machinery of government is so vast and complex, and participation within it often so small and local, that one's complicity with injustice becomes hidden within the system. According to the law of justice, for instance, complete self-sacrifice is demanded when one must act to remedy a clear injustice: "If I have unjustly wrested a plank from a drowning man, I must restore it to him though I drown myself." But when one is simply performing a minor function within a machine, rarely is one confronted with such a clear moral choice. Indeed, it is often thought a virtue to perform one's task irrespective of the function of the larger machine one is serving. Thoreau notes that when actions are taken that in themselves "command no more respect than men of straw or a lump of dirt"—say, the turning of a crank—the individuals performing such actions are "commonly esteemed good citizens." This is even more the case for those deemed to be leaders rather than servants of the state. For while the common rank of soldiers, captains, and constables serve the state with their bodies, "others—as most legislators, politicians, lawyers, ministers, and office-holders—serve the state chiefly with their heads; and, as they rarely make any moral distinctions, they are as likely to serve the devil, without *intending* it, as God." The phrase "without *intending* it" makes all the difference for Thoreau. Undoubtedly even those "worth only as horses and dogs" in their capacity as instruments of the machinery of state might, in their capacity as human beings, jump into a river to save a drowning man if presented with such a clear case of suffering.[97] Part of the tragedy of the state is that in its pursuit of expediency it either blinds its instruments to the suffering of others or, when such suffering becomes visible, cloaks its vice in an aura of virtue.

Yet just as the metaphor of the machine describes the rising system of domination in the modern state, it also points to the possibility for resistance. This possibility is captured in Thoreau's concept of friction. In a purely physical sense, friction represents the force resisting the relative motion of material elements sliding against each other, usually resulting in heat and gradual physical breakdown. Friction can be necessary and intentional, as when a belt relies on it to turn the gears of a steam engine, or unintentional and undesirable, as when the presence of friction on the moving parts of that engine causes it to wear down, overheat, and potentially explode. Understood in terms of the social economy of power, friction represents the active exertion of power itself within the specific points of the system, the moment when the free action of any individual is constrained, channeled, prevented, or encouraged by elements of the surrounding system. An economy of power without friction, for instance, is a contradiction in terms. As Foucault makes clear, "where there is power, there is resistance," such that "the points of resistance are present everywhere in the power network."[98] Power thus functions only in the context of friction. So too is resistance possible only at those points of friction at which power is exerted.

Thoreau's use of the metaphor of friction is impressive because of his willingness to admit the necessity of it within any economy of power. He rejects utopian notions of a frictionless society as pure fantasy: "All machines have their friction; and possibly this does enough good to counterbalance the evil. At any rate, it is a great evil to make a stir about it." Strikingly Thoreau uses the "Revolution of '75" as an example of a case of such an evil. Despite the fact that Americans believed they had a "right to refuse allegiance to, and to resist, the government" because its "tyranny or inefficiency" was "great and unendurable," Thoreau confesses he would not have counted himself among the revolutionaries at that time, not being terribly concerned about British taxation of commodities: "It is most probable that I should not make an ado about it, for I can do without them."[99] He thus introduces the concept of friction to explain his lack of proper revolutionary spirit. For Thoreau paying slightly higher prices for paper, tea, and other commodities was hardly cause for throwing off British rule and sacrificing thousands of lives in a war for independence. In his calculation (which here co-incides with the rule of efficiency) the loss of a percentage of one's income is fair compensation for public peace, prosperity, and security.

The factor that overrides the rule of expediency and activates the law of justice is the point at which friction becomes an explicit aim of the machine itself. There are, of course, many possible negative indirect consequences of any economy of power (perhaps the occasional accidental jailing or execution of an innocent man or woman) that can and must be tolerated if society is to exist at all. But the case is different when the entire machine is made to serve injustice. Thoreau explains: "if the injustice is part of the necessary friction of the machine of government, let it go, let it go: perchance it will wear smooth,—certainly the machine will wear out." However, "when the friction comes to have its machine, and oppression and robbery are organized, I say, let us not have such a machine any longer." Such is clearly the case for Thoreau in the face of the growing power of the slavocracy: "When a sixth of the population of the nation which has undertaken to be the ref-uge of liberty are slaves, and a whole country is unjustly overrun and conquered by a foreign army, and subjected to military law, I think that it is not too soon for honest men to rebel and revolutionize. What makes this duty the more urgent is the fact that the country so overrun is not our own, but ours is the invading army." Here was when the law of justice activated: "This people must cease to hold slaves, and to make war on Mexico, though it cost them their existence as a people."[100]

At this point of rhetorical commitment, Thoreau's perspective on the rheto-ric of action departs from long traditions of public advocacy, both then and now. The natural "political" impulse when faced with such injustice would be to take one's message both to the public and to the sources of power, making speeches, corralling votes, organizing petitions, and joining associations. Thoreau rejects all of these methods as uneconomical, however, both in the positive and the nega-tive senses of the economy of power. Such actions expend a great deal of energy, distract one from the care of the self, and do little to accomplish their explicit ends. Indeed Thoreau describes such political activity as itself being complicit in the machinery of the state. He expresses only contempt for petitioning:

> As for adopting the ways which the State has provided for remedying the evil, I know not of such ways. They take too much time, and a man's life will be gone. I have other affairs to attend to. I came into this world, not chiefly to make this a good place to live in, but to live in it, be it good or bad. A man has not everything to do, but something; and because he

cannot do *everything*, it is not necessary that he should do *something* wrong. It is not my business to be petitioning the Governor or the Legislature any more than it is theirs to petition me; and if they should not hear my petition, what should I do then? But in this case the State has provided no way; its very Constitution is the evil.

No better—and perhaps worse—were those who restricted their protest to giving "only a cheap vote, and a feeble countenance and Godspeed, to the right, as it goes by them." In the first case, voting is at best only an indirect expression of will. Voting "*for the right* is *doing* nothing for it. It is only expressing to men feebly your desire that it should prevail." But desire matters little in the functioning of a machine. The fact is that the winner of an election prevails through "the power of the majority," and the logic of the majority "never exceeds that of expediency." In the second case, no well-meaning, virtuous man would ever be nominated for president, anyway. The machinery of government extends beyond the limits of government itself and includes the newspapers and editors that surround it. Indeed the editors, "men who are politicians by profession," participate in the "selection of a candidate for the Presidency," seeking an individual who can sufficiently gather the votes of the majority by appealing to their baser instincts. A citizen who goes to the polls thus shows "that he is himself available for any purposes of the demagogue," and "his vote is of no more worth than that of any unprincipled foreigner or hireling native, who may have been bought."[101] Perhaps the cost to life of voting is less than that of petitioning, requiring only a few hours out of the day, but its result is counterproductive; it registers no protest at all, and worse, it sanctions the corrupt system that interprets democracy in terms of giving its citizens the choice of demagogues.

The problem with all of these methods is that they are based on an obsolete notion of power as sovereignty that pretends that it emanates from the judgments of an individual or group of individuals; but in the new economy of power, in which power is dispersed throughout the machine, effective resistance takes the form of precise and localized action that achieves maximum response with minimum effort. In his words, "Let your life be a counter-friction to stop the machine." Here, counter-friction represents a force that prevents some small but necessary part from doing its job, as when a gear freezes up entirely and prevents the movements of the entire mechanism. It is important to note, however, that this recommendation does not equate to the concept of throwing a wrench in the machine. A wrench is not a necessary component to a machine, but a foreign object hurled into it to sabotage it—much like proslavery activists destroyed the printing presses of abolitionists or antislavery activists clogged the streets with their bodies to prevent the extradition of a captured slave. Although Thoreau does not necessarily disapprove of these methods, what he means by counter-friction is something different—literally the effect of withholding one's support and refusing to perform the task demanded by the machine of state. One determines in what exact form he or she serves the functioning of the machine—as a spring, a pulley, a rope, a crank, or even a head—and refuses to perform that function so that the wheels no longer turn properly. This assumes that every citizen is already complicit in the machinery of the state in some way. Thoreau's counter-friction was to refuse to pay a tax demanded by the government, so that when the tax gatherer came to demand payment—to exert power and force Thoreau to turn his crank—he found that "the simplest, the most effectual, and, in the present posture of affairs, the indispensablest mode of treating with it on this head, of expressing your little satisfaction with and love for it, is to deny it then." If he did not actually forestall evil through this protest, or landed in prison as a consequence, at least "I do not lend myself to the wrong which I condemn."[102] That is enough to recommend the act according to the law of justice.

Thus the true audience for reform did not reside in Washington, D.C.; it lived next door, down the street, in the city, or in one's own house—in one's own self. The problem with most reformers was that, by taking for granted a sovereign notion of power, they felt that the only resistance worth doing was that which somehow directly confronted or challenged the sovereign, whether in the form of a petition or a vote. Consequently when such options are not available, they "sit down with their hands in their pockets, and say they know not what to do, and do nothing." Thoreau's reconceptualization of power is meant to give them something to do by focusing their rhetorical efforts on those individuals who are close to them rather than groups or institutions who are distant from their lives. From his perspective, "practically speaking, the opponents to a reform in Massachusetts are not a hundred thousand politicians at the South, but a hundred thousand merchants and farmers here, who are more interested in commerce and agriculture than they are in humanity, and are not prepared to do justice to the slave and to Mexico, *cost what it may.* I quarrel not with far-off foes, but with those who, near at home, coöperate with, and do the bidding of, those far away, and without whom the latter would be harmless."[103] This is no example of futile, idealistic self-promotion. This was a highly realistic, empirical strategy to restructure the operation of government machinery not by persuading its architect or engineer but by changing the nature of its moving parts.

The paradox was that the audience with the most power to effect change was the one most constrained by its own complicity with state power, whereas righteousness came easily to those who had the least to lose. On the one hand, "they who assert the purest right, and consequently are most dangerous to a corrupt state, commonly have not spent much time in accumulating property."

The most they have to lose is their body, which for Thoreau is but a little price to pay for retaining the purity of one's soul. On the other hand, "the rich man" is "always sold to the institution which makes him rich. Absolutely speaking, the more money, the less virtue; for money comes between a man and his objects, and obtains them for him. . . . Thus his moral ground is taken from under his feet."[104] Yet as Thoreau acknowledged in criticizing Northern merchants and farmers, moral actions by these same rich men were necessary to leverage influence in the state. The rhetorical challenge is thus to find a way for the virtuous but weak to influence the corrupt but powerful to force them to do right, or at least cease to do evil. The rhetoric of action that publicized the performance of right and exposed the corrupt expediency of the machinery of state was a method by which to shock and reform those "good citizens" who did not realize their own complicity with injustice.

Unfortunately Thoreau did not explicitly address this rhetorical challenge. Indeed, in his criticism of reformers, he seems to imply that (despite the performative contradiction) giving speeches and spending one's time on advocacy violates the arithmetic of the economy of power. He writes that if unjust laws exist, reformers ought not "to wait until they have persuaded the majority to alter them," but should rather "transgress them at once."[105] This apparent disdain for rhetorical action thus leads Johnstone to argue that Thoreau's essay contains a "rhetorical paradox" in that he "presents a political doctrine that requires the rejection of rhetoric as a form of strategic political activity, and so, the rejection of the essay itself as an instance of such activity."[106] In other words, because Thoreau seems to suggest that anything less than immediate transgression of the law "is inadequate from both a moral and a political standpoint," then "rhetoric as a political tool has no place in Thoreau's doctrine."[107] But of course since Thoreau is making this claim in a public lecture that was then reprinted as an essay—and thereby a case of rhetoric—the paradox suggests that he did not know what he was doing.

Once Thoreau's rhetorical performance is considered not as a contradiction but as an exemplar, however, it readily becomes clear that successful acts of civil disobedience require not only a personal transgression of law but also a rhetorical performance of that transgression in order to make the principle of its enactment a matter of public controversy. The way to gain influence over the levers, cranks, and pulleys of power is to force them, through the power of publicity, to make a clear public choice between the diabolical and the divine in which there is no longer any middle ground. Once again this act of separation is the necessary state of mind that must be produced in order that an individual might transcend to a new level and change their behavior in more than a superficial way. As a form of resistance to an unjust economy of power, the rhetoric of action not only conveys the sense of justice but, more important, makes people aware of their complicity with injustice in a way that challenges their self-conceptions as virtuous individuals and loyal citizens. When enough individuals collectively commit themselves to accept counter-friction, the machinery of injustice breaks down and reveals possibilities for freedom.

It would not be long before Thoreau had an opportunity to act on his principles, although this time without rhetorical publicity. In his journal of October 1, 1851, he recorded that he "just put a fugitive slave, who has taken the name of Henry Williams, into the cars for Canada." According to his entry, Williams had come to Thoreau by reference of Elijah Lovejoy and William Lloyd Garrison and had lodged in his home until money was forwarded to pay for the train. Thoreau records that he had "intended to dispatch him at noon through to Burlington, but when I went to buy his ticket, saw one at the depot who looked and behaved so much like a Boston policeman that I did not venture that time."[108] Easy to overlook in the nonchalant manner of his entry is the fact that Thoreau had, by the law of the land, committed a felony. In the Compromise of 1850, which had soured Emerson on his hero Daniel Webster, the price of admitting California as a free state and abolishing the slave trade in the District of Columbia was to institute the Fugitive Slave Act, by which Southern slave power exerted its force directly on the citizens in otherwise free states. Specifically the law mandated the return of any fugitive slave to its owner regardless of the laws of the state or locality, abolished the right to a jury trial, instituted financial incentives, gave U.S. marshals the right to deputize any citizen to assist in the capture of escapees, and subjected anyone found guilty of assisting a slave to heavy fine or imprisonment.

Thoreau would have been well aware of what he was doing by the end of 1851. Not soon after the law was passed, citizens of Massachusetts had felt its effects. On April 3, 1851, a seventeen-year-old boy named Thomas Sims was captured in Boston and held under guard in the federal courthouse. Despite the crowds that came out in support of his freedom, at four in the morning "three hundred soldiers escorted Sims through the jeering crowd who cried 'Shame!' at the soldiers but could not block their progress toward the docks, where Sims was put on a ship for Georgia"—where, after his arrival, he was "publicly whipped in Savannah on anniversary of the Battle of Lexington and Concord."[109] Thoreau's quiet assistance of Williams was his own way of transgressing unjust laws at a time when one had every right to be suspicious that any plain-clothed man on a train platform might be an officer of the state prepared to haul one off to prison—or a slave ship. Indeed not even a cabin in the Walden woods could one ever escape the long arm of the state.

The last step on Thoreau's way to "Plea for John Brown" was his hatred for this law, roused by the arrest and return of another runaway slave, Anthony Burns, on May 24, 1854. The timing of the arrest was especially controversial. A few days later, Congress passed the Kansas-Nebraska Act, which opened the Kansas and Nebraska territories to settlement (thus overriding multiple treaties with the Indians) while allowing any state to decide its status as free or slave by popular vote (thus negating the Missouri Compromise of 1820, which had forbidden slavery above the imaginary line of the parallel 36°30'). On May 26 a Boston mob tried to rescue Burns from the courthouse but failed when "a battalion of US artillery, four platoons of marines, the sheriff's posse, [and] twenty two companies of state militia" finally returned him to his owner at a total cost of forty thousand dollars in tax money.[110] That day Thoreau recorded in his journal: "Rather than thus consent to establish hell upon earth,—to be a party to this establishment,—I would touch a match to blow up earth and hell together. As I love my life, I would side with the Light and let the Dark Earth roll from under me, calling my mother and my brother to follow me."[111] A few months later, on July 4, Thoreau edited these words (saying more cautiously, "I need not say what match I would touch, what system endeavor to blow up") and included them in his lecture, delivered in Framingham and eventually republished in the *Liberator,* called "Slavery in Massachusetts."[112]

Although Thoreau's allusion to blowing up the state—thus adopting a more directly confrontational approach to resistance—seems to mark this essay as a distinct departure from "Resistance to Civil Government," it is actually more striking in the ways in which the logic is the same. The general rule by which the government operates remains expediency, necessarily so. Thoreau complains that people never seem to learn that "policy is not morality—that it never secures any moral right, but merely considers what is expedient." This is as it should be, as the "effect of a good government is to make life more valuable." But there remains a point at which expediency, pushed to the extreme, results in evils that must be remedied not by applying the rule of expediency but the law of justice, a "higher laws than the Constitution, or the decision of the majority." Such was the case with the Fugitive Slave Law, whose only aim was to rob "a poor innocent black man of his liberty for life." Turning his attention to the governor of Massachusetts, Thoreau then applied the same criteria of action as he did to himself in his earlier essay, arguing that "it was his business, as a Governor, to see that the laws of the state were executed; while, as a man, he took care that he did not, by doing so, break the laws of humanity." If such a case of injustice were demanded, Thoreau concluded, there would be only one thing that a man of principle could have done in that position—to "have *resigned* himself into fame." And if that action, did not stop the evil from occurring, at least he would have proven himself to still be a man and not a mere tool of the machine. But in the end, the governor proved to be a mere slave himself by doing the bidding of others. As Thoreau puts it through understatement, "in my opinion, he was not equal to the occasion."[113]

The difference in tenor with the earlier essay arises not by applying a different logic but by actually applying the arithmetic of his economy of power more rigorously. The Fugitive Slave Act compelled ordinary citizens to become the direct servants of slave power. In "Resistance to Civil Government," Thoreau had addressed the situation in which tangible support for slavery was still largely indirect, funded through taxes, commodities, or trade, thus making an equally indirect form of resistance more feasible. But as Unitarian minister Theodore Parker wrote, "We need not go to Charleston and New Orleans to see slavery; our own courthouse was a barracoon; our officers of this city were slave-hunters, and members of Unitarian churches in Boston are kidnappers."[114] Thoreau explicitly acknowledged this change in circumstance: "I had never respected the Government near to which I had lived, but I foolishly thought that I might manage to live here, minding my private affairs, and forget it. . . . I dwelt before, perhaps, in the illusion that my life passed somewhere only between heaven and hell, but now I cannot persuade myself that I do not dwell *wholly within* hell."[115] He thus found himself speculating on what it would be like to wake up and "discover suddenly that your villa, with all its contents, is located in hell, and that the justice of the peace is one of the devil's angels, has a cloven foot and forked tail."[116] It is impossible truly to escape complicity with the state, even in one's own thoughts: "Who can be serene in a country where both the rulers and the ruled are without principle? The remembrance of my country spoils my walk." But if this is so, then the cost to one's life in resistance becomes zero, because there is no true life to live when, as Thoreau concludes, even one's private "thoughts are murder to the State, and involuntarily go plotting against her."[117] It is at that point when the law of justice opens up new avenues of resistance that give a more extreme meaning to the word *counter-friction*.

One other notable aspect of "Slavery in Massachusetts" reinforces the necessity of rhetoric to Thoreau's theory of resistance. In considering available options for resistance, he recommends as "earnest and vigorous an assault on the Press" be made as possible, noting that "the press exerts a greater and more pernicious influence than the Church did in its worst period." The newspaper, he says, "is a Bible which we read every morning and every afternoon," and its "editor is a preacher whom you voluntarily support." The result is that "probably no country was ever ruled by so mean a class of tyrants as, with a few notable exceptions, are the editors of the periodical press in *this* country." This is, of course, a backhanded compliment. On the one hand, he criticizes their level of corruption and deceit while acknowledging on the other hand their enormous power to influence public opinion and action. It is important, however, to avoid concluding that Thoreau somehow disdains the press entirely as a medium and rejects it as a method of influence or reform (along with, presumably, conscious rhetorical advocacy). The opposite is clearly the case in his practice. Even as he condemned the majority of the newspapers (and by doing so advocated the method of the modern boycott, suggesting that "the free men of New England have only to refrain from purchasing and reading these sheets, have only to withhold their cents, to kill a score of them at once"), he acknowledges that there are "a few notable exceptions."[118] Then he names names: "The *Liberator* and the *Commonwealth* were the only papers in Boston, as far as I know, which made themselves heard in condemnation of the cowardice and meanness of the authorities of that city."[119] It is no accident that Thoreau's lecture was reprinted in the *Liberator*. His actions belied his belief that the press, once reformed, could be a rhetorical arm of justice. As he once said of government, so too he might say of the press: he does not demand that there be no press, but at once a better press—ideally with his article on the front page.

But the devil's angels did not stop their work for Thoreau; they were very busy across the nation after the passing of the Kansas-Nebraska Act. Throwing open the question of slavery to the popular sovereignty of individual states did not encourage enlightened democratic deliberation by citizens already a part of the state but rather encouraged a flood to these the states of proslavery or antislavery activists in order to tip the scales in one direction or another. Armed not only with ideology but also with shipments of rifles, "in Kansas, it seemed, democratic power would grow out of the barrel of a gun." Consequently, although antislavery settlers far outnumbered their opposition in Kansas, the elections of 1855, thanks to "plenty of intimidation, illegal vote counting, and other flagrant irregularities," resulted in thirty-six proslavery legislators' being elected to their opponents' three. Refusing to be intimidated, the free-state contingency accepted "crates of new model, breech loading Sharps' rifles sent out by sympathizers in New England" and organized a convention near Lawrence, where they drew up their own territorial constitution abolishing slavery—thus setting up a situation in which Kansas had two governments "with both sides armed to the teeth." On May 21, 1856, tensions came to a head as "proslavery forces of between five and eight hundred men, dragging with them four six-pounder brass cannons, lay siege to Lawrence." The free-staters, realizing they were outgunned, stood aside, and "the pro-slavery men went on a rampage, burning homes, ransacking shops, and smashing to bits the antislavery newspaper presses."[120] To avenge this defeat, on May 24, 1856, John Brown, four of his sons, and three other men associated with a free-state militia known as the Pottawatomie Rifle Company attacked farms of men allied with the proslavery cause, hacking to pieces with broad-swords anti-free-stater James Doyle and his two eldest sons (in front of Doyle's wife and younger child), law-and-order man Allen Wilkinson, and proslavery partisan William Sherman. By the end of the year, the entire nation was shocked by the events of "Bleeding Kansas."

The news continued to spoil Thoreau's walks. His August 30 entry in his journal expressed frustration and annoyance with the newspapers, feeling him-self pulled into affairs that would distract him from the pursuit of his own aims. Halfway through a lengthy entry that begins with his discovery of a "small cran-berry, *Vaccinium Oxycoccus,* which Emerson says is the common cranberry of the north of Europe," Thoreau detoured into a discussion of Kansas and the method by which to resist distractions:

> If you would really take a position outside the street and daily life of men, you must have deliberately planned your course, you must have business which is not your neighbors' business, which they cannot un-derstand. For only absorbing employment prevails, succeeds, takes up space, occupies territory, determines the future of individuals and states, drives Kansas out of your head, and actually and permanently occupies the only desirable and free Kansas against all border ruffians. The at-titude of resistance is one of weakness, inasmuch as it only faces an enemy; it has its back to all that is truly attractive. You shall have your affairs, I will have mine.[121]

In these passages Thoreau not only seems to reject the position taken in "Slavery in Massachusetts," but he also seems to go past "Resistance to Civil Government" all the way to the more self-absorbed *Week.* He argues, in effect, that the only way to determine the future of individuals and states is through complete and absorb-ing employment in one's own passionate pursuits, which he metaphorically la-bels the only truly free Kansas that can be protected against border ruffians. Thus it is a sign of weakness actually to confront directly an enemy, namely because it forces one to account for the position of that enemy and ignore all those pursuits that are truly worthwhile. Here is the kind of attitude toward "goodness" that Arendt criticizes as being completely outside the sphere of the political.

Yet when Brown suddenly appeared in Concord in February 1857, raising money for a vaguely defined plan to help slaves escape to Canada, Thoreau ap-peared with him within the sphere of the political. In fact Brown had lunch with the Thoreaus at their house, and "Thoreau was impressed with this Carlylean hero and made a small contribution, though he was annoyed that Brown would not say what exactly he wanted the money for."[122] Emerson was equally impressed, noting in his journal that Brown "believes on his own experience that one good, believing, strong-minded man is worth a hundred, nay twenty thousand men without character, for a settler in a new country; & that the right men will give a permanent direction to the fortunes of the state."[123] Clearly Brown knew how to speak Transcendentalism. Brown returned one last time to Concord in May 1859 for fundraising before disappearing once again. Thoreau did not hear of him again until he read the newspapers on October 19, 1859, about the raid on Harpers Ferry. On October 22 he wrote in his journal that "it is the best news that America has ever heard."[124] On November 12 he briefly described the colors of the sunset he had seen on the October 25, noting in retrospect that "it was hard for me to see its beauty then, when my mind was filled with Captain Brown. So great a wrong as his fate implied overshadowed all beauty in the world."[125] It seemed as if the border ruffians had once again crossed into Thoreau's free Kansas.

The reason Thoreau had not been able to recognize the beauty of that sunset was that he had turned away from his own "absorbing employment" to write a speech called "A Plea for Captain John Brown" to be delivered on October 30 at the Concord town hall. This was eleven days after hearing of the assault and Brown's arrest in the newspaper. But Thoreau hardly needed even that much time. He had been so struck with the immediacy and readiness by which not only the newspapers (as well as his neighbors) had condemned Brown's attacks that his October 19 journal entry journal had already produced a highly condensed version of the speech he eventually delivered, including its most controversial closing assertion: "Some eighteen hundred years ago Christ was crucified; this morning, perhaps, John Brown was hung. These are the two ends of a chain which I rejoice to know is not without their links."[126] In the text of his lecture, Thoreau then added: "He is not Old Brown any longer; he is an Angel of Light."[127] He had immediately set to work turning Brown into a symbol that could be put to rhetorical work against what he called "our foe," which "is the all but universal woodenness both of head and heart, the want of vitality in man, which is the effect of our vice."[128] Brown's action by principle, for Thoreau, finally created that entering wedge to separate the diabolical from the divine and force a divided house to choose a side.

Translating people and events in symbols was, of course, nothing new for the Transcendentalists; that was, in fact, their primary rhetorical strategy. But never before had such an explicitly violent act been so translated. In his October 19 journal entry, "he tackled the issue head-on when he accused critics of John Brown of hypocrisy by their own condoning of deeds of petty violence every day." As examples of this petty violence, Thoreau lists the "policeman's billy and handcuffs," the jail, the gallows, and the "the chaplain of the regiment."[129] Striking about these passages is how quickly Thoreau dismisses Brown's acts of violence as anything but extraordinary, placing them on the same ethical level as an act of self-defense (against a band of thieves or murderers) or the cumulative "deeds of petty violence" (in which almost all citizens are made complicit) that keep the machinery of government moving. For Thoreau it was not the level of violence (or absence thereof) in any act that made it moral or immoral; it was the virtue with which an act was performed and the aim toward which it was directed that made it worthy of encomium.

Nonetheless Thoreau intentionally downplayed Brown's violence in his lecture, emphasizing his principles and his character over his methods in order to make him more representative of the spirit of Transcendentalism. Thus when he quoted the same journal passages in his lecture, he eliminated any reference to violence as an instigating factor in his neighbors' remarks, noting only that they had responded to the first (erroneous) reports that "he was dead." Indeed Thoreau not only leaves out any mention of Brown's butchery in Kansas but also ignores entirely any details of the individuals taken hostage or killed at Harpers Ferry. He chooses instead to portray Brown (whom he refers respectfully to as "Captain Brown") as "a New England farmer, a man of great common sense, deliberate and practical as that class is, and tenfold more so." Brown was not a violent fanatic but rather a man of firm and high principles who adopted Spartan habits in order to fit "himself for difficult enterprises, a life of exposure." In short he was a hero cut in Thoreau's image: "A man of rare common sense and directness of speech, as of action; a transcendentalist above all, a man of ideas and principles,—that was what distinguished him. Not yielding to a whim or transient impulse, but carrying out the purpose of a life."[130] Thoreau uses this rhetorically cleansed image of Captain Brown to redefine Transcendentalism as the determination to carry out the purpose of a life in heroic action against the machinery of injustice.

Once the matter of violence is pushed to the side in this way, Thoreau could apply to Brown the same ethics and arithmetic of his economy of power as he had used in his earlier writing. Like them he juxtaposes the rule of expediency with the law of justice, condemning his neighbors for asking such questions as "Yankee-like, 'What will he gain by it?' as if he expected to fill his pocket by such an enterprise."[131] But such rules of expediency do not apply when at that moment "the slave ship is on her way, crowded with its dying victims; new cargoes are being added in mid ocean; [and] a small crew of slaveholders, countenanced by their large body of passengers, is smothering four millions under the hatches." As Thoreau had said in "Resistance to Civil Government," there are times when one has to do what is right at whatever cost to oneself. So too with Brown: "He did not value his bodily life in comparison with ideal things. He did not recognize unjust human laws, but resisted them as he was bid. For once we are lifted out of the trivialness and dust of politics into the region of truth and manhood." There was no real cost to such a sacrifice by Thoreau's arithmetic, because living in such a situation is not really living at all (at least insofar as one is a human being and not a mechanical instrument to be simply wound "down like a clock"). Better that one die a real death, having actually lived, than having "merely rotted or sloughed off, pretty much as they had rotted or sloughed along."[132] In these principles Thoreau is consistent. His praise of Brown's willingness to sacrifice his life for principle is no different than his praise of one who had given a plank to a drowning man even if it caused of his own drowning.

Had Brown killed no one but simply occupied the armory at Harpers Ferry, Thoreau's speech would have followed the same strategies of the rhetoric of action he had used in "Resistance," only praising the actions of Brown rather than himself. Indeed one might have attributed to Brown an early expression of civil disobedience. He was vocal in his opposition to slavery, organized a group of followers, raised funds in public, and ultimately violated the law in dramatic fashion that evoked a rapid and violent response by the government and captured the attention of the national press. Arendt, for instance, argues that "civil disobedience arises when a significant number of citizens have become convinced either that the normal channels of change no longer function, and grievances will not be heard or acted upon, or that, on the contrary, the government is about to change and has embarked upon and persists in modes of action whose legality and constitutionality are open to grave doubt." In reaction to the situation, "the civil disobedient, though he is usually dissenting from a majority, acts in the name and for the sake of a group; he defies the law and the established authorities on the ground of basic dissent, and not because he as an individual wishes to make an exception for himself and to get away with it."[133] In many ways this description is completely fitting for Brown, who acted in the name of the slaves and whose occupation of Harpers Ferry was such a tactical failure that it is plausible to speculate that his intent was not to succeed in his plan but to be captured and put on trial as a symbol. That Thoreau reacted to Brown's action by praising him as an "Angel of Light" and using subsequent events to expose the economy of power of an unjust government is perfectly consistent with the strategies of civil disobedience and the rhetoric of action.

But the fact that Brown did use violence added a disturbing element to Thoreau's rhetoric that departed from his earlier lectures and writings. He did not entirely sidestep the question of violence; he addresses the question head on in a single, powerful paragraph. Thoreau acknowledges that it was Brown's "peculiar doctrine that a man has a perfect right to interfere by force with the slaveholder, in order to rescue the slave." On this point he did not mince words about his own position: "I agree with him." For Thoreau the moral calculation was obvious: "Those who are continually shocked by slavery have some right to be shocked by the violent death of the slaveholder, but no others. Such will be more shocked by his life than by his death." In making this claim, Thoreau effectively valued the life of the slaveholder as one would value a wooden part in a machine designed for torture, the removal of which would emancipate so many blameless slaves from a life of abject misery. It effectively dehumanizes the slave owner and turns him into a pure object. To those who would prefer a philanthropy based in political advocacy, Thoreau retorted: "I speak for the slave when I say that I prefer the philanthropy of Captain Brown to that philanthropy which neither shoots me nor liberates me." Thoreau acknowledged that a man who is not a slave "may have other affairs to attend to," but he also recognized that circumstances might arise when all things became possible: "I do not wish to kill nor to be killed, but I can foresee circumstances in which both these things would be by me unavoidable." If society sanctions a million acts of small violence for the sake of injustice, why must it condemn a single large act of violence as necessarily unjust? After all, even Christ used violence: "The same indignation that is said to have cleared the temple once will clear it again. The question is not about the weapon, but the spirit in which you use it."[134] Thus it was that Christ and "Old Brown" could be found at two ends of the same chain, both using the tools of the oppressors to serve the cause of freedom.

The comparison between Jesus and Brown is problematic for an obvious reason—Jesus overturned tables for the sake of making a religious and rhetorical point. Brown assaulted Harpers Ferry in silence to obtain weapons for the sake of a violent revolution. The one openly and lovingly violated the law in order to expose its poverty and illuminate the existence of a higher, more divine law; the other secretly and violently attacked specific individuals in complete disregard for the law so as to reconstitute society through the barrel of a gun. Arendt, for instance, argues that violence stands in complete contradiction to the methods of civil disobedience, for the "necessary characteristic of civil disobedience is nonviolence."[135] Whereas civil disobedience shows a respect for the idea of law by openly violating an unjust one in hopes for its replacement by something better, violence shows disregard for the entire idea of law and authority it represents. Moreover, "violence is by nature instrumental."[136] Consequently it treats everything, including individuals, as a means to an end. When Thoreau justifies his own violent impulses, he thus treats the slave owner the same way that the slave owner treats the slave—as an object to be directly manipulated or eliminated rather than a subject to be addressed and persuaded. But once politics becomes reinterpreted through violence, and one's opposition becomes a mere physical obstacle to eliminate through the weapons of war, then the rhetoric of action is no longer needed; one needs only the propaganda of administration to start giving orders to direct action of pulleys, gears, and cranks.

Yet Thoreau drew back from this conclusion. His flirtations with violence in "Plea" are brief and largely confined to a distant hypothetical. His consistent effort throughout is to purify Brown to make him a fit symbol for his rhetoric of action whose purpose is not to champion the overthrow of the state through arms but rather the reformation of the public through speech. In effect Thoreau stripped Brown's act of the instrumental logic of violence and replaced it with the symbolic meaning of political action. This is possible with acts of violence. Even Arendt acknowledges that while "violence does not promote causes, neither history nor revolution, neither progress nor reaction," it can nonetheless "serve to dramatize grievances and bring them to public attention."[137] Brown's raid accomplished thus latter task with the help not only of Thoreau's speech but ironically the same newspapers that railed against its injustice, stupidity, and futility. By giving publicity to his perception and performance of right, the newspapers shocked and divided the conscience of the nation. As the *Richmond Enquirer* concluded, Brown's failed assault "has advanced the cause of Disunion more than any other event that happened since the formation of Government."[138] That is why Thoreau did not "plead for his life, but for his character—his immortal life; and so it becomes your cause wholly, and not his in the least."[139] He knew that Brown's power was not in his rifle; it was in the publicizing of his principle that could lay bare the brutality of the antebellum economy of power.

The impact that Brown's raid had on the nation was not long in coming. In a lecture called "The Last Days of John Brown," written for a celebration of his life held at his graveside in North Elba, New York, on July 4, 1860, and eventually published in the *Liberator,* Thoreau gave the last word on the power of the rhetoric of action. In contradistinction to the assumptions of rhetorical traditionalists, "years were not required for revolution of public opinion; days, nay, hours, produced marked changes in this case." Whereas before 1859 many were against violating established laws or antagonizing slave power, after Brown's raid the "North, I mean the *living* North, was suddenly all transcendental. It went behind the human law, it went behind the apparent failure, and recognized eternal justice and glory." The old formulas were cast off, and "original perceptions" of justice made clear.[140] Brown, despite having been hanged, was "more alive than he ever was. He has earned immortality. He is not confined to North Elba nor to Kansas. He is no longer working in secret. He works in public, and in the clearest light that shines on this land."[141] This was what happened when action from principle met the communication revolution: isolated events, actions, and people took on the quality of rhetorical symbols that once disseminated could divide a nation and start a war.

On the early morning of April 12, 1861, the forces of the new Southern Confederacy fired artillery on the small company of Union soldiers defending Fort Sumter near Charleston, South Carolina. The event began the American Civil War, which lasted for four years and cost six hundred thousand lives, including almost a third of the Southern white male population between eighteen and forty years old. The final breaking point of the Union had been the election of Abraham Lincoln to the presidency as the standard-bearer for the new Republican Party, formed less out of a moral hatred of slavery or support for the rights of blacks than in a "commitment to a 'free labor ideology,' grounded in the precepts that free labor was economically and socially superior to slave labor and that the distinctive quality of northern society was the opportunity it offered wage earners to rise to property-owning independence."[142] The election of Lincoln did not signal an all-out effort to abolish slavery in the South so much as a firm desire to limit its expansion and corrode its political influence, while at the same time making a full "commitment to the northern social order in its development and expansion."[143] The North did not instigate the war with the righteous indignation of Brown to purge the world of slavery and racism; it fought to proliferate a way of life that at its core was the ideology of free labor for white men, an ideology whose ultimate triumph through the strength of arms "culminated in unchallengeable bourgeois hegemony, moral and political."[144]

Thoreau, however, was largely unmoved by the start of the war. On December 3, 1860, after a visit from a coughing Bronson Alcott, he had come down with what he called influenza while out counting tree rings; the illness eventually deepened into bronchitis, which "kept him housebound all winter."[145] He preferred to expend what little energy he had on organizing his papers and reading about plant distribution and seed dispersion. His only extended statement about the war came in a letter to family friend Parker Pillsbury, who had requested a copy of *Walden* to give to a friend of his. (Thoreau did not have one, but he did have a copy of *Week* to send him.) But Thoreau included a warning along with it: "As for your friend, my prospective reader, I hope he ignores Fort Sumter, and 'Old Abe,' and all that; for that is just the most fatal, and, indeed, the only fatal weapon you can direct against evil, ever; for as long as you know of it, you are *particeps criminis*. What business have you, if you are 'an angel of light,' to be pondering over the deeds of darkness, reading 'the New York Herald,' and the like?" Of course, Thoreau admitted to having "heard of Sumter" and having read the *Tribune;* but he had tried to read Herodotus and Strabo "as hard as I can, to counterbalance it." Returning to the arithmetic of the economy of power by which futile distractions of public affairs that one cannot change or influence drain one's life and thereby inhibit one's power to pursue more noble ends, Thoreau adds his own beatitudes to the list of those delivered by Jesus in the Sermon on the Mount: "Blessed were the days before you read a President's Message. Blessed are the young, for they do not need the President's Message. Blessed are they who never read a newspaper, for they shall see Nature, and, through her, God."[146] The only entry in his journal for the month of April of that year is this: "April 23. Think I hear bay-wings. Toads ring."[147]

Thoreau died in his bed at 9 o'clock in the morning on May 6, 1862. Sam Staples, who had once put him in jail, remarked that he had never seen a man "dying with so much pleasure and peace." That morning his younger sister Sophia was reading from a section of *Week,* and Thoreau was looking forward to the book's narrative of the trip homeward. His last two audible words were *moose* and *Indian.*[148] Emerson, in his last sustained major piece of writing, composed and delivered a eulogy for him at the First Parish Meetinghouse on May 9, 1862. It was, according to Richardson, "Emerson's best, most personal biographical piece and remains the best single piece written on Henry Thoreau."[149] Much of the eulogy is descriptive of his character and habits, noting that he "declined to give up his large ambition of knowledge and action for any narrow craft or profession, aiming at a much more comprehensive calling, the art of living well." But Emerson also attended to his character as a "speaker and actor of the truth," who "was ever running into dramatic situations from this cause" and who "did not disappoint expectation, but used an original judgment on each emergency." As Emerson did with all of his character sketches, however, he ended on a critical note as well, complaining that "I cannot help counting it a fault in him that he had no ambition. Wanting this, instead of engineering for all America, he was the captain of a huckleberry party. Pounding beans is good to the end of pounding empires one of these days; but if, at the end of years, it is still only beans!"[150] A judgment could not be more fitting for a former disciple of Sampson Reed.

Perhaps the answer to this charge, however, can be found in the text of the eulogy itself. Three characteristics stand out. First, Emerson's Thoreau was less interested in the magnitude of an action or object than in the scope of the law it revealed. Emerson casually noted that for Thoreau, "there was no such thing as size. The pond was a small ocean; the Atlantic, a large Walden pond. He referred every minute fact to cosmical laws." To complain that Thoreau did not engineer for the United States because he hoed beans thus ignores the rhetorical power that came from expressing the laws, both natural and moral, that governed his experience with beans. Second, despite his lack of piety for size, he was a surveyor and was in the business of determining precise mathematical measurements and proportions, eventually developing the "habit of ascertaining the measures and distances of objects which interested him, the size of trees, the depth and extent of ponds and rivers, the height of mountains, and the air-line distance of his favorite summits." In comparison with Emerson's more dilettantish approach to science, Thoreau understood that predicting and measuring the effects of a thing required a detailed knowledge of actual relations and distances. Even a small stone can start an avalanche under the right conditions.

Lastly, Thoreau had a keen appreciation for how technology altered the sense of distance, compressing the great expanses of the world to such a small space that one no longer had to leave the boundaries of one's town for exotic experiences. Thoreau wrote in *Walden* of feeling "refreshed and expanded when the freight train rattles past me, and I smell the stores which go dispensing their odors all the way from Long Wharf to Lake Champlain, reminding me of foreign parts, of coral reefs, of Indian oceans, and tropical climes, and the extent of the globe."[151] In perhaps the most telling anecdote, Emerson related the following story:

> On one occasion he went to the University Library to procure some books. The librarian refused to lend them. Mr. Thoreau repaired to the President, who stated to him the rules and usages, which permitted the loan of books to resident graduates, to clergymen who were alumni, and to some other residents within a circle of ten miles radius from the College. Mr. Thoreau explained to the President that the railroad had destroyed the old scale of distances,—that the library was useless, yes, and President and College useless, on the terms of his rules,—that the one benefit he owed to the College was its library,—that, at this moment, not only his want of books was imperative, but he wanted a large number of books, and assured him that he, Thoreau, and not the librarian, was the proper custodian of these.

The end result was a rhetorical victory for Thoreau: "The President found the petitioner so formidable, and the rules getting to look so ridiculous, that he ended by giving him a privilege which in his hands proved unlimited thereafter."[152] Thoreau had used his knowledge of distance to leverage influence over a recalcitrant audience in order to give him access to power—that is, to the knowledge of fact, history, and law. He had not gone out into the world to conquer it; he had made the world come to him so he could understand it.

Thoreau grasped, perhaps more than any other Transcendentalist, how great changes came out of small events, and how the detailed inquiry into the law, history, and facts of the smallest entity could determine the course of history and the actions of a nation. A journal entry of September 22, 1851, narrated how he ventured into the Deep Cut to listen to the hum of the telegraph wire, putting his ear to one of the posts, noting that "every pore of the wood was filled with music, labored with the strain,—as if every fiber was affected and being seasoned or timed, rearranged according to a new and more harmonious law." That law was what Emerson had defined in his eulogy—that the old scale of distances had been destroyed. But to understand the meaning of this new law, Thoreau drew from the language of myth, creating a new myth for a new age:

Shall we not add a tenth Muse to the immortal Nine? And that the invention thus divinely honored and distinguished—on which the Muse has condescended to smile—is this magic medium of communication for mankind! To read that the ancients stretched a wire round the earth, attaching it to the trees of the forest, by which they sent messages by one named Electricity, father of Lightning and Magnetism, swifter far than Mercury, the stern commands of war and news of peace, and that the winds caused this wire to vibrate so that it emitted a harp-like an aeolian music in all the land through which it passed, as if to express the satisfaction of the gods in this invention. Yet this is fact, and we have yet attributed the invention to no god.[153]

In *Walden* Thoreau had famously complained that "our inventions are wont to be pretty toys, which distract our attention from serious things," and that even while a telegraph cord has been stretched across the Atlantic, "perchance the first news that will leak through into the broad, flapping American ear will be that the Princess Adelaide has the whooping cough."[154] But he also noted that to make "a railroad round the world available to all mankind is equivalent to grading the whole surface of the planet."[155] Just what would happen when humankind used its inventions for serious things, Thoreau rarely speculated upon; but he understood full well that when the world becomes flat, a thing done in one place can have impacts everywhere and simultaneously. To reform the world one had to harness the power of Mercury to disseminate truth, a weapon of reform that would represent amount to a Sharps' rifle of infinitely surer and longer range than anything imagined prior to the nineteenth century.

Conclusion

"Ethiopia shall stretch out her hand unto God"—
Frederick Douglass and the Legacy of Transcendentalism

Every Northern man who visits the old master class, the land owners and landlords of the South, is told by the old slaveholders with a great show of virtue that they are glad that they are rid of slavery and would not have the slave system back if they could; that they are better off than they ever were before, and much more of the same tenor. Thus Northern men come home duped and go on a mission of duping others by telling the same pleasing story. There are very good reasons why these people would not have slavery back if they could—reasons far more creditable to their cunning than to their conscience. With slavery they had some care and responsibility for the physical well-being of their slaves. Now they have as firm a grip on the freedman's labor as when he was a slave and without any burden of caring for his children or himself. The whole arrangement is stamped with fraud and is supported by hypocrisy, and I here and now, on this Emancipation Day: denounce it as a villainous swindle, and invoke the press, the pulpit and the lawmaker to assist in exposing it and blotting it out forever.

Frederick Douglass, "I Denounce the So-called
Emancipation as a Fraud," 1888

On April 16, 1888, Frederick Douglass stepped to a rostrum in Washington, D.C., to deliver an address commemorating the twenty-sixth anniversary of emancipation in the District of Columbia. It was also just a few days after the twenty-third anniversary of the April 9, 1865, surrender of Robert E. Lee to Ulysses S. Grant, which had ended the Civil War. Douglass had turned seventy that year, although his exact birthdate remained unknown to him his entire life. As he wrote in his *Narrative of the Life of Frederick Douglass:* "I do not remember to have ever met a slave who could tell of his birthday."[1] By then he had lived through slavery, freedom, war, emancipation, and reconstruction. In 1866 he had been buoyed with hope when the election turned out an overwhelming victory for radicals who could override any presidential veto of Reconstruction policy. "Radicalism," he had written, "so far from being odious, is now the popular passport to power." There had been those, of course, who had still denounced "the Negro for his prominence in this discussion," but Douglass had not thought one could deny the obvious fact: "The stern logic of events, which goes directly to the point, disdaining all concern for the color or features of men, has determined the interests of the country as identical with and inseparable from those of the Negro."[2] It was that policy, hopefully established by the radicals but progressively undermined and manipulated by former slaveholders through lies, that Douglass now condemned as a "swindle" and denounced as "a stupendous fraud—a fraud upon him, a fraud upon the world."[3]

Douglass, the elder statesman, was compelled to revive the forceful rhetoric of his youth because of a particular experience: mainly a visit that year to South Carolina and Georgia. The visit revealed to him the full degree to which emancipation had not improved the lives of African Americans in the two decades since the abolition of slavery. Douglass never believed that anything approaching true equality had ever been achieved through Reconstruction. It had been a constant theme in all of his speeches that "it is our lot to live among a people whose laws, traditions, and prejudices have been against us for centuries, and from these they are not yet free."[4] But at the same time, he consistently held out the hope that "prejudice, with all its malign accompaniments, may yet be removed by peaceful means; that, assisted by time and events and the growing enlightenment of both races, the color line will ultimately become harmless."[5] The conditions he witnessed in South Carolina and Georgia changed all of that. He described in detail the pervasive landlord and tenant laws skillfully devised to "crush out all aspiration, all hope of progress in the landless Negro."[6] The freedman was caught in a system that cheated him out of his earnings and imprisoned him in an endless cycle of debt until, through desperation, he resorted to theft to support his family and was inevitably "put to work for master in a chain gang, and he comes out, if he ever gets out, a ruined man."[7] Perhaps most offensive of all was the fact that Southern propaganda, spread "as far as the wings of the press and the power of speech can carry it," lay the blame for his condition squarely on his own shoulders. The consistent message was that the "Negro as a free man and a citizen is not yet solved" and that "he has shown himself unfit for the position assigned him by the mistaken statesmanship of the nation."[8] All of these facts revealed to Douglass the degree to which the "love of power," or what he called the "perpetual tendency of power to encroach upon weakness," had not died out in the South but had merely assumed a new, more insidious form that twisted the logic of emancipation into a new ideology of white supremacy.[9]

But in denouncing emancipation as a swindle and a fraud, Douglass was doing more; he was also criticizing that part of him that still held to the Transcendentalist faith that revolutionary change was possible, not only for the individual but also for the nation. He had used this faith in a lecture he had given on June 16, 1861, called "The Decision of the Hour," in which he urged the North to commit itself fully to fighting a war for the abolition of slavery and the establishment of freedom. In an argument that could have come straight from Emerson or Thoreau, Douglass argued that "the human mind is so constructed as that, when left free from the blinding and hardening power of selfishness, it bows reverently to the mandates of truth and justice. It becomes loyal and devoted to an idea." What was needed for that idea to become reality was action from principle. Indeed, he asserted, "all the progress towards perfection ever made by humankind, and all the blessings which are now enjoyed, are ascribable to some brave and good man, who, catching the illumination of a heaven-born truth, has counted it a joy, precious and unspeakable, to toil, suffer, and often to die for the glorious realization of that heaven-born truth."[10] Even as late as 1881, Douglass still asserted this faith. In a speech given in memory of John Brown at Harpers Ferry, West Virginia, he praised Brown for being just such a brave and good man. "Captain" Brown, he claims, "had evinced a conception of the sacredness and value of liberty which transcended in sublimity that of her own Patrick Henry and made even his fire-flashing sentiment of 'Liberty or Death,' seem dark and tame and selfish. Henry loved liberty for himself, but this man loved liberty for all men, and for those most despised and scorned, as well as for those most esteemed and honored."[11] This action of complete self-sacrifice, of "pure, disinterested benevolence," thus conveyed the "force of a moral earthquake," shocking the conscience of the nation and rallying it to freedom's cause.[12] "Mighty with the sword of steel," Douglass concluded, "he was mightier with the sword of the truth, and with this sword he literally swept the horizon."[13] And so the truth went marching on behind his dead body.

Or not. For despite Douglass's occasional flirtations with Transcendental eloquence, he was a firm realist about social change. He understood that dominant habits, once in place, are resistant to change and embed themselves in every institution and relationship in society. Even in his hopeful address "The Decision of the Hour," he recognized that "slavery, like all other gross and powerful forms of wrong which appeal directly to human pride and selfishness, when once admitted into the framework of society, has the ability and tendency to beget a character in the whole network of society surrounding it, favorable to its continuance. The very law of its existence is growth and dominion."[14] And in his 1883 "Address to the People of the United States" (in which he expressed optimism about the eventual abolition of the color line), he also recognized that more than a moral volcano is required to alter growth and powerful forms of wrong: "Time and events are required for the conversion of nations. Not even the character of a great political organization can be changed by a new platform. It will be the same old snake though in a new skin." So too with nations: "Though we had war, reconstruction and abolition as a nation, we still linger in the shadow and blight of an extinct institution. Though the colored man is no longer subject to be bought and sold, he is still surrounded by an adverse sentiment which fetters all his movements."[15] His experience in South Carolina and Georgia thus did not teach him any new principles of human behavior; it simply showed him the degree to which one set of principles seemed to be truer to the facts than others.

If Douglass challenged the Transcendentalist tendency to see all things as possible with heroic eloquence and accepted the fact that the work of reform required an organized and sustained struggle to condemn the habits of vice and cultivate the habits of virtue, he nonetheless held throughout his life a belief in the necessity of eloquence in that pursuit. Few things are more consistent in Douglass than the imperative to harness all the technology of the nineteenth century and exploit the power of the press and the pulpit both to alter public opinion and to influence the lawmaker. In his "Farewell Speech to the British People," delivered on March 30, 1847, before his return to the United States after friends had purchased his freedom, Douglass announced that he was returning to his home country "to unmask her pretensions to republicanism, and expose her hypocritical professions of Christianity; to denounce her high claims to civilization, and proclaim in her ears the wrong of those who cry day and night to Heaven."[16] But Douglass did not return unarmed. He exploited every resource of nineteenth-century technology to spread his message across the nation and around the globe: "the improvement in the facility for the transportation of letters to the post office, and steam navigation, as well as other means of locomotion—the extraordinary power and rapidity with which intelligence is transmitted from one country to another."[17] In particular he looked to turn those two greatest means of influencing public opinion to his own ends, for "it is in the pulpit and the press—and the publications especially of the religious press—that we are to look for our right moral sentiment."[18] Nothing had changed by the time he delivered his last major address, "Why Is the Negro Lynched?" in 1894. Almost half a century had passed, and yet Douglass still proclaimed that to end this scourge of racist violence, "let the Northern press and pulpit proclaim the gospel of truth and justice against the war now being made upon the Negro."[19] Using the Northern press and pulpit to proclaim the gospel of truth and justice against the vices of the United States is what the Transcendentalists had been doing all along.

When placed in juxtaposition with the titanic figure of Douglass, perhaps the greatest orator the United States produced in the nineteenth century, the rhetorical legacy of the Transcendentalists often seems small by comparison. One finds such a view expressed by none other than Emerson. In one of his last journal entries in 1871, he paused to reflect on the legacy of the Transcendentalists, a group that in his youth he believed was destined to become the recognized geniuses of their age and was to be reserved a place of public honor. But such was not to be: "How vain to praise our literature, when its really superior minds are quite omitted, & utterly unknown to the public. Sampson Reed is known only to his sect, which does not estimate him. And Newcomb is a subtiller [*sic*] thinker than is any other American. And Philip Randolph a deep & admirable writer, utterly unknown,—died unknown. Thoreau quite unappreciated, though his books have been opened & superficially read. Alcott, the scholars do not know how to approach, or how to discriminate his tentative & sometimes tiresome talking, from his insights."[20]

But who had time to interpret a tiresome talking of a man such as Alcott when the nation was healing from war and busy organizing itself for the pursuit of wealth? According to Rose the eclipse of Transcendentalism was due to a disjunction between their idealistic vision and the realities of the bourgeois order that had triumphed: "Capitalism came of age in America when it became clear that the Transcendentalists, and other radical reformers, had not been able to communicate to their contemporaries a belief in a social alternative, and had lost faith in themselves."[21] Gura argues that with the ascension of capitalistic individualism, "the other half of the Transcendentalists' dream, of a common humanity committed to social justice, fell by the wayside," ultimately giving way before the rise of the "Gilded Age and beyond."[22] Emerson's lament perhaps is thus better credited less to a failure of rhetoric and more to a shift in the national mind that could no longer hear their voice or make sense of their vision.

Despite all of this, the rhetoric of the Transcendentalists has endured. Perhaps one reason is that they represented the first sustained effort by American intellectuals to wrestle with what Burke would call the question of permanence and change, or of those moments of collective realization that "men build their cultures by huddling together, nervously loquacious, at the edge of an abyss."[23] Despite the empirical differences that come with vast spans of time, something in the attitude and context of the Transcendentalists resonates with the present day. Miller writes that "however few or confused or faltering were the so-called Transcendentalists, they were, often despite themselves, caught up in a crisis of the spirit and of the nation, a crisis that carries immense implications for the American predicament not only in their time but also in ours."[24] According to Packer, theirs was a time "born in a period of innocence and hope and grown to maturity in the time of wild experimentation," and although "they lived through a period of national humiliation, when every year brought new shame, they never lost faith in the ultimate triumph of the moral law."[25] There is thus something to be said for Emerson's claim that "there is no pure Transcendentalist," because Transcendentalism is really the expression of a certain attitude toward permanence and change, a contempt for and impatience of recalcitrant tradition, and a desire to harness the potential of new mediums of thought and action to constitute a new way of thinking, acting, and being.[26]

A central argument of this book has been that this attitude did not simply spring naturally from the spirit of genius or the force of the Over-Soul; the transcendental attitude arose in reaction to a specific set of complex changes encompassed in the communication, transportation, and market revolutions that released enormous new energies, both reactionary and progressive. The rhetoric, politics, and philosophy of the Transcendentalists were thus directed toward diagnosing the changes and developing new arts of living that purged old vices and emancipated new powers, both in the individual and in the collective. And while it is a vice of contemporary forgetfulness to look back on the Transcendentalists as if they were an effete circle of poets speaking only to one another in Emerson's salon, it is important to keep in mind that they represented some of the most widely known public intellectuals of their age. Reed was the foremost prophet of Emmanuel Swedenborg, Alcott the most controversial advocate for educational reform, Brownson the American forerunner of Marxist economic critique, Emerson the first American intellectual celebrity, Fuller the most forceful woman's voice in the nation, and Thoreau arguably one of the most influential advocates for environmentalism and civil resistance in American history. To argue that somehow Transcendentalist rhetoric was a failure is to judge their discourse by standards that lack an appreciation for history.

Once Transcendentalism is associated less with a group of people and more with a certain attitude expressed in eloquence, the spirit of Transcendentalism can be identified in someone such as Douglass, albeit combined with many competing attitudes that he drew upon when faced with different rhetorical situations. And so it is fitting that he provides the most succinct summary of the context that bought Transcendentalism (and so many other social movements of the early nineteenth century) into being. In the closing words of his famous 1852 Independence Day address, "The Meaning of July Fourth for the Negro," Douglass drew encouragement from what he called "the obvious tendencies of the age," which gave him optimism that the horrors of slavery may eventually be overcome:

> Nations do not now stand in the same relation to each other that they did ages ago. No nation can now shut itself up from the surrounding world, and trot round in the same old path of its fathers without interference. The time was when such could be done. Long established customs

of hurtful character could formerly fence themselves in, and do their evil work with social impunity. Knowledge was then confined and enjoyed by the privileged few, and the multitude walked on in mental darkness. But a change has now come over the affairs of mankind. Walled cities and empires have become unfashionable. The arm of commerce has borne away the gates of the strong city. Intelligence is penetrating the darkest corners of the globe. It makes its pathway over and under the sea, as well as on the earth. Wind, steam, and lightning are its chartered agents. Oceans no longer divide, but link nations together. From Boston to London is now a holiday excursion. Space is comparatively annihilated. Thoughts expressed on one side of the Atlantic, are distinctly heard on the other. The far off and almost fabulous Pacific rolls in grandeur at our feet. The Celestial Empire, the mystery of ages, is being solved. The fiat of the Almighty, "Let there be Light," has not yet spent its force. No abuse, no outrage whether in taste, sport or avarice, can now hide itself from the all-pervading light. The iron shoe, and crippled foot of China must be seen, in contrast with nature. Africa must rise and put on her yet unwoven garment. "Ethiopia shall stretch out her hand unto God."[27]

With the perspective that comes with time, it is apparent today that the problem of the Celestial Empire has not, in fact, been solved, and while the iron shoe and crippled foot may have passed into history, they have been replaced by other forms of oppression and suffering. And yet the hope that Ethiopia, and all other nations of the world, may stretch out their hands to God remains as alive as ever, for the forces that were binding together the world in the nineteenth century have continued unabated into the twenty-first. One can change but a few words in this description and see the contemporary world reflected back, both in its horrors and in its hopes.

It was the peculiar faith of the Transcendentalists that these many tendencies of their age could be controlled and directed by eloquence—that is, an art that transcended the conventional rules of rhetoric and sought to condense the insights of philosophy and science into a poetic discourse of rare beauty, depth, and power. In his journal Thoreau defined the art of writing as that which produces "sentences which suggest far more than they say, which have an atmosphere about them, which do not merely report an old, but make a new, impression; sentences which suggest as many things and are as durable as a Roman aqueduct," sentences "which lie like boulders on the page, up and down or across; which contain the seed of other sentences, not mere repetition, but creation."[28] Today, just as in Thoreau's time, such an ambition might seem poetically noble but rhetorically futile, an idealistic fantasy that is impotent before the overwhelming influence of propaganda and the press wielded by the wealthy and the powerful. Yet if it is true that such sentences cannot move a nation en masse, it is untrue that they are impotent to change an individual. If Transcendentalism means anything, it means that individuals matter to history. So perhaps the greatest legacy of the Transcendentalists is to give individuals confidence in their own genius and the courage to speak truth with beauty and power so they, like Ethiopia, might stretch forth their hands toward the farther shore.

NOTES

Introduction

1. Emerson, "American Scholar," 57.
2. Emerson, *Selected Journals: 1820–1842*, 357.
3. Emerson's journals, 665.
4. Ibid., 17, 126.
5. Ibid., 227.
6. Fliegelman, *Declaring Independence*, 26–28.
7. Engels observes, for instance, that "mob violence was the engine for social and political change in the 1760s and 1770s, and a way for poor and often disenfranchised citizens to make the fiction of popular sovereignty real." *Enemyship*, 5. A popular rhetoric certainly existed during this time that challenged the aristocratic notions of formulaic rhetoric, but it can hardly be said to be more than a passionate airing of grievances spoken with a simple directness.
8. Holmes, *Ralph Waldo Emerson*, 88.
9. Fliegelman, *Declaring Independence*, 29.
10. Ibid., 32.
11. Miller, introduction, 15.
12. Cranch, "Transcendentalism," 102.
13. Buell, introduction, xiii.
14. Emerson, *Nature*, 33.
15. Bloom, *Essayists*, 101.
16. Bloom, *Agon*, 108.
17. Ibid., 109.
18. Ibid., 4.
19. Ibid., 14.
20. Ibid., 171.
21. Ibid., 172.
22. Ibid., 171.
23. Ibid., 316.
24. Poirier, *Renewal of Literature*, 131.
25. Ibid., 132.
26. Ibid., 148.
27. Ibid.
28. Dewey, "Emerson," 190.
29. Rorty, *Philosophy and Social Hope*, 26.
30. Cavell, "What's the Use," 784.

31. Burke, *Attitudes toward History*, 166.
32. Cornford, *Origin of Attic Comedy*, 20.
33. Gura, *American Transcendentalism*, xi.
34. Myerson, introduction, xxix.
35. Thompson, "Emerson and the Democratization," 133–34.
36. Wydra, "Politics of Transcendence," 269. Similarly Emerson notes how the idealism associated with his own thought is nothing new: "This way of thinking, falling on Roman times, made Stoic philosophers; falling on despotic times, made patriot Catos and Brutuses; falling on superstitious times, made prophets and apostles; on popish times, made protestants and ascetic monks, preachers of Faith against the preachers of Works; on prelatical times, made Puritans and Quakers; and falling on Unitarian and conservative times, makes the peculiar shades of idealism which we know." Emerson, "Transcendentalist," 86.
37. Wydra, "Politics of Transcendence," 269.
38. Ibid.
39. Ibid.
40. Burke, *Language as Symbolic Action*, 200.
41. Burke, *Rhetoric of Motives*, 41.

Chapter 1: "Eloquence is the language of love"

1. Howe, *What Hath God Wrought*, 659.
2. Packer, *Transcendentalists*, 49.
3. Reed, "Genius," 21.
4. Ibid.
5. Ibid., 22.
6. Ibid., 25.
7. Ibid.
8. Wrobel, "Sampson Reed," 351–52.
9. Ibid., 352–53.
10. Emerson and Carlyle, *Correspondence*, 17.
11. Ibid.
12. Howe, *What Hath God Wrought*, 371.
13. Quoted in ibid., 369.
14. Emerson and Carlyle, *Correspondence*, 17.
15. Ibid.
16. Ibid., 19.
17. Ibid., 32
18. Ibid., 33.
19. Sellers, *Market Revolution*, 102.
20. Quoted in ibid., 87.
21. Quoted in ibid.
22. Howe, *What Hath God Wrought*, 485.
23. Jordan, "Sampson Reed," 295.
24. Quoted in ibid.
25. Ibid.
26. Japp, "Gift from Emerson," 628.

27. Sellers, *Market Revolution,* 237.

28. Weber, *Protestant Ethic,* 80.

29. Ibid.

30. Ibid.

31. Ibid., 23.

32. Ibid., 20.

33. Ibid., 170.

34. Ibid., 171.

35. Howe, *What Hath God Wrought,* 31–32.

36. Ibid., 38–39.

37. Reed, "Genius," 21.

38. Reed, "Growth of the Mind," 53–54.

39. Sellers, *Market Revolution,* 90.

40. Quoted in ibid., 78.

41. Ibid., 69.

42. Levine, *Half Slave,* 52.

43. Howe, *What Hath God Wrought,* 216.

44. Ibid., 217.

45. Ibid.

46. Warner, *Letters of the Republic,* 32.

47. Bailyn, *Ideological Origins of the American Revolution,* 1–2.

48. Anderson, *Imagined Communities,* 6.

49. Howe, *What Hath God Wrought,* 228.

50. Ibid., 225.

51. Ibid.

52. Ibid., 227.

53. Tocqueville, *Democracy in America,* 355.

54. Sellers, *Market Revolution,* 5.

55. Ibid.

56. Foner, *Free Soil,* 13.

57. Ibid.

58. Sellers, *Market Revolution,* 30.

59. Reed, "Growth of the Mind," 59.

60. Ibid., 53.

61. Reed, "Genius," 25.

62. Ibid., 22.

63. Niebuhr, *Essential Reinhold Niebuhr,* 147–54.

64. Ibid., 256.

65. Quoted in Kirk, Raven, and Schofield, *Presocratic Philosophers,* 287.

66. Reed, "Genius," 21.

67. Bloom, *Agon,* 175.

68. Nietzsche, *Philosophy in the Tragic Age,* 62.

69. Ibid.

70. Reed, "Growth of the Mind," 47.

71. Ibid., 45.

72. Ibid., 53.
73. Reed, "Genius," 24.
74. Ibid.
75. Ibid., 25.
76. Ibid.
77. Reed, "Growth of the Mind," 54.
78. Ibid., 54–55.
79. Ibid., 40.
80. Ibid., 41.
81. Ibid., 58.
82. Ibid., 27.
83. Emerson, *Selected Journals*, 887.
84. Ibid.
85. Ibid.
86. Ibid.
87. Wilentz, *Rise of American Democracy*, 640–41.
88. Ibid., 640.
89. Reed, "Genius," 24.

Chapter 2: "Jesus was a teacher"

1. Alcott, *Doctrine and Discipline*, 53.
2. Ibid.
3. Koster, *Transcendentalism in America*, 66.
4. Mott, "Education," 153.
5. Alcott, *Journals*, 51.
6. Mott, "Education," 169.
7. Freire, *Pedagogy of the Oppressed*, 72.
8. Ibid., 84.
9. Ibid., 88–89.
10. Ibid., 90.
11. Shepard, *Pedlar's Progress*, 94.
12. Mott, "Education," 158.
13. Zappen, *Rebirth of Dialogue*, 15.
14. Ibid., 14.
15. Alcott, *Doctrine and Discipline*, 37–38.
16. Ibid., 38.
17. Shepard, *Pedlar's Progress*, 18.
18. Ibid., 4.
19. Ibid., 19.
20. Dahlstrand, *Amos Bronson Alcott*, 18.
21. Shepard, *Pedlar's Progress*, 10.
22. Alcott, *Doctrine and Discipline*, 44.
23. Dahlstrand, *Amos Bronson Alcott*, 20–21.
24. Shepard, *Pedlar's Progress*, 33.

25. Dahlstrand, *Amos Bronson Alcott,* 20. A letter from fourteen-year-old Amos to his cousin William indicates the "arrogance and sense of superiority they felt in relationship with their peers": "Wolcott, August 27th, Saturday 1 PM 1814 Venerable Sir, Improving the present variety in writing to you, with the greatest pleasure; hoping to receive the receipt of a letter from you before long, concerning our Libraric Institution. Perhaps it is best to appoint in attendance at some proper place to consult on the project; but, sir, your opinion of the matter would be Satisfactory to me. Why not as well improve our money in that way, as to spend it in going to Balls, or some useless, Nonsensical Object! . . . I am Sir, Sincerely Yours, Amos B. Alcox." Cited in Dahlstrand, *Amos Bronson Alcott,* 21.

26. Butler, Wacker, and Balmer, *Religion in American Life,* 172.

27. Sellers, *Market Revolution,* 30.

28. Ibid.

29. Butler, Wacker, and Balmer, *Religion in American Life,* 172.

30. Alcott, *New Connecticut,* 126.

31. Quoted in Howe, *What Hath God Wrought,* 166.

32. Ibid., 169.

33. Sellers, *Market Revolution,* 210.

34. Howe, *What Hath God Wrought,* 172.

35. Dahlstrand, *Amos Bronson Alcott,* 23.

36. Ibid., 26.

37. Shepard, *Pedlar's Progress,* 36.

38. Ibid., 42.

39. Dahlstrand, *Amos Bronson Alcott,* 27.

40. Ibid., 28.

41. Shepard, *Pedlar's Progress,* 48.

42. Ibid., 42.

43. Ibid., 50.

44. Quoted in Sanborn and Harris, *A. Bronson Alcott,* 59.

45. Shepard, *Pedlar's Progress,* 70.

46. Dahlstrand, *Amos Bronson Alcott,* 31–32.

47. Ibid., 36.

48. Alcott, *Journals,* 4.

49. Ibid., 7.

50. Dahlstrand, *Amos Bronson Alcott,* 40.

51. Ibid.

52. Ibid., 109.

53. Myerson, introduction, xxxi.

54. Peabody, *Record of a School,* 26–27.

55. Bakhtin, *Dialogic Imagination,* 280.

56. Ibid.

57. Bakhtin, *Speech Genres,* 150.

58. Zappen, *Rebirth of Dialogue,* 2.

59. Bakhtin, *Problems in Dostoyevsky's Poetics,* 18.

60. Ibid., 6.

61. Wilson, "Aesthetics," 567.

62. Buell, *Literary Transcendentalism*, 200.

63. Hodder, *Emerson's Rhetoric of Revelation*, 120.

64. Peabody, *Record of a School*, 35.

65. Ibid., 36–37.

66. Heidegger, *On the Way to Language*, 63.

67. Ibid., 75.

68. Ibid., 80.

69. Packer, *Transcendentalists*, 58.

70. Bakhtin, *Dialogic Imagination*, 325.

71. Alcott, *Conversations with Children*, 199.

72. Ibid., 65n86.

73. Packer, *Transcendentalists*, 57.

74. Alcott, *Conversations with Children*, 142–43.

75. Ibid., 144.

76. Channing, "Likeness to God," 13.

77. Alcott, *Doctrine and Discipline*, 31.

78. Ibid., 35.

79. Ibid., 41.

80. Ibid.

81. Ibid., 47–48.

82. Ibid., 47.

83. Ibid., 38.

84. Ibid., 32.

85. Ibid., 36.

86. Ibid., 37.

87. Ibid., 46.

88. Ibid., 38.

89. Ibid., 37.

90. Hale, "Conversations," 42.

91. Buckingham, "Alcott's Conversations on the Gospels," 2.

92. Norton, "New School."

93. Alcott, *A. Bronson Alcott*, 189.

94. Alcott, *Journal*, 88.

95. Ibid., 95.

96. Ibid.

97. Alcott, *Doctrine and Discipline*, 54–55.

98. Alcott, *Journal*, 131.

99. Samuel May, quoted in Dahlstrand, *Amos Bronson Alcott*, 141.

100. Alcott, *Journal*, 131.

101. Emerson, "Divinity School Address," 142.

102. Alcott, *Journal*, 134.

103. Ibid., 52.

Chapter 3: "To break the fetters of the bound"

1. Sellers, *Market Revolution,* 354.
2. Quoted in ibid., 355.
3. Emerson, *Selected Journals,* 514.
4. Brownson, "Social Evils," 96.
5. Brownson, *New Views,* 194–96.
6. Ibid., 156.
7. Schlesinger, *Orestes A. Brownson,* 95, 96.
8. Burke, *On Symbols and Society,* 303.
9. Ibid., 307.
10. Ibid.
11. Emerson, *Journals and Miscellaneous Notebooks,* 305.
12. Aeschylus, *The Libation Bearers.*
13. Carey, *Orestes A. Brownson,* 2.
14. Brownson, *Convert,* 2.
15. Schlesinger, *Orestes A. Brownson,* 5.
16. Maynard, *Orestes Brownson,* 3.
17. Brownson, *Convert,* 2–3.
18. Carey, *Orestes A. Brownson,* 4.
19. Brownson, *Convert,* 4.
20. Ibid.
21. Butler, *In Search of the American Spirit,* 10.
22. Carey, *Orestes A. Brownson,* 3.
23. Brownson, *Convert,* 10.
24. Ibid., 12.
25. Ibid., 13.
26. Ibid.
27. H. Brownson, *Orestes A. Brownson,* 9–10.
28. Ibid., 10.
29. Grose, *Centennial History,* 133.
30. O. Brownson, "Independence Day Address," 117.
31. Ibid.
32. O. Brownson, *New Views,* 176–77.
33. O. Brownson, *Convert,* 41.
34. Robinson, *Unitarians,* 52.
35. O. Brownson, *Convert,* 51–52.
36. Maynard, *Orestes Brownson,* 20.
37. Carey, *Orestes A. Brownson,* 20.
38. O. Brownson, *Convert,* 58.
39. O. Brownson, "Essayist," 41.
40. O. Brownson, "Essay on the Progress of Truth," 1–2.
41. Ibid., 2.

42. Ibid., 4.

43. Frances Wright, quoted in Maynard, *Orestes Brownson*, 32–33.

44. O. Brownson, *Convert*, 123.

45. Ibid., 122–23

46. Ibid., 123.

47. Schlesinger, *Orestes A. Brownson*, 20.

48. Sellers, *Market Revolution*, 287.

49. Brownson, *New Views*, 190.

50. Schlesinger, *Orestes A. Brownson*, 21.

51. Sellers, *Market Revolution*, 287–88.

52. O. Brownson, "Free Enquirers," 54.

53. Schlesinger, *Orestes A. Brownson*, 22.

54. O. Brownson, "Social Evils," 95.

55. Rein, "New England Transcendentalists," 104.

56. Ibid., 111.

57. Ibid., 115.

58. Tompkins, "On 'Paradoxes,'" 40.

59. Ibid., 44.

60. Ray, "Role of the Orator," 216.

61. Burke, *Attitudes toward History*, 3.

62. Burke, *Rhetoric of Motives*, 45.

63. Burke, *On Symbols and Society*, 308.

64. Buell, "Transcendentalist Catalogue Rhetoric," 334.

65. Burke, *Rhetoric of Motives*, 20.

66. Ray, "Role of the Orator," 225.

67. Burke, *On Symbols and Society*, 307–8.

68. Maynard, *Orestes Brownson*, 44.

69. Hutchison, *Transcendentalist Ministers*, 42.

70. Schlesinger, *Orestes A. Brownson*, 30.

71. Gura, *American Transcendentalism*, 76.

72. Brownson, *New Views*, 186.

73. Grodzins, "Unitarianism," 52.

74. "Norton's Evidence" in the Miller Anthology, 205–10.

75. Ibid.

76. Brownson, *New Views*, 194.

77. F. H. Hedge, quoted in Schlesinger, *Orestes A. Brownson*, 46.

78. Gura, *American Transcendentalism*, 75.

79. Ibid.

80. Brownson, "Norton's Evidence," 208.

81. Brownson, *New Views*, 196.

82. Packer, *Transcendentalists*, 68.

83. Brownson, "Introductory Remarks," 3.

84. O. Brownson, "Democracy," 206.

85. Ibid., 208.

86. Ibid., 209.

87. Ibid., 226.
88. Ibid.
89. Ibid.
90. Burke, *On Symbols and Society,* 304–5.
91. Brummett, *Rhetoric in Popular Culture,* 177.
92. O. Brownson, "Democracy," 205.
93. Ibid., 211.
94. Ibid., 221.
95. Ibid., 214.
96. Ibid., 226.
97. Ibid., 209.
98. Ibid., 210.
99. Ibid., 234.
100. Butler, *In Search of the American Spirit,* 55.
101. O. Brownson, "Laboring Classes," 421.
102. Ibid., 438.
103. Ibid.
104. Ibid., 439.
105. Ibid.
106. Ibid., 438.
107. Ibid., 439.
108. Ibid., 434.
109. Ibid., 429.
110. Ibid., 431.
111. Ibid.
112. Ibid.
113. Ibid.
114. Ibid., 432.
115. Ibid., 435.
116. O. Brownson, "Emerson," 432. Miller anthology, "Emerson," 431–34.
117. O. Brownson, "Laboring Classes," 424–26.
118. Ibid., 425.
119. Ibid.
120. Ibid.
121. Ibid., 437.
122. Ibid.
123. Ibid.
124. Ibid., 439.
125. Ibid.
126. Ibid.
127. Adams, *Memoirs,* 345.
128. Maynard, *Orestes Brownson,* 92.
129. O. Brownson, "Laboring Classes II," 445.
130. Ibid., 446.
131. Schlesinger, *Orestes A. Brownson,* 111.

132. Ibid., 117.

133. Brownson, "Transcendentalism," in *Works*, 6:23.

134. Rose, *Transcendentalism*, 211.

135. Brownson, *Quarterly Review* 5.3 (1851): 383–410.

136. Gura, *Transcendentalism*, 265–66.

137. O. Brownson, "Progress of Society," 146.

Chapter 4: *"The transformation of genius into practical power"*

1. Von Frank, "Essays," 117.

2. Emerson, *Essays*, 27.

3. Gura, *American Transcendentalism*, 212.

4. Ibid., 131.

5. Emerson, *Selected Journals 1820–1842*, 147.

6. Emerson, *Essays*, 267.

7. Ibid., 185.

8. Black, "Excerpts from *Rhetorical Criticism*," 49.

9. Ibid., 53.

10. Ibid., 55.

11. Rein, "New England Transcendentalists," 115.

12. O. Brownson, "Emerson's Essays," 61.

13. Packer, *Transcendentalists*, 140.

14. Emerson, *Selected Journals 1820–1842*, 642.

15. Arendt, *Human Condition*, 19.

16. Emerson, *Selected Journals 1820–1842*, 1–4.

17. Ibid., 4.

18. Ibid., 12.

19. Burke, *Rhetoric of Motives*, 326, xiv, 21.

20. Burke, *Grammar of Motives*, 84.

21. Ibid., 85.

22. Emerson, *Selected Journals 1820–1842*, 2–3.

23. Rose, *Transcendentalism*, 65.

24. Emerson, *Selected Journals 1820–1842*, 1.

25. Richardson, *Emerson*, 21.

26. Ibid., 20–21.

27. Packer, *Transcendentalists*, 36.

28. Emerson, *Selected Journals 1820–1842*, 24–25.

29. Cole, *Mary Moody Emerson*, 164.

30. Richardson, *Emerson*, 27.

31. Woodberry, *Ralph Waldo Emerson*, 8.

32. Richardson, *Emerson*, 6.

33. Emerson, *Selected Journals 1820–1842*, 20.

34. Richardson, *Emerson*, 91.

35. Emerson, *Selected Journals 1820–1842*, 160.

36. Bloom, "Mr. America," 496–98.

37. Dolan, *Emerson's Liberalism*, 15–16, 7, 9.

38. Richardson, *Emerson*, 92.

39. Emerson, *Selected Journals 1820–1842*, 169.

40. Ibid., 172.

41. Ibid., 187.

42. Dant, "Composing the World," 22.

43. Ibid.

44. Buell, "Transcendentalist Catalogue Rhetoric," 327, 332.

45. Emerson, *Selected Journals 1820–1842*, 276.

46. Sellers, *Market Revolution*, 378.

47. Antczak, *Thought and Character*, 64.

48. Richardson, *Emerson*, 418.

49. Thompson, "America," 13. For instance during his 1836 series of twelve lectures titled "The Philosophy of History" held in Boston's Masonic Temple (in which he did his own advertising and sold tickets for two dollars through a bookstore), he averaged more than three hundred attendees for each lecture, leaving him a net profit of $350 after expenses.

50. Roberson, "Sermons," 326.

51. Bloom, *Agon*, 156,

52. Poirier, *Renewal of Literature*, 38.

53. Emerson, *Nature*, 36–37.

54. Pease, "Emerson," 59, 66.

55. Hodder, *Emerson's Rhetoric of Revelation*, 6, 142.

56. Cavell, *In Quest of the Ordinary*, 25.

57. Emerson, *Nature*, 42.

58. Ibid., 42–46.

59. Ibid., 44–45.

60. Ibid., 44–46.

61. Ibid., 47.

62. Packer, *Emerson's Fall*, 122.

63. Emerson, "Divinity School Address," 135, 137.

64. Ibid., 142.

65. Ibid.

66. Richardson, *Emerson*, 290.

67. Emerson, "Divinity School Address," 130.

68. Ibid.

69. Ibid., 145.

70. Ibid., 139.

71. Norton, "New School," 2.

72. Emerson, *Selected Journals 1820–1842*, 642.

73. Von Frank, "Essays," 106.

74. Robinson, *Emerson and the Conduct of Life*, 10.

75. Emerson, *Selected Journals 1820–1842*, 165.

76. Burke, *Counter-Statement*, 31.

77. Buell, "Reading Emerson," 59.

78. Burke, *Counter-Statement*, 31, 37.

79. Richardson, *Emerson*, 151.

80. Emerson, *Essays,* 18–19, 21.

81. Ibid., 21.

82. Ibid., 20.

83. Ibid., 6.

84. Ibid., 40.

85. Ibid., 29.

86. Ibid., 33.

87. Ibid.

88. Ibid.

89. Ibid., 37, 27, 31.

90. Cavell, *In Quest of the Ordinary,* 23.

91. Emerson, *Essays,* 27.

92. Ibid., 55.

93. Ibid., 58.

94. Ibid., 60, 58, 73.

95. Ibid., 69–71.

96. Von Frank, "Essays," 113.

97. Packer, *Transcendentalists,* 142.

98. Robinson, *Emerson and the Conduct of Life,* 22.

99. Packer, *Transcendentalists,* 143.

100. Emerson, *Essays,* 84.

101. Ibid.

102. Ibid., 82.

103. Ibid., 78–79.

104. Ibid., 83.

105. Ibid., 131.

106. Farrell, *Norms of Rhetorical Culture,* 25.

107. Emerson, *Essays,* 139, 141.

108. Ibid., 132.

109. Ibid.

110. Ibid., 132–33, 136.

111. Ibid., 149.

112. Ibid., 148–49.

113. Ibid., 155.

114. Ibid., 160.

115. Ibid., 159.

116. Ibid., 161.

117. Ibid., 160.

118. Ibid., 167.

119. Ibid., 180.

120. Ibid., 179.

121. Bloom, *Figures of Capable Imagination,* 63.

122. Emerson, *Essays,* 188.

123. Robinson, *Emerson and the Conduct of Life,* 28.

124. Emerson, *Essays,* 190.

125. Ibid., 180–81, 187.

126. Ibid., 183–85, 190.

127. Ibid., 198–99.

128. Ibid., 193.

129. Ibid., 196.

130. Ibid., 194.

131. Ibid., 198.

132. Ibid., 201.

133. Ibid., 215.

134. Ibid., 209.

135. Ibid., 210.

136. Ibid.

137. Ibid., 210–11.

138. Ibid., 211.

139. Ibid., 34.

140. Ibid., 211.

141. Ibid.

142. Ibid., 212.

143. O. Brownson, "Essays: By R. W. Emerson," 258.

144. O. Brownson, "Emerson's Essays," 70.

145. Dolan, *Emerson's Liberalism*, 23–24.

146. Kateb, *Emerson and Self-Reliance*, 178–79.

147. Bercovitch, *Rites of Assent*, 348.

148. Emerson, *Essays*, 218.

149. Arendt, *Between Past and Future*, 61, 13, 48.

Chapter 5: "The cause of tyranny and wrong everywhere the same"

1. Fuller, "New and Old World Democracy," 162–63.

2. Ibid., 164, 166.

3. Packer, *Transcendentalists*, 214.

4. Steele, *Transfiguring America*, 276, 293.

5. Steele, "Literary Criticism," 387.

6. Foucault, "Subject and Power," 138.

7. Foucault, "What Is Critique?" 266, 278.

8. Zwarg, *Feminist Conversations*, 197.

9. Steele, "Literary Criticism," 393.

10. Capper, *Margaret Fuller: Private Years*, 33.

11. Fuller, *Portable Margaret Fuller*, 474.

12. Camaiora, *Oliver Goldsmith*, 152.

13. Fuller, *Portable Margaret Fuller*, 474, 4–5, 478.

14. Von Mehren, *Minerva and the Muse*, 13.

15. Murray, *Margaret Fuller*, 17.

16. Fuller, *Portable Margaret Fuller*, 4.

17. Murray, *Margaret Fuller*, 20.

18. Ibid.

19. Ibid., 21.
20. Sellers, *Market Revolution,* 242.
21. Ibid.
22. Ibid., 237.
23. Ibid., 246.
24. Ibid., 243.
25. Foucault, *History of Sexuality,* 22, 114, 123.
26. Sellers, *Market Revolution,* 242.
27. Foucault, *History of Sexuality,* 92.
28. Murray, *Margaret Fuller,* 152.
29. Ibid., 45.
30. Ibid., 46.
31. Von Mehren, *Minerva and the Muse,* 26.
32. Cited in ibid.
33. Ibid.
34. Cited in ibid., 27.
35. Ibid., 34.
36. Murray, *Margaret Fuller,* 72.
37. Von Mehren, *Minerva and the Muse,* 54.
38. Murray, *Margaret Fuller,* 76.
39. Ibid.
40. Ibid., 75.
41. Ibid., 82.
42. Von Mehren, *Minerva and the Muse,* 75.
43. Foucault, "Ethics of the Concern of the Self," 26.
44. Capper, *Margaret Fuller: Private Years,* 191.
45. Gura, *American Transcendentalism,* 133.
46. Packer, *Transcendentalists,* 114.
47. Ibid.
48. Fuller, quoted in Myerson, *Transcendentalism,* 280.
49. Foucault, "Questions of Method," 249.
50. Fuller, quoted in Myerson, *Transcendentalism,* 282.
51. Belasco, "*Dial,*" 375.
52. Capper, *Margaret Fuller: The Public Years,* 17.
53. Ibid.
54. Ibid., 18–19.
55. Fuller, *Women in the Nineteenth Century,* 229.
56. Murray, *Margaret Fuller,* 196.
57. Von Mehren, *Minerva and the Muse,* 168.
58. Murray, *Margaret Fuller,* 197.
59. Kolodny, "Inventing a Feminist Discourse," 359, 360, 375.
60. Fuller, "Great Lawsuit," 1626–28, 1632.
61. Ibid., 1652.
62. Ibid., 1645.
63. Capper, *Margaret Fuller: The Public Years,* 121.

64. Foucault, "Masked Philosopher," 176.
65. Fuller, "Great Lawsuit," 1632.
66. Ibid.
67. Ibid., 1634.
68. Ibid., 1651.
69. Steele, *Transfiguring America,* 112.
70. Fuller, "Great Lawsuit," 1651, 1653.
71. Ibid., 1651.
72. Ibid., 1653.
73. Von Mehren, *Minerva and the Muse,* 168.
74. Fuller, "Great Lawsuit," 1654.
75. Quoted in Von Mehren, *Minerva and the Muse,* 171.
76. Kolodny, "Inventing a Feminist Discourse," 376, 356.
77. Von Mehren, *Minerva and the Muse,* 178.
78. Steele, *Transfiguring America,* 140.
79. Capper, *Margaret Fuller: The Public Years,* 123.
80. Burke, *Grammar of Motives,* 508.
81. Fuller, *Summer on the Lakes,* 136.
82. Ibid., 90.
83. Ibid., 106.
84. Ibid., 139.
85. Ibid., 143.
86. Ibid., 182.
87. Ibid., 190.
88. Von Mehren, *Minerva and the Muse,* 182.
89. Capper, *Margaret Fuller: The Public Years,* 154.
90. Von Mehren, *Minerva and the Muse,* 203.
91. Tuchinsky, *Horace Greeley's New-York Tribune,* 2.
92. Ibid.
93. Ibid., 64.
94. Von Mehren, *Minerva and the Muse,* 193.
95. Fuller, *Woman in the Nineteenth Century,* 328–29.
96. Capper, *Margaret Fuller: The Public Years,* 187.
97. Quoted in Mitchell, *Margaret Fuller's New York Journalism,* 31.
98. Von Mehren, *Minerva and the Muse,* 225.
99. Ibid., 218.
100. Fuller, "Asylum," 382.
101. Mitchell, *Margaret Fuller's New York Journalism,* 52.
102. Fuller, "These Sad but Glorious Days," 146.
103. Von Mehren, *Minerva and the Muse,* 257.
104. Capper, *Margaret Fuller: The Public Years,* 366.
105. Rapport, *1848,* ix.
106. Fuller, "These Sad but Glorious Days," 159–60f.
107. Ibid., 212.
108. Sperber, *European Revolutions,* 54, 109.

109. Stearns, *1848*, 46–47.
110. Hearder, *Italy in the Age of the Risorgimento*, 185.
111. Capper, *Margaret Fuller: The Public Years*, 321.
112. Von Mehren, *Minerva and the Muse*, 239.
113. Fuller, *"These Sad but Glorious Days,"* 153–55.
114. Anderson, *Imagined Communities*, 7, 36, 141.
115. Steele, *Transfiguring America*, 278, 292.
116. Ibid., 278, 292, 265.
117. Fuller, *"These Sad but Glorious Days,"* 154, 160–61.
118. Ibid., 228.
119. Ibid., 164.
120. Ibid., 159.
121. Ibid., 154.
122. Ibid., 240.
123. Capper, *Margaret Fuller: The Public Years*, 413.
124. Fuller, *"These Sad but Glorious Days,"* 240–41.
125. Capper, *Margaret Fuller: The Public Years*, 419.
126. Quoted in ibid., 418.
127. Reynolds and Smith, introduction, 26.
128. Fuller, *"These Sad but Glorious Days,"* 243–45.
129. Ibid., 245–47.
130. Ibid., 321–22.
131. Capper, *Margaret Fuller: The Public Years*, 510.
132. Quoted in Richardson, *Henry Thoreau*, 212.
133. Emerson, *Selected Journals 1841–1877*, 511–12.
134. Fuller, *Portable Margaret Fuller*, 523.
135. Fuller, *"These Sad but Glorious Days,"* 165.
136. Ibid., 211.
137. Cited in Marshall, *Margaret Fuller*, 385.
138. Steele, *Transfiguring America*, 293.

Chapter 6: "The perception and the performance of right"

1. Thoreau, "Plea," 269.
2. Thoreau, *Journal*, 584.
3. Thoreau, "Plea," 275.
4. Ibid., 264.
5. Ibid., 279.
6. Hyde, "Henry Thoreau," 142, 126, 127.
7. Dillman, *Essays*, 51, 35, 83–84.
8. Golemba, *Thoreau's Wild Rhetoric*, 232.
9. Milder, *Reimagining Thoreau*, 71.
10. Foucault, "Subject and Power," 128.
11. Worster, *Nature's Economy*, x.
12. Arendt, *Crisis of the Republic*, 56.
13. Mariotti, *Thoreau's Democratic Withdrawal*, xiii, 171.

14. Thoreau, "Resistance to Civil Government," 132.

15. Johnstone, "Thoreau and Civil Disobedience," 320.

16. Thoreau, "Resistance to Civil Government," 134.

17. McLuhan, *Understanding Media*, 254–55.

18. Harding, *Days of Henry Thoreau*, 8.

19. Ibid., 12.

20. Emerson, "Thoreau," 817.

21. Cited in Petrulionis, *Thoreau in His Own Time*, xiv.

22. Thoreau, *Walden*, 329.

23. Harding, *Days of Henry Thoreau*, 8.

24. Cited in ibid.

25. Ibid., 22.

26. Thoreau, *Walden*, 363.

27. Harding, *Days of Henry Thoreau*, 9.

28. Ibid., 10.

29. Ibid., 19–20.

30. Ibid., 26.

31. Ibid., 28–29.

32. Packer, *Transcendentalists*, 121.

33. Richardson, *Henry Thoreau*, 10.

34. Harding, *Days of Henry Thoreau*, 46, 49.

35. Channing and Sanborn, *Thoreau, the Poet-Naturalist*, 32.

36. H. Brownson, *Early Life*, 202.

37. Schlesinger, *Orestes A. Brownson*, 32.

38. Emerson, *Selected Journals 1820–1842*, 661.

39. Ibid., 576.

40. Richardson, *Henry Thoreau*, 18.

41. Thoreau, *Journal*, 3.

42. Ibid., 3.

43. Ibid., 3, 10.

44. Ibid., 20.

45. Richardson, *Henry Thoreau*, 31.

46. Ibid., 33.

47. Thoreau, *Service*, 15.

48. Robinson, *Natural Life*, 32.

49. Richardson, *Henry Thoreau*, 113.

50. Thoreau, *Journal*, 23.

51. Richardson, *Henry Thoreau*, 116.

52. Sullivan, *Thoreau You Don't Know*, 32.

53. Richardson, *Henry Thoreau*, 116.

54. Buell, *Environmental Imagination*, 8–10, 12.

55. Fink, "Thoreau and His Audience," 74–75.

56. Thoreau, *Correspondence*, 107, 76.

57. Fink, "Thoreau and His Audience," 77.

58. Richardson, *Henry Thoreau*, 132.

59. McLuhan, *Understanding Media*, 8, 248.

60. Thoreau, *Walden*, 395–96.

61. Richardson, *Henry Thoreau*, 146.

62. Packer, *Transcendentalists*, 165.

63. Emerson, "New England Reformers," 404.

64. Emerson, "Emancipation in the West Indies," 769.

65. Harding, *Days of Henry Thoreau*, 175.

66. Cain, *Historical Guide*, 34.

67. Johnson, "*Week*," 47.

68. Thoreau, *Week*, 221.

69. Ibid., 142.

70. Ibid., 318.

71. Ibid.

72. Ibid., 105–7.

73. Ibid., 106.

74. Ibid., 102–3.

75. Golema, *Thoreau's Wild Rhetoric*, 7.

76. Thoreau, "Winter Walk," 28.

77. Shulman, "Thoreau, Prophecy, and Politics," 128.

78. Hyde collection, "Natural History of Massachusetts," 1–24

79. Thoreau, *Walden*, 451, 389.

80. Arendt, *Human Condition*, 179–80, 192.

81. Arendt, *Promise of Politics*, 164, 167.

82. Arendt, *Human Condition*, 180.

83. Arendt, *Crises of the Republic*, 75.

84. Cavell, *Senses of* Walden, 47, 11, 85–86.

85. Ibid., 47.

86. Milder, *Reimagining Thoreau*, 71.

87. Thoreau, *Walden*, 363.

88. Neufeldt, *Economist*, 178.

89. Thoreau, *Walden*, 332.

90. Ibid., 347.

91. Ibid., 334.

92. Thoreau, "Resistance to Civil Government," 128–29.

93. Gougeon, "Thoreau and Reform," 201.

94. Howe, *What Hath God Wrought*, 748.

95. Ibid., 819.

96. Thoreau, "Resistance to Civil Government," 132, 127.

97. Ibid., 129, 127.

98. Foucault, *History of Sexuality*, 140–41.

99. Thoreau, "Resistance to Civil Government," 128.

100. Ibid., 132, 128.

101. Ibid., 133, 129–30.

102. Ibid., 133.

103. Ibid., 129.

104. Ibid., 131.

105. Ibid., 132.

106. Johnstone, "Thoreau and Civil Disobedience," 315.

107. Ibid., 320.

108. Thoreau, *Journal*, 85.

109. Packer, *Transcendentalists*, 222.

110. Richardson, *Henry Thoreau*, 314.

111. Thoreau, *Journal*, 265.

112. Thoreau, "Slavery in Massachusetts," 189.

113. Ibid., 190–91, 183.

114. Parker, "Fugitive Slave Law," 360.

115. Thoreau, "Slavery in Massachusetts," 192.

116. Thoreau, *Journal*, 267.

117. Thoreau, "Slavery in Massachusetts," 193.

118. Ibid., 187–88.

119. Ibid., 188.

120. Wilentz, *Rise of American Democracy*, 678, 686–89.

121. Thoreau, *Journal*, 403.

122. Richardson, *Henry Thoreau*, 370.

123. Emerson, *Selected Journals 1842–1877*, 674.

124. Thoreau, *Journal*, 585.

125. Ibid., 586.

126. Ibid., 585.

127. Thoreau, "Plea," 279.

128. Ibid., 268.

129. Thoreau, *Journal*, 584.

130. Thoreau, "Plea," 266, 262, 264.

131. Ibid., 266.

132. Ibid., 270–71, 277.

133. Arendt, *Crises of the Republic*, 74, 76.

134. Thoreau, "Plea," 276–77.

135. Arendt, *Crises of the Republic*, 77.

136. Arendt, *On Violence*, 51.

137. Ibid., 79.

138. Cited in Beck, *Creating the John Brown Legend*, 112.

139. Thoreau, "Plea," 279.

140. Hyde collection, "The Last Days of John Brown," 281–88.

141. Ibid., 288.

142. Foner, *Free Soil*, ix.

143. Ibid., 310.

144. Sellers, *Market Revolution*, 427.

145. Richardson, *Henry Thoreau*, 385.

146. Thoreau, *Familiar Letters*, 437–38.

147. Thoreau, *Journal*, 659.

148. Richardson, *Henry Thoreau*, 389.

149. Richardson, *Emerson,* 548.
150. Emerson, "Thoreau," 810, 812, 822, 823.
151. Thoreau, *Walden,* 417.
152. Emerson, "Thoreau," 823, 810, 812–13.
153. Thoreau, *Journal,* 81.
154. Thoreau, *Walden,* 364.
155. Ibid.

Conclusion

1. Douglass, *Autobiographies,* 15.
2. Douglass, "Reconstruction," 595–96.
3. Douglass, "I Denounce," 715.
4. Douglass, "Address," 673.
5. Ibid., 675.
6. Douglass, "I Denounce," 716.
7. Ibid., 718.
8. Ibid., 715.
9. Ibid., 713.
10. Douglass, "Decision of the Hour," 458–59.
11. Douglass, "John Brown," 641.
12. Ibid., 641, 639.
13. Ibid., 641.
14. Ibid., 642.
15. Douglass, "Address," 673.
16. Douglass, "Farewell Speech," 58.
17. Ibid., 70.
18. Ibid.
19. Douglass, "Why Is the Negro Lynched?" 773.
20. Emerson, *Selected Journals 1841–1877,* 897.
21. Rose, *Transcendentalism as a Social Movement,* 225.
22. Gura, *American Transcendentalism,* 306.
23. Burke, *Permanence and Change,* 272.
24. Miller, introduction, 7.
25. Packer, *Transcendentalists,* 274.
26. Emerson, "Transcendentalist," 88.
27. Douglass, "Meaning of July Fourth," 205.
28. Thoreau, *Journal,* 70.

BIBLIOGRAPHY

Adams, John Quincy. *Memoirs of John Quincy Adams: Comprising Portions of His Diary from 1765 to 1848.* Philadelphia: Lippincott, 1877.

Alcott, Amos Bronson. *A. Bronson Alcott: His Life and Philosophy.* Ed. F. B. Sanborn and William T. Harris. New York: Biblio & Tannen, 1965.

———. *Conversations with Children on the Gospels.* Boston: Munroe, 1836.

———. *The Doctrine and Discipline of Human Culture.* Boston: Munroe, 1836.

———. *The Journals of Bronson Alcott.* Boston: Little, Brown, 1938.

———. *New Connecticut.* Boston: Chadwyck-Healey Incorporated, 1996.

Anderson, Benedict. *Imagined Communities: Reflections on the Origin and Spread of Nationalism.* Rev. ed. London: Verso Books, 2006.

Antczak, Frederick. *Thought and Character: The Rhetoric of Democratic Education.* Ames: Iowa State University Press, 1985.

Arendt, Hannah. *Between Past and Future.* New York: Penguin, 1968.

———. *Crises of the Republic: Lying in Politics; Civil Disobedience; On Violence; Thoughts on Politics and Revolution.* New York: Houghton Mifflin Harcourt, 1972.

———. *The Human Condition.* 2nd ed. Chicago: University of Chicago Press, 1998.

———. *On Violence.* New York: Harcourt, 1970.

———. *The Promise of Politics.* New York: Schocken, 2009.

Bailyn, Bernard. *The Ideological Origins of the American Revolution.* Cambridge, Mass.: Belknap, 1992.

Bakhtin, Mikhail. *The Dialogic Imagination: Four Essays.* Trans. Caryl Emerson and Michael Holquist. Austin: University of Texas Press, 1981.

———. *Problems of Dostoevsky's Poetics.* Trans. Caryl Emerson. Minneapolis: University of Minnesota Press, 1993.

———. *Speech Genres and Other Late Essays.* Trans. Vern McGee. Austin: University of Texas Press, 1986.

Beck, Janet Kemper. *Creating the John Brown Legend: Emerson, Thoreau, Douglass, Child and Higginson in Defense of the Raid on Harpers Ferry.* Jefferson, N.C.: McFarland, 2009.

Belasco, Susan. "The *Dial.*" In *The Oxford Handbook of Transcendentalism,* ed. Joel Myerson, Sandra Harbert Petrulionis, and Laura Dassow Walls, 373–83. Oxford: Oxford University Press, 2010.

Bercovitch, Sacvan. *The Rites of Assent: Transformations in the Symbolic Construction of America.* New York: Routledge, 2014.

Black, Edwin. "Excerpts from *Rhetorical Criticism: A Study in Method.*" In *Readings in Rhetorical Criticism,* ed. Carl R. Burgchardt, 46–57. State College, Penn.: Strata, 1995.

Bloom, Harold. *Agon: Towards a Theory of Revision.* New York: Oxford University Press, 1982.

——. *Essayists and Prophets.* Philadelphia: Chelsea House, 2005.

——. *Figures of Capable Imagination.* New York: Seabury, 1976.

——. "Mr. America." In *Estimating Emerson: An Anthology of Criticism from Carlyle to Cavell,* ed. David LaRocca, 495–506. New York: Bloomsbury, 2013.

Brownson, Henry Francis. *Orestes A. Brownson's Early Life, from 1803 to 1844.* Detroit: Brownson, 1898.

Brownson, Orestes Augustus. *The Convert: or, Leaves from My Experience.* New York: Dunigan, 1857.

——. "Democracy." In *Works in Political Philosophy: Volume 2, 1828–1841,* ed. Gregory Butler, 203–36. Wilmington, Del.: ISI Books, 2007.

——. "Emerson's Essays." In *Estimating Emerson: An Anthology of Criticism from Carlyle to Cavell,* ed. David LaRocca, 61–70. New York: Bloomsbury, 2013.

——. "An Essay on the Progress of Truth." In *Works in Political Philosophy: Volume 2, 1828–1841,* ed. Gregory Butler, 1–34. Wilmington, Del.: ISI Books, 2007.

——. "The Essayist." In *Works in Political Philosophy: Volume 2, 1828–1841,* ed. Gregory Butler, 35–48. Wilmington, Del.: ISI Books, 2007.

——. "Essays: By R. W. Emerson." *Boston Quarterly Review* 4.2 (1841): 258.

——. "Free Enquirers." In *Works in Political Philosophy: Volume 2, 1828–1841,* ed. Gregory Butler, 53–56. Wilmington, Del.: ISI Books, 2007.

——. "The Fugitive Slave Law." In *The Works of Orestes A. Brownson: Politics,* ed. Henry Brownson, 17–38. Detroit: Thorndike Nourse, 1885.

——. "Independence Day Address at Dedham, Massachusetts." In *Works in Political Philosophy: Volume 2, 1828—1841,* ed. Gregory Butler, 111–24. Wilmington, Del.: ISI Books, 2007.

——. "Introductory Remarks." *Boston Quarterly Review* 1.1 (1838): 1–8.

——. "The Laboring Classes." In *Works in Political Philosophy: Volume 2, 1828–1841,* ed. Gregory Butler, 411–40. Wilmington, Del.: ISI Books, 2007.

——. "The Laboring Classes II." In *The Transcendentalists: An Anthology,* ed. Perry Miller, 436–46. Cambridge, Mass.: Harvard University Press, 1950.

——. *New Views of Christianity, Society, and the Church.* In *Works in Political Philosophy: Volume 2, 1828–1841,* ed. Gregory Butler, 149–202. Wilmington, Del.: ISI Books, 2007.

——. "Norton's Evidence." *Boston Quarterly Review* 2 (1839): 86–113.

——. "Progress of Society." In *Works in Political Philosophy: Volume 2, 1828–1841,* ed. Gregory Butler, 125–49. Wilmington, Del.: ISI Books, 2007.

——. "Social Evils and Their Remedy I," In *Works in Political Philosophy: Volume 2, 1828–1841,* ed. Gregory Butler, 93–100. Wilmington, Del.: ISI Books, 2007.

——. "Transcendentalism, or Latest Form of Infidelity." *Brownson's Quarterly Review* 2.4 (1845): 409–41.

Brummett, Barry. *Rhetoric in Popular Culture.* Thousand Oaks, Cal.: Sage, 2014.

Buckingham, Joseph T. "Alcott's Conversations on the Gospels." *Boston Daily Courier,* March 29, 1837, 2.

Buell, Lawrence. *The Environmental Imagination: Thoreau, Nature Writing, and the Formation of American Culture.* Cambridge, Mass.: Harvard University Press, 1996.

——. Introduction to *The American Transcendentalists: Essential Writings,* ed. Lawrence Buell, xi–xxiix. New York: Modern Library, 2006.

———. *Literary Transcendentalism: Style and Vision in the American Renaissance.* Ithaca, N.Y.: Cornell University Press, 1973.

———. "Reading Emerson for the Structures: The Coherence of the Essays." *Quarterly Journal of Speech* 58.1 (1972): 58–69.

———. "Transcendentalist Catalogue Rhetoric: Vision versus Form." *American Literature* 40.3 (1968): 325–39.

Burke, Kenneth. *Attitudes toward History.* Berkeley: University of California Press, 1984.

———. *Counter-Statement.* Berkeley: University of California Press, 1968.

———. *A Grammar of Motives.* Berkeley: University of California Press, 1969.

———. *Language as Symbolic Action: Essays on Life, Literature, and Method.* Berkeley: University of California Press, 1966.

———. *On Symbols and Society.* Ed. Joseph Gusfield. Chicago: University of Chicago Press, 1989.

———. *Permanence and Change: An Anatomy of Purpose.* Berkeley: University of California Press, 1965.

———. *A Rhetoric of Motives.* Berkeley: University of California Press, 1962.

Butler, Gregory. *In Search of the American Spirit: The Political Thought of Orestes Brownson.* Carbondale: Southern Illinois University Press, 1992.

Butler, Jon, Grant Wacker, and Randall Balmer. *Religion in American Life: A Short History.* Oxford: Oxford University Press, 2011.

Cain, William E. *A Historical Guide to Henry David Thoreau.* Oxford: Oxford University Press, 2000.

Camaiora, Luisa Conti. *Oliver Goldsmith: The Traveller and the Deserted Village.* Milan: EDUCatt-Ente per il diritto allo studio universitario dell' Università Cattolica, 2014.

Capper, Charles. *Margaret Fuller: An American Romantic Life; The Private Years.* Oxford: Oxford University Press, 1992.

———. *Margaret Fuller: An American Romantic Life; The Public Years.* Oxford: Oxford University Press, 2007.

Carey, Patrick W. *Orestes A. Brownson: American Religious Weathervane.* Grand Rapids, Mich.: Eerdmans, 2004.

Cavell, Stanley. *In Quest of the Ordinary: Lines of Skepticism and Romanticism.* Chicago: University of Chicago Press, 1994.

———. *The Senses of* Walden: *An Expanded Edition.* Chicago: University of Chicago Press, 1992.

———. "What's the Use of Calling Emerson a Pragmatist?" In *The Revival of Pragmatism: New Essays on Social Thought, Law, and Culture,* ed. Morris Dickstein, 72–80. Durham: Duke University Press, 1998.

Channing, William Ellery. "Likeness to God." In *Transcendentalism: A Reader,* ed. Joel Myerson, 3–20: Oxford: Oxford University Press, 2000.

Channing, William Ellery, and Franklin Benjamin Sanborn. *Thoreau, the Poet-Naturalist: With Memorial Verses.* Boston: Charles E. Goodspeed, 1902.

Cole, Phyllis. *Mary Moody Emerson and the Origins of Transcendentalism: A Family History.* New York: Oxford University Press, 1998.

Cornford, Francis Macdonald. *The Origin of Attic Comedy.* Garden City, N.Y.: Doubleday, 1961.

Cranch, Christopher Pearse. "Transcendentalism." In *The American Transcendentalists: Essential Writings*, ed. Lawrence Buell, 100–102. New York: Modern Library, 2006.

Dahlstrand, Frederick. *Amos Bronson Alcott: An Intellectual Biography*. Madison, N.J.: Fairleigh Dickinson University Press, 1982.

Dant, Elizabeth A. "Composing the World: Emerson and the Cabinet of Natural History." *Nineteenth-Century Literature* 44.1 (1989): 18–44.

Dewey, John. "Emerson: The Philosopher of Democracy." In *John Dewey, the Middle Works*, vol. 3, *1903–1906*, ed. Jo Ann Boydston, 184–92. Carbondale: Southern Illinois University Press, 1977.

Dillman, Richard. *Essays on Henry David Thoreau: Rhetoric, Style, and Audience*. West Cornwall, Conn.: Locust Hill, 1993.

Dolan, Neal. *Emerson's Liberalism*. Madison: University of Wisconsin Press, 2009.

Douglass, Frederick. "Address to the People of the United States." In *Selected Speeches and Writings*, 669–84.

——. *Autobiographies*. New York: Library of America, 1994.

——. "The Decision of the Hour." In *Selected Speeches and Writings*, 458–62.

——. "I Denounce the So-called Emancipation as a Stupendous Fraud." In *Selected Speeches and Writings*, 711–23.

——. "Farewell Speech to the British People, at London Tavern." In *Selected Speeches and Writings*, 54–74.

——. "John Brown." In *Selected Speeches and Writings*, 633–47.

——. "The Meaning of July Fourth for the Negro." In *Selected Speeches and Writings*, 188–205.

——. "Reconstruction." In *Selected Speeches and Writings*, 592–981.

——. *Selected Speeches and Writings*. Ed. Philip S. Foner. Chicago: Chicago Review Press, 2000.

——. "Why Is the Negro Lynched?" In *Selected Speeches and Writings*, 750–76.

Emerson, Ralph Waldo. "The American Scholar." In *Essential Writings*, 43–62.

——. "Divinity School Address." In *The American Transcendentalists: Essential Writings*, ed. Lawrence Buell, 129–46. New York: Modern Library, 2006.

——. "Emancipation in the West Indies." In *Essential Writings*, 753–78.

——. *The Essays of Ralph Waldo Emerson*. Cambridge, Mass.: Belknap, 1987.

——. *The Essential Writings of Ralph Waldo Emerson*. Ed. Mary Oliver. New York: Modern Library, 2009.

——. *Journals and Miscellaneous Notebooks of Ralph Waldo Emerson*. Vol. 7, *1838–1842*. Cambridge, Mass.: Harvard University Press, 1969.

——. *Nature*. In *The American Transcendentalists: Essential Writings*, ed. Lawrence Buell, 31–67. New York: Modern Library, 2006.

——. "New England Reformers." In *Essential Writings*, 402–18.

——. *Ralph Waldo Emerson: Selected Journals 1820–1842*. Ed. Lawrence Rosenwald. New York: Library of America, 2010.

——. *Ralph Waldo Emerson: Selected Journals 1841–1877*. Ed. Lawrence Rosenwald. New York: Library of America, 2010.

——. "Thoreau." In *Essential Writings*, 809–28.

——. "The Transcendentalist." In *The Essential Writings of Ralph Waldo Emerson,* ed. Mary Oliver, 81–98. New York: Modern Library, 2009.

Emerson, Ralph Waldo, and Thomas Carlyle. *The Correspondence of Thomas Carlyle and Ralph Waldo Emerson: 1834–1872.* Boston: Ticknor, 1886.

Engels, Jeremy. *Enemyship: Democracy and Counter-Revolution in the Early Republic.* East Lansing: Michigan State University Press, 2010.

Farrell, Thomas. *Norms of Rhetorical Culture.* New Haven, Conn.: Yale University Press, 1993.

Fink, Steven. "Thoreau and His Audience." In *The Cambridge Companion to Henry David Thoreau,* ed. Joel Myerson, 71–91. Cambridge: Cambridge University Press, 1995.

Fliegelman, Jay. *Declaring Independence: Jefferson, Natural Language, and the Culture of Performance.* Stanford, Cal.: Stanford University Press, 1993.

Foner, Eric. *Free Soil, Free Labor, Free Men: The Ideology of the Republican Party before the Civil War.* Oxford: Oxford University Press, 1971.

Foucault, Michel. *The Essential Foucault: Selections from the Essential Works of Foucault, 1954–1984.* Ed. Paul Rabinow and Nikolas Rose. New York: New Press, 1994.

——. "The Ethics of the Concern of the Self." In *Essential Foucault,* 25–42.

——. *The History of Sexuality.* Vol. 1, *An Introduction.* Trans. Robert Hurley. New York: Vintage, 1978.

——. "The Masked Philosopher." In *Essential Foucault,* 174–79.

——. "Questions of Method." In *Essential Foucault,* 246–58.

——. "The Subject and Power." In *Essential Foucault,* 126–44.

——. "What Is Critique?" In *Essential Foucault,* 263–78.

Freire, Paulo. *Pedagogy of the Oppressed.* New York: Continuum, 1970.

Fuller, Margaret. "Asylum for Discharged Female Convicts." In *Portable Margaret Fuller,* 381–86.

——. "The Great Lawsuit." In *The Norton Anthology of American Literature,* 6th ed., ed. Nina Baym, 1618–54. New York: Norton, 1996.

——. *Memoirs of Margaret Fuller Ossoli.* Ed. R. W. Emerson, W. H. Channing, and J. F. Clark. New York: Franklin, 1884.

——. *The Portable Margaret Fuller.* Ed. Mary Kelley. New York: Penguin, 1994.

——. *Summer on the Lakes.* In *Portable Margaret Fuller,* 69–227.

——. *"These Sad but Glorious Days": Dispatches from Europe, 1846–1850.* Ed. Larry J. Reynolds and Susan Belasco Smith. New Haven, Conn.: Yale University Press, 1991.

——. *Woman in the Nineteenth Century.* In *Portable Margaret Fuller,* 228–363.

Golemba, Henry L. *Thoreau's Wild Rhetoric.* New York: New York University Press, 1990.

Gougeon, Len. "Thoreau and Reform." In *The Cambridge Companion to Henry David Thoreau,* ed. Joel Myerson, 194–214. Cambridge: Cambridge University Press, 1995.

Grene, David, and Richmond Lattimore, eds. *Aeschylus.* University of Chicago Press, 1953.

Grodzins, Dean. "Unitarianism." In *The Oxford Handbook of Transcendentalism,* ed. Joel Myerson, Sandra Harbert Petrulionis, and Laura Dassow Walls, 50–69. Oxford: Oxford University Press, 2010.

Grose, Edward F. *Centennial History of the Village of Ballston Spa.* Troy, N.Y.: Ballston Journal, 1907.

Gura, Philip. *American Transcendentalism: A History.* New York: Hill & Wang, 2008.

Hale, Nathan. "Conversations with Children on the Gospels." *Boston Daily Advertiser and Patriot,* March 21, 1837, 54.

Harding, Walter. *The Days of Henry Thoreau.* New York: Knopf, 1965.

Hearder, Harry. *Italy in the Age of the Risorgimento 1790–1870.* New York: Routledge, 2014.

Heidegger, Martin. *On the Way to Language.* New York: Harper & Row, 1971.

Hodder, Alan D. *Emerson's Rhetoric of Revelation: Nature, the Reader, and the Apocalypse Within.* State College: Pennsylvania State University Press, 1989.

Holmes, Oliver Wendell. *Ralph Waldo Emerson.* Boston: Houghton, Mifflin, 1886.

Howe, Daniel Walker. *What Hath God Wrought: The Transformation of America, 1815–1848.* Oxford: Oxford University Press, 2009.

Hutchison, William R. *The Transcendentalist Ministers: Church Reform in the New England Renaissance.* New Haven, Conn.: Yale University Press, 2005.

Hyde, Lewis. "Henry Thoreau, John Brown, and the Problem of Prophetic Action." *Raritan* 22.2 (2002): 125–44.

Japp, Alex. "A Gift from Emerson." *Gentleman's Magazine* 253 (1882): 618–28.

Johnson, Linck C. "*A Week on the Concord and Merrimack Rivers.*" In *The Cambridge Companion to Henry David Thoreau,* ed. Joel Myerson, 40–56. Cambridge: Cambridge University Press, 1995.

Johnstone, Christopher Lyle. "Thoreau and Civil Disobedience: A Rhetorical Paradox." *Quarterly Journal of Speech* 60.3 (1974): 313–22.

Jordan, James O. "Sampson Reed: Emerson's Swedenborgian Druggist." *American Druggist and Pharmaceutical Record* 43 (1903): 295.

Kateb, George. *Emerson and Self-Reliance.* Thousand Oaks, Cal.: Sage, 1995.

Kirk, G. S., J. E. Raven, and M. Schofield, *The Presocratic Philosophers.* 2nd ed. Cambridge: Cambridge University Press, 1983.

Kolodny, Annette. "Inventing a Feminist Discourse: Rhetoric and Resistance in Margaret Fuller's Woman in the Nineteenth Century." *New Literary History* 25 (1994): 355–82.

Koster, Donald Nelson. *Transcendentalism in America.* Boston: Twayne, 1975.

Levine, Bruce. *Half Slave and Half Free: The Roots of Civil War.* Rev. ed. New York: Macmillan, 2005.

Mariotti, Shannon L. *Thoreau's Democratic Withdrawal: Alienation, Participation, and Modernity.* Madison: University of Wisconsin Press, 2010.

Marshall, Megan. *Margaret Fuller: A New American Life.* Boston: Houghton Mifflin Harcourt, 2013.

Maynard, Theodore. *Orestes Brownson: Yankee, Radical, Catholic.* New York: Hafner, 1971.

McKerrow, Raymie E. "Critical Rhetoric: Theory and Praxis." *Communication Monographs* 56.2 (1989): 91–111.

McLuhan, Marshall. *Understanding Media: The Extensions of Man.* Cambridge, Mass.: MIT Press, 1994.

Milder, Robert. *Reimagining Thoreau.* Cambridge: Cambridge University Press, 1995.

Miller, Perry. Introduction to *The Transcendentalists: An Anthology,* ed. Perry Miller, 3–14. Cambridge, Mass.: Harvard University Press, 1950.

Mitchell, Catherine. *Margaret Fuller's New York Journalism: A Biographical Essay and Key Writings.* Knoxville: University of Tennessee Press, 1895.

Mott, Wesley. "Education." In *The Oxford Handbook of Transcendentalism*, ed. Joel Myerson, Sandra Harbert Petrulionis, and Laura Dassow Walls, 153–71. Oxford: Oxford University Press, 2010.

Murray, Meg McGavran, *Margaret Fuller: Wandering Pilgrim.* Athens: University of Georgia Press, 2008.

——. Introduction to *Transcendentalism: A Reader,* ed. Joel Myerson, xxv–xxxvii. Oxford: Oxford University Press, 2000.

Neufeldt, Leonard. *The Economist: Henry Thoreau and Enterprise.* Oxford: Oxford University Press, 1989.

Niebuhr, Reinhold. *The Essential Reinhold Niebuhr: Selected Essays and Addresses.* Ed. Robert McAffee Brown. New Haven, Conn.: Yale University Press, 1986.

Nietzsche, Friedrich. *Philosophy in the Tragic Age of the Greeks.* Washington, D.C.: Regnery, 1962.

Norton, Andrews. "The New School in Literature and Religion." *Daily Advertiser and Patriot,* August 27, 1838.

Packer, Barbara. *Emerson's Fall: A New Interpretation of the Major Essays.* New York: Continuum, 1982.

——. *The Transcendentalists.* Athens: University of Georgia Press, 2007.

Parker, Theodore. "The Fugitive Slave Law." In *The American Transcendentalists: Essential Writings,* ed. Lawrence Buell, 357–61. New York: Modern Library, 2006.

Peabody, Elizabeth Palmer. *Record of a School: Exemplifying the General Principles of Spiritual Culture.* Boston: Russell, Shattuck, 1836.

Pease, Donald. "Emerson, Nature, and the Sovereignty of Influence." *Boundary 2* (1980): 43–74.

Petrulionis, Sandra Harbert. *Thoreau in His Own Time: A Biographical Chronicle of His Life, Drawn from Recollections, Interviews, and Memoirs by Family, Friends, and Associates.* Iowa City: University of Iowa Press, 2012.

Poirier, Richard T. *The Renewal of Literature: Emersonian Reflections.* New York: Random House, 1987.

Rapport, Mike. *1848: Year of Revolution.* New York: Basic Books, 2009.

Ray, Roberta K. "The Role of the Orator in the Philosophy of Ralph Waldo Emerson." *Communications Monographs* 41.3 (1974): 215–25.

Reed, Sampson. "Genius." In *Transcendentalism: A Reader,* ed. Joel Myerson, 21–26. Oxford: Oxford University Press, 2000.

——. "The Growth of the Mind." In *Transcendentalism: A Reader,* ed. Joel Myerson, 26–61. Oxford: Oxford University Press, 2000.

Rein, Irving J. "The New England Transcendentalists: Philosophy and Rhetoric." *Philosophy and Rhetoric* 1.2 (1968): 103–17.

Reynolds, Larry J., and Susan Belasco Smith. Introduction to Fuller, *"These Sad but Glorious Days,"* 1–38.

Richardson, Robert. *Emerson: The Mind on Fire.* Berkeley: University of California Press, 1996.

——. *Henry Thoreau: A Life of the Mind.* Berkeley: University of California Press, 1986.

Roberson, Susan L. "Sermons." In *The Oxford Handbook of Transcendentalism*, ed. Joel Myerson, Sandra Harbert Petrulionis, and Laura Dassow Walls, 319–29. Oxford: Oxford University Press, 2010.

Robinson, David M. *Emerson and the Conduct of Life: Pragmatism and Ethical Purpose in the Later Work*. New York: Cambridge University Press, 1993.

———. *Natural Life: Thoreau's Worldly Transcendentalism*. Ithaca, N.Y.: Cornell University Press, 2004.

———. *The Unitarians and the Universalists*. London: Greenwood, 1985.

Rorty, Richard. *Philosophy and Social Hope*. London: Penguin UK, 1999.

Rose, Anne. *Transcendentalism as a Social Movement, 1830–1850*. New Haven, Conn.: Yale University Press, 1981.

Sanborn, Benjamin, and William Torrey Harris. *A. Bronson Alcott: His Life and Philosophy*. Boston: Roberts Brothers, 1893.

Schlesinger, Arthur, Jr. *Orestes A. Brownson: A Pilgrim's Progress*. New York: Octagon Books, 1963.

Sellers, Charles. *The Market Revolution: Jacksonian America, 1815–1846*. Oxford: Oxford University Press, 1994.

Shepard, Odell. *Pedlar's Progress: A Life of Bronson Alcott*. Boston: Little, Brown, 1937.

Shulman, George. "Thoreau, Prophecy, and Politics," In *A Political Companion to Henry David Thoreau*, ed. Jack Turner, 124–50. Lexington: University Press of Kentucky, 2009.

Sperber, Jonathan. *The European Revolutions, 1848–1851*. Cambridge: Cambridge University Press, 2005.

Stearns, Peter. *1848: The Revolutionary Tide in Europe*. New York: Norton, 1974.

Steele, Jeffery. "Literary Criticism." In *The Oxford Handbook of Transcendentalism*, ed. Joel Myerson, Sandra Harbert Petrulionis, and Laura Dassow Walls, 384–95. Oxford: Oxford University Press, 2010.

———. *Transfiguring America: Myth, Ideology and Mourning in Margaret Fuller's Writing*. Columbia: University of Missouri Press, 2001.

Sullivan, Robert. *The Thoreau You Don't Know*. New York: Harper Collins, 2009.

Thompson, Roger. "America." In *Emerson in Context*, ed. Wesley Mott, 12–20. Cambridge: Cambridge University Press, 2013.

———. "Emerson and the Democratization of Plato's 'True Rhetoric.'" *Philosophy and Rhetoric* 48.2 (2015): 117–38.

Thoreau, Henry David. *The Correspondence of Henry David Thoreau*. Westport, Conn.: Greenwood, 1974.

———. *The Essays of Henry D. Thoreau*. Ed. Lewis Hyde. New York: Macmillan, 2002.

———. *Familiar Letters of Henry David Thoreau*. Ed. F. B. Sanborn. New York: Houghton, Mifflin, 1894.

———. *The Journal of Henry David Thoreau, 1837–1861*. New York: New York Review Books Classics, 2009.

———. "A Plea for Captain John Brown." In *Essays of Henry D. Thoreau*, 259–80.

———. "Resistance to Civil Government." In *Essays of Henry D. Thoreau*, 123–46.

———. *The Service*. Boston: Goodspeed, 1902.

———. "Slavery in Massachusetts." In *Essays of Henry D. Thoreau*, 179–94.

———. *Walden*. In *Thoreau: A Week on the Concord and Merrimack Rivers, Walden, The Maine Woods, Cape Cod*, 321–588. New York: Library of America, 1985.

——. *A Week on the Concord and Merrimack Rivers*. In *Thoreau: A Week on the Concord and Merrimack Rivers, Walden, The Maine Woods, Cape Cod,* 1–320. New York: Library of America, 1985.

——. "A Winter Walk." In *Essays of Henry D. Thoreau,* 25–42.

Tompkins, Phillip K. "On 'Paradoxes' in the Rhetoric of the New England Transcendentalists." *Quarterly Journal of Speech* 62.1 (1976): 40–48.

Tocqueville, Alexis de. *Democracy in America and Two Essays on America*. New York: Penguin, 2003.

Tuchinsky, Adam. *Horace Greeley's New York Tribune: Civil War–Era Socialism and the Crisis of Free Labor*. Ithaca, N.Y.: Cornell University Press, 2009.

Von Frank, Albert. "Essays: First Series." In *The Cambridge Companion to Ralph Waldo Emerson,* ed. Joel Porte and Saundra Morris, 106–20. Cambridge: Cambridge University Press, 1999.

Von Mehren, Joan. *Minerva and the Muse: A Life of Margaret Fuller*. Amherst: University of Massachusetts Press, 1994.

Warner, Michael. *The Letters of the Republic: Publication and the Public Sphere in Eighteenth-Century America*. Cambridge, Mass.: Harvard University Press, 1992.

Weber, Max. *The Protestant Ethic and the Spirit of Capitalism*. New York: Routledge, 1992.

Wilentz, Sean. *The Rise of American Democracy: From Jefferson to Lincoln*. New York: Norton, 2005.

Wilson, Eric G. "Aesthetics." In *The Oxford Handbook of Transcendentalism,* ed. Joel Myerson, Sandra Harbert Petrulionis, and Laura Dassow Walls, 559–71. Oxford: Oxford University Press, 2010.

Woodberry, George Edward. *Ralph Waldo Emerson*. New York: Macmillan, 1907.

Worster, Donald. *Nature's Economy: A History of Ecological Ideas*. Cambridge: Cambridge University Press, 1994.

Wrobel, Arthur. "Sampson Reed." In *The American Renaissance in New England: Third Series,* ed. Wesley Mott, 351–56. Woodbridge, Conn.: Bruccoli Clark Layman, 2001.

Wydra, Harald. "The Politics of Transcendence." *Cultural Politics* 7.2 (2011): 265–88.

Zappen, James Philip. *The Rebirth of Dialogue: Bakhtin, Socrates, and the Rhetorical Tradition*. Albany: SUNY Press, 2004.

Zwarg, Christina. *Feminist Conversations: Fuller, Emerson, and the Play of Reading*. Ithaca, N.Y.: Cornell University Press, 1995.

INDEX

ABOUT THE AUTHOR

NATHAN CRICK is a professor in the Communication Department at Texas A&M University. He is the author of *Rhetoric and Power: The Drama of Classical Greece,* and *Democracy and Rhetoric: John Dewey on the Arts of Becoming* (both published by the University of South Carolina Press), and *Rhetorical Public Speaking: Civic Engagement in the Digital Age.*